THE OFFENCES AGAINST THE STATE ACT 1939 AT 80

This timely edited collection brings together experts in the fields of legal history, criminal justice, human rights and counter-terrorism law to appraise Ireland's Offences Against the State Act on the eightieth anniversary of its enactment. The origins, development, invocation and extension of the powers contained in the legislation are analysed and critiqued using a broad range of methodologies.

The book engages fully with the 1939 Act's scope and complexity including consideration of the impact of the Act on issues as diverse as trial by jury, paramilitary organisations, organised crime, disclosure, the rules of evidence, freedom of expression and association, parliamentary oversight of legislation and adherence to international human rights norms. In addition, the interplay of the Act with the universal themes of normalcy, exceptionalism, contagion and due process are explored throughout.

This book will appeal to an audience beyond those with a particular interest in the Act itself. It combines historical and contemporary insights with theoretical and practical perspectives that will enrich the reader's understanding of emergency law, wherever it arises.

Volume 8 in Hart Studies in Security and Justice

Hart Studies in Security and Justice
Series editor: Liora Lazarus

The interplay between security and justice has always featured prominently in legal scholarship, but it has taken on a particular urgency since the new Millennium. The new scholarly questions that arise are theoretical, doctrinal and empirical, cutting across a range of traditional sub-disciplines within the legal academy. They address some of the most pressing legal issues of our time, such as the legal status of the 'the war on terror', the nature of states of exception, targeted killing, preventive pre-trial detention, mass surveillance and the numerous other threats that security poses to human rights, the rule of law and liberal democracy.

The purpose of this series is to engage with security and justice scholarship broadly conceived, and to promote a sophisticated and complex understanding of the important challenges it faces. The series is inclusive, promoting new and established scholars from a range of disciplines. It covers doctrinal, empirical, historical and theoretical work, as well as studies which focus on domestic, comparative and international dimensions of emerging security and justice fields. The series also strives to promote the most inclusive range of politics and methodologies, scrutinizing received wisdom and established paradigmatic approaches, and promoting an intellectual dialogue between its authors and the wider field of law as a whole.

Recent titles in this series:

Surveillance, Privacy and Trans-Atlantic Relations
Edited by David Cole, Federico Fabbrini and Stephen Schulhofer

Parliament's Secret War
Veronika Fikfak and Hayley J Hooper

Permanent States of Emergency and the Rule of Law
Alan Greene

The National Security Constitution
Paul F Scott

The Constitutional Structure of Europe's Area of 'Freedom, Security and Justice' and the Right to Justification
Ester Herlin-Karnell

Security and Human Rights
Benjamin Goold and Liora Lazarus

Coercive Human Rights: Positive Duties to Mobilise the Criminal Law under the ECHR
Edited by Laurens Lavrysen and Natasa Mavronicola

The Offences Against the State Act 1939 at 80

A Model Counter-Terrorism Act?

Edited by
Mark Coen

•HART•
OXFORD • LONDON • NEW YORK • NEW DELHI • SYDNEY

HART PUBLISHING

Bloomsbury Publishing Plc

Kemp House, Chawley Park, Cumnor Hill, Oxford, OX2 9PH, UK

1385 Broadway, New York, NY 10018, USA

29 Earlsfort Terrace, Dublin 2, Ireland

First published in Great Britain 2021

A catalogue record for this book is available from the British Library.

Library of Congress Cataloging-in-Publication data

Names: Coen, Mark, editor.

Title: The Offences against the State Act 1939 at 80 : a model Counter-Terrorism Act? / edited by Mark Coen.

Description: Oxford, UK ; New York, NY : Hart Publishing, an imprint of Bloomsbury Publishing, 2021. | Series: Hart studies in security and justice ; volume 8 | Includes bibliographical references and index.

Identifiers: LCCN 2020052055 (print) | LCCN 2020052056 (ebook) | ISBN 9781509931996 (hardback) | ISBN 9781509946761 (paperback) | ISBN 9781509932016 (pdf) | ISBN 9781509932009 (Epub)

Subjects: LCSH: Ireland. Offences against the State Act. | Political crimes and offenses—Law and legislation—Ireland.

Classification: LCC KDK1775 .O34 2021 (print) | LCC KDK1775 (ebook) | DDC 345.417/023—dc23

LC record available at https://lccn.loc.gov/2020052055

LC ebook record available at https://lccn.loc.gov/2020052056

ISBN: HB: 978-1-50993-199-6
ePDF: 978-1-50993-201-6
ePub: 978-1-50993-200-9

Typeset by Compuscript Ltd, Shannon

Foreword

As I look back on my legal life certain events remain etched in my legal memory. One is being invited while a young LLM student at the University of Pennsylvania to attend a meeting of the Brehon Law Society in Philadelphia in March 1982. (This was a society of Irish American lawyers practising in that city). I seethed and fumed as I heard speaker after speaker denounce the democratic institutions and laws of my own state: the existence of the Special Criminal Court and the detention provisions of section 30 of the Offences against the State Act 1939 were particular targets for opprobrium. For me it was then (and largely still is) a relatively black and white issue: seeing things perhaps through a lawyer's lens, this state had to deal with illegal organisations dedicated to overthrowing the democratic institutions of the state when these self-same organisations had taken it upon themselves to fight an illegal war in the name of the People of Ireland, even though this was completely contrary to Article 15.6 and Article 28.3 of the Constitution.

I recall that I wanted to stand up and respond to these speakers with (as I saw it) their intemperate and ill-informed views. My host urged restraint – I was gently reminded that I was, after all, there simply as a guest. Reluctantly, I held my tongue but I also reflected on what the response of the US speakers would have been if – perish the thought – America ever had to deal with a terrorism problem. The opportunity to deliver the response came some 23 years later when I was invited to speak at a session of the American Bar Association. This was a glittering affair, with a star-studded panel including several prominent American trial and appellate judges and prosecutors, all of whom had cut their teeth on the major post 9/11 cases, including some of the Guantanamo Bay habeas corpus cases.

I reminded the audience of my Brehon Law Society experience and wondered aloud whether those speakers who were so anxious to criticise the 48 hour detention provisions of section 30 of the 1939 Act, the non-jury Special Criminal Court and the opinion evidence provisions contained in section 2 of the Offences Against the State (Amendment) Act 1972 would now be willing to offer the same criticisms of the Guantanamo Bay regime and its system of military courts, special rules of evidence and limited access to habeas corpus. I sat down to muffled and desultory applause. While the contents of the speech were not well received, the discordant note which I had struck nonetheless won some grudging admiration from the other speakers. One leading US appellate judge – who later that year was short-listed for consideration for appointment to the US Supreme Court by President Bush – remarked in response: 'Touché, Mr. Hogan. But our situation is nevertheless different from yours …'. But was it? And does this exchange not show that the standard due process criminal law model of criminal justice which works so well in the context of largely peaceful and content societies is challenged by para-military violence and terrorism?

Other memories from an even earlier era come flooding back as well. As I entered the Law School at UCD in October 1976, I recall being struck at the time at the level of opposition on campus and in student debates to the Offences Against the State Act in general and to the Special Criminal Court in particular. (Much of this was in the context of the death sentences which that Court had imposed on Noel and Marie Murray in June 1976 following their conviction for the murder of Garda Michael Reynolds). Some of this seemed to evaporate when the Supreme Court subsequently set aside the conviction of the two accused for capital murder: see *People (DPP) v Murray* [1977] IR 360. But at the time much of what might be termed left wing agitprop directed against the Special Criminal Court had harped on about the Court's perceived lack of independence, its application of what was termed 'special rules of evidence' and the general erosion of the right to jury trial.

The more I studied criminal law, constitutional law and criminal procedure, the less convinced I was by this general critique. This was not to deny that there were aspects of the Offences Against the State Act 1939 which were either unconstitutional or unsatisfactory. Many of the difficulties associated with the powers of arrest under section 30 of the 1939 Act stemmed from the fact that there was no general statutory power of arrest for serious crimes until the entry into force in 1987 of section 4 of the Criminal Justice Act 1984 and that the application of section 30 itself rested on the scheduling of certain offences by the government under section 36 of the 1939 Act. This often meant in practice that the section 30 power was adapted by members of the Gardaí for use in circumstances for which it was ill designed: in its own way the judgment of the Supreme Court in *People (Director of Public Prosecutions) v Howley* [1989] ILRM 629 bears its own eloquent testimony to this.

In the end, however, many of those who so stridently opposed these measures in the 1970s and early 1980s perhaps have found in the interval that the tide went out and that they did not sufficiently take into account a series of changes in law and practice which ultimately changed the public mood. For a start, there is now a general consensus (which, admittedly, did not quite seem to exist in the 1970s and 1980s) that the traditional system of trial simply would not work in the context of illegal organisations. The words of McMahon J in *Redmond v Ireland* [2009] IEHC 201, summarising the evidence given by a senior Garda officer in the context of a challenge to the constitutionality of the opinion evidence provisions of section 3(2) of the Offences against the State Act 1972 also seem apposite in this context:

> Detective Superintendent O'Sullivan testified that he had served in An Garda Síochána for thirty-two years and had spent over twenty years involved in the investigation of subversive crime. His responsibilities are State security, the gathering and analysis of intelligence and the investigation of subversive crime within the jurisdiction. Referring to the increased activities and attacks of the IRA in the 1930s he explains the necessity for the introduction of the Offences Against the State Act in 1939. The IRA was declared to be an unlawful organisation and that suppression order still continues in this jurisdiction. In detailed evidence to the court he gave a brief history of the IRA and the emergence of a breakaway faction in around 1969, now known as the Provisional IRA. Having outlined the objectives of the IRA, he gave a description of the treatment meted out to people who are suspected of assisting police investigations, which included interrogations and torture, sometimes resulting in executions. The fact that it is an oath bound secret organisation divided into cells creates problems for the Gardaí making it very difficult to infiltrate the organisation and gather evidence to prosecute member volunteers. The organisation is very energetic [in] trying to identify members of the public who provide information to the police and are very assiduous in collecting evidence including closely examining

> books of evidence to identify any such persons. If anyone is identified in this manner it usually results in serious torture or death. This represents a serious problem for the Gardaí who bring prosecutions before the ordinary courts where witness and jury intimidation are not unknown.

While it is true that the Special Criminal Court can trace its forebears to the Military Tribunals set up under Article 2A in 1931, perhaps neither de Valera (as Taoiseach) nor Ruttledge (as Minister for Justice) have been given sufficient credit for the move away from the military court model of Article 2A which the 1939 Act commenced.

It was, of course, the case that the 1939 Act permitted military officers to sit on the Special Criminal Court and the Court continued to be staffed by such officers as late as the 1961–1962 period. But, as Thomas Mohr has pointed out in a characteristically profound analysis in Chapter 2 of this book, the 1939 Act had already made subtle and important changes in the move towards the present 'due process' style Special Criminal Court. Unlike the Article 2A Military Tribunal, there was now to be a right of appeal to the Court of Criminal Appeal (and, since 2014, the Court of Appeal) (section 44), the Special Criminal Court was now confined to applying the ordinary law relating to punishment and sentence (section 43(1)(a)) and the general practice and procedure and rules of evidence that pertained in the Central Criminal Court were to apply to the Special Criminal Court (section 41(4)). Just as importantly, the Special Criminal Court was to be the subject of specific legislation and Article 38.3 of the Constitution did not attempt to replicate the old Article 2A model of subjecting the rest of the Constitution to those provisions, thus paving the way for challenges – occasionally successful – to the constitutionality of the 1939 Act. (There appear to be have been three successful challenges to the constitutionality of provisions of that Act: *The State (Burke) v Lennon* [1940] IR 136 (section 55), *Cox v Ireland* [1992] 2 IR 503 (section 34) and *Damache v Director of Public Prosecutions* [2012] IESC 12, [2012] 2 IR 265 (section 29)).

The re-introduction of the Special Criminal Court in 1972 saw perhaps the most significant change of all: from then on the judges who served on the Court were either serving or retired judges. Further changes came unobtrusively in 1986 after the *Eccles* litigation (*Eccles v Ireland* [1985] IR 545) – thereafter all judges who were members of the Special Criminal Court would also be serving judges who were judges of the High Court, Circuit Court and District Court. Completing the picture, the result of the Supreme Court's decision in *Cox v Ireland* [1992] 2 IR 503 was that the consequences of a conviction in the Special Criminal Court were now no different from those of the ordinary courts by holding that section 34 of the 1939 Act and its forfeiture provisions were unconstitutional. And in *Murphy v Ireland* [2014] IESC 19, [2014] 1 IR 198 the Supreme Court moved away from over 40 years of case-law to hold that at least in some circumstances the Director of Public Prosecutions does have to give reasons for her decision to prosecute the accused in the Special Criminal Court.

Apart, therefore, from the occasional loose ends, we have largely seen the emergence of the 'due process' model of the Special Criminal Court. The protests of the 1970s and 1980s have largely disappeared because the Court has demonstrated itself to be a professional court which applies the ordinary rules of criminal procedure, criminal evidence and substantive criminal law. Given that it also provides a reasoned basis for its conclusions and is subject to ordinary appellate review by the Court of Appeal (see, *eg*, *People (Director of Public Prosecutions) v Murphy* [2017] IECA 6), there is, in truth, little to object to from the point of view of fairness, due process and the rule of law.

The public, moreover, well know that the risk of jury intimidation is a very real one and seems prepared to pay the price of dispensing with jury trial where security considerations warrant this, even if this has also meant that the mandate of the Court has been extended to deal with organised crime as well as the traditional challenge posed by illegal organisations.

The foregoing represent some personal reflections prompted by a consideration of the stimulating series of essays gathered around the theme of the Offences Against the State Act 1939 and the Special Criminal Court. The reader will find a wealth of industry and analysis, coupled with a survey of often tangled – and sometimes obscure – statutory provisions and case-law. The general and legal historical dimensions to these questions – whether it be before or after the seminal dates of 1922, 1937–1939, 1969–1972 or 1994 and thereafter – features prominently. All of this makes the book an essential *vade mecum* for those interested in the complex case-law which the 1939 Act has generated. I accept that kind sentiments of this nature are commonly found in Forewords and Prefaces, but the reader may be assured that these essays are all of a superlative quality.

I hope I may again be permitted to conclude on a personal note. It is a measure of the passage of years on my part that only one of the contributors is older than I. It is fitting, accordingly, that, having been re-united briefly with him during the conference which formed the basis for this book, I should pay a special tribute to the acknowledged doyen of all UK legal scholars who have engaged with this topic, Professor Clive Walker, Emeritus Professor of Criminal Justice at the University of Leeds. Where he has led, many have followed.

Gerard Hogan
Advocate General, Court of Justice of the European Union
Luxembourg
8 September 2020

Acknowledgements

Fergal Davis originally approached me with the idea of a project to mark the eightieth anniversary of the Offences Against the State Act. The chapters in this volume were presented in draft form at the Society of Legal Scholars (SLS) Annual Seminar 2019, which was held at the Sutherland School of Law at University College Dublin in October 2019. I gratefully acknowledge the financial support of the SLS, which made a memorable two-day event possible. My thanks in particular to Professor Paula Giliker and Sara Bladon of the Society.

I wish to thank Professor Imelda Maher for her support of this project and my colleagues Una Kelly and Aoife Ryan for their great assistance in the organisation and smooth running of the seminar.

Kate Whetter, Linda Staniford, Emma Platt and Rosie Mearns of Hart Publishing were consummate professionals. I thank them for their helpfulness, dedication and courtesy. I am grateful also to the series editor, Dr Liora Lazarus, for her support.

One of the highlights of the seminar was that it reunited two collaborators, Gerard Hogan and Clive Walker, 30 years after the publication of their seminal work, *Political Violence and the Law in Ireland*. It is worth recalling that in addition to his background as an eminent constitutional scholar, Advocate General Hogan was a member of both the Constitution Review Group (1996) and the Committee to Review the Offences Against the State Acts 1939–1998 (2002), two bodies that had much to say about the matters discussed in this volume. I can think of no person better placed to write the Foreword, and I thank him for doing so.

I was blessed with a cohort of enthusiastic, engaged and responsive authors. I thank them for the time and energy they have invested in the project.

Finally, my love and gratitude to Conor Noonan, who supports me in everything.

Mark Coen
August 2020

Contents

List of Contributors

Ivana Bacik is Reid Professor of Criminal Law, Criminology and Penology at Trinity College Dublin and a Senator for the University of Dublin constituency.

Liz Campbell is Francine V McNiff Chair of Criminal Jurisprudence at Monash University.

Mark Coen is a Lecturer in Law at the Sutherland School of Law, University College Dublin.

Yvonne Daly is an Associate Professor at the School of Law and Government, Dublin City University.

Laura Donohue is a Professor of Law at Georgetown University.

Alan Greene is a Senior Lecturer in Law at the University of Birmingham.

Claire Hamilton is Professor of Criminology at Maynooth University.

Alice Harrison is a Lecturer in Law at Maynooth University and a practising barrister.

Liz Heffernan is an Associate Professor at the School of Law, Trinity College Dublin.

Niamh Howlin is an Associate Professor at the Sutherland School of Law, University College Dublin.

Nicola McGarrity is a Senior Lecturer and Director of the Terrorism Law Reform Project at the University of New South Wales.

Jamie McLoughlin is a PhD student at the Sutherland School of Law, University College Dublin.

Thomas Mohr is an Associate Professor at the Sutherland School of Law, University College Dublin.

Fionnuala Ní Aoláin is Regents Professor, University of Minnesota Law School and Professor of Law, The Queens' University of Belfast. She is also the United Nations Special Rapporteur on the Protection and Promotion of Human Rights and Fundamental Freedoms while Countering Terrorism.

Eoin O'Connor is an Adjunct Assistant Professor at the School of Law, Trinity College Dublin, and a practising barrister.

Clive Walker is Professor Emeritus of Criminal Justice Studies at the University of Leeds.

Table of Cases

Table of Legislation

National Instruments (All Jurisdictions)

International and European Instruments

Introduction

MARK COEN

THE OBJECTIVE OF this volume is to examine the origins and evolution of the Offences Against the State Act 1939, 80 years after its enactment. The chapters that follow seek to capture the scope of the legislation and critique its content, application and impact. For eight decades the Act has been highly controversial and perennially topical. Associated most closely with independent Ireland's struggle against paramilitary subversives, it has also been invoked in contexts as diverse as wartime black marketeering and twenty-first century organised crime. Its title emphasises 'the State' and its provisions are replete with words that underline the illegitimacy of the activities it seeks to suppress. Its sections envisage that the institutions of government could be subject to 'usurpation', 'obstruction' and 'interference' and that persons and groups opposed to those institutions will engage in conduct that is 'unauthorised', 'unlawful', 'treasonable' or 'seditious'. In equipping the state to defend itself against attacks up to and including an existential threat, the Act (and its subsequent amendments) makes sweeping modifications to the 'normal' substantive and procedural law of a common law jurisdiction. It is perhaps not surprising that legislation that permits internment without trial and the trial of civilians by a court composed of military officers has provoked controversy. While neither of these powers has been invoked in recent times, they remain available alongside other contentious provisions still in use, including those relating to non-jury trials for serious offences and the reception of police belief evidence, to name but two.

The Special Criminal Court is perhaps the most contested and most emblematic feature of the Act, and the photograph on the cover of this volume is of its three judges' chairs. It is an image that seems to capture both the Court's exceptionality and its embeddedness in the legal system. Almost 50 years since it was last established, the Court endures in an Ireland that would be unrecognisable to the judges who sat on it in 1972. Characterised in 1937 as 'a monstrous blot on the Constitution',[1] memorably derided as 'a sentencing tribunal',[2] and criticised on an ongoing basis by respected national and international organisations, successive governments have refused to countenance its discontinuation. Indeed, as several contributors to this volume observe, the jurisdiction of the Court has been extended in the twenty-first century and a second Court created. Even modest proposals to amend aspects of the law relating to the Court's

[1] A O'Rahilly, *Thoughts on the Constitution* (Dublin, Browne and Nolan Limited, 1937) 50.

[2] That description in an article in *The Irish Times* gave rise to contempt of court proceedings; see *State (DPP) v Walsh and Conneely* [1981] IR 412.

operation, such as those pertaining to the security of tenure of its judges[3] and the automatic sending of certain offences for trial there,[4] have been ignored. In June 2020, the caretaker government stated that it intended to initiate a review of the operation of the Offences Against the State Acts, including the Special Criminal Court. While one could be sceptical about such a proposal, given the degree to which the excellent Hederman report of 2002[5] has been ignored, it nevertheless demonstrates the enduring topicality of the legislation and the concerns it arouses. Its cameo role in the general elections of 2016 and 2020 attests to this also.[6] In short, the Offences Against the State Act, and in particular the Special Criminal Court, have been staples of political discourse in Ireland for 80 years.

Although it is a statute rooted in the Irish experience, I hope that international readers will also find much to interest them in this collection. From the beginning, the Act had an important inter-state dimension. Part of the rationale for the creation of the legislation was to contain terrorist threats emanating from Ireland that would erupt abroad and in so doing damage our relations with another jurisdiction, namely Great Britain. In addition, the 1939 Act makes for an interesting case study because it is an omnibus anti-terrorism statute that made radical inroads on settled legal principles and did so many decades before similar developments in other common law countries. In an editorial in 1972, *The Times* of London cautioned against the introduction of similar legislation in Great Britain, on the basis that both the 1939 Act and Northern Ireland's Special Powers Act demonstrated that 'recourse to unaccustomed powers of coercion [and] the suspension of normal rights and safeguards, may confuse and embitter opinion in a way that actually works to the advantage of those against whom the special measures are directed'.[7] These words remain strikingly relevant in a world that struggles to calibrate its response to cross-border radicalisation and extremism while safeguarding civil liberties and human rights.

Three of the chapters in this volume provide historical context on the Offences Against the State Act. In Chapter 1, Niamh Howlin examines the patchwork of emergency measures that existed in the pre-Independence period. It is evident from a thematic analysis that under British rule Ireland was subjected to a vast array of extraordinary laws that foreshadowed many of the features of the 1939 Act, such as those relating to unlawful organisations, special courts and detention without trial. Thomas Mohr's essay (Chapter 2) reviews emergency law in the period from 1922 to 1937, uncovering a wide array of legal devices and approaches, including legislating by Resolution, temporary and permanent legislation, as well as implicit and explicit amendments of

[3] *Report of the Constitution Review Group* (Dublin, Stationery Office, 1996) 199; *Report of the Committee to Review the Offences Against the State Acts 1939–1998* (Dublin, Government Publications, 2002), hereinafter Hederman Report, 9.39–9.40 and 9.55–9.56.

[4] Hederman Report, 9.57.

[5] See n 3 above.

[6] C Little, 'The Irish General Election of February 2016: Towards a New Politics or an Early Election?' (2017) 40(2) *West European Politics* 479, 482; P Ryan, C Quinn and H O'Connell, 'General Election 2020 Prime Time Debate: Leaders Clash over Housing and Special Criminal Court', *The Irish Independent*, 4 February 2020, available at: www.independent.ie/irish-news/election-2020/general-election-2020-prime-time-debate-leaders-clash-over-housing-and-special-criminal-court-38927804.html (accessed 13 August 2020).

[7] 'A Special Powers Act?', *The Times*, 1 March 1972, 15.

the Constitution of the Irish Free State. The chapter demonstrates how both the 1939 Act and its underlying constitutional framework were informed by what their drafters learned from the emergency law experience of the first 15 years of the state. Mark Coen (Chapter 3) continues the historical theme by arguing that the experience of trial by jury under British rule and in the two decades immediately after independence has given rise to an ambivalent attitude to the jury in Irish political and judicial circles. The operation of special courts is not subjected to an intense level of scrutiny by Irish state actors, because the institution of trial by jury is merely tolerated, not revered.

As was discussed above, the Special Criminal Court looms large in any discussion of the Offences Against the State Act, and so it is with this collection. While it features throughout the book, it is a special focus of five of the 13 chapters. The extraordinary nature of the Court can become diluted by familiarity, but Fionnuala Ní Aoláin (Chapter 4) articulates it in a way that is fresh and arresting. The discussion is illuminated by statistical data that speaks to the Court in action, including its use of Garda opinion evidence. Nicola McGarrity's essay (Chapter 5) situates the Special Criminal Court in comparative perspective by reference to a schema that interrogates fundamental aspects of its practice. One striking feature that emerges from the chapter is the extent to which Ireland was in the vanguard of having modified trials for terrorism cases, an issue which many countries have only comprehensively confronted in the past 20 years. The use of Garda belief evidence in trials for membership of unlawful organisations is the subject of Chapter 6, written by Liz Heffernan and Eoin O'Connor. The origins, operation and legal challenges to this controversial provision are examined against the backdrop of constitutional rights and the European Convention on Human Rights. As the authors indicate, the changed nature of the legal and investigative landscape since the introduction of belief evidence raises the question if a credible case can be made for its continued use today. Alice Harrison considers the current approach of the Special Criminal Court to disclosure in Chapter 7 and surveys the appellate case law it has engendered. The hybrid nature of the Court as finder of law and fact is to the forefront of this essay, which concludes with an appraisal of how the disclosure process could be reformed. The trial of non-subversive offences in the Special Criminal Court has given rise to much controversy over the years and has been heightened since the advent of the organised crime provisions of the Criminal Justice (Amendment) Act 2009. This is the subject of Chapter 8, by Liz Campbell. A comparative methodology highlights the unusual nature of Ireland's response to concerns about jury intimidation (essentially a presumption in favour of trial by a special court for particular offences). Drawing on the experience of other jurisdictions, the chapter illustrates how a rational and evidence-based discussion about protecting jurors should be conducted.

Two chapters address discrete activities that are the subject of regulation by the 1939 Act, namely unlawful organisations and freedom of expression. Clive Walker and Jamie McLoughlin (Chapter 9) consider the legislation's approach to the proscription of unlawful organisations. This departs from the pre-1939 statutory formula, which depended on the banning of named groups by statutory instrument, but also allows for the naming of individual organisations in suppression orders. In addition to critiquing the existing system, the chapter considers how it has been amended to enable the prosecution of membership offences committed outside the state by Irish citizens or residents. As the authors point out, this is a topical issue at the time of writing, with the ongoing case of Lisa Smith receiving prominent media coverage. The impact of the Act on freedom of expression is the subject of Laura Donohue's essay (Chapter 10). Offences such as the possession of incriminating, treasonable or seditious documents and the ban on newspaper publicity for organisations subject to suppression orders are contextualised by reference to similar offences contained in legislation prior to 1939. The suitability of such provisions for a world in which communication by extremist elements is instant, anonymous, informed by algorithms and unhindered by national boundaries is discussed.

Chapters 11 and 12 are concerned with oversight of the Offences Against the State Act. Yvonne Marie Daly (Chapter 11) reviews the criticisms that have been levelled at the legislation by international human rights bodies and the adverse findings that have been made in relation to its provisions by the United Nations Human Rights Committee and the European Court of Human Rights. The chapter also evaluates the impact of Ireland's international human rights obligations on the domestic courts and legislature, noting that they can be deployed cynically, for example by cloaking measures that erode rights in acceptable language. In Chapter 12, Ivana Bacik brings her unique insight as a parliamentarian to bear on the Act. The annual parliamentary review of aspects of the Offences Against the State Act attracted an unusual amount of publicity and media commentary in 2020, as it appeared that a government might not be formed in time to renew particular provisions. In addition to its discussion of parliamentary oversight, the chapter also includes a personal reflection on the author's practice as a barrister in the Special Criminal Court when it sat in its previous location in the historic Green Street Courthouse. Accounts such as these are important for the historical record.

The final two chapters are linked by their consideration of the themes of emergency and normalcy. Alan Greene (Chapter 13) discusses the relationship between the state of emergency envisaged by Article 28.3.3 of the 1937 Constitution and the quasi-emergency measures contained in the Offences Against the State Act. The chapter concludes with a number of recommendations that could be implemented to resolve the rather blurred lines that currently permit emergency measures without the necessity for a declaration of constitutional emergency. The final chapter, by Claire Hamilton (Chapter 14), address the theme of 'contagion'; the extent to which measures introduced in a specific emergency context seep into more general use and come to be assimilated and regarded as the norm. The chapter situates this phenomenon in both the domestic and the international spheres and in doing so synthesises questions of criminal justice policy, rights and judicial culture.

After the passage of an eventful 80 years, it is natural to wonder what the next decade or two will bring in relation to the Offences Against the State Act. If the statute's past is any predictor, it seems unlikely that the coming years will be uncontroversial. The prosecution of Irish citizens for terrorist offences committed abroad will be an emerging issue to monitor. The improving political fortunes of Sinn Féin and the likelihood that that party will form a significant part of a future government, could herald dramatic changes. Conversely, there may be attempts to further embed the architecture of the Offences Against the State Act in the legal system, by redesigning and renaming its features so that they are no longer referred to as 'special' or regarded as deviations from the norm. In light of the historical tendency to ignore reform suggestions, including those emanating from official review groups, the prospect of official engagement with the recommendations proposed in many of the chapters in this book appears slight. The 1939 Act has proven remarkably durable, immune to a torrent of domestic and international critique. But the role of the academic commentator is not merely to make reform recommendations, however laudable that exercise may be. It is also to document phenomena, identify trends and place issues in context and perspective. Regardless of future developments, the Offences Against the State Act (or a replacement not yet imagined) will continue to provide fertile ground for those activities in the years to come.

1

The Prehistory of the Offences Against the State Act

NIAMH HOWLIN

I. INTRODUCTION

The Offences Against the State Act 1939 (OASA) is part of a continuum of special legislative measures introduced to suspend normal criminal justice procedures in Ireland. The Special Criminal Court was not the first specially constituted tribunal created by legislation to deal with specific types of crime, for example, and prohibitions on the membership and activities of certain groups were not novel. Many of the provisions of the OASA echo, either in substance or in language, earlier legislative interventions. Ireland was often the subject of coercive legislation or emergency measures.[1] As Crossman has pointed out, '[t]he repeated use of special legislation to suppress popular disorder in Ireland and the failure to provide any permanent remedy has been a recurrent theme of Irish history'.[2] These legislative interventions were usually responses to specific criminal justice challenges, which were in turn usually consequences of political situations.

This chapter is not a comprehensive overview of all emergency legislation passed for Ireland in the late eighteenth and nineteenth centuries. Rather, it is, together with Chapter 2, an attempt to contextualise the OASA as one of a long line of 'special' measures deemed necessary for Ireland.

II. 'COERCIVE' LEGISLATION IN IRELAND

Coercion, in Dicey's view, meant 'the enforcement of law by arbitrary and exceptional methods which tend to diminish the securities for freedom possessed by ordinary citizens'.[3] It has been observed that Ireland was governed by 'special' legislation for most

[1] I have written elsewhere about the frequency with which Ireland's criminal trial system came under scrutiny in the 19th century; eg N Howlin, 'The Politics of Jury Trials in Nineteenth-Century Ireland' (2015) 3(2) *Comparative Legal History* 272 and N Howlin *Juries in Ireland* (Dublin, Four Courts Press, 2017), ch 1.

[2] V Crossman, 'Emergency Legislation and Agrarian Disorder in Ireland 1821–41' (1991) 27(108) *Irish Historical Studies* 309.

[3] AV Dicey, *England's Case Against Home Rule* (London, Murray, 1886) 179.

of the nineteenth century.[4] Farrell estimates that between 1801 and 1921 Parliament passed 105 emergency or coercion Acts,[5] and John Spencer told the House of Lords at the end of the century, 'I believe that in 87 years there have been 87 Coercion Acts or renewal of Coercion Acts.'[6] Although these figures tend to focus on legislation passed by the Parliament at Westminster after the Act of Union, this is a somewhat artificial starting-point. As Connolly notes, emergency legislation introduced at the end of the eighteenth century for the suspension of habeas corpus and the suppression of rebellion was still in force at the time of the Act of Union in 1801.[7]

To get a clearer overall picture of the nature of emergency legislation in Ireland, this chapter takes the mid-eighteenth century as its starting point. A search through the statute books indicates over 100 Acts which could be deemed 'coercive' between 1765 and 1887. To be considered 'coercive', this analysis includes Acts which suspended or superseded the ordinary functioning of the criminal justice system. This might be through the suspension of 'ordinary' procedure, the introduction of new procedures, the creation of new offences, or an increase in punitiveness. I have focused on Acts which were specifically passed to deal with criminal justice challenges in Ireland, rather than Acts which, after 1801, applied to other parts of the UK also.[8]

Whichever figure one takes, it is evident that emergency or extraordinary criminal legislation was in fact far from extraordinary for most of the period under consideration. As Bowman observes, 'Following the Act of Union of 1800, Ireland, supposedly an integral part of the United Kingdom, was to be covered by much special legislation.'[9] For several decades around the turn of the nineteenth century, for example, there was an average of one 'coercion' or emergency Act per year. Despite the frequency with which such measures were introduced, Crossman makes the point that governments generally proceeded with some reluctance and usually attempted to make use of ordinary legal procedures to restore law and order.[10] Indeed, some of the Acts discussed in this chapter were the subject of scrutiny and criticism, both in the houses of Parliament and beyond.

Sometimes the legislature explicitly acknowledged, in the legislative preambles, the shortcomings of the ordinary criminal law in dealing with particular offences at a specific point in time. This usually reads as something of a justification for the restrictive measures being introduced. For example, an Act passed in 1775 noted that previous legislation 'hath been found insufficient'.[11] Other preambles stated a determination not to allow persons involved in political or agrarian violence to hide behind the ordinary

[4] Ibid, 309.

[5] M Farrell, *Emergency Legislation: The Apparatus of Repression* (Derry, Field Day, 1986) 5.

[6] Hansard, vol 17, col 5, House of Lords (5 September 1893).

[7] SJ Connolly, 'Aftermath and Adjustment' in WE Vaughan (ed), *A New History of Ireland: V: Ireland Under the Union 1801–70* (Oxford, Oxford University Press, 1989) 8.

[8] Also included in the tally are amending and continuing Acts.

[9] T Bowman, 'Ireland: Rebellion and Counter-Insurgency, 1848–1867' (2019) 30(4–5) *Small Wars & Insurgencies* 895, 900.

[10] Crossman, 'Emergency Legislation' (n 2) 312–3.

[11] An Act to Prevent and Punish Tumultuous Risings of Persons within this Kingdom, and for other purposes therein mentioned (15 & 16 Geo III c 21), referred to as the Whiteboy Act 1775. This was amended in 1796 by An Act to Amend An Act Passed in the 15th and 16th Years of His Majesty's Reign, Entitled, An Act to Prevent and Punish Tumultuous Risings of Persons Within this Kingdom, and for Other Purposes Therein Mentioned 1796 (36 Geo III c 32).

laws and procedures. For example, the preamble to the Local Disturbances, etc (Ireland) Act 1833[12] noted that unlawful activities 'frustrate[d] the ordinary modes of criminal prosecution'. It went on to explain that the laws currently in force were 'inadequate' for 'prompt and effectual suppression of the said mischiefs …'. This sentiment was repeated in section 13, which declared that 'the ordinary Tribunals may in certain cases in proclaimed districts be inadequate to the prompt and effectual punishment of the offences …'.[13] As Comerford points out, the Lord Lieutenant in the 1880s, Earl Spencer, 'fundamentally disliked exceptional coercive measures'.[14] However, the Prevention of Crime (Ireland) Act 1882[15] noted in its preamble that 'by reason of the action of secret societies and combinations for illegal purposes in Ireland the operation of the ordinary law has become insufficient for the repression and prevention of crime'.

III. THEMES OF CONTROL

Most academic consideration of coercive legislation has been from a historical rather than a legal or legal-historical viewpoint[16] and there has been relatively little scrutiny of the provisions of such legislation by lawyers.[17] Chronological or narrative accounts of many of the Acts have been presented by various historians of the nineteenth century, providing invaluable analysis of the contexts in which such Acts were passed.[18] Indeed, as Mulloy observed in 1986, '[i]t is easier and more illuminating to examine certain specific Acts rather than to attempt a complete account of the entire interlocking system of coercion'.[19]

Nevertheless, in this chapter I take a thematic rather than a chronological approach to examining the eighteenth- and nineteenth-century precursors to the OASA. A number of themes emerge, which can be grouped into two broad categories: specific offences and special powers. The special powers include detention without trial, suspension of habeas corpus, special courts, curfews, powers of search and seizure and alteration to criminal procedure. The offences relate to restrictions on assembly, membership of organisations or the swearing of oaths, the control of arms, the press or printed matter, and failure to cooperate with the authorities. These categories of powers and offences have been broadly drafted to allow for high-level analysis within the confines of a short chapter.

[12] 3 & 4 Wm IV c 4, preamble.

[13] Ibid, s 13.

[14] RV Comerford, 'The Parnell Era, 1883–91' in WE Vaughan (ed), *A New History of Ireland: VI: Ireland Under the Union 1870–1921* (Oxford, Oxford University Press, 1989) 58.

[15] 45 & 46 Vic c 25.

[16] See, eg, Comerford, 'The Parnell Era' (n 14).

[17] Several works which focus on the Special Criminal Court do not probe its history and antecedents further back than 1922 – eg A Harrison, *The Special Criminal Court: Practice and Procedure* (Dublin, Bloomsbury Professional, 2019) ch 1 and F Davis, *The History and Development of the Special Criminal Court 1922–2005* (Dublin, Four Courts Press, 2009).

[18] See, eg, Crossman, 'Emergency Legislation' (n 2); Perry L Curtis, *Coercion and Conciliation in Ireland 1880–1892: A Study in Conservative Unionism* (Princeton, Princeton University Press, 1963); Bowman, 'Ireland' (n 9) 900–901.

[19] E Mulloy, *Emergency Legislation: Dynasties of Coercion* (Derry, Field Day, 1986) 8.

IV. OFFENCES UNDER THE COERCION ACTS

A common feature of coercive legislation was the introduction of new offences to counter specific unlawful activities.

A. Unlawful Organisations and Unlawful Oaths

Secret societies were an established feature of Irish life in the late eighteenth and early nineteenth centuries, particularly in rural areas. Early groups were often referred to as Whiteboys, and they protested against such issues as enclosure of common land, tithes and other agrarian issues.[20] Ribbonmen were generally distinguished by the wearing of ribbons in their hats, and other groups included the Oakboys, the Hearts of Steel and the Peep O'Days. The existence of such groups, as well as more visible groups such as the Orange Order, proved to be a challenge to maintaining law and order, and from the 1760s legislation sought to curtail their activities and existence. Legislation also sought to prevent the members of such groups from taking or administering what were known as unlawful oaths. An Act to prevent 'tumultuous risings', known as the Whiteboy Act, was passed in 1765,[21] and another was passed ten years later.[22] The 1765 Act did not name the targeted groups, but focused more on their activities than on official membership, making many activities felonies without benefit of clergy. It made it an offence 'by force, violence or menaces' to 'impose or tender any oath or oaths … on any other person or persons, in order thereby to engage or compel him, her or them to commit or conceal any unlawful Act'.[23] The 1775 Act made specific reference to 'persons calling themselves White Boys, and others'. The Riot Act 1787 imposed a punishment of transportation for life for administering unlawful oaths, and transportation for seven years for taking such oaths.[24]

In the 1790s, the United Irishmen were established to agitate for parliamentary reform and religious equality. From 1797 until around 1803, the tensions in Irish society manifested as localised armed rebellions, with groups such as the Defenders active around the country.[25] The Insurrection Act 1796[26] imposed the death penalty for administering unlawful oaths, stating that the penalties imposed by the Riot Act 1787[27] were 'insufficient

[20] See generally M Beames, *Peasants and Power: The Whiteboy Movements and Their Control in Pre-Famine Ireland* (Sussex, The Harvester Press, 1983).

[21] An Act To Prevent for the Future Tumultuous Risings of Persons Within this Kingdom, and for Other Purposes Therein Mentioned 1765 (5 & 6 Geo III c 8).

[22] Whiteboy Act 1775 (15 & 16 Geo III c 21).

[23] Whiteboy Act 1765 (5 & 6 Geo III c 8) s 6.

[24] An Act to Prevent Tumultuous Risings and Assemblies, and for The More Effectual Punishment of Persons Guilty of Outrage, Riot and Illegal Combinations, and of Administering and Taking Unlawful Oaths 1787 (27 Geo III c 15) s 6.

[25] See T Garvin, 'Defenders, Ribbonmen and Others: Underground Political Networks in Pre-Famine Ireland' (1982) 96(1) *Past & Present* 96, 133.

[26] An Act More Effectually to Suppress Insurrections, and Prevent the Disturbance of the Public Peace 1796 (36 Geo III c 20).

[27] Tumultuous Risings Act 1787 (27 Geo III c 15).

to deter wicked and designing men from administering and taking such oaths'. In 1807, the 1787 punishments were reinstated.[28]

Legislation prohibiting the membership of specific groups and the taking and administering of oaths continued to be passed during the nineteenth century.[29] The Unlawful Oaths (Ireland) Act 1810[30] contained expansive definitions of the nature of such oaths and prohibited a range of activities such as administering or causing to be administered such oaths; tendering or causing them to be tendered, or being present, aiding and assisting at the administering or tendering of such oaths. It also included causing, procuring or inducing others to take oaths, through 'threats, promises, persuasions, or other undue means'.[31] In 1823 an Act provided that any 'society, association, brotherhood, committee, lodge, club or confederacy' requiring members to take an unlawful oath was deemed to be an 'unlawful combination and confederacy'.[32] This legislation sought to repress sectarian violence, and was primarily aimed at Orange societies. Membership of such groups was prohibited, and persons could be convicted on the evidence of 'one or more credible witness or witnesses'.[33] The Unlawful Oaths Act 1823 was extended and amended by the Unlawful Societies (Ireland) Act 1839.[34] This Act expanded the definition of an 'unlawful combination and confederacy' to include any society whose members were known to one another by 'secret sign or signs, or password or passwords, by way of question and answer or otherwise'. It also included societies formed with an aim to purchase, distribute, fund or procure arms.[35] These provisions were continued by legislation in the context of the activities of Young Ireland in the 1840s and the Fenians in the 1860s.[36]

The Protection of Life and Property in Certain Parts of Ireland Act 1871[37] was enacted specifically to target membership of the Ribbon Society in certain counties. Persons suspected of involvement could be arrested and detained without trial. This power was widely drafted to include not only membership but also 'directly or indirectly maintaining correspondence or intercourse with [the society], or of aiding, abetting, or supporting by contribution of money or otherwise'.[38]

The Prevention of Crime (Ireland) Act 1882[39] was passed in the aftermath of the Phoenix Park murders in May 1882, when the Chief Secretary and Under Secretary were assassinated by members of a secret society known as the Invincibles.[40] The Act prohibited

[28] Insurrection and Disturbances (Ireland) Act 1807 (47 Geo III c 13), s 3.
[29] See also An Act for the Suppression of the Rebellion Which Still Unhappily Exists Within this Kingdom 1799 (39 Geo III c 11).
[30] 50 Geo III c 102.
[31] Unlawful Oaths (Ireland) Act 1810 (50 Geo III c 102), preamble.
[32] Unlawful Oaths Act 1823 (4 Geo IV c 87).
[33] Ibid, s 3.
[34] 2 & 3 Vic c 74.
[35] Ibid, s 1.
[36] The Unlawful Combinations (Ireland) Act 1848 (11 & 12 Vic c 89); the Unlawful Oaths (Ireland) Act 1851 (14 & 15 Vic c 48); the Unlawful Oaths (Ireland) Act 1856 (19 & 20 Vic c 78); and the Unlawful Oaths (Ireland) Act 1862 (25 & 26 Vic c 32).
[37] 34 & 35 Vic c 25.
[38] Ibid, s 7.
[39] 45 & 46 Vic c 25 s 9.
[40] See F Larkin, 'Lord Frederick Cavendish and the Phoenix Park Murders of 1882' (2014) 22(3) *History Ireland* 28; T Corfe, *The Phoenix Park Murders: Conflict, Compromise and Tragedy in Ireland, 1879–1882* (London, Hodder and Stoughton, 1968); I Hernon, *Assassin!: 200 Years of British Political Murder* (London, Pluto Press, 2007) 109–127.

membership of associations formed 'for the commission of crimes; or carrying on operations for or by the commission of crimes; or for encouraging or aiding persons to commit crimes'.[41] The Criminal Law and Procedure (Ireland) Act 1887,[42] a permanent measure, was enacted in the context of the Land War and the Plan of Campaign.[43]

B. Restrictions on Assembly

Legislation in the late eighteenth century frequently imposed restrictions on gatherings, either for specific purposes, at specific times or in specific numbers. The Whiteboy Act 1765[44] prohibited groups of five or more from gathering at night to perpetrate attacks on individuals or damage to property. A similar prohibition was contained in an Act of 1771.[45] The Whiteboy Act 1775 made it an offence to 'knowingly incite, encourage or promote' unlawful assemblies 'by sound of drum, horn, music, fire, shouting or other signal'.[46] The Riot Act 1787[47] targeted groups of twelve or more. Failing to disperse when ordered by a justice of the peace or other official was a felony without benefit of clergy and could lead to a sentence of death. During the turbulent 1790s, the Insurrection Act 1796 made it an offence to assemble 'unlawfully and tumultuously' during the day. Those who did so were liable to be drafted into the Navy.[48]

The early 1820s once more saw famine and unrest in the Irish countryside.[49] The Insurrection Act 1822[50] targeted secret agrarian societies such as the Whiteboys, Ribbonmen, Rockites and Caravats.[51] The Act prohibited 'tumultuous assemblies' and assembling in public houses,[52] with offenders liable to be sentenced to seven years' transportation.[53] The Unlawful Oaths Act 1823[54] made it a specific offence to allow an unlawful meeting to take place in one's home.

[41] 45 & 46 Vic c 25, s 34.

[42] 50 & 51 Vic c 20, s 2. This was a permanent measure, still in force at the time of the Anglo-Irish war.

[43] According to Jackson, it did in fact help to undermine the Plan of Campaign. A Jackson, *Ireland 1798–1898: Politics and War* (Oxford, Oxford University Press, 1999) 134.

[44] Whiteboy Act 1765 (5 & 6 Geo III c 8), preamble.

[45] An Act For the More Effectual Punishing Wicked and Disorderly Persons Who Have Committed or Shall Commit Violences and do Injuries to the Persons or Properties of Any of His Majesty's Subjects in the Counties of Antrim, Down, Armagh, City and County of Londonderry and County of Tyrone, or Any of Them, Who Shall Deliver or Publish Threatening Letters, or Shall Resist or Oppose the Levying the Public Taxes In the Said Counties, or Any of Them, and For the More Sure and Speedy Bringing to Justice Certain Offenders Therein Mentioned 1771 (11 & 12 Geo III c 5).

[46] Whiteboy Act 1775 (15 & 16 Geo III c 21), s 23.

[47] Tumultuous Risings Act 1787 (27 Geo III c 15), preamble.

[48] Insurrection Act 1796 (36 Geo III c 20), s 31.

[49] See JS Donnelly, *Captain Rock: The Irish Agrarian Rebellion of 1821–1824* (Madison, University of Wisconsin Press, 2009).

[50] 3 Geo IV c 57. Continued by the Insurrections (Ireland) Act 1823 (4 Geo IV c 58) and the Insurrections, etc (Ireland) Act 1824 (5 Geo IV c 105).

[51] For more on these secret organisations see K Hughes and D McRaild, *Ribbon Societies in Nineteenth-Century Ireland and its Diaspora: The Persistence of Tradition* (Liverpool, Liverpool University Press, 2018).

[52] See also Insurrection Act 1796 (36 Geo III c 20), s 31.

[53] Later, in 1870, legislation allowed the Lord Lieutenant to order the closure of public houses in proclaimed districts: Peace Preservation (Ireland) Act 1870 (33 & 34 Vic c 9), s 24.

[54] 3 Geo IV c 87, s 7.

In 1825 an Act was passed with the prevention and dispersal of unlawful assemblies as its main aim.[55] This legislation targeted groups and committees seeking redress for 'grievances in church or state'. This was squarely aimed at the growing Catholic Emancipation movement. Membership of such an organisation was a misdemeanour punishable by fine or imprisonment.[56] Two Justices of the Peace could command meetings of such organisations to disperse.[57] The 1825 Act was relatively benign compared with the Dangerous Assemblies (Ireland) Act 1829,[58] which explicitly targeted the Catholic Association. This organisation was considered 'dangerous to the public tranquillity and inconsistent with the exercise of regular government,' and was 'utterly suppressed and prohibited'. In addition, the Lord Lieutenant could suppress other associations or assemblies by proclamation.[59]

As well as prohibiting assemblies generally, legislation also prohibited certain marches and processions; usually these Acts targeted parades and marches by the Orange Order.[60] The Party Processions (Ireland) Act 1832[61] prohibited meetings, parades and processions 'for the purpose of celebrating or commemorating any festival, anniversary, or political event relating to ... any religious or other distinctions ... between any classes of his majesty's subjects'.[62] Such processions were deemed to be 'calculated to create and perpetuate animosities'. Also prohibited were provocative banners, emblems, flags, or symbols, provocative music, and weapons or firearms. Justices of the peace were empowered to disperse such processions,[63] and persons who did not obey orders to disperse within 15 minutes were liable to one month's imprisonment (or three months for subsequent offences).[64] Another Party Processions Act was passed in 1850 along similar lines.[65] In 1860 legislation was passed prohibiting the display of banners or flags designed to provoke animosity.[66] It also prohibited provocatively 'publicly meeting and parading with other Persons, or the playing of any Music, or discharging any Cannon or Firearm in any Public Street, Road, or Place'.[67]

As Crossman notes, 'one of the most notable features of repressive legislation of the 1820s and 1830s was the extent to which it was designed to meet a particular challenge to

[55] The Unlawful Societies (Ireland) Act 1825 (6 Geo IV c 4). In 1793 legislation had been passed specifically to prohibit the election or appointment of representative assemblies: An Act to Prevent the Election or Appointment of Unlawful Assemblies, under Pretence of Preparing or Presenting Public Petitions, or Other Addresses to His Majesty or the Parliament 1793 (33 Geo III c 29), preamble.

[56] Unlawful Societies (Ireland) Act 1825 (6 Geo IV c 4), s 5.

[57] Ibid, s 4. Versions of this provision were included in several subsequent enactments, including the Dangerous Assemblies (Ireland) Act 1829 (10 Geo IV c 1).

[58] 10 Geo IV c 1.

[59] Ibid, s 2.

[60] See generally N Maddox, '"A Melancholy Record": The Story of the Nineteenth-Century Party Processions Acts' (2004) 39(1) *Irish Jurist* 243 and A Tock Morrisette, 'Preventing the Parade: The Party Processions Acts in Ireland and Canada' (2018) 48(2) *American Review of Canadian Studies* 110.

[61] 2 & 3 Wm IV c 118. This was to be in force for five years. The Party Processions (Ireland) Act 1838 (1 & 2 Vic c 34) continued it for a further five years.

[62] 2 & 3 Wm IV c 118, s 1.

[63] Ibid, s 2.

[64] Ibid, s 3.

[65] Party Processions (Ireland) Act 1850 (13 & 14 Vic c 2).

[66] Party Emblems (Ireland) Act 1860 (23 & 24 Vic c 141), s 2.

[67] Ibid.

peace and order'.[68] The Tithe War[69] was a period of violent opposition to the payment of tithes by Roman Catholics to the Anglican Church of Ireland.[70] Targeting anti-tithe groups, the Local Disturbances, etc (Ireland) Act 1833[71] allowed the Lord Lieutenant to prohibit or suppress any 'association, assembly, or body of persons in Ireland which he or they shall deem to be dangerous to the public peace or safety, or inconsistent with the due administration of the law …'. The legislation was aimed at 'tumultuous movements of large bodies of evil-disposed persons, who have, by their numbers and violence, created such general alarm and intimidation as materially to impede the due course of public justice'. The legislation also made it an offence to communicate with illegal associations by the 'making of any beacon, bonfire, light, fire, flash, blaze, or any signal by smoke, or by any rocket, firework, flag, firing of any gun or other fire-arms, or by blowing of horns, or by ringing of any church, chapel, or other bell'.[72]

The 1880s saw considerable unrest and violence in the Irish countryside. The Prevention of Crime (Ireland) Act 1882[73] empowered the Lord Lieutenant to proscribe meetings 'which he has reason to believe to be dangerous to the public peace or the public safety.' It was also an offence to take part in any unlawful assembly or riot, or to commit an aggravated crime of violence.[74]

C. Controlling Arms

Limiting the availability of weapons and ammunition was another legislative tactic frequently employed in Ireland. The Whiteboy Act 1775, for example, allowed for the seizure of unlicensed arms held by papists.[75] The Insurrection Act 1796[76] contained detailed provisions for the local registration of arms,[77] and the Insurrection and Disturbances (Ireland) Act 1807[78] provided for summary trial by special commission and seven years' transportation for persons unlawfully carrying arms. As well as licensing requirements, a number of Arms Acts sought to restrict the importation of arms.[79]

[68] Crossman, 'Emergency Legislation' (n 2) 309.

[69] RF Foster, 'Ascendancy and Union', in RF Foster (ed), *The Oxford History of Ireland* (Oxford, Oxford University Press, 2001) 156.

[70] See *Report from the Select Committee on the State of Ireland* (HC 1831, 12 – xvi) 677.

[71] 3 & 4 Wm IV c 4. Continued and modified by the Local Disturbances, etc (Ireland) Act 1834 (4 & 5 Wm IV c 48).

[72] Ibid, s 27.

[73] 45 & 46 Vic c 25, s 10.

[74] Ibid, s 8. Unlawful assemblies were also prohibited by the Criminal Law and Procedure (Ireland) Act 1887 (50 & 51 Vic c 20), s 2.

[75] Whiteboy Act 1775 (15 & 16 Geo III c 21), s 15.

[76] Insurrection Act 1796 (36 Geo III c 20), s 6.

[77] Tumultuous Risings Act 1787 (27 Geo III c 15) s 10 made it an offence to forcibly seize arms or ammunition, or to provide arms and ammunition for unlawful purposes.

[78] 47 Geo III c 13, s 19.

[79] See, eg, An Act to Prevent the Importation of Arms, Gunpowder and Ammunition into this Kingdom; and the Removing and Keeping of Arms, Gunpowder and Ammunition Without Licence 1793 (33 Geo III c 2); the Possession of Arms (Ireland) Act 1807 (47 Geo III c 54); the Arms (Ireland) Act 1813 (53 Geo III c 78); the Arms (Ireland) Act 1817 (57 Geo III c 21); the Arms (Ireland) Act 1820 (1 Geo IV c 47); the Arms (Ireland) Act 1822 (3 Geo IV c 4); the Arms (Ireland) Act 1823 (4 Geo IV c 14); and the Arms, etc (Ireland) Act 1843 (6 & 7 Vic c 74).

Later in the nineteenth century, general emergency statutes made reference to arms and weapons – for example, the Peace Preservation (Ireland) Act 1835[80] made it a misdemeanour to carry or conceal firearms in certain circumstances.[81]

D. Controlling the Press and Printed Materials

Control of written information or communications was also a feature of several statutes. Under the Insurrection Act 1796, persons 'hawking' any seditious 'hand bill, paper or pamphlet' were liable to be punished.[82] Similar provisions were contained in the statutes of 1807[83] and 1822.[84]

The proliferation of newspapers by the second half of the nineteenth century meant that legislation targeting handbills was no longer sufficient. Legislation in 1870 stated that newspapers containing treasonable or seditious matters were to be forfeited to the state.[85] A similar provision was contained in the Prevention of Crime (Ireland) Act 1882.[86]

E. Threatening Letters

Specific references were made in several eighteenth-century statutes to the use of threatening letters. For example, an Act which applied to a number of Ulster counties in the 1770s mentioned the practice of sending 'letters with fictitious names, and some without name, to several persons, demanding arms and money'.[87] The Act made it an offence 'to knowingly send, deliver, affix in any public place, or otherwise publish, or cause to be sent, delivered, affixed or otherwise published' any threatening or extorting letter. Other legislation focused on the use of public notices designed to threaten or incite.[88]

In response to the tithe-related violence of the 1830s, the Tumultuous Risings (Ireland) Act 1831[89] made it an offence to print, write, post, publish, circulate, send, or deliver threatening notices, letters or messages. It was quite broad in scope, encompassing inciting riots or unlawful meetings, or 'threatening any Violence, Injury, or Damage' to persons or property; 'demanding any money, arms, weapons or weapon, ammunition, or other matter'. It also included letters or notices 'directing or requiring any person to do or not to do any act, or to quit the service or employment of any person, or to set or to give

[80] 5 & 6 Wm IV c 48 s 8.

[81] See also the Prevention of Crime (Ireland) Act 1848 (11 & 12 Vic c 2); The Peace Preservation (Ireland) Act 1870 (33 & 34 Vic c 9), s 7; the Peace Preservation (Ireland) Act 1875 (38 & 39 Vic c 14), s 1; and the Peace Preservation (Ireland) Act 1881 (44 & 45 Vic c 5), s 5.

[82] Insurrection Act 1796 (36 Geo III c 20), s 32. It is interesting to note that different penalties were provided for male and female offenders. Men and boys could be drafted into the Navy, and women could be imprisoned for up to three months.

[83] Insurrection Disturbances (Ireland) Act 1807 (47 Geo III c 13), s 26. This did not distinguish between men and women.

[84] Insurrection Act 1822 (3 Geo IV c 57).

[85] Peace Preservation (Ireland) Act 1870 (33 & 34 Vic c 9), s 30.

[86] 45 & 46 Vic c 25, s 13.

[87] Insurrection in Ulster Act 1771 (11 & 12 Geo III c 5), preamble.

[88] Tumultuous Risings Act 1787 (27 Geo III c 15), s 9.

[89] 1 & 2 Wm IV c 44.

out any land'.[90] Aiding and abetting such letters or notices was deemed a transportable offence.[91] Earlier legislation targeting secret societies had also prohibited the sending of threatening letters.[92]

F. Other Offences

While the offences relating to unlawful assemblies, organisations and oaths covered most of what was included in the eighteenth- and nineteenth-century coercion legislation, from time to time other offences were legislatively proscribed. Sometimes these were drafted as specific responses to outbreaks of violence, usually in rural areas. The Whiteboy Act 1775, for example, prohibited disguises and face-coverings in an attempt to curb the activities of secret societies.[93] The Riot Act 1787 prohibited the damage and destruction of places of worship,[94] as well as the digging or erection of 'any grave, gallows or gibbet, or any instrument for inflicting bodily pain or punishment'.[95]

Legislation in 1831, enacted during the tithe agitation, applied to 'any person who shall compel or menace any one to quit his farm or employment, or shall assault or break into any habitation, or injure property, or carry away horses …'.[96] Such offenders were liable to be punished either by transportation (for life, 14 years or 7 years), or imprisonment with or without hard labour for up to three years. Men could also be whipped 'once, twice, or thrice publicly or privately'. Jailbreaking and rescuing prisoners were explicitly criminalised by legislation in the 1760s[97] and the 1830s.[98]

Some statutes were passed prohibiting certain types of violence or imposing harsher penalties for certain types of violence in Ireland. For example, legislation in 1773 and 1783 targeted assaults with sharp weapons, known as 'houghing', often perpetrated against soldiers.[99] The Assaults (Ireland) Act 1839[100] was enacted because 'the use of stones and of loaded sticks and loaded whips, in the commission of assaults, has been productive of grievous injury and sometimes loss of life in Ireland'. This Act provided that assaults with certain types of weapon could lead to fines of between ten shillings and five pounds on summary conviction.

The Prevention of Crime (Ireland) Act 1882[101] contained some very broadly drafted offences in an attempt to combat the practice of boycotting. It was an offence to use

[90] 1 & 2 Wm IV c 44, s 3.

[91] Ibid, s 6. Under the Peace Preservation (Ireland) Act 1870 (33 & 34 Vic c 9), s 15, warrants could be issued in proclaimed districts to allow searches for documents in the handwriting of persons suspected of writing threatening letters.

[92] Whiteboy Act 1775 (15 & 16 Geo III c 21), s 3.

[93] Ibid, s 2.

[94] Tumultuous Risings Act 1787 (27 Geo III c 15), s 5.

[95] Ibid, s 8.

[96] Tumultuous Risings (Ireland) Act 1831 (1 & 2 Wm IV c 44), s 2. This Act amended the Whiteboy Act 1775 (15 & 16 Geo III, c 21) by mitigating the death penalty in favour of transportation or imprisonment.

[97] Whiteboy Act 1765 (5 & 6 Geo III c 8), s 4.

[98] The Tumultuous Risings (Ireland) Act 1831 (1 & 2 Wm IV c 44), ss 4 and 5.

[99] An Act to Prevent Malicious Cutting and Wounding, and to Punish Offenders Called Chalkers 1773 (13 & 14 Geo III c 45); An Act for the More Effectual Discovery And Prosecution Of Offenders Called Houghers, and for the Support And Maintenance of Soldiers or Others Houghed, Maimed and Disabled by Such Offenders 1783 (23 & 24 Geo III c 56).

[100] 2 & 3 Vic c 77. Continued by the Assaults (Ireland) Act 1849 (12 & 13 Vic c 38).

[101] 45 & 46 Vic c 25.

intimidation or to incite another to use intimidation to prevent others from doing things they were lawfully entitled to do, or to force them to do things from which they could lawfully abstain. Intimidation under the 1882 Act included both actions and spoken words 'calculated to put any person in fear of any injury or danger to himself, or to any member of his family, or to any person in his employment, or in fear of any injury to or loss of his property, business, or means of living'. Persons summarily convicted of these offences faced up to six months' imprisonment, with or without hard labour.[102] Similar provisions were contained in Balfour's Criminal Law and Procedure (Ireland) Act 1887.[103] This Act also contained specific offences of forcibly taking possession of a house, or wilfully obstructing or resisting sheriffs or other officials in the execution of their duties.[104]

V. POWERS UNDER THE COERCION ACTS

Many of the Acts discussed here allowed for the 'proclamation' by the Lord Lieutenant that a particular district or county was in a disturbed state. The provisions of the coercive legislation then usually applied only in these 'proclaimed' districts.

A. Detention without Trial

According to Costello, by the mid-seventeenth century habeas corpus was being used as 'a mechanism for the bail or release of prisoners who had been committed for criminal offences, and were still awaiting trial in breach of the common law entitlement to an expeditious trial'.[105] The Habeas Corpus Act 1782[106] provided for the suspension of the right of habeas corpus by proclamation of the Lord Lieutenant, but this power was never invoked.[107] Habeas corpus was used on a number of occasions during the late 1790s by prisoners being detained without charge.[108] Instead of being suspended by proclamation, it was suspended by legislation in 1797.[109]

The 1797 Act was the first of fifteen Habeas Corpus Suspension Acts. Legislation restricting habeas corpus was in effect for most of the first decade of the Union.[110] Subsequent legislation was passed during times of violent disturbance in the 1820s,[111] the late 1840s[112] and in the 1860s.[113] Each Act was drafted along the same lines. However, as

[102] Ibid, ss 21, 22.

[103] 50 & 51 Vic c 20, s 2. This was a permanent measure, still in force at the time of the Anglo-Irish war.

[104] Ibid.

[105] K Costello, *The Law of Habeas Corpus in Ireland: History, Scope of Review and Practice under Article 40.4.2 of the Irish Constitution* (Dublin, Four Courts Press, 2006) 2.

[106] 21 & 22 Geo III c 11, s 16.

[107] Costello, *The Law of Habeas Corpus* (n 105) 19.

[108] Ibid, 17–19.

[109] Habeas Corpus Suspension Act 1797 (37 Geo III c 1).

[110] Eg, Habeas Corpus Suspension (Ireland) Act 1803 (43 Geo III c 116); Habeas Corpus Suspension (Ireland) Act 1805 (45 Geo III c 4).

[111] Habeas Corpus Suspension (Ireland) Act 1822 (3 Geo IV c 2).

[112] Habeas Corpus Suspension (Ireland) Act 1848 (11 & 12 Vic c 35) and Habeas Corpus Suspension (Ireland) Act 1849 (12 & 13 Vic c 2). The context was the Young Ireland rebellion; see Bowman, 'Ireland' (n 9).

[113] The context this time was the Fenian rebellion; see Bowman, 'Ireland' (n 9). Habeas Corpus Suspension (Ireland) Act 1866 (29 & 30 Vic c 1); Habeas Corpus Suspension (Ireland) Act 1866 (29 & 30 Vic c 119);

Costello points out, these statutes neither completely suspended the operation of habeas corpus at common law, nor did they directly suspend all of the rights in the Habeas Corpus Act 1782.[114] Instead, they indirectly superseded the prisoner's right to submit a petition for trial,[115] by enabling the Lord Lieutenant to detain persons suspected of treason (or treasonable practices) without initiating a criminal prosecution.[116] There was no requirement in the Habeas Corpus Suspension Acts that there be a situation of invasion or rebellion. Crossman describes the suspension of habeas corpus as a 'tried and trusted' remedy for criminal justice challenges in nineteenth-century Ireland.[117] This was so much so that by the early twentieth century there was what Costello describes as a 'recognition in Irish legal culture of habeas corpus as a high-priority civil right'.[118]

In addition to restrictions on habeas corpus, several Acts also provided for arrest and detention without trial. The Protection of Person and Property (Ireland) Act 1881[119] allowed for arrest and detention on suspicion of being guilty of treasonable offences. It also applied to persons suspected of committing any crime of violence or intimidation in a proclaimed district, or inciting violence or intimidation. The detention of such persons could be reviewed by the Lord Lieutenant every three months.[120] Persons detained under these provisions were to be treated as prisoners awaiting trial and not as convicted prisoners.[121]

Some legislation specifically targeted 'strangers' or non-residents found in proclaimed districts. The Insurrection Act 1796,[122] for example, empowered Justices of the Peace to commit to gaol any stranger in a district who was unable to satisfactorily account for 'his place of abode, the place from whence he came, his manner of livelihood, and his object or motive for remaining or coming into the county, town or city'. Similar powers were contained in subsequent legislation, including the Insurrection and Disturbances (Ireland) Act 1807,[123] the Peace Preservation (Ireland) Act 1870[124] and the Prevention of Crime (Ireland) Act 1882.[125]

Habeas Corpus Suspension (Ireland) Act 1867 (30 & 31 Vic c 1); Habeas Corpus Suspension (Ireland) Act 1867 (30 & 31 Vic c 25); Habeas Corpus (Ireland) Act 1868 (31 & 32 Vic c 7); Protection of Life and Property (Ireland) Act, 1871 (34 & 35 Vic c 25).

[114] Costello, *The Law of Habeas Corpus* (n 105) 20.

[115] Contained in the Habeas Corpus Act 1782 (21 & 22 Geo III c 11) s 6.

[116] Costello, *The Law of Habeas Corpus* (n 105) 20.

[117] Crossman, 'Emergency Legislation' (n 2) 314.

[118] Costello, *The Law of Habeas Corpus* (n 105) 20. See *Re Sullivan* (1888) 22 LR Ir 98 and *Egan v Macready* [1921] 1 IR 265. The former related to detention during the Plan of Campaign in 1887, and the latter influenced the decision to include habeas corpus in the Free State Constitution. Both cases are discussed in Costello, *The Law of Habeas Corpus* (n 105) 22–27.

[119] 44 & 45 Vic, c 4, s 1.

[120] 44 & 45 Vic, c 4, s 1(5).

[121] Ibid, s 1(3). This meant that the prison rules relating to convicted prisoners did not apply.

[122] Insurrection Act 1796 (36 Geo III c 20), s 15.

[123] (47 Geo III c 13), s 9. The person detained could be required to produce a surety for their good behaviour. These powers were restated in the Unlawful Oaths (Ireland) Act 1810 (50 Geo III c 102), s 7.

[124] 33 & 34 Vic c 9, s 25; continued by the Protection of Life and Property in Certain Parts of Ireland Act 1871 (34 & 35 Vic c 25), which conferred extensive powers to detain persons suspected of involvement with secret societies. Both Acts were continued by the Peace Preservation (Ireland) Acts Continuance Act 1873 (36 & 37 Vic c 24) and, with amendments, by the Peace Preservation (Ireland) Act 1875 (38 & 39 Vic c 14).

[125] 45 & 46 Vic c 25, s 12. See H Humphries, *The Prevention of Crime (Ireland) Act 1882: 45 and 46 Vic, Cap 25, With A Review on the Policy, Bearing and Scope of the Act* (Dublin, Hodges Figgis, 1882).

B. Special Courts

The removal of powers of trial and punishment from the ordinary courts was a method frequently employed to deal with rebellion and revolt. In the late eighteenth century, special military tribunals were authorised for the trial of civilians and a state of martial law existed. This continued after the passing of the Act of Union.[126] The legislation meant that courts martial could be convened and impose death sentences. By 1803 it was deemed necessary to pass further legislation. The Suppression of Rebellion (Ireland) Act 1803 noted in its preamble that 'a treasonable and rebellious spirit of insurrection now unfortunately exists in Ireland, and hath broken out into acts of open murder and rebellion'.[127] Courts martial were also legislated for in the 1830s[128] during the Tithe War.

Aside from courts martial, emergency legislation sometimes also provided for special courts within the civil system, usually known as special sessions[129] or extraordinary sessions of the peace.[130] These sessions generally had all the same powers as a regular civil court.[131]

One of the most significant pieces of legislation to provide for trial by special tribunal was the Prevention of Crime (Ireland) Act 1882.[132] Comerford describes it as providing the government with 'a comprehensive armoury of most of the powers that had been used against crime and agitation during the nineteenth century'.[133] It was designed to circumvent the difficulties in securing convictions in the regular criminal courts for offences connected with the land agitation. It authorised the establishment of special commissions of three judges of the superior courts. Unanimity was required for a conviction, and reasons had to be stated.[134] These measures proved to be extremely controversial, nowhere less so than among the judiciary. The superior court judges were opposed to the measure, to the extent that one judge resigned over the issue.[135]

C. Rules of Evidence and Procedure

The widespread use of intimidation and violence against informers and witnesses often served to frustrate attempts at conviction. Several Acts allowed statements made by witnesses who were subsequently murdered to be admissible.[136] Legislation around this

[126] Suppression of Rebellion (Ireland) Act 1801 (41 Geo III, c 14), preamble; continued by the Suppression of Rebellion (Ireland) Act 1801 (41 Geo III c 61).

[127] Suppression of Rebellion, etc (Ireland) Act 1803 (43 Geo III c 117), preamble; continued by the Suppression of Rebellion, etc (Ireland) Act 1803 (43 Geo III c 9).

[128] The Local Disturbances, etc. (Ireland) Act 1833 (3 & 4 Wm IV c 4), s 13; continued and modified by the Local Disturbances, etc (Ireland) Act 1834 (4 & 5 Wm IV c 48).

[129] Insurrection Act 1796 (36 Geo III c 20) s 16; Insurrection and Disturbances (Ireland) Act 1807 (47 Geo III c 13); Unlawful Combinations (Ireland) Act 1814 (54 Geo III c 180).

[130] Insurrection Act 1822 (3 Geo IV c 57); Peace Preservation (Ireland) Act 1835 (5 & 6 Wm IV c 48).

[131] Peace Preservation (Ireland) Act 1835 (5 & 6 Wm IV c 48), preamble.

[132] 45 & 46 Vic c 25.

[133] RV Comerford, 'The Politics of Distress' in WE Vaughan (ed) *A New History of Ireland: VI: Ireland Under the Union 1870–1921* (Oxford, Oxford University Press, 1989) 50.

[134] Ibid, ss 1(3), 1(4).

[135] This was Baron Fitzgerald of the Court of Exchequer. See Howlin, 'The Politics of Jury Trials' (n 1) 223.

[136] Insurrection Act 1796 (36 Geo III c 20), s 12; Insurrection and Disturbances (Ireland) Act 1807 (47 Geo III c 13); Unlawful Oaths (Ireland) Act 1810 (50 Geo III c 102), s 5.

time also allowed the use of specific defences: the Insurrection and Disturbances (Ireland) Act 1807[137] explicitly allowed for the defence of necessity for persons accused of taking or administering an unlawful oath.[138] This principle was retained in the Unlawful Oaths (Ireland) Act 1810.[139] By contrast, the Insurrection Act 1796[140] had precluded the use of this defence unless the oath-taker came forward to inform within ten days.

From time to time legislation allowed for the removal of trials from one county to another,[141] in contravention of the common law principle that defendants should be tried in the county where an alleged offence had taken place. Removal of the trial to another county was thought to reduce the possibility of witnesses and jurors being threatened, influenced or intimidated.[142]

D. Curfews

If the Lord Lieutenant proclaimed a district to be disturbed, certain personal liberties could be restricted. Proclamations often entailed the imposition of a curfew, in attempts to restrict the nocturnal activities of secret societies.[143]

E. Powers of Search and Seizure

Powers to search private dwellings were a feature of several eighteenth- and nineteenth-century Acts, including the Whiteboy Act 1775[144] and the Insurrection Act 1796.[145] Many of these provisions were mirrored in 1807[146] and 1822.[147] The late 1840s saw the outbreak of a short-lived rebellion led by the Young Irelanders,[148] leading to the passing of another emergency Act. The Prevention of Crime (Ireland) Act 1848[149] mirrored the earlier legislation in allowing for searches of private property and seizure of weapons.[150]

[137] 47 Geo III c 13.

[138] Insurrection and Disturbances (Ireland) Act 1807 (47 Geo III c 13), s 4.

[139] 50 Geo III c 102, s 2.

[140] Insurrection Act 1796 (36 Geo III c 20), s 2.

[141] Eg, the Insurrection in Ulster Act 1771 (11 & 12 Geo III c 5) allowed for cases to be tried by 'the good and lawful men of the body of the county of Dublin'.

[142] See, eg, the Trial of Offences (Ireland) Act 1833 (3 & 4 Wm IV c 79); the Peace Preservation (Ireland) Act 1870 (33 & 34 Vic c 9); the Prevention of Crime (Ireland) Act 1882 (45 & 46 Vic c 25 s 6); and the Criminal Law and Procedure (Ireland) Act 1887 (50 & 51 Vic c 20).

[143] Eg, the Insurrection Act 1796 (36 Geo III c 20), s 17; the Insurrection and Disturbances (Ireland) Act 1807 (47 Geo II, c 13), s 11; the Unlawful Combinations (Ireland) Act 1814 (54 Geo III, c 180); the Insurrection Act 1822 (3 Geo IV, c 57); the Local Disturbances, etc (Ireland) Act 1833 (3 & 4 Wm IV c 4) s 22; the Peace Preservation (Ireland) Act 1835 (5 & 6 Wm IV c 48); and Prevention of Crime (Ireland) Act 1882 (45 & 46 Vic c 25).

[144] Whiteboy Act 1775 (15 & 16 Geo III c 21), s 15.

[145] Insurrection Act 1796 (36 Geo III c 20), s 10.

[146] Insurrection and Disturbances (Ireland) Act 1807 (47 Geo III c 13), s 17.

[147] Insurrection Act 1822 (3 Geo IV c 57).

[148] Bowman, 'Ireland' (n 9) 897 describes the 1848 rebellion as 'a fairly miserable affair'.

[149] The Prevention of Crime (Ireland) Act 1848 (11 & 12 Vic c 2), ss 13 and 14.

[150] See also The Peace Preservation (Ireland) Act 1870 (33 & 34 Vic c 9) and the Peace Preservation (Ireland) Act 1881 (44 & 45 Vic c 5) s 1, continued by the Peace Preservation (Ireland) Continuance Act 1886 (49 & 50 Vic c 24).

VI. CONCLUSION

The OASA deals with a range of specific offences as well as criminal justice procedures and processes. These include secret societies; unlawful organisations; unauthorised military activities; administering unlawful oaths; printing, possessing or disseminating certain documents; the prohibition of public meetings; special courts and internment. This chapter demonstrates that the Act is firmly rooted in a tradition of special or emergency legislation enacted to deal with specific law and order challenges in Ireland.[151] There were many commonalities between the earlier legislation and the OASA, in terms of both the types of activities and groups proscribed, and the alterations to the mechanics of criminal justice. Of course, that is not to say that there was nothing new in the OASA, and other contributors to this book illustrate who and what the Act originally targeted, and how this changed over time.[152]

Despite what seems to be an unending litany of special punitive measures enacted for Ireland, Crossman points out that:

> No government turned to extraordinary measures lightly. They were, after all, an admission of failure and although they might provide a temporary respite ministers had no illusions about their long-term effect ... Ministers disliked presenting such measures to parliament and the political difficulties involved should not be underestimated.[153]

She makes the point that emergency legislation was not passed on a whim, but after the 'ordinary' criminal law was seen to have failed. One member of the House of Lords observed, presumably with the benefit of some hindsight in 1893, that 'exceptional legislation, as we know, is not a cure for a deep-rooted and deep-seated evil'.[154] The same commentator noted the 'demoralising effect' such legislation could have. It is worth adding that the 'ordinary' rules of criminal procedure and evidence, the principles of substantive criminal law, and the courts' power of punishment were not insignificant tools for the maintenance of public order. Special measures often proved controversial, not only amongst those who were targeted, but also by those tasked with administering these laws.

[151] It is worth pointing out that the enforcement and application of these laws was at times patchy.
[152] See L Campbell, Chapter 8 and L Donohue, Chapter 10, this volume.
[153] Crossman, 'Emergency Legislation' (n 2) 312–3.
[154] Hansard, vol 17, col 4, House of Lords (5 September 1893), Earl Spencer.

2

Precursors to the Offences Against the State Act – Emergency Law in the Irish Free State

THOMAS MOHR

I. INTRODUCTION

IN 1939, FUTURE Taoiseach John A Costello insisted that the Offences Against the State Bill presented to the Oireachtas had been copied 'practically verbatim' from emergency measures enacted during the lifetime of the Cumann na nGaedheal Government that had held power between 1922 and 1932.[1] The emergency measures in question were the Public Safety Acts 1923 to 1927, the Treasonable Offences Act 1925 and Article 2A of the 1922 Constitution that had been inserted by means of constitutional amendment in 1931. Of course, Costello had a powerful interest in asserting this claim as he had held the office of Attorney General between 1926 and 1932 and became a leading member of the parliamentary opposition after Cumann na nGaedheal was incorporated into Fine Gael in 1933. The accusation of plagiarism served the dual purpose of allowing Costello's Fine Gael party to take credit for many provisions of the 1939 Bill while, at the same time, exposing the Fianna Fáil Government to charges of hypocrisy for having opposed these provisions while they were in opposition.

Costello's claim, made during the course of partisan parliamentary debates, was, of course, an exaggeration. Nevertheless, it cannot be denied that a substantial number of provisions of the Offences Against the State Act 1939 (OASA) were based on provisions from legislation enacted during the Free State period that preceded the enactment of the 1937 Constitution. For example, the impact of the Treasonable Offences Act 1925 on the OASA can be seen in the latter's provisions on the usurpation of the functions of government, illegal drilling, secret societies within the army and police force and in dealing with unlawful oaths.[2] The provision in Section 28 of the OASA prohibiting meetings in the vicinity of the Oireachtas was based on a provision dropped from the 1925 Act.[3]

[1] *Dáil Debates*, vol 74, col 1408, 2 March 1939.

[2] See Treasonable Offences Act 1925, ss 4, 5, 7, 8, and 9 and Offences Against the State Act 1939, ss 6, 15, 16 and 17.

[3] Treasonable and Seditious Offences Bill 1925, s 7. *Dáil Debates*, vol 10, col 287, 18 February 1925.

The influence of the Public Safety Act 1927 and Article 2A of the 1922 Constitution can be seen in the provisions of the OASA concerning censorship of publications, closure of buildings, prohibition of public meetings and treatment of unlawful associations.[4] Costello's allegation of plagiarism must have been particularly galling to de Valera's government which appears to have gone to some effort to reword provisions that had been derived from earlier emergency measures before inclusion in the OASA.[5] Despite these efforts at rearrangement, the links between important provisions of the OASA and those of preceding emergency measures remained obvious.

This chapter does not examine the lengthy drafting process that led to the creation of the OASA. A detailed examination of this drafting process would, of necessity, be lengthy and highly technical.[6] Instead, this chapter examines the most significant emergency measures passed during the lifetime of the Irish Free State (1922 to 1937) that influenced the drafting of the OASA. This examination raises the issue of whether controversial provisions produced during the Free State period became 'normalised' with repeated use and the passage of time which, in turn, facilitated their reproduction in the OASA. The second theme of this chapter examines the historical experience of the emergency measures passed during the Free State period. This theme deserves attention because the OASA was not merely influenced by the textual provisions of the emergency measures that preceded it but also by the successes and failures of these measures.

II. EMERGENCY LAW AND THE ORIGINS OF THE STATE

Howlin has shown, in the preceding chapter of this volume, that Ireland experienced a continuous stream of emergency legislation throughout the eighteenth and nineteenth centuries.[7] Many of the themes of emergency legislation in the eighteenth and nineteenth centuries, in particular the control of unlawful associations, remained equally relevant after 1922. The basic tools used by emergency legislation after 1922 would also have been familiar to those who drafted emergency legislation in the eighteenth and nineteenth centuries. These included the use of detention without trial, enhanced police powers of search and seizure together with special rules on evidence. As seen in the previous chapter, the use of special courts, including military courts capable of trying civilians, was a familiar theme to lawyers in the centuries that preceded the birth of the Irish state. This was a trend that would continue into the early twentieth century.

The very title 'Offences Against the State' assumes the existence of a self-governing and autonomous Irish state whose continued survival and vitality is dependent upon protection from internal dissidents. Indeed, the origins of the Irish state in the early twentieth century are inseparable from a history of emergency law. Involvement in the

[4] Eg, see Public Safety Act 1927, ss 4, 7, 9; Constitution (Amendment No 17) Act 1931, ss 19, 22, 27; and Offences Against the State Act 1939, ss 10, 18, 24 and 25.

[5] NAI Department of the Taoiseach, S10454B, M Moynihan to S Roche, 25 January 1939. See also JJ Lee, *Ireland 1912–1985 – Politics and Society* (Cambridge, Cambridge University Press, 1989) 220–1 and F Davis, *The History and Development of the Special Criminal Court, 1922–2005* (Dublin, Four Courts, 2007) 65–6.

[6] Accounts of the drafting process can be found in S Ó Longaigh, *Emergency Law in Independent Ireland, 1922–1948* (Dublin, Four Courts, 2006) 221–6 and Davis, *Special Criminal Court* (n 5) 64–7.

[7] N Howlin, Chapter 1, in this volume.

First World War saw the enactment of the Defence of the Realm Act 1914 and the British reaction to the 1916 uprising was heavily influenced by the framework of this statute and subsequent amending legislation.[8] The armed struggle between Crown forces and the IRA that occurred between 1919 and 1921 saw the enactment of the Restoration of Order (Ireland) Act 1920 which resulted in the introduction of martial law in many parts of the island. This conflict formally ended with the signing of the document popularly known as 'the Treaty' in Ireland (henceforth '1921 Treaty' in this chapter) on 6 December 1921. The settlement offered by the 1921 Treaty raised hopes of breaking the long historical cycle of emergency legislation in Ireland. These hopes were dashed on 28 June 1922 when the shelling of the Four Courts heralded the outbreak of the Irish Civil War.

The 1922 Constitution of the Irish Free State was drafted during a brief period of optimism immediately after the signing of the 1921 Treaty when the events of 28 June 1922 still seemed inconceivable. One of the most noteworthy features of the Constitution was the inclusion of several human rights provisions. These were far more extensive than anything that appeared in the Constitutions of the Dominions to which the infant Irish state was linked under the terms of the 1921 Treaty.

It is sometimes asserted that Irish experience of emergency laws in the eighteenth and nineteenth centuries, as outlined by Howlin,[9] prompted the inclusion of constitutional safeguards for individual liberty in the 1922 Constitution.[10] Similar considerations may have influenced the drafters in creating the Constitution's emergency provisions which were phrased in terms of constraints on the powers of the state. For example, there were limits on the use of courts martial on members of the armed forces (Article 71) and on the removal of trial by jury (Article 72). Article 70 provided that 'extraordinary courts shall not be established, save only such Military Tribunals as may be authorised by law for dealing with military offenders against military law'. This provision also made clear that 'The jurisdiction of Military Tribunals shall not be extended to or exercised over the civil population save in time of war, or armed rebellion, and for acts committed in time of war or armed rebellion, and in accordance with the regulations to be prescribed by law.' The powers of the state in an emergency could only be determined by implication from these limiting provisions. There were no general provisions permitting the suspension or overriding of key constitutional provisions in times of war or armed rebellion.[11]

Two historical points require clarification to facilitate understanding of this account of emergency law passed between 1922 and 1937. The first concerns the amendments of the 1922 Constitution that are mentioned in this chapter. It is important to understand that the 1922 Constitution could be amended by Acts of the Oireachtas throughout its lifetime. The text of Article 50 of that Constitution provided that constitutional

[8] Eg, see A Hardiman, 'Shot in Cold Blood: Military Law and Irish Perceptions in the suppression of the 1916 Rebellion' in G Doherty and D Keogh (eds), *The Long Revolution: the 1916 Rising in Context* (Cork, Mercier, 2008) 225.

[9] N Howlin, Chapter 1, in this volume.

[10] Eg, see L Kohn, *The Constitution of the Irish Free State* (Dublin, Allen and Unwin, 1932) 130.

[11] The impact of war and rebellion on specific aspects of the Constitution were anticipated by Art 6 (personal liberty) and Art 70 (limits on the use of extraordinary and military courts). Limits on the state's active participation in war were included in Art 49. The relevant provisions of Art 6 were held to be merely declaratory of the pre-existing state of the law with respect to entitlement to habeas corpus and its limitation in times of war and armed rebellion. *R (O'Brien) v Minister for Defence* [1924] 1 IR 32. See also Kohn, *Constitution* (n 10) 134.

amendments could only be made if approved in a referendum. However, a change to the text of Article 50 shortly before it came into force permitted amendment by ordinary legislation for the first eight years of the lifetime of the 1922 Constitution. The Oireachtas would later pass the Constitution (Amendment No 16) Act 1929 which extended the transitional period from 8 to 16 years. The legality of this extension was confirmed in 1934 by the majority judgment in the case of *State (Ryan) v Lennon*.[12]

The second historical point that requires clarification concerns the origins of the Irish Free State itself. The signature of the 1921 Treaty on 6 December 1921 initiated a year-long period of transition. This transition witnessed a gradual handover of responsibility from British authorities to the Irish Provisional Government. An assembly called the 'Provisional Parliament', but also known as the 'Constituent Assembly', was elected for the embryonic state. As a Provisional Parliament it lacked full legislative powers. Its main function as a Constituent Assembly was to pass the draft Constitution of the Irish Free State, which would be enacted in parallel with legislation passed in London.[13] This period of transition ended on 6 December 1922 when the Constitution came into force and, in the eyes of lawyers, the 26 counties officially left the UK and formed the Irish Free State.[14] The outbreak of Civil War on 28 June 1922 occurred right in the middle of this year of transition. Consequently, an embryonic Irish state, that was still developing its core institutions, faced the ultimate challenge to its existence while lacking the legal tools to respond to it.

III. ARMY (EMERGENCY POWERS) RESOLUTION

How could the embryonic state pass emergency legislation to deal with the crisis when its Parliament lacked full legislative powers? Hugh Kennedy, legal advisor to the Provisional Government, wrestled with this challenge within the restrictive framework of British law and under the shadow of the draft Irish Constitution, whose basic structure had now taken shape although it was not yet in force. The Provisional Government had already adopted a system of creating a form of temporary legislation known as 'Decrees' and ten of these were passed between April and October 1922.[15] Yet, the adoption of a Provisional Government Decree was deemed unsuitable for emergency measures dealing with public order. This was because it was believed that the Provisional Parliament could only pass temporary legislation that dealt with 'matters of administration' that the British had already transferred to it.[16] These did not include emergency legislation dealing with public order.

[12] [1935] IR 170.

[13] See Constitution of the Irish Free State (Saorstát Éireann) Act 1922 enacted in Dublin and Constitution of the Irish Free State Act 1922 (Session 2) enacted by Westminster.

[14] See T Mohr, 'Law and the Foundation of the Irish State on 6 December 1922' (2018) 59 *Irish Jurist* 31–58.

[15] NAI, Department of the Taoiseach, S1735, legislative powers of the Provisional Parliament, 13 September 1922. Hugh Kennedy developed the procedure to be followed in enacting these Provisional Government decrees. See UCD Archives, Kennedy Papers, P4/227. It should be noted that the first and second incarnations of Dáil Éireann had also purported to pass legislation between 1919 and 1922 and these were later known as 'Dáil decrees'. See B Farrell, 'The Legislation of a Revolutionary Assembly: Dáil Decrees, 1919–1922' (1975) 10 *Irish Jurist* 112.

[16] See the Provisional Government (Transfer of Functions) Order 1922 (1922 No 315), a British Order in Council that followed the enactment of the Irish Free State (Agreement) Act 1922.

Hugh Kennedy severed this Gordian knot by having the Provisional Parliament pass an instrument that was given the title of a 'Resolution' instead of being called an 'Act' or a 'Decree'.[17] In addition, Kennedy recommended the presentation of these emergency provisions as parliamentary confirmation of powers already inherent in the Provisional Government.[18] Nevertheless, Leo Kohn has concluded that the Resolution was 'in effect, if not in form, a parliamentary measure'.[19]

The Army (Emergency Powers) Resolution passed by the Provisional Parliament permitted the establishment of a system of military courts whose reach extended beyond those who considered themselves combatants in the Civil War. It also imposed controls on the ownership of firearms. The military courts were empowered to inflict sanctions that included fines, imprisonment, penal servitude and even the death penalty.[20] It was expected that existing prisons could not contain the number of anticipated internees and the Provisional Government seriously considered approaching the British Government to lease the island of St Helena to hold them.[21] This proposal proved impractical but rumours of the plan did leak into the public domain.[22] Nevertheless, over 11,000 people were interned in the Irish Free State between 1922 and 1924.[23]

Although the Army (Emergency Powers) Resolution was passed during the depths of the Civil War, its adoption did not pass without protest. The introduction of the Resolution in the Provisional Parliament coincided with the presentation of what would become Article 70 of the draft Constitution that sought to place severe limits on the use of military courts to try civilians. Challenges as to the legality of the Resolution and its system of military courts were raised by the opposition in the Provisional Parliament. The powers granted to the military tribunals under the Resolution were described as a 'blank cheque' and comparisons were made with military courts in the Soviet Union, an analogy that would be raised with respect to almost every piece of emergency legislation enacted in the 1920s and 1930s.[24] Opposition TDs also raised questions as to what laws these military courts would enforce.[25] Cathal O'Shannon, a leading member of the Labour party, voiced his doubts by declaring 'I question very much the validity of passing a resolution like this by the Dáil, and I challenge the legal gentlemen in this Assembly to justify it from a legal and Constitutional point of view.'[26] Nevertheless, the Provisional Government enjoyed a strong parliamentary majority, thanks to the absence of TDs who opposed the 1921 Treaty, and the Resolution passed without difficulty. The Provisional Government lost no time in exercising its powers and establishing the anticipated military courts.[27]

[17] NAI, Department of the Taoiseach, S1735 and UCD Archives, Kennedy Papers, P4/946, Supplemental Opinion, 13 September 1922. See also NAI, Provisional Government Minutes, G1/3, 15 September 1922.

[18] NAI, Department of the Taoiseach, S1735 and UCD Archives, Kennedy Papers, P4/946, Supplemental Opinion, 13 September 1922. This method of enacting emergency measures also circumvented the awkward question of obtaining royal assent required for formal legislation.

[19] Kohn, *Constitution* (n 10) 144.

[20] *Dáil Debates*, vol 1, col 802–4, 27 September 1922.

[21] NAI, TSCH/1/1/3/1, Provisional Government Minutes, 18 September 1922.

[22] Eg, see *Dáil Debates*, vol 1, col 919, 28 September 1922 and col 1829, 20 October 1922.

[23] NAI, Department of the Taoiseach, S1369/4, number of prisoners (political), 21 May 1924.

[24] *Dáil Debates*, vol 1, col 813 and 851, 27 September 1922.

[25] Eg, ibid at col 811–7.

[26] Ibid at 825.

[27] Legal challenges to these courts were defeated in *R (Johnstone) v O'Sullivan* [1923] 2 IR 13 and *R (Childers) v Adjutant-General of the Forces of the Irish Provisional Government* [1923] 1.

IV. THE PUBLIC SAFETY ACTS 1923

On 30 April 1923 anti-Treaty forces declared a unilateral ceasefire. On 24 May 1923 they declared their intention to dump arms and ordered their combatants to return to their homes. Nevertheless, the military courts established by Army (Emergency Powers) Resolution continued to operate and most persons who had been interned were not released. The legal basis of the Army (Emergency Powers) Resolution had always lacked clarity and been open to challenge.[28] The Irish Government slowly came to the realisation that emergency legislation passed by the new Oireachtas of the Irish Free State was urgently required to provide legal cover to the continued use of military courts and internment and to create new powers of arrest and detention.

In June 1923 the Public Safety (Emergency Powers) Bill was finally introduced in the Oireachtas in the shadow of habeas corpus actions that had already been initiated in the courts.[29] Despite the urgency of the proposed legislation, the concerns expressed by the opposition in the newly-constituted Oireachtas over the sweeping powers contained in the Bill ensured that its progress was neither swift nor easy. Kevin O'Higgins, Minister for Home Affairs, justified the measure by arguing that although the Civil War was now over 'the peace, such as it is, is a false peace' and 'the calm is a calm of exhaustion and not of peace'.[30] The opposition condemned the proposed powers in biblical terms as 'out-Heroding Herod',[31] made analogies with the Court of Star Chamber and provided unflattering comparisons with emergency measures enacted by the Parliament of Northern Ireland.[32] The provisions of the 1923 Bill that permitted the infliction of flogging attracted particular attention and ensured that it would be popularly known as the 'Flogging Bill'.[33]

The provisions of the 1923 Bill were debated in some detail. Many amendments were moved by the opposition and progress through the Oireachtas proved to be slow. Nevertheless, the prospect of successful litigation forced the Irish Government to rapidly accelerate their plans to create properly constituted emergency legislation. The case of *R (O'Brien) v Minister for Defence* saw an internee, Nora Connelly O'Brien, take a case to the Court of Appeal on the basis that the state of war that had underpinned her detention had now come to an end.[34] A decision in her favour would place the detention of all interned prisoners in doubt. The government anticipated serious difficulties and so, on 1 August 1923, the final stages of the Public Safety (Emergency Powers) Bill 1923 were rushed through the Oireachtas and it was given royal assent the very same day.

The unseemly haste of the final stages of the enactment of the Public Safety (Emergency Powers) Act 1923 had unfortunate consequences. The state attempted to contest the release of Nora Connolly O'Brien, one of the many prisoners who still remained in military custody, on the basis of the new legislation.[35] Unfortunately, the

[28] *R (Childers) v Adjutant-General of the Forces of the Irish Provisional Government* [1923] 1 IR 5.
[29] *Dáil Debates*, vol 3, col 1984–6, 15 June 1923.
[30] Ibid, col 2501, 26 June 1923.
[31] Ibid, col 1987, 15 June 1923.
[32] Ibid, col 2513–4 and 2527, 26 June 1923.
[33] See, eg, *Dáil Debates*, vol 4, col 740 and 762, 12 July 1923.
[34] [1924] 1 IR 32.
[35] Ibid, 35.

Court of Appeal held that the Public Safety (Emergency Powers) Act 1923 was unconstitutional as its enactment had not followed the procedures laid down by Article 47 of the 1922 Constitution.[36] Consequently, the Oireachtas enacted a second statute that was passed in just one day and would be known as the Public Safety (Emergency Powers) (No 2) Act 1923. This legislation re-enacted the text of the original Act but also provided that the requirements of Article 47 would not apply to this statute.[37]

The first and second Acts of 1923 aimed at providing legal justification for a policy of internment that was already in place. The government insisted that this was a temporary measure and the Public Safety (Emergency Powers) (No 2) Act 1923 was set to expire on 1 February 1924. As time wore on it became apparent that the policy of internment could not be wound down by this deadline. O'Higgins argued the continued practice of jury intimidation together with hunger strikes and other obstructive tactics by prisoners had slowed the pace of winding down internment.[38] Consequently, it was decided to enact the Public Safety (Powers of Arrest and Detention) Temporary Act 1924 and the Public Safety (Punishment of Offences) Temporary Act 1924. The Public Safety (Powers of Arrest and Detention) Temporary Act 1924 extended the period in which opponents of the state could be interned until 1 February 1925.[39] This was the subject of a legal challenge in *R(O'Connell) v Military Governor of Hare Park Camp* but, on this occasion, the constitutionality of the relevant legislation was upheld.[40] The Public Safety (Punishment of Offences) Temporary Act 1924 allowed for a trial to be moved to a court in another part of the state, a measure designed to deal with the risk of jury intimidation.[41] The Oireachtas also enacted the Enforcement of Law (Occasional Powers) Acts 1923 and 1924 to enforce civil law remedies in the unsettled circumstances that prevailed in the aftermath of the Civil War.

Although the period of internment had been extended to 1 February 1925 it was, in practice, gradually wound down over the course of 1924. By July 1924 the few remaining prisoners in military custody were transferred to ordinary prisons.[42] The conclusion of the Civil War, the gradual winding-down of the policy of internment and new laws aimed at opponents of the state did result in a reduction in armed violence after 1924. Yet, the problem of armed violence never entirely disappeared. State officials tended to blame continuing high rates of unemployment for this unfortunate reality rather than any initiative by opponents of the state.[43]

[36] Article 47 provided for a period of seven days after the enactment of a Bill in which two-fifths of the Dáil and a majority in the Seanad might make a written demand that the Bill be suspended and possibly placed before the people in a referendum. This provision would not apply if both Houses of the Oireachtas declared the Bill to be 'necessary for the immediate preservation of the public peace, health or safety'. This procedure had not been followed with respect to Public Safety (Emergency Powers) Act 1923.

[37] Public Safety (Emergency Powers) (No 2) Act 1923, s 2.

[38] *Dáil Debates*, vol 5, col 1939–47, 14 December 1923. For an assessment of jury intimidation in this period see M Coen, '"The work of some irresponsible women": Jurors, Ghosts and Embracery in the Irish Free State' (2020) 38(4) *Law and History Review* 777–810.

[39] Public Safety (Powers of Arrest and Detention) Temporary Act 1924, s 10. See NAI Department of the Taoiseach, S3463.

[40] [1924] 2 IR 104.

[41] Public Safety (Punishment of Offences) Temporary Act 1924, s 8.

[42] NAI, Department of the Taoiseach, S1369/4, Secretary, Department of the President to Secretary, Department of Justice, 17 July 1924.

[43] Ó Longaigh, *Emergency Law* (n 6) 55.

V. PERMANENT MEASURES 1925 TO 1926

In 1926 a number of armed attacks on Garda stations resulted in calls for a revival of the power of the government to declare temporary periods of emergency that would justify the reintroduction of internment.[44] The result was the enactment of the Public Safety (Emergency Powers) Act 1926 that passed through the Oireachtas with more muted opposition than had greeted earlier emergency provisions. Those who did oppose this measure tended to argue that the government already had sufficient powers to deal with the purported emergency. The weakness of opposition to the Act may be explained by the more moderate powers it contained in comparison to earlier measures. Although it did provide for internment, there were, at least, no references to flogging or the death penalty in the 1926 Act. In any case, there was little time for opposition as this measure was signed into law just three days after its introduction in the Dáil and brought into force by proclamation one day later.[45] Despite the relative weakness of opposition, the 1926 Act ran into trouble less than a month after it came into force. Although the government attempted to present the release of a large number of internees detained under the 1926 Act as a gesture of goodwill, it also admitted that some members of the Garda Síochána in County Waterford had abused their authority and severely beaten some internees.[46] Even the normally unapologetic Kevin O'Higgins, now Minister for Justice, seemed shocked and expressed 'deep regret and a feeling of humiliation'.[47] The Act was designed to remain in force for periods of three months following a proclamation issued by the government and was allowed to lapse on 19 February 1927.[48] The ineffective 1926 Act was soon overshadowed by legislation granting far more radical powers and was finally repealed by the OASA.[49]

Political, in addition to legal, considerations demanded the enactment of the Firearms Act 1925 and the Treasonable Offences Act 1925. The former was needed to replace the Firearms Act 1920 which was politically undesirable as it had been enacted as part of the campaign by Crown forces during the conflict of 1919–1921. It also replaced a temporary Irish statute known as the Firearms (Temporary Provisions) Act 1924 that had been enacted in some haste. The enactment of the Treasonable Offences Act 1925 was also politically desirable as treason had previously been defined by reference to the British monarch.[50] Both measures also sought to modernise the law in their respective areas.

Kevin O'Higgins described the core provisions of the Treasonable Offences Act 1925 as 'the State's answer to those who challenge its life'.[51] It was promoted as a permanent feature in the architecture of the state, in contrast to the temporary nature of the Public

[44] NAI, Department of the Taoiseach, S2257 and *Dáil Debates*, vol 17, cols 39–41, 16 November 1926.

[45] The Public Safety (Emergency Powers) Bill was introduced to the Dáil on 16 November 1926. See *Dáil Debates*, vol 17, col 39, 16 November 1926. NAI, Department of the Taoiseach, S2262, Proclamation by the Executive Council of Saorstát Éireann, 20 November 1926.

[46] *Dáil Debates*, vol 17, col 697, 15 December 1926.

[47] Ibid.

[48] Public Safety (Emergency Powers) Act 1926, s 1(2) and NAI, Department of the Taoiseach, S2262, note by Michael McDunphy, 11 February 1927.

[49] Offences Against the State Act 1939, s 5.

[50] Eg, see preamble, Treason Felony Act 1848.

[51] *Dáil Debates*, vol 10, col 275, 18 February 1925.

Safety Acts.[52] Attempts to intimidate servants of the state or to incite mutiny or desertion among the police or military were specified as serious offences. The 1925 Act also placed limitations on the right to silence and, in certain circumstances, placed the burden of proof on the accused.[53]

One of the most striking features of the 1925 Act was a latent fear, reflected in key provisions, of a repetition of the events of 1919 when the first Dáil Éireann declared itself an Irish legislature in defiance of Westminster, proceeded to appoint its own government, demanded allegiance from the IRA and even created its own system of courts. Attempts to repeat such acts would now attract serious penalties under the 1925 Act. The original wording of the Bill introduced in the Oireachtas was uncompromising in criminalising claims to be a President, Vice-President, minister of an alternative government or claims of being a member of the military, police or civil service under a 'pretended government purporting to be established in Saorstát Éireann otherwise than under and by virtue of the Constitution'.[54] The final wording maintained these offences but focused on attempts to usurp government authority and functions in place of the original wording that attempted to criminalise the adoption of government titles.[55]

VI. THE ASSASSINATION OF KEVIN O'HIGGINS

On 10 July 1927, a seminal event occurred in Irish history when Kevin O'Higgins was assassinated while walking alone to mass. O'Higgins held the posts of Vice-President, Minister for Justice and Minister for External Affairs and had long been considered the 'strong man' of the Cumann na nGaedheal Government.[56] He had piloted all the emergency legislation passed up to the date of his death through the Oireachtas. The Irish state had never before, and has never since, endured the murder of a such a high profile political figure. The government, several of whose members were ill at the time, immediately suspected the worst and concluded that the assassination was part of a wider conspiracy to murder government ministers. WT Cosgrave told the Dáil that 'This crime has not been committed by private individuals against Kevin O'Higgins.'[57] Instead, he spoke of the event as 'the political assassination of a pillar of the State' and concluded that it was 'the fruit of the steady persistent attack against the State and its fundamental institutions'.[58] Thomas Johnson, leader of the Labour party and of the official opposition that sat in the Oireachtas, echoed these sentiments when he concluded 'none can doubt that it was intended as a blow at the new State'.[59] Decades later it was revealed that the shooting was an opportunistic event by individual members of the IRA who managed to intercept O'Higgins while he was without a bodyguard.[60] This was not known in 1927

[52] Ibid, cols 272–3.
[53] Treasonable Offences Act 1925, ss 9(2) and 10(3).
[54] Treasonable and Seditious Offences Bill 1925, s 4(1)(b). *Dáil Debates*, vol 10, col 279, 18 February 1925.
[55] Treasonable Offences Act 1925, ss 4, 5 and 6. *Dáil Debates*, vol 10, cols 1255–65, 19 March 1925.
[56] Lee, *Ireland 1912–1985* (n 5) 153.
[57] *Dáil Debates*, vol 20, col 757, 12 July 1927, Assassination of the Vice-President.
[58] Ibid.
[59] Ibid, col 758.
[60] T de Vere White, *Kevin O'Higgins* (Dublin, Anvil, 1986) 256 and JP McCarthy, *Kevin O'Higgins – Builder of the Irish State* (Dublin, Irish Academic Press, 2006) 287–9.

and government reaction was based on a conviction that the assassination was part of a wider plot against the state. Although the Army Council of the IRA denied involvement in the assassination, the Irish Government remained convinced that a section of that organisation must have been responsible.[61] Cosgrave made his government's policy clear when he expressed the determination 'to meet this form of terrorism as we met other forms of terrorism, and we shall not falter until every vestige of it is wiped out from the land'.[62] The enactment of the Public Safety Act 1927 must be seen as an emotive response to the assassination of a colleague amid genuine fears that it was just one manifestation of a wider campaign to undermine the state.

The government argued that the provisions of the 1927 Act represented the minimum powers that were necessary to prevent further attacks and demonstrate that 'revolutionary changes in the Constitution are not likely to be achieved by deeds of violence'.[63] Cosgrave even concluded that the Bill might be 'too moderate in parts'.[64] The opposition Labour party, while acknowledging the seriousness of the assassination, insisted that the state was not in immediate danger and added that there was no evidence that the level of threat had changed since the enactment of the Public Safety (Emergency Powers) Act 1926.[65] Once again, analogies with the laws of the Soviet Union were raised in a vain effort to resist enactment of the 1927 Act.[66]

The most significant measures contained within the 1927 Act included enhanced Garda powers together with provisions aimed at suppression of 'unlawful associations' and their activities. New police powers allowed Garda superintendents to issue their own search warrants.[67] Some of the offences relating to unlawful associations placed the burden of proof onto the accused.[68] Parents and guardians of persons under 16 who were convicted of membership of unlawful associations could be imprisoned under certain circumstances.[69] Refusing to recognise an Irish court was criminalised as contempt of court and those who did so might be denied legal representation.[70] WT Cosgrave justified this provision by arguing:

> It is perfectly absurd that persons who enjoy the protection and security of the Constitution and the State should openly flout its authority when charged with serious crime. It may satisfy certain neurotic people, but I think it would be healthy to give these neurotics less opportunity for satisfying their desire for the sensational.[71]

Persons convicted of misdemeanours under the 1927 Act or any offence under the Treasonable Offences Act 1925 who were or had been in public employment would lose their jobs or pensions.[72] The 1927 Act also provided extensive powers of censorship in the

[61] *Dáil Debates*, vol 20, col 838, 26 July 1927.
[62] Ibid, col 757, 12 July 1927.
[63] Ibid, col 842, 26 July 1927.
[64] Ibid.
[65] Ibid, cols 842–9.
[66] Ibid, col 847.
[67] Public Safety Act 1927, s 14.
[68] Ibid, ss 6, 7 and 18.
[69] Ibid, s 18.
[70] Ibid, s 17.
[71] *Dáil Debates*, vol 20, col 841, 26 July 1927.
[72] Public Safety Act 1927, s 19.

field of publishing, in the printing of documents and in the importation of newspapers and periodicals.[73] Yet, the centrepiece of the new legislation was the creation of new special courts to try offenders, a feature that had not been seen since the military courts created by the 1922 Army (Emergency Powers) Resolution.[74] The original plan for the special courts envisaged in 1927 left open the possibility of their being staffed by three judges of the superior courts or by three officers of the defence forces.[75] However, some judges of the superior courts objected and the strength of their resistance resulted in the removal of any prospect of substantial judicial involvement.[76] The result was a reversion to the established model of reliance on the defence forces to staff special courts.[77]

The most lasting consequence of the Public Safety Act 1927 was its impact on the 1922 Constitution. Fears of constitutional challenges to a measure that had been drafted in haste resulted in the use of an unprecedented constitutional device. Section 3 of the Act provided 'Every provision of this Act which is in contravention of any provision of the Constitution shall to the extent of such contravention operate and have effect as an amendment for so long only as this Act continues in force of such provision of the Constitution.' A legal challenge to this means of constitutional amendment was defeated in the High Court in *Attorney General v McBride*, which found that it conformed to the strict requirements of Article 50 concerning the amendment of the Constitution.[78] Nevertheless, Hanna J made his feelings clear when he stated that he had reached this conclusion 'with great hesitation'.[79] Hanna J delivered an unambiguous message to the Irish Government when he declared 'it is a precedent that should not be followed'.[80]

In time, resistance to many of the extreme provisions of the 1927 Act, together with the gradual realisation that O'Higgins' assassination was not part of a wider plot, limited the practical impact of this legislation. The government soon encountered difficulties with a provision that permitted the deportation of persons associated with unlawful associations but made no distinction between Irish citizens and foreign nationals and gave no guidance as to where these expelled persons would actually go.[81] The British Government assumed that most deportees would end up in the UK and warned that this provision might threaten the principle of free movement between their country and the

[73] Ibid, ss 9, 10, 11 and 12.

[74] Ibid, ss 20 to 28.

[75] NAI, Department of the Taoiseach, S5486, Public Safety Bill 1927, s 22(1).

[76] See NAI, Department of the Taoiseach, S5486, decision of Cabinet, 26 July 1927 and *Dáil Debates*, vol 20, col 841, 26 July 1927 and cols 1405–6 and 1449–50, 3 August 1927 and *Seanad Debates*, vol 9, cols 361–3, 10 August 1927. Public Safety Act 1927, s 22 provided that one out the three members of a special court was to be 'a person certified by the Attorney-General to have legal knowledge or experience' who might or might not be an officer in the defence forces. This provision left open the possibility of some judicial involvement in these special courts. This was a feature taken from the Army (Emergency Powers) Resolution 1922.

[77] Public Safety Act 1927, s 22. Section 24 of the 1927 Act demanded that all convictions and sentences be confirmed by an officer of the defence forces not below the rank of colonel who had been nominated for this role by the Irish Government.

[78] [1928] IR 451.

[79] Ibid, 456.

[80] Hanna J wrote, extra judicially, that the Public Safety Act 1927 had been the subject of 'very severe criticism' without mentioning that he was one of the principal sources of this criticism. H Hanna and D Pringle, *The Statute Law of the Irish Free State* (Dublin, Alex Thom, 1929) 45.

[81] Public Safety Act 1927, s 13.

Irish Free State.[82] The military courts envisaged by the 1927 Act never actually functioned. Although the 1927 Act was originally intended to remain in place for seven years this period was later cut down to five, a length of time that corresponded with the anticipated lifespan of the government.[83] As events transpired, criticism levelled at the 1927 Act and the gradual realisation that the level of threat was not as high as originally anticipated ensured that it was repealed at the end of 1928.[84]

VII. THE INSERTION OF ARTICLE 2A INTO THE 1922 CONSTITUTION

The origin of the Public Safety Act 1927 was based on a single identifiable event, the murder of Kevin O'Higgins. The same could not be said for the next major piece of emergency law in the Irish Free State, the insertion of a new Article 2A into the Constitution in 1931. The justification most often provided was a number of high profile murders including those of Garda Superintendent John Curtin, who had taken action against IRA activities, and of John Ryan and Patrick Carroll, who were suspected of giving information to the Gardaí concerning such activities.[85] In reality, a variety of considerations lay behind this measure including jury and witness intimidation, juries declining to convict out of fear or sympathy, a belief that the powers vested in the Garda Síochána were insufficient, reluctance on the part of the judiciary to enforce the Treasonable Offences Act 1925 and a number of high profile acquittals of members of the IRA. Fears of communist organisation in the Irish Free State were also raised to justify the need for a new emergency law.[86] Attempts were made to deal with difficulties concerning juries in the Juries (Protection) Act 1929, but these were not deemed sufficient by the government and, in any case, this problem was seen as one amongst many.[87] The government also experienced persistent lobbying by the Commissioner of the Garda Síochána, Eoin O'Duffy, for new emergency measures. O'Duffy, argued that members of the IRA should be placed 'outside the protection of a Constitution, which at the time they are attacking and sheltering behind, and placing them in a position uninfluenced by the constitutional rights of citizenship'.[88]

How could those who challenged the Constitution be placed outside the ambit of the rights provisions contained within that Constitution? The original proposal for the emergency measures of 1931 was to achieve this by means of a slightly modified version of the device used to place the Public Safety Act 1927 beyond the reach of constitutional scrutiny.[89] In the end, a new scheme was developed to avoid the criticism that the 1927

[82] NAI Department of the Taoiseach, S5486, Foreign Secretary to Minister for External Affairs, 2 November 1927.

[83] Public Safety Act 1927, s 1(2). See *Dáil Debates*, vol 20, cols 1119–32, 28 July 1927.

[84] Public Safety Act 1928, s 1.

[85] NAI, Department of the Taoiseach S4469/17, speech by President, 14 October 1931. See also *Dáil Debates*, vol 40, cols 33–6, 15 October 1931.

[86] Eg, see *Dáil Debates*, vol 40, cols 37–8 and 40, 15 October 1931.

[87] Ibid, cols 42–3.

[88] UCD Archives, FitzGerald Papers, P80/857, O'Duffy to Roche, 27 July 1931.

[89] The criticism of the form of amendment used in the Public Safety Act 1927 is likely to have influenced the change of name of the 1931 measure from the 'Treasonable Offences Bill 1931' to 'Constitution (Amendment No 17) Bill, 1931'. NAI, Department of the Taoiseach, S4469/17, short title, undated.

Act had attracted. Instead of placing the 1931 emergency measure above the Constitution it was decided to place it inside the Constitution itself. Consequently, this emergency measure was enacted as Constitution (Amendment No 17) Act 1931. This constitutional amendment inserted extensive emergency provisions into a new Article 2A of the Constitution.[90] It also provided that Article 2A would prevail over all subsequent provisions of the Constitution.[91]

The centrepiece of Article 2A was the creation of a military court that was hastily provided with the awkward name of the 'Constitution (Special Powers) Tribunal'. This tribunal would be staffed by five members of the defence forces and sat in Collins Barracks, Dublin. The tribunal was empowered to try persons charged with a wide range of offences and had the power to impose a higher penalty than that provided by law if this were deemed 'necessary or expedient'.[92] This included the power to impose the death penalty even when the law specified a lesser punishment for the relevant offence.[93] The tribunal also had unlimited discretion in imposing punishment for uttering perjured statements during proceedings.[94] There was no right of public access to trials and members of the press required special permission to attend.[95] In addition, there was no right of appeal from the decisions of the tribunal although the Executive Council did enjoy the power to grant a pardon or remit a sentence.[96] Government ministers had extensive discretion in deciding whether or not a particular act could constitute an offence that could be tried by the tribunal.[97]

The Constitution (Special Powers) Tribunal, although important, was just one of many facets of Article 2A. Enhanced powers were granted to the Garda Síochána and the defence forces.[98] There were also provisions for outlawing subversive associations.[99] In addition, there were powers to declare periodicals to be seditious, powers to prohibit public meetings and close buildings.[100] An unusual provision provided the Governor General with the power to appoint individuals to occupy seats in both houses of the Oireachtas if a member failed to attend as a result of unlawful imprisonment, threats or intimidation or as a consequence of death or physical incapacity resulting from an unlawful act.[101] Finally, some of the provisions of Article 2A had retrospective effect.[102] The range and variety of powers awarded to multiple organs of the state reflected the wide range of reasons that underlay the entrenchment of Article 2A within the Constitution.

[90] Constitution (Amendment No. 17) Act 1931, s 1.

[91] Constitution (Amendment No 17) Act 1931, Sch, Pt 1, s 2 provided 'Article 3 and every subsequent Article of the Constitution shall be read and construed subject to the provisions of this Article, and in case of inconsistency between this Article and the said Article 3 or any subsequent Article, this Article shall prevail.'

[92] Constitution (Amendment No 17) Act 1931, s 7(1).

[93] Ibid.

[94] Ibid, s 9.

[95] Ibid, s 5(2).

[96] Ibid, ss 6(5) and 12.

[97] Ibid, Appendix to the Foregoing Article, s 7.

[98] Eg, Constitution (Amendment No 17) Act 1931, Pt III.

[99] See Constitution (Amendment No 17) Act 1931, Pt IV.

[100] Ibid, ss 24, 26 and 27.

[101] Ibid, s 25.

[102] See, eg, Constitution (Amendment No 17) Act 1931, s 11 and Appendix to the Foregoing Article.

Although opposition parties criticised Article 2A, it is worth noting that constructive resistance in the Oireachtas was mainly voiced by independent and Labour representatives in the Dáil and Seanad. These TDs and senators emphasised the impact that Article 2A would have on the human rights provisions of the Constitution and the text of the Constitution as a whole. Senator JT O'Farrell concluded:

> This is the most drastic Bill that has ever been introduced here because it is an amendment of the Constitution and it sets aside every guarantee that is normally given to each citizen in every civilised democratic country.[103]

The Constitution (Amendment No 17) Act 1931 passed without a single amendment after an extremely time-constrained debate in the Oireachtas. It came into force just before the Cumann na nGaedheal Government lost power in early 1932.[104] This reality ensured that de Valera's position on Article 2A became the source of particular scrutiny. The Fianna Fáil party opposed the measure in 1931, suspended its operation when it came into power in 1932 and even released some prisoners who had been convicted and sentenced by the Constitution (Special Powers) Tribunal.[105] Yet, in 1933 key aspects of Article 2A were revived and would be used against various incarnations of the Army Comrades Association, popularly known as the 'Blueshirts', in addition to persons associated with the IRA.[106] This dramatic change of stance resulted in thinly veiled criticism from the Supreme Court while considering legal challenges to the detention and trial of prisoners under Article 2A.[107]

The courts were not just a useful forum in criticising the record of successive Irish governments with respect to Article 2A. They also proved to be very active in scrutinising the actions and jurisdiction of the Constitution (Special Powers) Tribunal. This was remarkable because Article 2A had been drafted with the clear intention of preventing any challenges to the Tribunal from appearing before the courts. It provided that the decisions of the Constitution (Special Powers) Tribunal could not be appealed before the courts.[108] Article 2A also provided that the 'Tribunal shall not be restrained or interfered with in the execution of its jurisdiction or powers under this Article by any court.'[109] However, these provisions could not prevent a number of successful legal challenges on the basis that the Tribunal had acted outside of the powers and jurisdiction granted to it by Article 2A.[110] These successes encouraged other litigants to go further and mount a legal challenge to the constitutional amendments that underpinned Article 2A in the case of *State (Ryan) v Lennon*.[111] This proved to be a step too far and this challenge to Article 2A was rejected by the majority of the Supreme Court notwithstanding the celebrated dissenting judgment delivered by Kennedy CJ.[112]

[103] *Seanad Debates*, vol 14, col 1997–8, 16 October 1931.
[104] Constitution (Operation of Article 2A) Order 1931 (SI 72/1931).
[105] Constitution (Suspension of Article 2A) Order 1932 (SI 11/1932).
[106] Constitution (Operation of Article 2A) Order 1933 (SI 91/1933).
[107] *State (Ryan) v Lennon* [1935] IR 170 at 235.
[108] Constitution (Amendment No 17) Act 1931, s 6(5).
[109] Ibid.
[110] See *In re O'Duffy* [1933] IR 550, *State (O'Duffy) v Bennett* [1935] IR 70 and *State (Hughes) v Lennon* [1935] IR 128. See also the unsuccessful challenge in *State (McCarthy) v Lennon* [1936] IR 485.
[111] [1935] IR 170.
[112] Ibid.

VIII. EMERGENCY LAW UNDER A NEW CONSTITUTIONAL ORDER

In 1934, de Valera appointed a special 'Constitution Committee' charged with the task of recommending desirable reforms to the Free State Constitution. The position enshrined in Article 70 of the 1922 Constitution, which only provided for conditions of peace and conditions of outright war, was clearly untenable. The Constitution Committee concluded that 'it was essential that power should be provided to enable the Executive to deal with conditions of disorder not amounting to actual rebellion or state of war'.[113] It explored alternative mechanisms whereby the invocation of emergency measures, including the use of special or extraordinary courts, could be recognised and regulated by the Constitution.[114] In 1935 it was decided to enact a new constitution to replace the Constitution of the Irish Free State.[115] When a draft Constitution was made public on 1 May 1937 it became clear that the new document contained far more extensive emergency provisions than those contained in the 1922 Constitution.[116] The 1922 Constitution had been drafted in a brief period of idealism that did not fully anticipate all of the challenges to come. In early 1922 the new Irish Provisional Government had no experience of administering emergency law and even lacked the knowledge that such law would be needed outside the obvious context of a full military conflict. This knowledge and experience was available to the drafters of the Constitution that would come into force in 1937. The provisions of Article 28 of the new Constitution, designed to deal with times of war or armed rebellion, were supplemented by provisions in Article 38 that provided for the creation of special criminal courts and military tribunals, while Article 39 defined the crime of treason. In 1939 the Oireachtas enacted a new Treason Act to replace the Treasonable Offences Act 1925. Although there was scope for practical improvements, a substantial part of the impulse behind this legislation was political. The 1925 Act, which still made reference to the Governor General, was seen as being interlinked with the provisions of the 1922 Constitution. De Valera insisted 'The moment the [1937] Constitution was enacted by the people treason had a new meaning' and added that 'treason must no longer be understood in terms of allegiance to foreign Powers'.[117]

The enactment of the new Constitution brought to a conclusion the work of the Constitution (Special Powers) Tribunal whose existence had been dependent on the now defunct Article 2A of the former Constitution. There were provisions for 'special courts' in Article 38 of the 1937 Constitution and, unlike the equivalent provisions in the 1922 Constitution, their use would not be limited to times of 'war and armed rebellion'. These special courts could be established 'for the trial of offences in cases where it may be determined in accordance with such law that the ordinary courts are inadequate

[113] NAI, Department of the Taoiseach, S2979, second meeting, 29 May 1934; third meeting 1 June 1934 and first draft, 9 June 1934.

[114] NAI, Department of the Taoiseach, S2979, rough draft of a proposed scheme to replace Art 2A of the Constitution, 14 June 1934 and report of the Constitution Committee 1934, Appendix B, 3 July 1934 and Davis, *Special Criminal Court* (n 5) 59–61.

[115] D Keogh and A McCarthy, *The Making of the Irish Constitution 1937* (Cork, Mercier, 2007) 75 and G Hogan, *The Origins of the Irish Constitution, 1928–1941* (Dublin, Royal Irish Academy, 2012) 152.

[116] The draft Constitution was published in many newspapers on 1 May 1937. Eg, see *Irish Independent*, 1 May 1937, 8–9.

[117] *Dáil Debates*, vol 74, cols 966–7, 23 February 1939.

to secure the effective administration of justice, and the preservation of public peace and order'.[118] Detailed provision for a 'Special Criminal Court' was finally enacted in the OASA.

IX. A PROCESS OF NORMALISATION?

The history of emergency law in the Irish Free State could be presented in terms of a series of legislative acts that had a cumulative impact in normalising provisions that were once widely perceived as repugnant to the principles of rule of law and individual liberty. This line could be drawn all the way from the Army (Emergency Powers) Resolution of 1922 to the enactment of the OASA. There is evidence to support such a thesis. For example, Kevin O'Higgins contrasted the 'extraordinary difficulty' he had encountered in getting provisions of the Public Safety Act 1923 and the Enforcement of Law (Occasional Powers) Act 1923 through the Oireachtas with the relative ease with which almost identical provisions were accepted in the Treasonable Offences Act 1925.[119] O'Higgins ascribed this trend to the extent to which 'the Dáil has developed in a political sense towards maturity'.[120] Recent scholarship has contrasted a perceived period of heavy Oireachtas criticism of emergency law in the 1920s and early 1930s with an apparent waning of political opposition in this area by 1939.[121]

This apparent process of 'normalisation' could also be seen as having preceded the creation of the Irish Free State as many of the most controversial provisions of emergency law enacted after 1922 actually had their roots in the years immediately before the creation of the state. For example, in 1921, the Irish Court of King's Bench held in *R v Allen* that the civil courts have no power to interfere with the decision of a military court in a martial law area during a time of war or armed rebellion.[122] Although Leo Kohn would describe this as a 'truly revolting decision'[123] it was replicated in *R (Childers) v Adjutant-General of the Forces of the Irish Provisional Government*[124] and its influence was extended beyond any definite period of war or armed rebellion in the provisions of the Public Safety Act 1927 and Article 2A.[125]

Although there is evidence to support a thesis of gradual normalisation, any such conclusion must be seen as subject to a number of important caveats. First, it is difficult to quantify opposition to legislative provisions. Even parliamentary debates, which are just one of many fora for opposition to legislative measures, are an unreliable source. This problem is exacerbated by the reality that members of the opposition within the Oireachtas were permitted less time to analyse and criticise emergency legislation as the

[118] Constitution of Ireland, 1937, Art 38.3.1.
[119] *Dáil Debates*, vol 10, cols 1261–2, 19 March 1925.
[120] Ibid, 1262.
[121] Eg, see Ó Longaigh, *Emergency Law* (n 6) 285 and 288.
[122] [1921] 2 IR 241.
[123] Kohn, *Constitution* (n 10) 141.
[124] [1923] 1 IR 5
[125] Public Safety Act 1927, s 25(5) and Constitution (Amendment No 17) Act 1931, s 6(5). A similar argument could be made with respect to the impact of the decision in *Ex Parte Marais* [1902] AC 109 on the provisions of Article 70 of the 1922 Constitution. See Kohn, *Constitution* (n 10) 145–6.

Irish Free State advanced in age. The Public Safety Act 1923 initially proceeded through the Oireachtas at a leisurely pace that allowed for detailed debate. After four days of lengthy analysis and debate at committee stage the Dáil had only advanced through the first five sections of the Bill. This provided ample opportunities to criticise the contents of this prospective legislation. The prospect of pending litigation caused the government to curtail this slow but detailed scrutiny of the 1923 Bill. This proved to be the beginning of an enduring trend. It may be recalled that the Public Safety (Emergency Powers) Act 1926 was enacted just three days after its introduction in the Dáil and brought into force by proclamation one day later.[126] The debates on the future Public Safety Act 1927 were also curtailed in order to get the Bill through the Dáil before Fianna Fáil TDs took the oath prescribed in the Constitution and occupied their seats in the house. Their presence might have jeopardised the Bill which completed its last stages in the Dáil within minutes of Fianna Fáil TDs taking their seats.[127] The enactment of Constitution (Amendment No 17) Act 1931, that inserted Article 2A into the 1922 Constitution, provides the most extreme example of curtailment of debate. The Oireachtas debates on this wide-ranging measure were limited to just three days, which, of course, had to be divided between the Dáil and the Seanad.[128] In addition, the impact of the 1927 Act and Article 2A on the integrity of the 1922 Constitution demanded considerable attention and further limited analysis of their substantive provisions in the Oireachtas.

The curtailment of debate on the most controversial emergency provisions passed between 1922 and 1937 render it difficult to judge whether these provisions had become less controversial and had even become normalised with the passage of time. The debates on the OASA experienced less constraints in terms of time but greater constraints in terms of parliamentary opposition. The considerable number of provisions of the OASA that had been influenced by legislation passed by Cumann na nGaedheal, a party that was incorporated into Fine Gael in 1933, limited the ability of the main opposition party to criticise much of its content.

These considerations render it difficult to judge whether controversial aspects of the OASA, which had their roots in earlier legislation, had been rendered less controversial or had even become normalised with the passage of time, at least in terms of the opposition that they generated. This analysis is further complicated by the reality that parliamentary debates are not the only forum for opposition to emergency law. For example, the government received many letters of protest from local authorities, societies and members of the public that condemned the emergency measures passed between 1922 and 1939.[129]

[126] NAI, Department of the Taoiseach, S2262, Proclamation by the Executive Council of Saorstát Éireann, 20 November 1926

[127] The Public Safety Bill 1927 completed its final stage in Dáil Éireann at *Dáil Debates*, vol 20, col 1602, 4 August 1927, a declaration as to the non-application of Article 47 of the Constitution to the Bill was passed at *Dáil Debates*, vol 20, cols 1603–9, 4 August 1927. Fianna Fáil TDs took their seats at *Dáil Debates*, vol 20, col 1609, 4 August 1927.

[128] Constitution (Amendment No 17) Act 1931 was introduced in the Dáil on 14 October 1931 and was signed into law on 17 October 1931. See *Dáil Debates*, vol 40, col 24, 14 October 1931. NAI, Department of the Taoiseach, S4469/17, Secretary of Department of the President to Clerk of Dáil Éireann, 10 October 1931.

[129] For example, letters of protest with respect to the Public Safety Act 1927 can be found in NAI, Department of the Taoiseach, S5486; with respect to Constitution (Amendment No 17) Act 1931 in NAI, Department of the Taoiseach, S2267 and with respect to the Offences Against the State Act 1939 in NAI, Department of the Taoiseach, S11129.

The analysis becomes easier when viewed from the perspective of support rather than that of opposition. The enactment of the OASA might have been completed by a Fianna Fáil Government, but many of its most controversial provisions had their roots in legislation passed while the leadership of Fine Gael had been in power. This ensured that these emergency provisions were rooted in the identities of the two political parties that would dominate the life of the state for almost a century. In these circumstances, it is hardly surprising that the OASA would remain in force without realistic prospects of substantive reform at the dawn of a new twenty-first century.

X. CONCLUSION

The outbreak of the Irish Civil War in 1922 ensured that there would be no break in the long history of emergency legislation in Ireland highlighted by the preceding chapter of this volume.[130] The emergency legislation of the Free State period had many links to the past but also had a powerful impact on the future. There is no doubt that the OASA was heavily influenced by it. Yet, a narrative that presents the OASA as an unbroken accumulation of the legislation that preceded it would be deceptive and inaccurate. Although the OASA had much in common with its predecessors there were also important differences. For example, the OASA did not permit the Special Criminal Court to impose penalties in excess of those provided by law.[131] In addition, the OASA broke with the precedents of the 1926 Act, the 1927 Act and Article 2A by allowing for appeals in certain circumstances from the decisions of the Special Criminal Court to the ordinary courts.[132] Also, the OASA did not purport to override provisions of the 1937 Constitution as the 1927 Act and Article 2A had done with respect to the 1922 Constitution. These differences reflect the great advantage enjoyed by the drafters of the 1937 Constitution in having the benefit of all the experience of dealing with emergency law that had been accumulated under the preceding Constitution. This ensured that the 1937 Constitution expressly provided for the creation of special courts whereas, previously, such courts could only be created by temporarily amending or overruling the provisions of the 1922 Constitution. Recognition that the OASA did not represent an unbroken accumulation of the legislation that preceded it guards against facile comparisons that ignore vital differences of context. For example, it would not be a fair comparison to contrast the refusal of superior court judges to sit on the special courts proposed under the 1927 Public Safety Act with the presence of judges on the existing Special Criminal Court. Academic or journalistic works that ignore or minimise such realities should be treated with justifiable scepticism.

The benefit of experience also had an impact on the constitutional context in which the OASA operates, which is very different to the context that underpinned its

[130] See N Howlin, Chapter 1, this volume.

[131] However, the Minister for Justice can make special provisions as to the carrying out of the sentence and custody of persons convicted by the Special Criminal Court. Offences Against the State Act 1939, s 50(3) and (4).

[132] Under the Offences Against the State Act 1939, s 44, appeals went to the Court of Criminal Appeal. This jurisdiction moved to the Court of Appeal as mandated by the passing of the 33rd Amendment of the 1937 Constitution in 2013 and the enactment of the subsequent Court of Appeal Act 2014.

predecessors. The 1922 Constitution viewed the provision of emergency powers in binary terms that envisaged periods of peace and periods of war and failed to envisage emergency situations between these two poles. Consequently, the 1922 Constitution was perceived to lack the flexibility required to deal with intermediate situations and was treated as a barrier to be overcome by successive governments in the 1920s and 1930s. This reality was reflected in the emergency measures passed during the lifetime of the Irish Free State and seriously diminished prospects for the survival of the 1922 Constitution. By the time the Constitution Committee convened in 1934 it was clear that the binary approach adopted by the 1922 Constitution was unsustainable. Consequently, the 1937 Constitution was drafted with the benefit of the knowledge and experience that the dissident challenge was not going to disappear with the passage of time alone. These considerations ensured that the 1937 Constitution contained more detailed emergency provisions than its predecessor, for example in Articles 28 and 38. These articles anticipated further provisions in the form of legislation which, however controversial, would remain subservient to the text of the 1937 Constitution. All this ensured that the OASA was enacted with the benefit of key provisions contained in earlier legislation drafted in the 1920s and 1930s but also with the benefit of the mistakes made during the difficult and traumatic infancy of the state.

3

A Certain Ambivalence: Independent Ireland and Trial by Jury

MARK COEN*

IN FEBRUARY 1935, the Dáil debated the second stage of the Courts of Justice Bill 1934. One of its more controversial clauses attempted to permit majority verdicts in criminal cases on a permanent basis.[1] In opposing this change, the Fine Gael Deputy (and barrister) Daniel McMenamin spoke in favour of the jury system and its requirement of a unanimous verdict.[2] However, he felt bound to acknowledge a problem with trial by jury: 'It may be said … that it is English law, but there are a lot of things English that are not bad – even the coal on a winter's day. The system has stood the test of time. It is not necessarily bad because it is English.'[3]

One of the criticisms levelled most frequently and vociferously at the Offences Against the State Act 1939 (OASA) as amended is the exceptions it permits to jury trial. This chapter attempts to distil the attitude of the Irish state to trial by jury, as revealed by its approach to the institution and derogations therefrom. The jury is an accepted part of the legal system with a constitutionally protected position.[4] It attracts neither significant praise nor significant criticism in public discourse. It is something that is taken for granted, a piece of machinery that whirrs unobtrusively in the background. The state treats it with a certain ambivalence. This chapter seeks to demonstrate this attitude of ambivalence and contends that it is heavily influenced by the country's historically complicated and difficult relationship with this mode of trial. Past problems inform an official mindset

* I would like to thank Thomas Mohr for his helpful comments on a previous draft of this chapter.

[1] Section 73 of the Bill as initiated provided that a verdict of nine jurors would be sufficient. This provision faced significant opposition and was later removed from the Bill. Majority verdicts had been allowed in criminal cases by the Juries (Protection) Act 1929, s 5(1). The Act was presented as an emergency measure and s 13 stated that it would expire on 30 September 1931. However, the operation of the 1929 Act was extended by section 1 of the Juries (Protection) Act 1931 for a further two years. After the expiry of this second piece of legislation majority verdicts were not permitted in Irish criminal trials for over 50 years: Criminal Justice Act 1984, s 25 provides that a verdict of ten jurors is sufficient. Majority verdicts were permitted in civil cases from 1924 onwards: Courts of Justice Act 1924, s 95.

[2] Writing in 1956, Lord Devlin strongly defended the unanimous verdict, stating that a majority verdict indicated the existence of a reasonable doubt: P Devlin, *Trial by Jury* (London, Stevens & Sons, 1956) 56. Majority verdicts were introduced in England and Wales in the Criminal Justice Act 1967, s 13.

[3] *Dáil Debates*, 21 February 1935, vol 54, col 2275.

[4] Article 38.5 of the Constitution of Ireland.

that tolerates jury trial in the absence of alternatives, but which is conservative about change and suspicious of reforms that would reduce the discretion of the sate to employ special, non-jury courts. The colonial associations of trial by jury, though never referred to today, informed some of the antipathy to the system in official circles in the decades after independence. Arguably, those associations continue to subconsciously affect how trial by jury is perceived and discussed by legislators and judges. Among the definitions provided for the word 'ambivalence' by the Oxford English Dictionary is '[t]he condition of having contradictory or mixed feelings, attitudes or urges regarding a person or thing'.[5] The chapter will demonstrate that this captures the relationship between the Irish state and trial by jury, and that it has replaced a sometimes hostile attitude to the institution in the decades immediately after independence in 1922.

I. THE ROOTS OF AMBIVALENCE: THE PRE-INDEPENDENCE EXPERIENCE

Much has been written about the history of trial by jury in Ireland under British rule.[6] One of the major themes that emerges from that scholarship is that the system was not regarded as satisfactory by either the British authorities or the predominantly Catholic population of the country.[7] The narrative is one of British claims that Irish juries refused to return verdicts in accordance with the evidence and were subject to intimidation, and indigenous counter claims that jury processes were manipulated by the authorities in order to achieve convictions. The dynamic in other countries under British rule was similar; while the Empire-builders viewed the jury as the embodiment of British justice and fairness, the people of colonised countries did not always agree, often perceiving it to be blighted by 'arbitrary authority and racism'.[8]

Howlin has noted that throughout the nineteenth century, officials and commentators questioned whether trial by jury was appropriate to Irish conditions, which were increasingly characterised by sustained political unrest.[9] There was agrarian disorder for much of the century. In addition to trials arising from land disputes, political trials were also highly contentious. Conviction rates for all categories of offence were lower in Ireland than in England. Johnson argues that this may have been a bi-product of the close links between people in a small rural country, in contrast to the greater anonymity of life in Britain.[10] However, the differential in conviction rates between the two countries was

[5] *OED Online* (Oxford, Oxford University Press, 2020).

[6] For a comprehensive account of juries in 19th century Ireland, see N Howlin, *Juries in Ireland: Laypersons and Law in the Long Nineteenth Century* (Dublin, Four Courts Press, 2017).

[7] See, eg, JF McEldowney, 'Some Aspects of Law and Policy in the Administration of Criminal Justice in Nineteenth-Century Ireland' in JF McEldowney and PO Higgins (eds), *The Common Law Tradition: Essays in Irish Legal History* (Dublin, Irish Academic Press, 1990) 117; N Howlin, 'The Politics of Jury Trials in Nineteenth-Century Ireland' (2015) 3(2) *Comparative Legal History* 272.

[8] R Vogler, 'The International Development of the British Empire' (2001) 72 *Revue Internationale de Droit Pénale* 525, 525. See also Y Murphy, 'The Role of the Judge and Jury in Criminal Cases' in J Sarkin and W Binchy (eds), *The Administration of Justice: Current Themes in Comparative Perspective* (Dublin, Four Courts Press, 2004) 109, 110.

[9] N Howlin, 'English and Irish Jury Laws: A Growing Divergence 1825–1833' in M Brown and S Donlan (eds), *The Laws and Other Legalities of Ireland, 1689–1850* (London, Ashgate, 2011) 117, 122.

[10] D Johnson, 'Trial by Jury in Ireland, 1860–1914' (1996) 17(3) *Journal of Legal History* 270, 277.

particularly marked in respect of violent crimes.[11] Jurors seldom returned convictions for forcible possession, the reoccupation of land from which the accused tenant had been removed.[12]

While some acquittals officially regarded as perverse may have been actuated by sympathy for the accused persons, the intimidation of jurors was regarded as a major problem and occurred throughout the century. Because of this jurors often failed to present when summoned.[13] In 1838, 32 magistrates sitting in Tipperary wrote a letter to the Lord Lieutenant citing increasing difficulties in the administration of justice, including the intimidation of jurors.[14] The methods of those seeking to influence jurors were varied, and included 'signed or anonymous letters; public notices; verbal threats; damage to property, including livestock; or physical altercations'.[15] An article from the middle of the century proclaimed: '… Ireland and trial by jury, as they both are at present, are mutually unsuited'.[16] The author argued that the jury had been subverted by the Irish people:

> The unceasing endeavour of the Roman Catholic part of the people is to convert the juror, by intimidation, into a mere instrument for the acquittal of criminals. Trial by jury is not valued as a guarantee for the due observance of the law, but for its evasion.[17]

In order to counter what it perceived to be the widespread intimidation of jurors and to eliminate anti-prosecution bias insofar as possible, the Crown used a number of tactics. These strategies gave rise to a general feeling among the populace that British justice was unfair and corrupt.[18] The first Crown strategy was to ask jurors to 'stand by' – in effect, an unlimited power of peremptory challenge.[19] It was 'not uncommon'[20] for the Crown to exercise its power to stand by in respect of 30 to 50 jurors per trial. Second, the prosecution sometimes resorted to special juries, composed of persons of 'higher social standing'[21] than those on the common jury lists. A third strategy invoked by the authorities with a view to increasing the likelihood of conviction was to change the venue of a trial from the area in which an offence had allegedly been committed. In Johnson's words: 'Changing the venue and using special jurors inevitably meant that many Catholic defendants found themselves being tried … by predominantly Protestant jurors of a superior social class outside their own locality.'[22] Jury packing was a fourth strategy open to officials seeking to influence a jury verdict, and was linked to the use of special juries,

[11] Ibid, 279.
[12] Ibid, 271.
[13] N Howlin, '"The Terror of their Lives" Irish Jurors' Experiences' (2011) 29(3) *Law and History Review* 703, 721.
[14] P Bew, *Ireland: The Politics of Enmity, 1789–2006* (Oxford, Oxford University Press, 2007) 146. The Lord Lieutenant denied the existence of the problems in his reply. Ibid, 147.
[15] Howlin, *Juries in Ireland* (n 6) 158.
[16] 'Trial by Jury in Ireland' (1848) 19 *The Living Age* 12. *The Living Age* was a weekly American publication founded in 1844. No author is given for this article.
[17] Ibid.
[18] McEldowney, 'Some Aspects of Law and Policy' (n 7) 154.
[19] See JF McEldowney, '"Stand by for the Crown": An Historical Analysis' [1979] *Crim LR* 273.
[20] Johnson, 'Trial by Jury in Ireland' (n 10) 284.
[21] N Howlin, 'Merchants and Esquires: Special Juries in Dublin 1725–1833' in G O'Brien and F O'Kane (eds), *Georgian Dublin* (Dublin, Four Courts Press, 2008) 97.
[22] Johnson, 'Trial by Jury in Ireland' (n 10) 286.

the composition of which was easier to manipulate than trial juries.[23] Howlin observes that the degree to which jury packing actually occurred is very difficult to ascertain[24] but her research demonstrates that the issue was widely discussed and provided ample material for pamphlet-writers and cartoonists.[25] Fifth, despite the hallowed status of trial by jury in British law, it was often temporarily replaced by other modes of trial in pre-independence Ireland.[26] The suspension of trial by jury in particular areas was among the grievances that the Irish Parliamentary Party enumerated in a 1902 pamphlet explaining why the mood of Ireland was one of 'rightful discontent and disaffection'.[27]

The degree to which the courts were viewed as integral to British domination of Ireland may be seen in the campaigns waged against them during the War of Independence, which occurred between 1919 and 1921. Republicans established a system of indigenous and local courts presided over by members of Sinn Féin and popularly known as Dáil Courts.[28] Kotsonouris explains the context:

> Dáil Eireann was being forced to accept the consequences of its pretensions. If it was the democratic government of the people, then it had to be prepared, like every other government, to use the coercion and sanction necessary to impose the collective will.[29]

The overall aim was to deprive the British courts system of business, and therefore relevance. Several years later Meredith J, by then a judge of the High Court, observed approvingly that the judges of the Dáil Courts had 'frustrated [the] attempt'[30] to abolish juries in criminal cases. He himself had been instrumental in ensuring that juries were used in trials on indictment in those courts, at least in the latter stages of their operation.[31] In addition to the setting up of the Dáil Courts, there was a campaign aimed at making the British courts system unworkable in Ireland. Some jurors were physically prevented from attending assizes to which they had been summoned.[32] In Galway, prospective jurors were sent a circular urging them not to attend the assizes and Irish Republican Army (IRA) members called out their names at the train station and ordered them to return home.[33] Cork jurors held a meeting in the City Hall and resolved not to attend assizes or

[23] Howlin, 'Merchants and Esquires' (n 21) 104–105.

[24] Howlin, *Juries in Ireland* (n 6) 156.

[25] Two cartoons relating to jury packing are reproduced in Howlin, *Juries in Ireland* (n 6) (unnumbered central pages).

[26] See N Howlin, Chapter 1, and T Mohr, Chapter 2, this volume.

[27] *Ireland and the Coronation: Why Ireland is Discontented* (London, United Irish League of Great Britain, 1902) 8.

[28] The name of the courts reflected the fact that they had been established by Dáil Eireann, the parliamentary assembly (regarded as illegal by the British Government) which Sinn Féin MPs attended in Dublin after the 1918 general election, instead of taking their seats in Westminster.

[29] M Kotsonouris, *Retreat from Revolution: The Dáil Courts, 1920–24* (Dublin, Irish Academic Press, 1994) 25.

[30] *The Attorney General of the Irish Free State v Sean T O'Kelly* [1928] 1 IR 308, 322.

[31] Kotsonouris, *Retreat from Revolution* (n 29) 73. James Creed Meredith was President of the Supreme Court in the revolutionary (or Dáil) courts and later served as a judge of the High Court and Supreme Court of the Irish Free State. For further information about Meredith, see D O'Donnell, 'A Partial or Uneven Administration of the Law: Lawyers, the Law and the Importation of Arms into Ireland, 1914' (2015) 53(1) *Irish Jurist* 100, 103–107.

[32] 'Intimidation of Waterford jurors: "Held up" on the way to assizes', *The Irish Times*, 8 July 1920.

[33] 'Jurors "held up"', *The Irish Times*, 20 July 1920.

pay fines for non-attendance.[34] In September 1921, Dáil Eireann instructed county councils to stop compiling jury lists.[35] Jurors were applauded by Pim J for their attendance in 'trying times' in late July 1922,[36] but in September the Dublin City Sub-Sheriff reported that he frequently had to send the police in search of absent jurors.[37]

This short overview illustrates that for at least a century preceding Irish independence there was British exasperation with the Irish jury system. Nationalists resented both the strategies used by the Crown to attempt to increase the likelihood of jury convictions and the suspensions of jury trial that occurred intermittently. A culture of interfering with the jury system and undermining the administration of justice became established among the people. It is however noteworthy that juries featured, at least to some degree, in the revolutionary courts established during the War of Independence. The endurance of the jury despite official frustration with its perceived shortcomings would be a strong feature of independent Ireland.

II. TRIPPING THE POLICEMAN: 1922 TO 1937

The issue of what type of courts structure would operate in the new state was one of some importance. Kevin O'Higgins, Minister for Home Affairs, ruled out the long-term use of the 'hastily devised'[38] Dáil Courts and also warned against a knee-jerk dismissal of the courts system devised by the British.[39] The Free State Constitution provided for a Supreme Court, a High Court and courts of local and limited jurisdiction.[40] Jury trial was enshrined in the Constitution, Article 72 of which provided:

> No person shall be tried on any criminal charge without a jury save in the case of charges in respect of minor offences triable by law before a Court of Summary Jurisdiction and in the case of charges for offences against military law triable by Court Martial or other Military Tribunal.

Hanly has suggested two rationales for the retention of trial by jury by the fledgling state. First, it may have been assumed that the difficulties that bedevilled the jury system prior to independence would cease with self-government.[41] Second, the lawyers who advised the drafters were schooled in the common law tradition and thus accepted the place of the jury in the legal order.[42] A Judiciary Committee was appointed to consider the establishment of courts 'in fulfilment of the Constitution'.[43] W T Cosgrave, President of the Executive Council,[44] urged the members of the Committee to take a broad,

[34] 'Meeting of Cork jurors: Refusal to pay fines', *The Irish Times*, 12 August 1920.

[35] 'Dail Eireann and franchise and jurors' lists', *The Irish Times*, 3 September 1921.

[36] 'Jurors Complimented', *The Irish Times*, 28 July 1922.

[37] 'Perfect jury lists: No more phantom jurors', *The Irish Times*, 12 September 1922.

[38] T de Vere White, *Kevin O'Higgins* (Dublin, Anvil Books, 1986) 136.

[39] Ibid, 136–137.

[40] Article 64 of the Irish Free State Constitution.

[41] C Hanly, 'The 1916 Proclamation and Jury Trial in the Irish Free State' (2016) 39(2) *Dublin University Law Journal* 373, 386.

[42] Ibid.

[43] *Report of the Judiciary Committee* (Dublin, Stationery Office, 1923) 5.

[44] This was the name given to the position of Prime Minister under the 1922 Constitution of the Irish Free State. It was replaced by the title 'Taoiseach,' an old Irish title meaning chieftain or leader, in the Constitution of Ireland, 1937.

'untrammelled'[45] approach to its terms of reference. Among the topics which he stated 'must anxiously engage [their] attention'[46] were: 'the centralisation or decentralisation of the Courts, the numbers and grades of Judges … and officials, and their respective qualifications for office, and manner of selection [and] the method of trial by jury'.[47] Of all the issues mentioned in the Judiciary Committee's terms of reference, jury trial was the most neglected in its report.[48] The Committee appeared to envisage that the criminal trial jury would continue as before, and it is mentioned only in passing in its report.[49] The Dáil Courts were wound up by 1925[50] and the Courts of Justice Act 1924 provided the statutory basis for the new courts, the scheme for which largely followed the Judiciary Committee's recommendations.[51]

The Free State Government soon discovered that attitudes to law-breaking that had been formed under British rule would not vanish overnight. As the anonymous correspondent of the British Empire journal *The Round Table* put it:

> Those who were in open rebellion against British Law in 1920 and 1921, and had themselves encouraged lawlessness in their struggle for what they believed to be freedom, found it no easy task to assume the new *rôle* of guardians of the law and upholders of its majesty.[52]

Einrí Ó Frighil, Secretary of the Department of Home Affairs in the 1920s, echoed this when he said that the state was still viewed as 'the tyrant that wants to hang and imprison people'.[53] The government believed that jurors were not entirely trustworthy, whether because of anti-state bias stemming from the Civil War, sympathy with the situation or politics of accused persons, or because they were subject to intimidation. Ó Frighil identified a belief in jurors 'that the State can afford to lose prestige and even security better [than] the prisoner can afford to lose life and liberty'.[54] A writer in *The Round Table* agreed with Ó Frighil's analysis, observing: 'The habits of centuries cannot be eradicated in a year. It has always been the custom in Ireland to trip the policeman and help the criminal to escape.'[55]

Some of the commentary of state officials on juries began to sound eerily like that of their British predecessors. Writing in June 1923, the State Solicitor for County Monaghan, John Keenan, reported that no convictions were returned at Castleblayney Quarter Sessions. This was in spite of careful screening of the jury panel by the Gardaí, who showed the names of prospective jurors to the victims of crime whose cases were

[45] *Judiciary Committee* (n 43) 5.

[46] Ibid.

[47] Ibid.

[48] The report was 26 pages long and was compiled in four months. Its major focus was the jurisdiction of the new courts and the tenure and remuneration of the judges who would preside over them.

[49] Passing reference is made to the criminal jury in the passages dealing with the provision of stenographers in the Circuit and High Courts. *Judiciary Committee* (n 43) 16 and 22. A short paragraph discusses the jury in civil cases, recommending that it consist of 12 persons with a majority of 9 being sufficient to return a verdict. Ibid, 20. This recommendation was implemented by the Courts of Justice Act 1924, s 95.

[50] The story of the winding up of the Dáil Courts is fully recounted in M Kotsonouris, *The Winding Up of the Dáil Courts, 1922–1925: An Obvious Duty* (Dublin, Four Courts Press, 2004).

[51] Law Reform Commission, *Consolidation and Reform of the Courts Acts* (Dublin, LRC 46-2007, 2007) 8.

[52] 'The Irish Free State: An Ex-Unionist View', (1925) 16(61) *The Round Table* 29, 31.

[53] S Ó'Longaigh, *Emergency Law in Independent Ireland 1922–1948* (Dublin, Four Courts Press, 2006) 34.

[54] Ibid.

[55] 'Ireland As It Is', (1923) 13(50) *The Round Table* 254, 258.

to be heard so that they could highlight anyone who might be prejudiced against them. Reflecting on the acquittals returned by the juries, Keenan stated:

> The cases were clearly proven, any unprejudiced person would have found the prisoners guilty … The Jurymen have lost all sence [sic] of distinguishing right from wrong and seem to consider most offences no crime at all. In one of the cases in which the Jury disagreed the prisoners were of a very humble class living in a back lane in Carrickmacross and were not the type of persons likely to have any friends on the Jury or likely to be able to influence a single juryman.[56]

Mr Keenan suggested that an increase in the property rating qualification for jurors 'might have better results.'[57] In a similar vein, the State Solicitor for Tipperary expressed his frustration at the acquittals being returned by juries in that county, many of which he regarded as perverse: '[C]ountry jurors disregard their oaths. There is little or no sense of civic duty in the country.'[58]

Nor were judges above criticising juries in the early years of the state. In 1928 O'Byrne J rebuked a jury which could not agree whether a Republican accused who failed to plead was 'mute of malice or by the visitation of God'.[59] He voiced his belief that the jury 'had acted in disregard of the oath they had taken, and in disregard of the law under which they lived, and in disregard of the rights and well-being of the citizens of the State'.[60] A Divisional High Court found by a majority that the editor of the newspaper, *The Nation*, had committed a contempt of court by criticising O'Byrne J's comments. According to Hanna J: 'The main object of both the articles is obviously to incite or induce juries to act in the same improper manner as the jurors reprimanded by the learned judge.'[61] The editor, the future President of Ireland, Seán T O'Kelly, was fined £100 and ordered to pay costs.[62]

As under British rule, the prosecution of cases with a political dimension presented acute challenges for the authorities. Offences under the Treasonable Offences Act 1925, such as participation in illegal military exercises and unlawful organisations, were triable by jury. In a parallel with the nineteenth century experience, it is probable that juror sympathy with accused persons in political cases influenced some acquittals and that jury intimidation played a role in others. An organised campaign of jury intimidation was conducted by the Republican women's organisation Cumann na mBan between

[56] Report of the State Solicitor for County Monaghan, 15 June 1923. National Archives of Ireland TAOIS S/3120. This letter was circulated to the Executive Council (cabinet of the Irish Free State) on 19 June 1923. I am grateful to Donal Coffey for bringing this file to my attention.

[57] Ibid.

[58] O'Longaigh, *Emergency Law* (n 53) 69.

[59] A procedure under s 54(4) of the Juries Act 1927. The requirement for a separate jury to be empanelled to determine why a prisoner was not pleading was removed on a temporary basis by s 6 of the Juries (Protection) Act 1929, and permanently by s 80 of the Courts of Justice Act 1936.

[60] *The Attorney General of the Irish Free State v Sean T O'Kelly* [1928] 1 IR 308, 310.

[61] Ibid, 330.

[62] Ibid, 333. The case was discussed recently by McKechnie J in *Walsh v Minister for Justice and Equality* [2019] IESC 1, paras 20–21. For more examples of judges criticising jurors, see 'Another Leitrim Jury Disagrees: Judge Sheehy's Comment', *The Irish Independent*, 29 June 1934, 11; 'Judge Sealy on Abolition of Juries: Remarkable Statement', *The Irish Independent*, 17 November 1934, 7; 'Judge Ignores Roscommon Jury's Verdict', *The Irish Times*, 17 January 1946, 5.

1926 and 1934.[63] In 1929 the Irish Republican Army murdered Albert Armstrong, a witness in a criminal trial, and wounded John White, a juror. The government enacted the Juries (Protection) Act 1929, a temporary piece of legislation which aimed to make jury intimidation more difficult. Its provisions included the introduction of majority verdicts, anonymity for jurors and a statutory offence of juror interference.[64]

The regular confidential reports about policing sent by Garda Commissioner Eoin O'Duffy[65] to the government often referred to the conduct of juries. Writing in the aftermath of the IRA attacks on Armstrong and White, O'Duffy took a stern view of the juries that refused to convict in political cases: 'Let us make no mistake about it, from the point of view of their outlook on so-called political crime, the Irish public is rotten. Their sense of citizenship is negligible.'[66] In a later report from 1931, the Commissioner included a paragraph that could have been written in Dublin Castle in the 1880s:

> The laws of this State are laws meant for a civilised people, a normal people. They are largely the laws ruling England. That country is fortunate in having behind her hundreds of years of internal tranquillity. For hundreds of years no organised political body has attempted to violently overthrow her Government. The people, too, have a highly developed civic sense and moral courage which is entirely lacking here. If there is anybody in this country who thinks that this state can be ruled by the present laws he is making a cardinal error.[67]

O'Duffy was in receipt of reports penned by Garda Superintendents in districts around the country, extracts from which he sometimes included in his own report to the government. In 1931 he included several extracts from these policemen urging that trial by jury be replaced in cases involving subversive activity with trial by military tribunal or judges sitting alone. Such a call was made by Superintendent Curtin of Tipperary, who wrote in the aftermath of acquittals in an illegal drilling case:

> [I]t is useless to have anything in the nature of a political case ever again tried in this South Riding of Tipperary. The result of this case should, I respectfully suggest, give rise for [sic] serious thought to abolish the Jury system in cases of a political nature. As far as the Garda were concerned in this case all possible [sic] was done at every stage of the case to make it successful and no pains were spared.[68]

Typed across the top of this report are the words 'Superintendent Curtin's last report. Written two hours before he was murdered.'[69] As is noted elsewhere in this volume, this murder provided yet another impetus for the government to introduce trial by military tribunal by inserting Article 2A into the Constitution.[70]

Following the transition to a Fianna Fáil Government in 1932, constitutional reform was high on the political agenda. In 1934 the Constitution Committee produced a

[63] For more on the campaign and its protagonists, see M Coen, '"The work of some irresponsible women": Jurors, Ghosts and Embracery in the Irish Free State' (2020) 38(4) *Law and History Review* 777–810.

[64] Section 13 of the 1929 Act provided that it would expire on 30 September 1931. However, it was continued in force for another two years by the Juries (Protection) Act 1931, s 1.

[65] O'Duffy was Garda Commissioner from September 1922 to February 1933.

[66] Confidential Report by Commissioner, Garda Síochána, for period ended 31 March 1929, University College Dublin Archives (UCDA) Desmond Fitzgerald papers P80/856.

[67] Confidential Report by Commissioner, Garda Síochána, for period ended 31 May 1931, UCDA P80/856.

[68] Report of Superintendent Curtin dated 20 March 1931, UCDA P80/856.

[69] Ibid.

[70] See T Mohr, Chapter 2, this volume.

report on possible amendments of the existing Constitution for the consideration of the government.[71] The Committee clearly enumerated the articles which it 'regarded as fundamental'[72] and which it believed should 'be rendered immune from easy alteration'.[73] Among the provisions it regarded as fundamental were those concerned with electoral procedures, the courts structure and rights such as the inviolability of the dwelling and freedom of speech. Also included in this category was Article 70 which provided for trial in due course of law and restricted the jurisdiction of military tribunals to persons subject to military law.[74] However, Article 70 did not refer to trial by jury. This was dealt with in Article 72, which was placed in Appendix C, away from the important provisions in Appendix A. Article 72 provided that no person would be tried on a criminal charge without a jury save in the case of minor offences and offences against military law. The Committee stated that it did not regard the jury as fundamental in a democracy in which the independence of the judiciary was constitutionally protected; the modern, more equitable relationship between the citizen and the state meant that trial by jury had 'lost its original importance'.[75] Without elaborating further, the Committee asserted that trial by jury had recently attracted criticism in England and America. It also referred approvingly to the practice of trial by magistrates.

In an emotive and jingoistic aside, the Committee observed of the jury: '[I]n our State it cannot even claim to be a spontaneous national growth.'[76] The import of the Committee's belief that trial by jury should not form a fundamental aspect of a future Constitution was then revealed. Presumably motivated by a desire that distinctively Irish institutions should develop in the young state, it recommended that it should be made clear in the constitutional text that the country was not bound 'to the English system of requiring a jury of twelve and an [sic] unanimous verdict'.[77] More crucially, it recommended that the designation of an offence as 'minor' by the Oireachtas would not be open to constitutional challenge.[78] Had the Committee's proposals been adopted, trial by jury would have occupied a very vulnerable position in the constitutional order. With a lower status than other constitutional provisions, the Oireachtas could have circumvented its operation by characterising offences as 'minor'. Doubts in official circles about the merits of the jury system persisted until just before the coming into force of the new Constitution. In 1936 the Attorney General of the Fianna Fáil Government, Conor Maguire, who later became Chief Justice, stated in the Dáil: '[T]he Anglo-Saxon method … of trial by jury has failed.'[79] He referred to the campaign of jury intimidation to justify this comment. The pointed manner in which the English origins of trial by jury were often referred to

[71] The report of the Committee is reproduced in full in G Hogan, *The Origins of the Irish Constitution: 1928–1941* (Dublin, Royal Irish Academy, 2012) 74–100.

[72] Ibid, 74.

[73] Ibid.

[74] Suggested provisions allowing for special courts were provided in Appendix B. The Committee acknowledged that Art 70 might have to be revised if those provisions were adopted. Ibid, 87.

[75] Ibid, 92.

[76] Ibid.

[77] Ibid, 93.

[78] Ibid.

[79] *Dáil Debates*, 13 August 1936, vol 63, col 2901.

in the 1920s and 1930s is consistent with contemporary discourse that viewed the laws carried over from pre-independence times as unsuited to a new Irish state.[80]

The recommendations of the Review Committee in relation to trial by jury were not followed in the drafting of the 1937 Constitution and, in Hogan's words: 'if anything, the new Constitution strengthened and reinforced the right to jury trial'.[81] Given the antipathy towards the jury evident in official and political sentiment prior to the enactment of the new Constitution (and the absence of any public praise for the institution) it is unclear why trial by jury survived. The leading accounts of the drafting of the Constitution do not discuss why it was included, or whether its omission was seriously considered.[82] It has been suggested that the constitutional status of trial by jury was borne out of 'the bitter Irish race memory'[83] of the corrupt administration of criminal justice under British rule and the concomitant need for 'safeguard against future tyranny'.[84] However, this explanation is not very convincing because a state-manipulated jury system was perceived to be one of the problems afflicting the legal system prior to independence. It also seems to jar with the frustrations being voiced about the institution in official circles in the years leading up to the drafting of the new Constitution. Other potential reasons for the retention of the jury suggest themselves. Abolition of the jury would have entailed the design of an alternative system, a difficult and unwelcome task in addition to drafting the Constitution itself. Any such change was likely to be vigorously opposed by the legal profession and the judiciary. It could also have been portrayed by opponents of the new Constitution as an attack by the government on the rights of the citizen, jeopardising the acceptance of the text by a majority in a referendum.[85] Finally, it may have been felt that the provision for special courts in Article 38.3 solved the difficulties, from the state's point of view, that had arisen in relation to jury trials in 'political' or subversive cases.

III. POST-1937 JURY AMBIVALENCE

Official antipathy to trial by jury did not cease after the coming into force of the Constitution. Stephen Roche, Secretary of the Department of Justice (and one of the

[80] See T Mohr and J Schweppe, 'Irish Scholarship, Irish Law and the Irish Association of Law Teachers' in T Mohr and J Schweppe (eds), *30 Years of Legal Scholarship* (Dublin, Thomson Round Hall, 2011) 3, 3–7. Indeed, as late as 2013, a retired Supreme Court judge wrote: 'It would be churlish not to admit that one good thing we inherited from the English was the common law system.' See H Geoghegan, 'The Three Judges of the Supreme Court of the Irish Free State, 1925–36: Their Backgrounds, Personalities and Mindsets' in FM Larkin and NM Dawson (eds) *Lawyers, the Law and History: Irish Legal History Society Discourses and Other Papers, 2005–2011* (Dublin, Four Courts Press, 2013) 29, 34.

[81] Hogan, *Origins* (n 71) 359–360.

[82] D Keogh, *The Making of the Irish Constitution: Bunreacht na hEireann* (Cork, Mercier Press, 2007) and G Hogan, *The Origins of the Irish Constitution: 1928–1941* (Dublin, Royal Irish Academy, 2012).

[83] *People (DPP) v O'Shea* [1982] 1 IR 384, 432, per Henchy J.

[84] JD Jackson, K Quinn and T O'Malley, 'The Jury System in Contemporary Ireland: In the Shadow of a Troubled Past' in N Vidmar (ed), *World Jury Systems* (Oxford University Press, Oxford, 2000) 283, 289.

[85] The Constitution was ultimately endorsed by 56.52% of those who voted in the plebiscite held on 1 July 1937, with 43.48% voting against.

drafters of the Constitution) favoured the abolition of juries in all criminal cases.[86] In December 1939, he wrote:

> The fact is that trial by jury has no real roots in this country and is quite unsuited for dealing with our most serious form of crime, *viz.*, political crime. Instead of recognising that fact frankly, we have put up the pretext that occasionally – once in ten years or so – we may find to our surprise that juries will not convict in political cases, whereupon the Government makes proclamations under the Offences Against the State Act.[87]

In the following decades, hostility to trial by jury in official circles appears to have abated. The merits and fate of the institution were popular topics in debating societies.[88] However, public statements from politicians and judges praising trial by jury are difficult to find. A 1965 editorial in *The Irish Press* discussing the recommendations of the Committee on Court Practice and Procedure in relation to jury service described the jury as 'one of our more valuable heritages [sic]'.[89] This was a noteworthy endorsement of trial by jury by a newspaper controlled by the de Valera family. The following year the presidential election candidate and future Chief Justice, T F O'Higgins, reflected on jury trial at a public meeting: 'Whatever the origin of the jury system, it is a system particularly suited to our needs and as such must be retained.'[90] It is noteworthy that O'Higgins felt the need to acknowledge the unpalatable English origins of the jury in the context of emphasising the value of the institution. Arguably, hostility and frustration about trial by jury in the upper echelons of the Irish state gave way to ambivalence, and this ambivalence can be identified in respect of the judiciary and politicians. The indicia of this ambivalence will be briefly outlined in respect of both branches of government.

A. The Judiciary

Judges who preside over trials on indictment in Ireland hold juries in high esteem and are supportive of the jury system.[91] However, it is possible to detect other, more mixed, signals also, particularly from the appellate judiciary. These could be particularised as an absence of public pronouncements from judges on the merits and value of trial by jury, and a failure to scrutinise departures from the constitutional norm of jury trial with sufficient rigour.

English judges like nothing better than delivering (generally laudatory) lectures on the subject of trial by jury. The most celebrated and quoted of these is, of course,

[86] S Ó Longaigh, 'Emergency Law in Action, 1939–1945' in D Keogh and M O'Driscoll (eds), *Ireland in World War Two: Neutrality and Survival* (Cork, Mercier Press, 2004) 63, 66.

[87] Ibid, 65.

[88] See, eg, 'Trial by Jury: Technical Students' Debate', *The Irish Times*, 26 January 1937, 4; 'Debate on "Trial by Jury"', *The Irish Times*, 14 March 1941, 6; 'Right to Trial by Jury', *The Irish Press*, 2 January 1945, 3; 'Jury System Praised by Counsel', *The Irish Times*, 8 November 1950, 3.

[89] 'Jury Service', *The Irish Press*, 19 November 1965, 11.

[90] 'Jury System is Safeguarding the Individual', *The Irish Press*, 4 March 1966, 5.

[91] M Coen, N Howlin, C Barry and J Lynch, *Judges and Juries in Ireland: An Empirical Study* (2020, UCD); Murphy, 'The Role of the Judge and Jury in Criminal Cases' (n 8) 110.

Lord Devlin's Hamlyn Lectures, in which he described the jury as 'the lamp that shows that freedom lives'.[92] There have been others, with less memorable encomiums, such as Watkins LJ's lecture containing the statement that 'the destruction of trial by jury would be an act … of grim foreboding for the continuance of freedom as we know it'.[93] In the past decade or so, speeches on trial by jury, sometimes raising issues of concern or suggesting reforms, but overwhelmingly positive in tone, have been given by Lord Phillips,[94] Lord Judge,[95] Moses LJ,[96] Hallett LJ[97] and Sir Brian Leveson,[98] among others.[99] These speeches demonstrate an active interest in trial by jury among the senior judiciary of England and Wales. The only lecture on trial by jury given by an Irish judge since independence appears to be that given by the late O'Hanlon J and subsequently published as an article, in which he described trial by jury as an 'anachronism in the modern constitutional democracy'[100] and called for its replacement by a court composed of three judges. When reflecting on the dearth of extrajudicial statements on trial by jury, it should be borne in mind that Ireland is a considerably smaller jurisdiction than England and Wales, with fewer judges. The giving of lectures by judges on aspects of the legal system is also not as well-established a convention here.[101] Nevertheless, the contrast between the jurisdictions in terms of extrajudicial discussion of trial by jury is undeniable.

A stronger argument that there is judicial ambivalence about the importance of trial by jury in Ireland can be made by reference to the judiciary's approach to challenges to various aspects of the Special Criminal Court regime. The wide degree of latitude accorded to the executive in that regard has been evident since the decision of the Supreme Court in *Re McCurtain*,[102] where it was held that the judges of the Special Criminal Court could be military officers. This was notwithstanding the wording of Article 38.4.1, which suggests that civilians may only be tried by military tribunal in a time of war or armed rebellion.[103] Equally, although the Constitution makes the inadequacy of the ordinary courts a condition precedent to the establishment of the Special Criminal Court, the

[92] Devlin, *Trial by Jury* (n 2) 164.

[93] T Watkins, 'Trial by Jury: A Time for Re-Appraisal' (1985) 16 *Cambrian Law Review* 5,16. See also Lord Griffiths, 'The History and Future of the Jury' (1987) 18 *Cambrian Law Review* 5.

[94] N Phillips, 'Trusting the Jury', 23 October 2007, available at: https://webarchive.nationalarchives.gov.uk/20100406123501/http:/www.judiciary.gov.uk/docs/speeches/lcj_trusting_juries_231007.pdf.

[95] I Judge, 'Jury Trials', 19 November 2010, available at: https://webarchive.nationalarchives.gov.uk/20131203071051/http://www.judiciary.gov.uk/Resources/JCO/Documents/Speeches/speech-lcj-jury-trials-jsb-lecture-belfast.pdf.

[96] A Moses, 'Summing Down the Summing up', 23 November 2010, available at: https://webarchive.nationalarchives.gov.uk/20130114062220/http://www.judiciary.gov.uk/Resources/JCO/Documents/Speeches/speech-moses-lj-summing-down-summing-up.pdf.

[97] H Hallet, 'Trial by Jury – Past and Present', 20 May 2017, available at: www.judiciary.uk/wp-content/uploads/2017/05/hallett-lj-blackstone-lecture-20170522-1.pdf.

[98] B Leveson, 'Criminal Trials: The Human Experience', 13 June 2019, available at: www.judiciary.uk/wp-content/uploads/2019/06/Sir-Brian-Leveson-UCL-Valedictory-lecture.pdf.

[99] In his speech (n 96 above), Moses LJ also referred to speeches on trial by jury delivered in 2010 by Hooper LJ and Lord Brown.

[100] RJ O'Hanlon, 'The Sacred Cow of Trial by Jury' (1990) 25(1) *Irish Jurist* 57, 68.

[101] There is no Irish equivalent of the official English webpage for judicial speeches, for example. See www.judiciary.uk/announcement-type/speeches/.

[102] [1941] IR 83.

[103] Article 38.4.1 states: 'Military tribunals may be established for the trial of offences against military law alleged to have been committed by persons while subject to military law and also to deal with a state of war or armed rebellion.'

courts have held that they have no role in reviewing the government's determination that the threshold of inadequacy has been reached.[104]

What Hogan and Walker termed 'judicial reluctance'[105] to intervene has been particularly marked in relation to cases seeking curial scrutiny of the Director of Public Prosecution's power to transfer trials for non-scheduled offences to the special court.[106] As Walsh notes, this discretion of the DPP has profound consequences, because where the offence involved is non-minor the Director's certificate removes the constitutional right to trial by jury that the accused would otherwise enjoy.[107] In caselaw that arguably undervalues the right in issue, the courts have held that the decision of the Director to make that decision is only judicially reviewable on the very narrow ground of bad faith.[108] The fact that the courts have set the threshold for reviewability so high when the decision-maker, the Director, will be a party to the criminal prosecution, suggests ambivalence about the status of trial by jury. The decision of the Supreme Court in *Murphy v Ireland*[109] presented an opportunity to advance the protection of accused persons and vindicate their right to fair procedures in relation to the determination of mode of trial. Although the Court held that the DPP should provide reasons for sending a non-scheduled offence forward for trial in the Special Criminal Court, the principle is of no value because the Court qualified it into oblivion by saying that national security could be invoked as a justification for not providing reasons. O'Donnell J was clearly conscious of the historical context of non-jury trial in Ireland, stating:

> It is an important, though a regrettable fact, that for almost the entire life of the Constitution, and indeed since the foundation of the State, legislation providing for some form of emergency powers and trial in a Special Criminal Court has been part of the legislative code of this State. That, in turn, reflects a fact which cannot be avoided, that, since the foundation of the State, there have been organisations active within it, at different times, and with different degrees of force, which have denied the legitimacy of the State and the administration of justice within it, and consider violence, criminal conduct, and, if necessary, the intimidation and/or persuasion of witnesses and jurors, as acceptable tactics in pursuit of their aims.[110]

It can thus be seen that the turbulent history outlined earlier in this chapter casts a long shadow. It creates a reluctance on the part of the judiciary to be interventionist in relation to the rights-compliance of the special court system. This approach may be motivated by a fear of meddling in security issues, but it can give the impression of an ambivalence to jury trial.

B. Politicians

Irish politicians have been extremely apathetic in relation to trial by jury, particularly in the area of law reform. It took the decision of the Supreme Court in *de Búrca*

[104] *Kavanagh v Ireland* [1997] 1 ILRM 321.

[105] G Hogan and C Walker, *Political Violence and the Law in Ireland* (Manchester, Manchester University Press, 1989) 185.

[106] Offences Against the State Act 1939, ss 46, 47(2) and 48(a), as amended.

[107] D Walsh, *Walsh on Criminal Procedure* (Dublin, Thomson Reuters, 2016) 1499.

[108] *Kavanagh v Ireland* [1997] 1 ILRM 321, 360, per Barrington J.

[109] [2014] 1 IR 198.

[110] Ibid, 213.

and Anderson v AG[111] to force the wholesale redrawing of the jury composition rules to accord with the constitutional requirement that juries be drawn from a pool that is representative of the community.[112] The law on juries has not been revisited in any substantial way since the enactment of the Juries Act 1976, in spite of major social and cultural changes brought about by developments including immigration and advances in transport and technology. A Law Reform Commission report from 2013 containing many uncontroversial and sensible recommendations has not been implemented and is currently being considered by a Justice Sector Working Group on Juries. In the absence of legislative reform, it is quite possible that the jury pool does not meet the *de Búrca* criteria of representativeness. This is particularly so if vast swathes of professional people, many employed in the public service, are availing of their 'excusable as of right' privileges under the 1976 Act.[113]

The legislature has also ignored many well-considered and reasoned reform suggestions in relation to non-jury trial. The criticisms of Ireland's special court regime by international human rights organisations are discussed elsewhere in this volume.[114] The political class has refused to modify the system in light of this sustained adverse commentary. It has also ignored the recommendations of two domestic bodies, namely the Constitution Review Group (CRG) and the Hederman Committee on the Offences Against the State Acts. In its 1996 report, the CRG conducted a thorough analysis of all aspects of the Constitution. In relation to special courts, among the recommendations was that Article 38.3 be amended so that special courts could only be established 'for a fixed period as prescribed by law'.[115] An amendment of Article 38.6, providing that the judges of such courts would have the same guarantees in relation to tenure, salaries and independence as other members of the judiciary was also recommended.[116] Neither recommendation has been implemented. The operation of the Special Criminal Court was one of the issues considered by the Hederman Committee, which published its report in 2002. A majority of the Committee recommended the retention of the Court, citing its continued necessity in both subversive and non-subversive contexts.[117] A minority of the Committee expressed the view that the Special Criminal Court should be dispensed with on the basis that a trial without a jury for serious offences contravened fundamental 'constitutional values and human rights norms'.[118]

Among the major recommendations of the Committee were that the 1939 Act be amended so that a resolution establishing a special court would lapse after three years unless positively affirmed by the Oireachtas[119] and that a decision of the Director of Public Prosecutions to send an accused for trial in such a court would be subject to review

[111] [1976] 1 IR 38.

[112] The Juries Act 1976 was enacted in the aftermath of the *de Búrca* decision, which found that the exclusion of people who did not satisfy a property rating qualification and the de facto exclusion of women from jury service was unconstitutional.

[113] The excusable as of right categories are contained in Pt II of the First Schedule of the Juries Act 1976.

[114] See Y Daly, Chapter 11, this volume.

[115] *Report of the Constitution Review Group* (Dublin, Stationery Office, 1996) 198.

[116] Ibid, 199.

[117] *Report of the Committee to Review the Offences Against the State Acts 1939–1998* (Dublin, Government Publications, 2002), hereinafter Hederman Report, 9.38.

[118] Ibid, para 9.89.

[119] Ibid, para 9.44.

by a serving Supreme Court judge.[120] In recommending these reforms the Committee was clearly of the view that the existing legislative provisions were imbalanced in favour of the executive and insufficiently protective of the right to trial by jury for non-minor offences. Another recommendation included an amendment to the 1939 Act disallowing members of the Defence Forces from acting as judges of the Court.[121] The Committee also reiterated the CRG recommendation in relation to the tenure, independence and salaries of Special Criminal Court judges.[122] These recommendations, which would have involved some reduction in executive power while still allowing the Special Criminal Court to function, have not been implemented.

In her contribution to this volume, Ivana Bacik discusses the parliamentary oversight role of the Oireachtas in relation to the OASA. There are several crucial limitations to this mechanism. First, it relates only to certain aspects of the legislative framework and does not, for example, entail a regular, wholesale review of whether the entire statutory scheme or even just the Special Criminal Court should be continued in existence. Second, as Bacik observes in her chapter, the government does not provide detailed information as to why the various provisions should be continued in force. Third, Irish governments generally have a majority of the seats in both Houses of the Oireachtas, with their deputies and senators 'whipped' to vote for the government position. If the executive is in favour of renewing the provisions, a different voting outcome from the legislature is highly unlikely. Taking these limitations into account, the review mechanism does not seem particularly meaningful or effective. At most, it permits Opposition members of the Oireachtas to draw attention to the unimplemented recommendations of the Hederman Report and criticism of the Special Criminal Court by domestic and international human rights bodies. While such debate is of some value, it achieves very little in practice.

IV. CONCLUSION

This chapter has argued that a collective official attitude of ambivalence to trial by jury is discernible in Ireland. It is evinced by legislative inaction in relation to reform of the jury system and the much-criticised derogations from it, and the deferential approach of the judiciary in cases challenging the operation of the Special Criminal Court. There is a dearth of official Irish pronouncements celebrating or extolling trial by jury. More substantively, ambivalence may be inferred from political and judicial failures to vindicate the constitutional right involved to the greatest extent possible. The argument is not that the existence of a special, non-jury court demonstrates an ambivalence to trial by jury, but that the absence of official recognition that the current system could be improved upon to maximise the right to trial by jury does so. Successive governments have been keen to maintain very broad discretion in relation to special courts and have ignored the recommendations of official domestic reviews, the critiques of academics and the censure of international human rights institutions. The judiciary, in turn, has made plain

[120] Ibid, para 9.76.

[121] Ibid, para 9.39. No member of the Defence Forces has acted as a judge of the current Court since its establishment in 1972.

[122] Hederman Report (n 117) para 9.56.

that recourse to non-jury courts is a matter for government, with minimal curial oversight. It is questionable if this is the appropriate standard of review for departures from 'an important constitutional right of the citizen and a constitutional obligation on the State'.[123]

There are probably several reasons that might explain why Irish politicians and judges have engaged with these issues in these ways. For example, politicians may perceive a lack of electoral interest in review and reform of the Juries Act or the system of non-jury trial. They may feel that current legal arrangements are working well and should not be disturbed, because of the serious issues at stake. Judges may be reluctant to make constitutional findings that would curtail the use of special courts, lest they are blamed if jurors are intimidated or worse. They may also be disinclined to do anything that could be interpreted as casting aspersions on the fairness of the Special Criminal Court, which is composed of their judicial colleagues. As in most areas of life, a myriad of considerations and values are in play. Ambivalence to trial by jury is but one of the attitudes that may be discerned in Ireland's approach to the trial of serious offences. Its origins lie in unhappy experiences of that foreign legal transplant both before and after independence. Its effects are reluctant acceptance of jury trial, wide-ranging political discretion to derogate from it and a marked disinclination to engage in its reform.

[123] *Murphy v Ireland* [2014] 1 IR 198, 214, per O'Donnell J.

4

The Special Criminal Court: A Conveyor Belt of Exceptionality

FIONNUALA NÍ AOLÁIN*

THE RESORT TO special courts by democratic states is rarely a standalone legal response. Rather, the establishment of specially empowered courts is part of a broader assault on due process rights which does not always stay quarantined in the exceptional legal sphere.[1] Exceptional courts form the bridge between rules that permit multiple latitudes vis-a-vis arrest, detention and rules that extend and bound the imprisonment of persons convicted and sentenced in such fora. The decision to abandon ordinary legal process epitomises the apex of a matrix of the extraordinary for states. Special Courts are particularly attractive to the state because they promise greater flexibility in court operation, personnel, procedural rules, and outcomes for governments who may feel that ordinary courts will be rigid or are constitutionally limited in their capacity to process certain defendants as they would wish. There is also comparative evidence,[2] that because Special Courts try a small class of 'selected out' individuals the 'public' is less interested in the outcomes and such courts will be subject to less scrutiny. In short, Special Courts promise states the possibility of greater control over the legal process, a highly attractive proposition when faced with violent challengers, sustained internal violence or substantial opposition to the political and constitutional order.

* I note specific thanks for the data collection and analysis carried out by Adrienne Reilly and Ita Connolly, and for the intellectual and practical contributions of Professor Colm Campbell to this research. Research assistance was carried out by Bonny Birkeland. Statistical analysis was carried out with the support of Dr Ryan Halen. Views expressed in this article are personal to the author.

[1] F Ní Aoláin, 'The Individual Right of Access to Justice in Times of Crisis: Emergencies, Armed Conflict, and Terrorism' in F Francioni (ed), *Access to Justice as a Human Right* (Oxford, Oxford University Press, 2007) 57–93; F Ní Aoláin, 'Lawyers, Military Commissions and the Rule of Law in Democratic States' in Lennon, King and McCartney (eds), *Counter-Terrorism, Constitutionalism and Miscarriages of Justice* (Oxford, Hart Publishing, 2018) 117–33; F Ní Aoláin, 'Restriction on the Jurisdiction of Military Courts' in Caledo, Haldemann and Unger (eds), *The United Nations Principles to Combat Impunity: A Commentary* (Oxford, Oxford University Press, 2018) 315–323.

[2] See, eg, DPJ Walsh, 'Arrest and Interrogation: Northern Ireland'(1981) 9(1) *Journal of Law and Society* 37–62; Although undercut by the publicity and public attention which the military tribunals established to process Guantanamo detainees have garnered; C Campbell and I Connolly, 'A Model for the War Against Terrorism? Military Intervention and the 1970 Falls Curfew' (2003) 30(2) *Journal of Law and Society* 341–375.

The context of exceptional court creation may vary,[3] but a common thread that marks these courts out from their ordinary counterparts is the sense of greater internal latitude and compromises on their operative frameworks.

I have noted elsewhere that the legal basis and operation of these courts is critical for governments.[4] These are not lawless courts. They are deeply rooted and legitimised by legal rules and are frequently defended by reference to their legal pedigrees.[5] The rule of law matters greatly, at least at a formal and symbolic level for democratic governments.[6] Thus, even in the creation of such courts, certain conventions are observed. This is not least because the international human rights treaties to which such states are signatories affirm the centrality of 'competent, independent and impartial tribunal[s] established by law'.[7] Despite the practical reality that such courts may depart significantly from the protections available to individuals in ordinary courts, the appearance of legal form and conventions has a significant symbolic and practical legitimising effect for these courts. This chapter proceeds by using the Irish Special Criminal Court as a case study of how Special Courts are established, legitimised and endure (Section I). The analysis then proceeds to address the practice of the Special Criminal Court drawing on a unique data set compiled by the author (Section II). The data presented will focus specifically on the evidential basis for the conviction of persons charged with terrorist offences in Ireland, underscoring the broader point of this analysis that Special Courts are part of a continuum of compromises on the rule of law and regular legal process. The conclusion will reflect on the modalities of juridical exceptionality and address its peculiarities in Ireland.

I. EXCEPTIONAL COURTS IN IRELAND

Emergency powers and Special Courts were not new prior to the enactment of the 1937 Constitution.[8] Such powers were an inherent and integral part of the colonial structure

[3] F Ní Aolain & O Gross, *Guantanamo and Beyond: Exceptional Courts and Military Commissions in Comparative Perspective* (Cambridge, Cambridge University Press, 2013).

[4] Ní Aoláin, 'Lawyers, Military Commissions' (n 1).

[5] J Hafetz, 'The Guantanamo Effect and Some Troubling Implication of Limiting Habeas Rights Domestically' (2007) 10 *City University of New York Law Review* 351, 351–60; JK Elsea, 'The Military Commissions Act of 2006: Analysis of Procedural Rules and Comparison with Previous DOD Rules and the Uniform Code of Military Justice' (CRS Report for Congress 2007) www.fas.org/sgp/crs/natsec/RL33688.pdf accessed 28 March 2020; AN Guiora, 'Military Commissions and National Security Courts After Guantanamo' (2008) 103 *Northwestern University Law Review, Colloquy*.

[6] O Gross and F Ní Aoláin, *Law in Times of Crisis: Emergency Powers in Theory and Practice* (Cambridge University Press, 2006).

[7] International Covenant on Civil and Political Rights (adopted 16 December 1966, entered into force 23 March 1976) 999 UNTS 171 (ICCPR) art 14.

[8] By way of background see N Howlin, Chapter 1 and T Mohr, Chapter 2, this volume. The inclusion of a Military Tribunal in the post-partition Constitution is significant. Article 70 noted that extraordinary courts were not to be established 'save only such Military Tribunals as may be authorised by law for dealing with military offences against military law'. Constitution of the Irish Free State Act (Saorstát Eireann) 1922, Art 70. The jurisdiction of this court was not to be extended over the civilian population unless in a time of war or armed rebellion or for acts committed during either. It should be noted that there is a dearth of statutory legislation which covers the use of emergency law in Ireland prior to the 1937 Constitutional provision for the establishment of a Special Criminal Court. See C Campbell, *Emergency Law in Ireland 1918–1925* (Oxford, Clarendon Press, 1994); M Robinson, *The Special Criminal Court* (Dublin University Press, 1974) 22.

in Ireland, central to the maintenance of military and political control on the island.[9] However, the Constitution codified the establishment of Special Courts and gave them a unique standing in the emerging Irish legal order. Article 38.3 states that:

> 1° Special courts may be established by law for the trial of offences in cases where it may be determined in accordance with such law that the ordinary courts are inadequate to secure the effective administration of justice, and the preservation of public peace and order.
>
> 2° The constitution, powers, jurisdiction and procedure of such special courts shall be prescribed by law.[10]

The Special Criminal Court is a hybrid Court by virtue of its dual military and civilian status. This defining feature is legitimised by parallel recognition of the role of military courts in Article 38(4)(1) of the Constitution where it stipulates that military courts can be established 'for the trial of offences against military law alleged to have been committed by persons while subject to military law and also deal with a state of war or armed rebellion'. Moreover, Article 43(1)(c) allows for jurisdiction in order to facilitate '[t]he detention of and to detain in civil or military custody … any person sent, sent forward, transferred, or otherwise brought for trial by that Court'. The dual inclusion of provisions for both military and exceptional courts confirms the strong executive model contained in the constitutional ordering, as well as a prescient fear of instability and conflict stemming from the deeply divisive civil war and its long legal and political shadows.

It was unclear initially how a Special Court was to be facilitated in practice.[11] The then government chose to pass the Offences Against the State Act 1939 (OASA), which included in Part V the ability for a Special Court to be established by government proclamation where it is deemed that 'the ordinary courts are inadequate to secure the effective administration of justice, and the preservation of public peace and order'.[12] The exceptional nature of these courts included that they were juryless and had accompanying emergency statutory legislation providing for both the composition of the court,[13] and the nature of the offences to be processed.[14]

The first Special Criminal Court was established in August 1939 in response to the threat manifested by the outbreak of World War II. The Court was operative between 1939–46 and 1961–62 and all cases were heard by military officers.[15] The hearings, in the main, related to paramilitary activity by the Irish Republican Army. However, even then the Court also dealt with miscellaneous criminal activity as well as presiding over formally defined military trials. These proceedings did not go unchallenged and were

[9] Campbell, *Emergency Law in Ireland* (n 8).

[10] Constitution of Ireland 1939 (Bunreacht Na hÉireann), Art 38.3.1–2.

[11] GW Hogan and C Walker, *Political Violence and the Law in Ireland* (1989) 177: 'Article 28.3.3 also gave constitutional immunity to any law which is expressed to be "for the preservation of public safety and the preservation of the state in time of war and armed rebellion". Article 28.3.3° allowed for government to take emergency action in the case of actual invasion or in a time of war but it was also clear that these powers might not of themselves be sufficient in the case of a European conflict in which Ireland was not a belligerent. A constitutional amendment together with the Emergency Powers Bill had already been drafted by January 1939 to compensate for this apparent gap. The Treason Act, 1939, and the OASA, 1939, were passed by June 1939.'

[12] Offences Against the State Act (OASA) 1939, s 35. See Robinson, *The Special Criminal Court* (n 8), for a general overview of provisions for establishing a special criminal court and relevant statute.

[13] Constitution of Ireland 1939, Art 38; OASA, s 39.

[14] OASA, Pt II. Section 47(2) enables the Director of Public Prosecutions (DPP) to send non-scheduled offences to be tried before the Special Criminal Court providing the appropriate certificate is given. OASA, s 47(2).

[15] Section 39(3) provides for military officers to hear cases before the Special Criminal Court. OASA, s 39(3).

controversial both legally and politically whenever they came into session.[16] The Special Criminal Court was closed down entirely by government proclamation which terminated the Part V powers of the 1939 Act in 1962.[17]

The contemporary Special Criminal Court emerged in May 1972 in response to the political violence emanating from the conflict in Northern Ireland. It has, since then, operated continuously as part of the court structure of the Republic of Ireland.[18] Unlike the Special Courts which operated from 1939–62 where military officers presided, the Court has, in the main, consisted of regularly appointed judges, although barristers and solicitors and military officers are still by law eligible to hear trials. It is presided over by the President of the High Court and the rules of evidence are those applied in the Central Criminal Court subject to modifications. In practice this includes *voir dire* proceedings,[19] admissibility of evidence and witness evidence.[20] The very fact of any trial (terrorist or other) being located in the Special Criminal Court has a significant effect on the nature, form and experience of trial for legal representatives and defendants alike.[21] Notably, Article 41(1) of the OASA on procedure states that:

> Every Special Criminal Court shall have power, in its absolute discretion, to appoint the times and places of its sittings, and shall have control of its own procedure in all respects, and, shall for that purpose make, with the concurrence of the Minister for Justice, rules regulating its practice and procedure and may in particular provide by such rules for the issuing of summonses, the procedure for bringing (in custody or on bail) persons before it for trial, the admission or exclusion of the public to or from its sitting, the enforcing of the attendance of witnesses, and the production of documents. (summarise and critique).[22]

[16] F Davis, *The History and Development of the Special Criminal Court 1922–2005* (Dublin, Four Courts Press, 2007) 42–55.

[17] The Court closed on 2 October 1962.

[18] Robinson, *The Special Criminal Court* (n 8) 25: 'On the 26th May 1972 the Government made a proclamation which was published in *Iris Oifigiuil*, bringing Part 5 of the 1939 Act into effect.'

[19] *People (DPP) v McGowan* [1979] IR 45; *People (DPP) v McMahon* [1984] ILRM 461. To overcome fairness concerns it has been argued that inadmissible evidence should be heard by a separate chamber other than that of the sitting judges on the Court. However, in *DPP v Special Criminal Court*, Carney J reasoned why this would not be appropriate:

> It is the function of every professional judge to adjudicate on the admissibility of evidence prejudicial to an accused person and *to exclude it from his mind* if it is not admissible according to the rules of evidence. I would not see it as necessary for another chamber of the court to deal with the matter. (italics added).

See A Harrison, Chapter 7, this volume.

[20] Specific controversy has sustained about the admissibility of membership evidence. Section 3(2) of the Offence Against the State (Amendment) Act 1972 provides the following:

> Where an officer of the Garda Síochána, not below the rank of Chief Superintendent, in giving evidence in proceedings relating to an offence under the said Section 21, states that he believes that the accused was at a material time a member of an unlawful organisation, the statement shall be evidence that he was then such a member.

Section 26 of the 1939 Act is seen as precursor to this section. It relates to incriminating documents and a Chief Superintendents belief that a document is incriminating. Section 21 of the 1939 Act is also supported by the Offences Against the State (Amendment) Act 1998, s 2 where inferences can be drawn for failure to answer a material question. Note the concerns articulated by *Report of the Committee to Review the Offences Against the State Acts 1939–1998* (Dublin, Government Publications, 2002), hereinafter Hederman Report. See L Heffernan and E O'Connor, Chapter 6, this volume.

[21] OASA, s 41(4).

[22] Ibid, s 41(1).

An overarching difference between the Special Criminal Court and the Central Criminal Court, is its non-jury status. The significance of non-jury trials and the impact of such trials in common law systems on the rights of defendants and the integrity of the legal system as a whole has been well-canvassed.[23] Juryless trials create significant obstacles to ensuring that the fundamental evidential rules supporting criminal trials are observed in a regular way. Specifically, Anglo-American common law rules of evidence include prohibitions on hearsay and requirement that any confessions be both voluntary and supported by independent corroboration of the crime.[24] These rules, in particular, come under particular stress in non-jury common law courts. While the Diplock (non-jury) trials in Northern Ireland garnered significant international attention and opprobrium,[25] by contrast, the Irish Special Criminal Court has largely escaped public and international legal scrutiny.[26] The fact of ongoing conflict, high-profile trials, systematised review of counter-terrorism legislation and sustained legal challenge to the Diplock system meant that there were multiple entry points to contestation. The Republic of Ireland presented fewer such high-profile opportunities and the high degree of its acceptance and validity in 'ordinary' legal circles further enabled its longevity and its legitimacy.

II. ANALYSING THE RELATIONSHIP OF ARREST AND DETENTION TO THE SPECIAL CRIMINAL COURT

The data presented in this chapter is part of a larger empirical research project conducted by the author and colleagues over two decades. Using official court records, to which access was granted by the President of the High Court, the researchers recorded details of individual biographies (age, gender, employment status, education), interrogation timelines, access to lawyers, and specifics of evidence attributed to the accused. Thereafter, SPSS cross-tabulations were generated based on literature and/or inductive reasoning from the data to track the process from initial arrest, though interrogation, charging and trial.[27] A unique facet of this overall project is its longitudinal dimension, involving access to approximately 50 individual cases of persons tried under national security-specific

[23] SC Greer and A White, *Abolishing the Diplock Courts: The Case for Restoring Jury Trial to Scheduled Offences in Northern Ireland* (London, Cobden Trust, 1986); J Jackson and S Doran, *Judge Without Jury, Diplock Trials in the Adversary System* (Oxford, Clarendon Press, 1995); B Dickson, *The Legal System of Northern Ireland* 3rd edn (SLS Legal Publications, 1993); F Ní Aoláin and C Campbell, 'Managing Terrorism' (2018) 9 *Journal of National Security Law and Policy* 367, 367–412.

[24] D Glazier, 'Precedents Lost: The Neglected History of the Military Commission' (2005) 46 *Virginia Journal of International Law* 5, 54–55.

[25] D Walsh, 'Civil Liberties in Northern Ireland' in P Wallington (ed), *Civil Liberties 1984* (Oxford, Oxford University Press, 1984) 325; Human Rights Watch, 'Northern Ireland: Continued Abuses by All Sides' (Report 1994) www.hrw.org/sites/default/files/reports/UK943.pdf accessed 28 March 2020; Lawyers Committee for Human Rights, *Human Rights and Legal Defense in Northern Ireland: The Intimidation of Defense Lawyers* (New York, Lawyers Committee for Human Rights, 1993).

[26] With some notable exceptions, see eg, Amnesty International found at www.amnestyusa.org/countries/ireland/; and the Irish Council on Civil Liberties found at: www.iccl.ie/tag/special-criminal-court/.

[27] The trial of one individual is referred to as a 'case'; several such cases could be tried on one indictment, and in each case the defendant might have faced a number of charges. For each case, a data sheet listing such variables as time of arrest, place of arrest and other relevant criteria was completed by referring to the 'Book of Evidence' and the court files. The author was given research access to these files and had ethical and security clearance to undertake the research.

provisions in Irish law in cohorts from 1974–2008. The research strategy in this project sought to ensure that the methodologies employed in respect of the Special Criminal Court were compatible with earlier and contemporary studies of the Diplock courts,[28] permitting future assessment of their collective operation over a period of nearly four decades.

This chapter addresses two principle questions:

(1) What kind of evidence formed the basis for trial in cases before the Special Criminal Court?
(2) What impact did the use of Garda (police) statement evidence have on the outcomes of trials?

These questions allow for some reflection on broader conceptual questions, namely: (1) What are the forms of layered exceptionality evidenced in the day-to-day operation of the Special Criminal Court?; and (2) In the longer term, what does a longitudinal study over the length of the Court's existence say about the role of legal institutions and the effect of legal culture on a state's resort to exceptional Courts and exceptional procedural rules?

A. Trials and Evidence in the Special Criminal Court

The (re)-instatement of the Court in 1972 constituted an exceptional legal measure, discarding the general right to trial by jury to trial by judges alone, notwithstanding the absence of any compelling evidence of jury tampering, jury bias or jury intimidation.[29] As I have articulated at length elsewhere,[30] exceptional courts generally come with a panoply of associated legal measures, which shape the positionality of persons charged with terrorism offences (or other offences) before they ever reach the court. These include regulations concerning extended detention, access to counsel, and conditions of confinement. Other regulatory measures are directed specifically to the functioning of the trial itself. These are primarily but not exclusively rules of evidence and procedure including reversals of the burden of proof, the use of abrogated procedures, allowances for admitting intelligence evidence, and prosaic reliance on confessional evidence. Finally, such courts are generally accompanied by changes to sentencing rules and stipulations concerning detention post-conviction. All of these measures in the criminal law arena can be further layered with civil and financial penalties as well as administrative measures when the response to violent challengers, conflict and terrorism is layered across multiple legal orders.

In Ireland, the public posture of the Special Criminal Court was as the front-line adjudicator of persons charged with terrorist offences,[31] though in practice the Court

[28] See, eg, T Hadden, K Boyle and P Hillyard, *Ten Years on in Northern Ireland* (London, Cobden Trust, 1980); Ní Aoláin and Campbell, 'Managing Terrorism' (n 23).

[29] D Walsh, 'The Impact of the Antisubversive Laws on Police Powers and Practices in Ireland: The Silent Erosion of Individual Freedom' (1989) 62 *Temple Law Review* 1099.

[30] See n 1.

[31] Human Rights Committee, 'Summary Record of the 1239th meeting of the Human Rights Committee' (20 July 1993) UN Doc CPR/C/SR.1239 paras 13–14.

became a shortcut to facilitate the trial of persons charged with offences associated with organised criminal gangs.[32] One particular feature of the Court was its reliance on procedural and evidentiary shifts which were employed with a view to facilitating convictions. Many Special Courts, including the Diplock Courts in Northern Ireland permitted reliance on confessional evidence, which was linked to persistent concerns about torture, inhuman and degrading treatment in interrogation contexts. For a brief period, parallel practices were identified in the Republic of Ireland but more substantive changes to the evidential terrain in the Special Criminal Court significantly replaced the reliance on confessions.[33]

I now turn to explore the substantial evidentiary measures that accompanied the Court's functioning. The critical legal change as regards the introduction of evidence was the shift to the use of Garda opinion evidence in the Special Criminal Court in 1972.[34] The rationale to modify rules of evidence was based primarily on the threat posed by non-state armed groups to the functioning of trials.[35] Specifically, abrogation of trials by jury were framed around claims of potential intimidation by the organisations to which the accused persons were believed to be associated. In parallel, assertions that persons accused of terrorism had received terrorist training enabling them to withstand coercive questioning and thus limiting the capacity to elicit evidence also facilitated the introduction of Garda opinion evidence. Thus, to 'assist any prosecution under section 21 [of the 1939 Offences Against the State Act] … certain evidential shortcuts' were provided.[36]

Two primary shortcuts were first provided by the OASA, under sections 23 and 26. Section 23 enabled 'incriminating documents' found on a person or their property to be used as evidence of membership of an illegal organisation.[37] It was consolidated by section 26, which facilitated the use of Garda opinion evidence in the context of documentary evidence, specifically if the origin or production of the document was at issue.[38] Both provisions were subject to significant contestation.[39] Litigation focused on fair trial concerns highlighted the reversal of the burden of proof in membership prosecutions,

[32] See L Campbell, Chapter 8, this volume.; Davis, *The History and Development* (n 16).

[33] Amnesty International, *Report of an Amnesty International Mission to Northern Ireland, 28 November–6 December 1977* (London, Amnesty International Publications, 1978); A Mulcahy, 'The Impact of the Northern "Troubles" on Criminal Justice in the Irish Republic in Criminal Justice in Ireland' in P O'Mahony (ed), *Criminal Justice in Ireland* (Institute of Public Administration, 2008) 288.

[34] See L Heffernan and E O'Conner, Chapter 6, this volume.

[35] This rationale was articulated in the Hederman Report (n 20), 6.51 (Use of opinion evidence and other special evidential rules).

[36] Hogan and Walker, *Political Violence* (n 11) 248.

[37] See, eg, 'The People (Director of Public Prosecutions) v. Treanor' *The Irish Times* (30 July 1980) (where the accused were convicted of membership of an illegal organisation where they had been found in possession of a document described as 'Instructions for training officers, IRA'); 'The People (Director of Public Prosecutions) v. Carroll' *The Irish Times* (8 December 2001) (where documents containing information on home-made explosives and improvised mix were found in the accused's bedroom).

[38] 'Where in any criminal proceedings the question whether a particular treasonable document, seditious document or incriminating document was or was not published by the accused (whether by himself or in concert with other persons or by arrangement between himself and other persons) is in issue and an officer of the Garda Síochána not below the rank of Chief Superintendent states on oath that he believes that such document was published (as the case may be) by the accused or by the accused in concert with other persons, such statement shall be evidence … that the accused published such document as alleged in the said statement on oath of such officer.' OASA s 26.

[39] See, eg, *O'Leary v Attorney General* [1993] 1 IR 102 (HC), [1995] 1 IR 254 (SC).

particularly when such prosecutions were pursued on the basis of documentary evidence alone. The Supreme Court upheld the constitutionality of section 23, premised on highly convoluted reasoning which upheld de facto broad inferences substantiating membership of unlawful organisations, based on the possession of documents.[40]

An innovation in section 26 saw Garda opinion evidence further extended and consolidated by section 3(2) of the 1972 Offences Against the State Act.[41] This provision, is one of the most notorious in the Act and sets out:

> Where an officer of the Garda Síochána, not below the rank of Chief Superintendent, in giving evidence in proceedings relating to an offence under the said section 21, states he believes that the accused was at a material time a member of an unlawful organisation, the statement shall be evidence that he was then such a member.

Practically, the most contentious legal issue was whether the opinion of the Chief Superintendent alone was sufficient to sustain a conviction. The Supreme Court held in *People (Director of Public Prosecutions) v Ferguson*,[42] that such reliance was possible (though not in that particular case). Subsequent cases upheld the constitutionality of Garda opinion evidence.[43] Although *Ferguson* was the operative standard in the time period assessed by this data analysis, the courts have now moved to a position of requiring corroboration of belief evidence,[44] which is a positive step forward but does not entirely dispose of the evidential and human rights challenges that follow from the use of opinion evidence in terrorism trials.

This background to the regulation of evidence under constitutional and statutory law in Ireland is the basis for proceeding to examine the study's data on the operation of the Special Criminal Court. Table 1 (below) sets out the array of evidential sources relied upon by the Prosecution drawn on the 50 cases forming the basis of this study. The descriptive overview confirms that a broad range of evidence was available to the Court (forensic, eyewitness, fabric, camera and DNA) and (obviously) multiple evidential sources were available in multiple cases. This snapshot belies the assumptions that tangible and material evidence was unavailable to the Gardaí and the prosecution in cases involving terrorism. As such, it suggests, as a preliminary matter, that the case for the need to maintain inferences and Garda opinion evidence was significantly overstated,

[40] Ibid.

[41] Section 3(1)(a) and (b) of the Act essentially pertain to the speech or acts by the accused person from which reasonable inferences may be drawn that she is a member of an unlawful organisation. Offences Against the State Act 1972, s 3(1)(a)–(b).

[42] Notably, O'Higgins CJ, while not convinced that the belief was sufficient in the case before the Court, laid out some very broad perimeters:

> With regard to an expression of belief, obviously the weight to be attached to it depends on a wide variety of matters; the person who expressed the belief, the circumstances in which it was expressed and, in particular, whether the expression of belief was challenged or not.

People (Director of Public Prosecutions) v Ferguson, Court of Criminal Appeal, 27 October 1975.

[43] *O'Leary v Attorney General* [1993] 1 IR 102. Objections to the reliance on Garda evidence included that it was treated as a unique (and unwarranted) category of expert opinion which is otherwise generally required to limit itself to factual data based on ascertainable and empirical facts; that experts are 'not allowed, to give evidence on the ultimate issue, in this case whether or not the accused is a member of an illegal organisation, and finally that the Chief Superintendent's opinion may be based on hearsay and other inadmissible evidence'.

[44] *People (DPP) v Redmond* [2015] 4 IR 84.

as a policy and empirical matter. Moreover, this snapshot also suggests that given the very small number of cases where inferences or opinion might prove useful, pragmatic justifications for its use were based on a limited factual assessment and should not have overtaken the significant constitutional and evidential objections made concerning these types of evidence.

Table 1 Evidence Descriptive Statistics

Statistics	Garda Testimony	Civilian Eyewitness	Forensic	Fingerprint	Fabric	DNA	Camera	Number of Different Sources
Number of Observations	44	46	46	43	37	46	48	32
Mean	0.5	0.5434783	0.9347826	0.1860465	0.0540541	0.021739	0.104167	2.53125
Median	0.5	1	1	0	0	0	0	2.5
Stn. Dev	0.5057805	0.5036102	0.2496374	0.3937496	0.2292434	0.147442	0.308709	1.190944
Min	0	0	0	0	0	0	0	0
Max	1	1	1	1	1	1	1	5
Coding	All Binary							Count

Table 2 below sets out the correlation of the reliance of Garda opinion evidence with other data sources in 32 relevant cases. Essentially, this analysis maps the extent to which there were other independent sources of evidence available to back-up and demonstrate some statistical significance to the use of Garda opinion evidence. While this analysis does not test the strength of other evidential sources, it does chart the capacity of Garda opinion evidence as the basis for conviction as being something more than chance.

Table 2 Garda Opinion Correlations with Other Evidence Sources

	Garda Opinion Relied Upon
Civilian Witness	0.1773
Forensics	0.1276
Fingerprint	0.1304
Fabric	–0.0162
DNA	
Camera	0.0593
Number of Evidence Sources	0.586
Observations with relevant data: 32	

Table 2 lists the correlations between whether the Garda officers' testimony was considered evidence and other evidence sources. Each independent source of evidence seems to have little relation to whether or not the Garda opinion was also relied upon, given the rather low correlations (in absolute terms, <0.3). Instead, there is a fairly strong correlation between Garda opinion and just the number of evidence sources; where there are more separate sources of evidence, Garda opinion is more likely to be relied upon as evidence. This seems to indicate that the Garda opinion is primarily relied upon when there are several other sources of evidence as well. This finding leads to a number of salient observations. First, the traditional evidentiary sources (eg forensics, witnesses, DNA), atypically for criminal crimes were viewed as insufficient on their own to base a conviction for terrorism offences. Second, that the reliance on Garda opinion evidence has become 'baked into' the system in a way that hardwired its consistent use, notwithstanding the strength of other evidence available to support a conviction for terrorism-related offences.

Table 3 Charges by Garda Opinion

	Charges		
Garda Opinion	**Membership**	**Principal**	**Total**
Not Relied Upon	1	21	22
	2%	48%	50%
Relied Upon	18	4	22
	41%	9%	50%
Total	19	25	44
	43%	57%	100%

Table 3 illustrates the breakdown of charge outcomes across Garda opinion categories. The difference is fairly stark. In only 1 out of 19 cases in which membership charges were brought was the Garda opinion not relied upon as evidence. In contrast, in only 4 out of the 25 cases in which principal charges were brought the Garda opinion was relied on. Thus, in 95 per cent of membership cases, the Garda opinion was relied on in comparison to 20 per cent of principal cases. The previous relation between Garda opinion and other evidence sources may stem from the relationship between membership cases and number of evidence sources.

Table 4 Outcome by Garda Opinion

	Outcome			
Garda Opinion	**Not Guilty**	**Mixed**	**Guilty**	**Total**
Not Relied Upon	1	14	7	22
	2%	32%	16%	50%
Relied Upon	5	2	15	22
	11%	5%	34%	50%
Total	6	16	22	44
	14%	36%	50%	100%

Table 4 describes the breakdown of verdict outcomes by Garda opinion. Overall, it appears that Garda opinion entered as evidence has a polarising effect on verdicts. Without relying on the Garda opinion, cases are much more likely to result in a mix of guilty and not guilty outcomes which tracks the expected outcomes we would see in 'regular' criminal cases. Cases in which Garda opinion was relied on appear to have significantly 'purer' outcomes (not guilty/guilty), with the predominant outcome being guilty, making the use of Garda opinion evidence consistently correlated with guilty pleas. The outcome of such polarisation, relied upon in practice would yield a preference to utilise Garda opinion, given the perceived 'risks' in negative outcomes (ie, non-convictions) if it were not used. This underscores again, the hardwiring of reliance on exceptional evidentiary rules to deliver conviction outcomes for the Court. It also points to a phenomenon consistent with 'case hardening' in non-jury trial were judges become comfortable with the use of opinion evidence over time and cease to view it as exceptional,[45] with consequent effects for the protection of due process and procedural rights in terrorism related trials in Ireland.

Table 5 Affiliation by Charges

Paramilitary Affiliation	Charges		
	Membership	Principal	Total
No Affiliation	0	2	2
	0%	4%	4%
Paramilitary Affiliation	19	26	45
	40%	55%	96%
Total	19	28	47
	40%	60%	100%

Table 5 underscores the importance of membership as a key category of management and processing in the Special Criminal Court. Membership, of course, has a distinct relationship with evidential rules, as the use of Garda opinion evidence overlaps with membership charging and successful convictions. The absence of other strong evidence of membership (as it is a category of *belonging* rather than a per se act of harm) may also explain the different rates of conviction in membership compared with principle categories. Membership carries sentences of three months to eight years,[46] and this sentencing range may also explain the relative ease with which judges acquiesced in the use of opinion evidence as the penalties were considered less severe (although it is notable that the tariff for terrorism membership has increased over time, a trend not unique to Ireland). By contrast, conviction of principal roles (eg directing and unlawful organisation, possession of firearms or training persons in the use of a firearm) carry sentences in the range of 6–15 years, the length and severity of sentencing providing a barrier to reliance on garda evidence primarily or alone.

Table 6 Sentence Length by Paramilitary Affiliation

Affiliation	Number of Observations	Mean Sentence	Median Sentence	Stn. Dev	Min	Max
No Affiliation	2	3.25	3.25	2.474874	1.5	5
Paramilitary Affiliation	38	4.638158	5	2.009015	0	10

[45] J Jackson and S Doran, *Judge Without Jury, Diplock Trials in the Adversary System* (Oxford, Clarendon Press, 1995).

[46] OASA, s 21(2), as amended by the Criminal Justice (Terrorist offences) Act 2005. The sentence depends on the particular case but for a first-time offender a custodial sentence of 4 or 5 years would not be unusual.

Table 6 illustrates the significant difference in sentencing consequences for those deemed to be engaged in a paramilitary organisation and those who were 'ordinary decent criminals' (ODCs). For persons with no affiliation to a paramilitary organisation the mean sentence is 3.2 years. For those with paramilitary affiliation that mean is 4.6 years demonstrating that sentence lengths will be significantly lengthier when membership is charged. While the number of cases in the data set that pertain to non-paramilitary offenders is low, nonetheless this provides an important window on the consequences of being charged with a membership offence under the OASA or membership of an unlawful organisation. It confirms the broader point that the exceptionality of such Special Courts is not merely academic but also points to the specific liberty and rights consequences for individuals prosecuted, adjudicated and convicted within the confines of the Irish Special Criminal Court.

III. CONCLUSION

There is a contradiction at the heart of a Special Court. To employ the designation 'court' is to mark the institution out as judicial, clearly distinguishable from an administrative tribunal; the court is to be a vehicle for justice rather than for the convenient disposal of the state's enemies. Yet to be 'special' implies a departure, a derogation. In the Irish context, as this chapter reveals in one specific aspect, namely the use of evidence, trials in the Special Criminal Court live comfortably with significant departures from the norms of accepted procedure in the regular criminal courts, and such departures are intrinsic to the functioning of the Court. It is worth underscoring that such departures were not marginal to the efficacy of the Court, demonstrated by the data on the widespread use of Garda opinion evidence, the results (convictions for membership) and the outcomes, namely steeper sentences for those convicted of membership through the use of such evidence.

The Special Court, explicitly or implicitly, exists in a state of exception (expressed in the 'special' of its title). At its most extreme, this points to special courts existing in a state of relative anomie; less far down the scale are special courts departing from standards conventionally considered as characteristic of the juridic (for instance trying vaguely drawn charges). Here it remains critical to note that the Irish Special Criminal Court is juridically based, and formally functions within the rule of law. Critically, that appearance and form of legality matter significantly to its legitimacy. But appearance and form, while virtuous at a political level, do not safeguard the legal. The very point of the exceptional is that the core rule of law protections and fundamental guarantees of human rights are compromised in the reach to exceptional regulation. The challenges of anomie and the juridic in the operation of special courts therefore reveals and expresses a fault-line found in the state of emergency or exception generally. While Ireland is not in a formal emergency situation (and has not had any claim to such a legal status, at a very minimum since the passage of the Good Friday Peace Agreement)[47] the maintenance of this Court essentially hardwires the legal exception into the contemporary criminal

[47] See A Greene, Chapter 13, this volume.

justice system. The Irish Special Criminal Court underscores both the juridic weakness and the consequences of anomie in enabling and facilitating a continuum of exceptionality, including but not limited to the absence of a jury in a common law criminal court and the deep regression on evidential rules to enable conviction of the accused.

The importance of exposing these fault lines as the conflict in Northern Ireland has receded is that the Special Criminal Court, unlike its Diplock counterpart, remains operative and utilised. It has, like many exceptional mechanisms first deployed to confront an emergency, continued to thrive past the formal end of the circumstances which birthed it.[48] Its exceptional rules have become normalised and accepted by a significant portion of the legal and judicial professions, that have got used to its value in processing certain kinds of individuals and groups. The ease and comfort of its acceptance should not detract from its continued and sustained exceptionality, both in terms of the absence of trial by jury and the abrogation of evidence rules. The problem with emergencies and exceptional law is that their tendency to persist mutes the general abhorrence of the loss to the rule of law and human rights protections that accompany them. This reflection underscores the continuum of exceptionality associated with the Court that has persisted in Ireland. I make the case that the empirical and legal basis for such exceptionality was not made historically and certainly would struggle to have traction in the contemporary.

[48] See C Hamilton, Chapter 14, this volume.

5

Terrorism Trials and the Offences Against the State Acts in Comparative Perspective

NICOLA McGARRITY

I. INTRODUCTION

IN PREVIOUS SCHOLARSHIP, this author has set out a schema for understanding how criminal trials have been modified in response to the threat of terrorism, especially in, but not limited to, the period since the 11 September 2001 terrorist attacks.[1] That schema consists of an examination of the fora in which terrorism trials are held, the identity of the decision-maker, the applicable procedures at trial and, finally, the rules of evidence. The Irish experience represents a useful way of framing a discussion of these modifications. This is because, throughout the twentieth and twenty-first centuries, the Irish Offences Against the State Acts have explored many of the options that have been adopted globally. Indeed, Kilcommins and Vaughan have argued that Ireland is 'a lodestar for other jurisdictions … in terms of a devaluation in due process values'.[2]

This chapter is divided into four substantive Parts which roughly correspond with each aspect of the schema. Part II examines the fora in which terrorism trials are held. Part III considers the identity of the decision-maker. Parts IV and V examine modifications to the applicable procedures and the rules of evidence respectively. Each Part begins by providing a comparative overview of global approaches to the relevant aspect of the schema. It then turns to examine the approach (or, more accurately, approaches) which Ireland has taken throughout the twentieth and twenty-first centuries. This progression from the general to the specific highlights the extent to which Ireland's experience has truly been unique. It is notable that whilst the Irish response insofar as the forum in which terrorism trials are held and the identity of the decision-maker are concerned has been exceptional, far more modest modifications have been made to the applicable trial procedures and rules of evidence.

[1] N McGarrity, 'Trial Procedure in Response to Terrorism' in D Brown, JI Turner and B Weisser (eds), *The Oxford Handbook of Criminal Process* (Oxford, Oxford University Press, 2019) 653–678.

[2] S Kilcommins and B Vaughan, 'A Perpetual State of Emergency: Subverting the Rule of Law in Ireland' (2004) 35 *Cambrian Law Review* 56.

II. FORA FOR TERRORISM TRIALS

A. Comparative Overview

In considering the types of fora in which terrorism trials are conducted, it is apt to think of them as existing on a spectrum. This spectrum reflects the extent to which the chosen forum is consistent with the approach taken for other criminal offences. At one end of the spectrum is the prosecution of terrorism offences before the ordinary civilian criminal courts. Whilst it would be difficult to find even *two* countries which agree upon the precise structure, composition and procedures applying to such courts, the essential point to be made is that they are generalist in character and deal with the full range of criminal offences. The utilisation of the ordinary civilian criminal courts reflects an acknowledgement on the part of the relevant state that terrorism is not so exceptional as to necessitate it being prosecuted in a special forum. Instead, the ordinary criminal courts are equally as equipped to deal with terrorism-related activities as they are any other criminal offence.

Given that conducting trials in the ordinary civilian criminal courts represents the status quo insofar as the prosecution of criminal offences is concerned, it is unsurprising that this is the approach which has been taken by many (if not most) countries. This is especially so in respect of Western democracies, such as the UK and Canada, that have a long history of respecting the rule of law and protecting fundamental human rights. One example of a country with a particularly strong commitment to the use of the ordinary civilian criminal courts for offences against the state is Germany. This commitment has been maintained despite the reluctance of the domestic courts to prioritise national security over the right to a fair trial.[3] Of course, a country's continued reliance upon the ordinary civilian criminal courts does not mean that no changes have been made to court processes in response to the specific challenges posed by terrorism. As will be highlighted later in this chapter, a considerable number of countries have made significant changes to the procedural arrangements and rules of evidence applicable at trial.

At the other end of the spectrum is the use of exceptional courts. This differs in that it is premised upon a perception of offences against the state as being so distinct from other criminal activities that the ordinary criminal courts are an inappropriate forum in which to conduct trials for terrorism offences. This is so regardless of any modifications which are made to the procedural arrangements and rules of evidence applicable at trial. It follows from this perception that an alternative forum is required. Duffy notes that the adoption of a specialist court or tribunal for trying people suspected of involvement in terrorism offences has become 'a feature of international practice in a surprising number of States'.[4]

In some cases, the alternative forum has taken the form of a military tribunal. The specific issues raised by the involvement of members of the armed forces in the trials of

[3] See, eg, the quashing of the conviction of Mounir El Motassedeq for terrorism offences. A detailed discussion of this case is contained in T Kost, 'Mounir El Motassadeq – A Missed Chance for *Weltinnenpolik*?' (2007) 8(4) *German Law Journal* 443.

[4] H Duffy, *The 'War on Terror' and the Framework of International Law* (Cambridge, Cambridge University Press, 2015) 214.

civilians will be addressed in Part III below. In some jurisdictions, new military tribunals have been established specifically to deal with terrorism offences and other offences against the state. Most famously, a Military Order issued by the President of the United States on 13 November 2001 bestowed power upon military commissions (as distinct from the tribunals under the Uniform Code of Military Justice which apply to people under military jurisdiction) to try non-citizen enemy combatants held in the Guantanamo Bay detention camps.[5] In other jurisdictions, especially in the Middle East, the military tribunals which have been utilised already existed. The Eminent Jurists Panel on Terrorism, Counter-Terrorism and Human Rights of the International Commission of Jurists has identified two ways in which this has occurred:

> In many countries, pre-existing regimes of martial law, or states of siege, provided for the trial of civilians by military courts. In other countries, emergency laws transferred jurisdiction to try certain terrorist or subversive offences from civilian to military courts.[6]

These tribunals represent an exceptional response not because they were created specifically to address the threat posed by terrorism, but rather in their extension beyond the enforcement of military discipline and the prosecution of members of the armed forces.

In contrast to the creation of new military tribunals or the extension of the jurisdiction of existing military tribunals, other countries have chosen to establish new courts within the civilian criminal justice system specifically for the purpose of dealing with terrorism offences and other offences against the state. Whilst it might be assumed that such courts are less contentious than military tribunals, the United Nations Human Rights Committee has cautioned that the use of such courts should similarly be 'limited to cases where the State party can show that … [they are] necessary and justified by objective and serious reasons, and … the regular civilian courts are unable to undertake the trials'.[7] This is because 'the trial of civilians in [such] courts may raise serious problems as far as the equitable, impartial and independent administration of justice is concerned'.[8] Like military tribunals, their effect is to create a parallel system of justice for one category of criminal offences.

It is undeniable that there may be legitimate reasons – and this is implicitly acknowledged by the United Nations Human Rights Committee – for establishing an exceptional civilian criminal court. These include that the complexity of terrorism trials requires a particular type of judicial expertise or that exceptional courts enable the fast-tracking of lengthy terrorism prosecutions without affecting the progression of ordinary criminal trials. Furthermore, in Somalia, specialist civilian criminal courts have been established in

[5] GW Bush, 'Detention, Treatment and Trial of Certain Non-Citizens in the War Against Terrorism', Executive Order Military Order of 13 November 2001.

[6] Eminent Jurists Panel on Terrorism, Counter-Terrorism and Human Rights, International Commission of Jurists, *Assessing Damage, Urging Action* (2009) 34 www.refworld.org/docid/499e76822.html (accessed 27 July 2020).

[7] United Nations Human Rights Committee, General Comment No 32, *Right to Equality Before Courts and Tribunals and to a Fair Trial*, 23 August 2007, 6–7. Similar statements have been made by regional bodies such as the Inter-American Commission on Human Rights: Inter-American Commission on Human Rights, *Resolution on Terrorism and Human Rights*, 12 December 2001.

[8] United Nations Human Rights Committee, General Comment No 32, *Right to Equality Before Courts and Tribunals and to a Fair Trial*, 23 August 2007, 6.

response to the vulnerability of the ordinary courts to attacks by Al Shabaab terrorists.[9] It is important, however, to closely scrutinise the reasons which are provided for establishing exceptional courts to ensure that they are not used as a veil for illegitimate motives. In the Pakistani context, for example, the creation of Anti-Terrorism Courts by the Anti-Terrorism Act 1997 was justified on the basis that it would result in 'speedy justice, unencumbered by the procedural niceties of the regular court system'.[10] However, the strict time constraints which applied (seven days for the prosecutorial investigation and seven days for the trial itself), as well as the potential for trials to be conducted in absentia, pointed to the real purpose of these courts as being to dispose of the cases of political opponents with limited fanfare.[11]

Sitting somewhere in the middle between maintaining the status quo and utilising exceptional (whether specialist civilian or military) courts is the centralisation of terrorism-related functions within the ordinary civilian criminal courts. What this involves is the identification of groups of judges within these courts with exclusive responsibility for presiding over terrorism trials. This is the approach which Spain adopted in the late 1970s, with France following suit in the early 1980s. In the former, serious crimes which carry a maximum penalty of at least five years' imprisonment, such as terrorism, are prosecuted before the Sala de lo Penal of the Audiencia Nacional.[12] In France, a special section of counter-terrorism investigating magistrates in Paris presides over serious terrorism trials.[13] In both of these jurisdictions, centralisation is best understood as part of a gradual (and undeniably positive) movement away from the historical use of military tribunals to address terrorism. In addition to its utility as a political compromise in countries where there is ongoing scepticism about the ability of the ordinary civilian criminal courts to address terrorism, centralisation has a number of practical benefits which roughly mirror those of exceptional courts discussed above. These include: 'unification of criteria and a certain distance from the scene of the conflict'; 'better understanding of the problems that the prosecution of terrorist acts pose, [thus] improving efficiency'; and 'security can be enhanced by focusing protection in a single seat and in a small number of judges and prosecutors'.[14]

Whilst these are undoubtedly worthy goals, centralisation is not unproblematic. As with exceptional courts, centralisation is premised upon an assumption that a parallel system of criminal justice is necessary in order to adequately address terrorism. Alain Marsoud, a former French parliamentarian, stated that 'there must be a balance between individual liberty on the one hand and the efficiency of the system to protect the public

[9] Human Rights Watch, 'Human Rights Priorities for Somalia's New Government', 2 May 2017 www.hrw.org/news/2017/05/02/human-rights-priorities-somalias-new-government (accessed 27 July 2020).

[10] C Kennedy, 'The Creation and Development of Pakistan's Anti-Terrorism Regime, 1997–2002' in S Limaye, R Wirsing, M Malik (eds), *Religious Radicalisation and Security in South Asia* (Asia Pacific Centre for Security Studies, 2004) 389.

[11] This legislation was examined by the Supreme Court in *Mehram Ali v Federation of Pakistan*, PLD 1998 SC 1445.

[12] For further detail, see R Alonso and F Reinares, 'Terrorism, Human Rights and Law Enforcement in Spain' (2005) 17(1) *Terrorism and Political Violence* 267.

[13] F Foley, *Countering Terrorism in Britain and France: Institutions, Norms and the Shadow of the* Past (Cambridge, Cambridge University Press, 2013) 193–194.

[14] MA Rueda and MA Boldova, 'Spain' in K Roach (ed), *Comparative Counter-Terrorism Law* (Cambridge, Cambridge University Press, 2015) 314.

on the other. In an ideal world, I would choose the first, but this is not an ideal world, and when dealing with Islamic extremists we have to be brutal sometimes'.[15] With that in mind, centralised systems have often modified the applicable procedures and rules of evidence to facilitate convictions. However, even where no such modifications have been made, the Eminent Jurists Panel on Terrorism, Counter-Terrorism and Human Rights of the International Commission of Jurists has highlighted the challenges posed by centralisation for the independence and impartiality of the courts. It notes that 'given the constant interaction between investigators and prosecutors specialising in terrorism cases, appearing before the same judges, all involved may gradually come to see themselves as part of the State's counter-terrorism machinery'.[16]

Most insidiously, centralisation offers a means of achieving the same goals as the creation of exceptional courts but with far less political and public controversy. In Egypt, for example, there is a long history of exceptional courts being utilised to stifle political dissent. Under Article 97 of the Constitution of the Arab Republic of Egypt, which was adopted in 2014, 'no person may be tried except before the ordinary judge and exceptional courts are prohibited'. However, this protection has largely proved to be meaningless with the establishment of special circuits within the Egyptian criminal courts and courts of first instance which are presided over by so-called 'ordinary' judges.[17] Given examples like this, centralisation should be treated with caution and adopted only where clear evidence has been presented of its necessity. Even then, rather than formally legislating for a centralised approach, it would be preferable to leave it to the leadership of the relevant courts to determine whether it is necessary and appropriate for individual judges to develop their expertise in the terrorism context by presiding over multiple terrorism trials. This ensures that the discretion remains with an independent and impartial judiciary, rather than the politically-motivated legislature.

B. The Irish Experience

The use of exceptional courts to prosecute offences against the state has a long history in Ireland.[18] However, it was not until the early 1930s that such courts were given constitutional status. In 1931, the Irish Free State Constitution (which was adopted in October 1922) was amended to include a new Article 2A. This provided for the trial of people before the Constitution (Special Powers) Tribunal.[19] Importantly, this tribunal, which

[15] Quoted in M Perry and HE Negrin (eds), *The Theory and Practice of Islamic Terrorism: An Anthology* (New York, Palgrave MacMillan, 2008) 15–16.

[16] Eminent Jurists Panel on Terrorism, Counter-Terrorism and Human Rights, *Assessing Damage, Urging Action* (2009) 142 www.refworld.org/docid/499e76822.html (accessed 27 July 2020). For a more positive perspective upon this interaction between the judiciary and law enforcement, see A Garapon, 'The Oak and the Reed: Counter-Terrorism Mechanisms in France and the United States of America' (2006) 27(5) *Cardozo Law Review* 2041, 2055 ('[t]he specific profile of the counter-terrorist magistrates derives its effectiveness from both being a judge and being in permanent contact with the police, thus accumulating great personal knowledge and experience in such matters. The judge may also receive information through informal discussions with the police').

[17] *Counter-Terrorism Law (Decree Law No. 94 for the Year 2015)*, Art 50.

[18] This is discussed by N Howlin, Chapter 1, this volume.

[19] An overview of the emergency provisions in the Irish Free State is discussed by T Mohr, Chapter 2, this volume.

was in essence a military tribunal, was not permanent. It only came into effect upon the making of an order by the Executive Council. Despite withstanding several judicial challenges,[20] Article 2A was not incorporated into the new Constitution of Ireland which came into force in December 1937. Article 38 did, however, provide for the creation of '[s]pecial courts … for the trial of offences in cases where it may be determined in accordance with such law that the ordinary courts are inadequate to secure the effective administration of justice, and the preservation of public peace and order'. In contrast to the detailed content in Article 2A of the Irish Free State Constitution, this Article merely provided that '[t]he constitution, powers, jurisdiction and procedure of such special courts shall be prescribed by law'.

Only a very short period of time elapsed before Article 38 was relied upon. In June 1939, just prior to the outbreak of World War II, the Offences Against the State Act 1939 (OASA) was passed. Part V of this Act sets out the composition and functions of the Special Criminal Court, as well as stating that it – like its predecessor, the Constitution (Special Powers) Tribunal – only comes into force upon the making of an order by the government. Such an order was made on 22 August 1939, and the Special Criminal Court was established two days later.

It was also within the power of the government to determine, by way of statutory instrument, which offences fell within the jurisdiction of that Court. It could make an order in relation to offences of any particular class or kind or under any particular enactment if satisfied that the ordinary courts were inadequate to secure the effective administration of justice and the preservation of public peace and order.[21] Even where an offence was not scheduled, but the Attorney-General (and now the Director of Public Prosecutions)[22] was satisfied of the aforementioned criterion, they could order that a person brought before an ordinary court be transferred to the Special Criminal Court for trial.[23] The uncertainty as to which offences would ultimately be tried before the Court has been an ongoing cause of concern for the United Nations Human Rights Committee.[24] It commented in July 2000 that '[t]he law establishing the Special Criminal Court does not specify clearly the cases which are to be assigned to that Court but leaves it to the broadly defined discretion of the Director of Public Prosecutions'.[25]

Recognising that there may be circumstances (either domestic or international) in which extraordinary measures were required, Article 28 of the Irish Constitution left it open for the Oireachtas to enact any laws which were 'for the purpose of securing the public safety and the preservation of the State in time of war or armed rebellion'. Nothing in the Constitution could be taken to invalidate such laws.[26] It was with this provision in mind that a national emergency was declared on 3 September 1939, and

[20] See, eg, *State (Ryan) v Lennon* [1935] IR 170.

[21] OASA, s 36.

[22] The powers of the Attorney-General in relation to criminal matters were vested generally in the Director in s 3(1) of the *Prosecution of Offences Act 1974*.

[23] OASA, s 46.

[24] This is discussed by Y Daly, Chapter 11, this volume.

[25] United Nations Human Rights Committee, *Report of the Human Rights Committee*, Vol 1 (2000) [436]. The mechanisms by which a case may be brought before the Special Criminal Court are discussed by L Campbell, Chapter 8, this volume.

[26] This is discussed by A Greene, Chapter 13, this volume.

the Emergency Powers Act 1939 and Emergency Powers (Amendment) (No 2) Act 1940 were enacted. Whilst the former Act continued to prohibit the trial by court martial of people not subject to military law, this provision was repealed a year later. In its place, the amending Act allowed the Executive Council to order that specific offences be tried before a military court from which no appeal was allowed.[27] Such an order was made later that year, and a military court remained in place between 1940 and 1943. Whilst no order re-establishing the court has been made by the government, it was not until 1 September 1976 that the state of emergency was finally rescinded by the Oireachtas.

The Special Criminal Court lasted only six years and was dismantled shortly after the end of World War II in 1946. As will be discussed in more detail in Part III below, the Court was – like the military court – also staffed by military officers during this period. However, in contrast to the military court, it was reintroduced on two subsequent occasions. First, in November 1961, in response to the resumption of paramilitary activities by the Irish Republican Army several years earlier. The jurisdiction of the Court was expressed by the then Taoiseach as being limited to offences 'arising from this armed conspiracy of violence'.[28] On this occasion, the Court remained in place for less than a year. On 2 October 1962, the government ordered that it be disestablished. More recently, in May 1972, the government again ordered the re-establishment of the Court and, 47 years on, it continues to operate. As at October 2015, the workload of the Court was so great, with a delay of almost two years for the trial of cases, that the decision was made to establish a Special Criminal Court No 2.[29] It is unclear what the future of the No 2 Court is. With case numbers steadily dropping since shortly after its establishment, it was announced in August 2019 that it would be wound down.[30] However, this has not yet eventuated.

Whilst there are legitimate questions about the necessity for the Court in the post-ceasefire period,[31] the Supreme Court nevertheless rejected a challenge to its constitutionality in *Kavanagh v Government of Ireland*.[32] It ruled that it was for the government of the day to determine whether the ordinary courts were inadequate to secure the effective administration of justice, and this determination would be subject to judicial review only in exceptional circumstances. A different decision was reached by the United Nations Human Rights Committee. In April 2001, the Committee found that the applicant's right to equality had been violated because Ireland had failed to demonstrate

[27] The constitutionality of this law is discussed in RJ O'Hanlon, 'Special Courts and Military Tribunals under the Constitution of Ireland: Powers of the President in Relation to Emergency Legislation' (1965) 31(1) *Irish Jurist* 1–6, 3–4.

[28] Quoted in Committee to Review the Offences Against the State Acts, 1939–1998 and Related Matters, *Report of the Committee to Review the Offences Against the State Acts, 1939–1998 and Related Matters* (2002) hereinafter Hederman Report, 4.30.

[29] 'Second Special Criminal Court established to deal with backlog of cases', *Irish Examiner*, 28 October 2015, www.irishexaminer.com/breakingnews/ireland/second-special-criminal-court-established-to-deal-with-backlog-of-cases-702868.html (accessed 27 July 2020).

[30] C Gallagher, 'Second Special Criminal Court to Suspend Operation Amid Falling Case Numbers', *The Irish Times*, 24 August 2019, www.irishtimes.com/news/crime-and-law/second-special-criminal-court-to-suspend-operation-amid-falling-case-numbers-1.3995590 (accessed 27 July 2020).

[31] See 'FactCheck: Who wants to get rid of the Special Criminal Court', *The Journal*, 10 February 2016, www.thejournal.ie/ge16-election-2016-ireland-fact-check-special-criminal-court-2594422-Feb2016/ (accessed 27 July 2020).

[32] [1996] 1 IR 321. This case is discussed by Y Daly, Chapter 11, this volume.

that the decision to try him before the Special Criminal Court 'was based on reasonable and objective grounds'.[33] A year earlier, that same Committee had concluded in its Country Report for Ireland that '[s]teps should be taken to end the jurisdiction of the Special Criminal Court'.[34]

III. IDENTITY OF THE DECISION-MAKER

A. Comparative Overview

The status quo identified in Part II of this Chapter was that criminal trials take place in the ordinary civilian criminal courts. This provided the yardstick against which to determine which countries have adopted an exceptional approach insofar as the fora for terrorism trials is concerned. An analysis of the second aspect of the schema is more complex in that there is no immediately apparent point of reference. This is because of the distinct approaches associated with the common law and civil law legal systems with respect to the identity of the decision-maker. On the one hand, there is a long tradition in common law countries of using juries to decide matters of fact in serious criminal cases. In contrast, civil law systems have historically relied upon a professional judge or panel of professional judges to determine the guilt or innocence of the defendant.

Nevertheless, insofar as it is possible to generalise, the trend in response to the threat of terrorism has been to move away from the use of juries. Pressure to do so has come from both sides of the courtroom. Concerns have been expressed by defendants and their counsel about the potential for juror stereotypes about the nature of terrorism and its relationship to particular religious and political groups to undermine the fairness of the trial process.[35] However, the most persuasive arguments against trial by jury have typically come from prosecutors and other representatives of the state. In Russia, for instance, which only introduced trial by jury in 1993 as one of the cornerstones of the post-Soviet Union era, a pattern of unjustified acquittals associated with close familial ties in the southern regions of Russia was used to justify its repeal just 15 years later.[36] The inability to secure convictions – and the assertion that this was due to strongly held political views within the civilian population – was also at the heart of the decision to suspend jury trial for terrorism offences in Northern Ireland in the 1970s.[37]

[33] *Kavanagh v Ireland*, Communication No 819/1998, 4 April 2001, 10.3.

[34] United Nations Human Rights Committee, *Report of the Human Rights Committee*, Vol 1 (2000), 437. This call was repeated in the Committee's 2008 Report, and by the United Nations Human Rights Council's Special Rapporteur on the Situation of Human Rights Defenders in 2013. See *Mission to Ireland (19–23 November 2012)*, 36.

[35] M Pelly, 'Why Turnball and accused terrorist Alqudsi wanted no jury at trial', *The Australian*, 24 June 2016, available at www.theaustralian.com.au/business/legal-affairs/why-turnbull-and-accused-terrorist-alqudsi-wanted-no-jury-at-trial/news-story/f6cca648340b030961da3664d8814516.

[36] A Gurinskaya, 'Trial by Jury in Russia: From the Cornerstone of the Judicial Reform to the Constitutional History Artifact' (2015) 17(1) *Journal of Criminal Justice and Security* 70.

[37] Lord Diplock, *Report of the Commission to Consider Legal Procedures to Deal with Terrorist Activities in Northern Ireland* (1972) Cmnd 5185. See also L Donohue, 'Terrorism and Trial by Jury: The Vices and Virtues of British and American Criminal Law' (2007) 59 *Stanford Law Review* 1326. A further reason for the decision to suspend jury trial was the perceived risk of jury intimidation from persons associated with paramilitary organisations.

In addition to moving away from reliance upon trial by jury, the other modification which has often been made in response to the terrorist threat is to include members of the military in the decision-making process. It is unsurprising that judges of military tribunals are generally required to have experience in, or, at the very least, detailed knowledge of, the armed forces. However, the use of military judges is not limited to such courts. Many of the exceptional civilian courts which have been established to address the threat posed by terrorism also frequently include one or more military judges. This is, for example, the case in Jordan. The Jordanian State Security Court sits as a panel of three judges; two military judges appointed by the Prime Minister based on the recommendation of the Head of the Joint Chiefs of Staff of the armed forces and a civilian judge designated by the Juridical Council.[38]

The utilisation of military judges to try civilians has been strongly criticised by the European Court of Human Rights as undermining the independence and impartiality of the criminal justice system. It commented that '[w]hat is at stake is the confidence which the courts in a democratic society must inspire in the public and above all, as far as criminal proceedings are concerned, in the accused.'[39] The fundamental issue is that judges who are currently members of the armed forces may prioritise national security over the defendant's right to a fair trial. Furthermore, as noted by the European Court of Human Rights in *Incal v Turkey*, the participation of a military judge raises legitimate fears that a court might allow itself to be unduly influenced by considerations which have nothing to do with the facts of the case.[40] It is notable that the Court reached this conclusion notwithstanding the fact that the military judge was sitting on a civilian National Security Court alongside two civilian judges.

In a 1994 report, the Centre for the Independence of Judges and Lawyers bluntly stated that military judges 'are not independent'.[41] This was reinforced by the European Court of Human Rights in *Incal*, where the Court found that the military judge lacked independence from the executive branch of government for three reasons. First, they 'still belong to the army, which in turn takes its orders from the executive'.[42] Second, 'they remain subject to military discipline'.[43] Third, '[d]ecisions pertaining to their appointment are to a great extent taken by the administrative authorities and the army'.[44] Insofar as the last of these is concerned, for confidence in the independence and impartiality of the criminal justice system to be maintained, it is imperative that judges have security of tenure. Hamilton, one of the Founding Fathers of the Constitution of the United States, wrote that anything less than life tenure would 'be fatal to [the courts'] necessary independence' as a body of judges which held office at the pleasure of the executive and/or

[38] Jordanian National Center for Human Rights, Response to Questionnaire Prepared by the Special Rapporteur on the Independence of Judges and Lawyers (2018) www.ohchr.org/Documents/Issues/IJudiciary/JudicialCouncils/Jordon_NHI.docx (accessed 27 July 2020).

[39] *Incal v Turkey* (1998) 28 EHRR 449, 71.

[40] Ibid, 72.

[41] Centre for the Independence of Judges and Lawyers, *Attacks on Justice: The Harassment and Persecution of Judges and Lawyers* (1994) 254.

[42] *Incal v Turkey* (1998) 28 EHRR 449, 68.

[43] Ibid.

[44] Ibid.

legislature would be 'unwilling to hazard the displeasure' of these branches of government by making an unpopular decision.[45]

B. The Irish Experience

Under Article 2A of the Irish Free State Constitution, the membership of the Constitution (Special Powers) Tribunal consisted of five officers of the Defence Forces not below the rank of Commandant.[46] They were appointed by, and removable at the will of, the Governor-General acting on the advice of the Executive Council. The Irish Constitution, on its face, seemed to envisage a very different role for the Special Criminal Court. This was especially so given that Article 38 also provided for the establishment of a separate body of military tribunals for the trial of offences against military law alleged to have been committed by persons while subject to military law, or to deal with a state of war or armed rebellion. However, there were nevertheless some similarities. First, the Irish Constitution, whilst generally protecting the right to trial by jury for criminal offences, carved out an exception for trials before the Special Criminal Court.[47] The European Commission of Human Rights concluded in *X and Y v Ireland* that this was not, in and of itself, a contravention of Article 6 of the European Convention on Human Rights and Fundamental Freedoms.[48] Nevertheless, the fundamental importance of trial by jury is recognised in Ireland's constitutional framework.[49]

Second, under s 39 of the OASA, the Special Criminal Court was to be made up of an uneven number of at least three people who are: judges of the High Court, Circuit Court or District Court; barristers or solicitors of at least seven years standing; or an officer of the Defence Forces not below the rank of Commandant. It is notable that military officers served on the Courts from 1939 to 1946, and 1961 to 1962.[50] This, in combination with detention in military custody and the conduct of the trial in a military barracks, led to one defendant, MacCurtain, seeking (albeit unsuccessfully) an order for habeas corpus on the basis that the Court was in reality a military tribunal and not a genuine Special Criminal Court.[51]

Finally, even though only civilian judges have been appointed to the Court since its reestablishment in 1972, concerns continue to be expressed about the closeness of its relationship with the executive branch of government. In *Eccles v Ireland*, a constitutional challenge was brought to the OASA on this basis.[52] The applicant focused upon

[45] *The Federalist* No 78, 377.

[46] *Constitution (Amendment No 17) Act 1931*, s 4(2).

[47] *1937 Constitution*, Art 38(5).

[48] Application No 8299/78, Admissibility, 10 October 1980, DR 22, 551–75.

[49] See K Quinn, 'Jury Trial in Republic of Ireland' (2001) 72(1/2) *Revue Internationale de Droit Penal* 197–214. The historical and contemporary ambivalence of Ireland to trial by jury is discussed by M Coen, Chapter 3, this volume.

[50] B Kissane, 'Defending Democracy? The Legislative Response to Political Extremism in the Irish Free State, 1922–39' (2004) 34(134) *Irish Historical Studies* 171.

[51] RJ O'Hanlon, 'Special Courts and Military Tribunals under the Constitution of Ireland: Powers of the President in Relation to Emergency Legislation' (1965) 31(1) *Irish Jurist* 2.

[52] *Eccles v Ireland* [1985] IR 545.

sections 39(2) (judges may be appointed and removable at will by the Government) and 39(4) (remuneration is determined by the Minister for Finance and may differ between members of the Court). This was rejected by the Supreme Court (albeit using somewhat circular logic) on the basis that the Special Criminal Court was able to prevent and correct any interference with its judicial independence as this would constitute an attempt to 'frustrate the constitutional right of persons accused before the Court to a trial in due course of law'.[53] In responding to a subsequent complaint by Eccles, the European Commission of Human Rights referred to the conclusion it had reached in *X and Y v Ireland* that the Special Criminal Court was an independent and impartial decision-making body. It then went on to look at the 'realities' of the concrete case before it, and found that the executive powers of appointment, removal and remuneration had not been used in such a way as to undermine the Court's independence and impartiality.[54] In addition to the abandonment of military judges, a further positive move which was made by the government in 1985, and which deals with some of the essence of the issues raised by Eccles, is to no longer rely upon retired judges.[55] Such reliance was problematic in that these judges did not have security of tenure.

IV. PROCEDURES

A. Comparative Overview

Amongst those countries which have made modifications to the ordinary civilian criminal process in response to the threat of terrorism (and it must be recognised that there are a number of countries which have not), two distinct categories can be identified. On the one hand, there are those jurisdictions which have emphasised the establishment of new decision-making entities, either for terrorism trials generally (such as Ireland itself) or for the trials of non-citizens (such as the US). The other category consists of those jurisdictions which have chosen to focus upon modifications to the applicable procedures and rules of evidence. Of course, these categories are by no means exclusive. The US, for example, has not only established extra-territorial military tribunals for prosecuting non-citizens accused of terrorism offences, but has also made modifications to the manner in which domestic terrorism trials are conducted before the ordinary civilian criminal courts. Nevertheless, it is generally possible to categorise countries according to the approach to which they have given the most weight. What is critical is that we are not blinded to the more technical, but no less important, modifications to the applicable procedures and rules of evidence by the more blatant changes made by countries falling into the first category. Whilst the United Nations Human Rights Committee emphasises that the ordinary criminal courts should only be abandoned in exceptional circumstances, it also states

[53] Ibid, 549.

[54] Application No 12839/87, 9 December 1988.

[55] F Gartland, 'State Papers: Concerns over retired judges serving on court', *The Irish Times*, 31 December 2015 www.irishtimes.com/news/politics/state-papers-concerns-over-retired-judges-serving-on-court-1.2480564?mode=sample&auth-failed=1&pw-origin=https%3A%2F%2Fwww.irishtimes.com%2Fnews%2Fpolitics%2Fstate-papers-concerns-over-retired-judges-serving-on-court-1.2480564 (accessed 27 July 2020).

that regardless of the character of the court, it must 'genuinely afford the full guarantees stipulated in Article 14' and the other articles of the International Covenant on Civil and Political Rights.[56] This is where the analysis in Parts IV and V of this Chapter comes in.

The modifications which have been made to trial procedures globally in response to the threat of terrorism may be divided into three broad categories. The first of these is the restriction of open justice. Whilst it is a central tenet of criminal justice in liberal democracies for the public to be able to scrutinise the trial process, it is not uncommon for this to be restricted (either by the legislature or as part of the inherent jurisdiction of the courts to control proceedings) in terrorism trials. The principle of open justice is not absolute and there may be circumstances in which it is appropriate to exclude the public, for example, where national security is threatened by the disclosure of particular information. However, the criteria upon which the decision to close the court is based should be narrowly framed so that it captures only those situations where confidentiality is strictly necessary.

There is a case to be made for some level of confidentiality to apply to military tribunals. This is because their core function, namely, to address breaches of military law by military personnel, is necessarily intertwined with operational matters. However, it is inappropriate to maintain such secrecy where the jurisdiction of the military courts is extended to civilians who are not subject to military discipline. The lack of public scrutiny of proceedings before these courts is exacerbated by the limited accountability mechanisms which typically apply to military agencies. These problems are particularly apparent in countries with a poor record insofar as the protection of fundamental human rights is concerned. For example, in a recent report into human rights practices in the Sudan, the US Department of State noted the '[m]ilitary trials, which sometimes were secret and brief, lacked procedural safeguards'.[57]

The US itself has not been immune from criticism in this regard. In relation to the system of military commissions established to try detainees held at Guantanamo Bay, a report produced by the Brennan Center for Justice at the New York University School of Law, noted that there is nothing in the rules which 'imposes[s] strict limits on the scope of the closure' or 'insures that secrecy concerns will not needlessly impair the public's right to know'.[58] Importantly, whilst the issue of secrecy is particularly significant in respect of military tribunals, it is not limited to these tribunals or, indeed, to exceptional courts generally. In *Guardian News and Media Ltd v AB and CD*, which involved the trial of Erol Incedal and Mounir Rarmoul-Bouhadjar for terrorism offences, the UK Court of Appeal controversially concurred with the decision of the trial judge that the majority of the proceedings (with the exception of the reading of the charges to the jury, the identities of the defendants, and the handing down of the verdicts) should

[56] United Nations Human Rights Committee, General Comment No 13, *Equality Before the Courts and the Right to a Fair and Public Hearing by an Independent Court Established by Law*, 13 April 1984.

[57] United States Department of State, *2019 Country Reports on Human Rights Practices: Sudan* (2019), 13 www.state.gov/reports/2019-country-reports-on-human-rights-practices/sudan/ (accessed 27 July 2020).

[58] S Turner and S Schulhofer, *The Secrecy Problem in Terrorism Trials* (Brennan Centre for Justice, 2005) www.brennancenter.org/sites/default/files/2019-08/Report_The_Secrecy_Problem_Terrorism_Trials.pdf (accessed 27 July 2020) 62.

occur in closed court.[59] This case was described by the Court as 'exceptional' because 'there is a significant risk … that the administration would be frustrated were the trial to be conducted in open Court … [because] the Crown might be deterred from continuing with the prosecution'.[60]

The second category of modifications concerns the right to silence. International courts have consistently recognised that this is an international standard which lies at the heart of the notion of a fair trial. The historically protected status of the right to silence stems from its connection to the privilege against self-incrimination.[61] This, in turn, is closely linked to the presumption of innocence in that it 'presupposes that the prosecution in a criminal case seeks to prove their case against the accused without resort to evidence obtained through methods of coercion or oppression in defiance of the will of the accused'.[62] It is upon the prosecution alone that the task of establishing the guilt of the defendant lies. In the final substantive Part of this chapter, mention will be made of the use of torture to coerce admissions for defendants and other witnesses. This is one of the most obvious and egregious ways in which the right to silence may be undermined by the state and its agents. It is not, however, the only mechanism for doing so.

It is relatively common in the civil context for coercive questioning powers to be bestowed by legislation upon administrative bodies charged with, for example, investigating government corruption.[63] However, the right to silence has been vigorously protected by the courts in the criminal context because it safeguards against abuses of power by those in authority and ensures the preservation of the basic concepts of justice and fairness.[64] Australia is something of an outlier in this regard in that the Australian Security Intelligence Organisation may request a judicial warrant authorising the questioning of a person for up to 24 hours where there are 'reasonable grounds for believing that [it] will substantially assist the collection of intelligence that is important in relation to a terrorism offence'.[65] It is a criminal offence to fail to comply with the terms of the warrant. However, even in Australia, the potential for coerced information to be used in criminal proceedings is limited by the existence of a use immunity.

The third category of modifications to the procedures operating in terrorism trials relates to the defendant's access to legal counsel. The United Nations Human Rights Committee has noted that '[t]he availability or absence of legal assistance often determines whether or not a person can access the relevant proceedings or participate them in

[59] [2015] 1 Cr App R 46, 16 and 20–21. The Court did note that the mere reference by the state to 'considerations of national security' was not a sufficient justification in and of itself for closing the court, and that this 'must be justified on the facts' and be no 'greater than necessary': 2 and 5.

[60] Ibid, 14.

[61] Article 14(3)(g) of the *International Covenant on Civil and Political Rights* relevantly states that everyone is entitled 'not to be compelled to testify against himself or to confess guilt'.

[62] *Saunders v United Kingdom* (1997) 23 EHRR 313, 68.

[63] In Australia, for example, these bodies include the Australian Crime Commission, the Australian Securities and Investments Commission, the Independent Commission Against Corruption, the New South Wales Crime Commission and Royal Commissions.

[64] See A Gray, 'The Right to Silence: Using American and European Law to Protect a Fundamental Right' (2013) 16(4) *New Criminal Law Review* 527–567.

[65] *Australian Security Intelligence Organisation Act 1979* (Commonwealth) Part III, Division 3.

a meaningful way.'[66] Thus, it is critical that a defendant is not barred by legal or practical constraints from obtaining legal assistance. In the anti-terrorism context, however, the reality is that very significant inroads into the right to legal representation have been made. At the most extreme end of the spectrum is the denial of access to legal counsel altogether. The International Commission of Jurists notes that '[t]his denial of proper legal representation is illustrated by the fact that the so-called fourteen "high value detainees" never had access to counsel until well after their transfer [from secret overseas prisons run by the CIA] to Guantánamo Bay' in September 2006.[67] These detainees included Khalid Sheikh Mohammed, the self-confessed mastermind of the September 11 terrorist attacks, who had been captured in Pakistan more than three years previously, in March 2003.

Such limitations upon access to legal representation are not limited to extraterritorial detention arrangements. Legislation recently adopted by Tunisia allows the prosecutor to order that a defendant be detained for up to 15 days without legal representation or access to a judicial officer.[68] Furthermore, in France, there is a considerable delay before a person arrested on terrorism charges is permitted to access legal advice. They are not permitted to speak to a lawyer for three (or, if an extension is granted, four) days and, even then, only for 30 minutes.[69] The explanation for this approach is that 'access to legal counsel is only delayed for the purposes of the inquiry having regard to the seriousness of the offences in question'.[70] To put it another way, it is 'essential to establishing the truth' and 'proportional to the seriousness of the circumstances and the complexity of the offences committed'.[71] However, the International Commission of Jurists rejects this explanation as 'not persuasive'.[72] This is because 'the seriousness [of] the offence of which an individual is accused does not in itself provide rational justification for restriction on access to a lawyer'.[73]

B. The Irish Experience

The Irish experience in establishing special courts and utilising military judges is unusual amongst Western democracies. Its approach has been far more modest insofar as modifications to the applicable procedures and rules of evidence are concerned. In this sense,

[66] United Nations Human Rights Committee, General Comment No 32, Right to Equality before Courts and Tribunals and to a Fair Trial, 23 August 2007.

[67] Eminent Jurists Panel on Terrorism, Counter-Terrorism and Human Rights, International Commission of Jurists, *Assessing Damage, Urging Action* (2009) 61 www.refworld.org/docid/499e76822.html (accessed 27 July 2020).

[68] Human Rights Watch, *Tunisia: Counterterror Law Endangers Rights: Legislate Safeguards Against Abuse*, 31 July 2015, available at www.hrw.org/news/2015/07/31/tunisia-counterterror-law-endangers-rights.

[69] Human Rights Watch, *In the Name of Security: Counterterrorism Laws Worldwide since September 11* (2012) 73.

[70] Committee Against Torture, *Fourth to Sixth Periodic Reports of States Parties Due in 2008: France*, 30 June 2008 www.refworld.org/category,CAT,FRA,4b1645252,0.html (accessed 27 July 2020) [68].

[71] Ibid, 67.

[72] International Commission of Jurists, Submission to the Committee Against Torture on the 6th Periodic Report of France, April 2010 https://tbinternet.ohchr.org/Treaties/CAT/Shared%20Documents/FRA/INT_CAT_NGO_FRA_44_8774_E.pdf (accessed 27 July 2020) 3–4.

[73] Ibid.

Ireland clearly falls into the first category identified above, that is, countries which have emphasised the establishment of new decision-making entities. It is beyond the scope of this chapter to engage in a thorough investigation of the political, social and cultural reasons behind Ireland's choice of approach. Suffice to say that there is a considerable body of literature which points to widely-held concerns about the potential for terrorists to interfere in ordinary civilian criminal trials by, for example, intimidating the participants. It is at least arguable that the establishment of new decision-making entities represented a rational attempt to resolve these problems.

The Special Criminal Court, whilst having limited (and, as discussed in Part II, selective) jurisdiction, had considerably more in common with the ordinary civilian criminal courts than did the Constitution (Special Powers) Tribunal which preceded it or the military tribunal under the Emergency Powers (Amendment) (No 2) Act 1940 in operation in the early 1940s. Section 41 of the OASA provides that 'the practice and procedure applicable … in the Central Criminal Court shall, so far as practicable, apply to the trial of a person by the Special Criminal Court'. The words 'so far as practicable' indicate that this rule is not absolute and, in fact, section 41 goes on to explicitly states that the Court 'shall have control of its own procedure in all respects' and make rules 'regulating its practice and procedure'.

To date, the various iterations of the Special Criminal Court Rules have made no attempt to modify the ability of a defendant to access legal representation (with the exception of providing for legal aid in certain circumstances). More direct attention has, however, been given to the principle of open justice. The most recent iteration of the Special Criminal Court Rules, adopted in 2016, states that '[t]he Court shall be an open Court to the sittings of which the public generally shall have access'.[74] This does not mean that there may never be restrictions upon access. As is the case in proceedings before the ordinary civilian courts, any person – other than a bona fide representative of the media – may be excluded where 'it is desirable in the interests of justice, or for the protection of the accused or any other person … because of the special nature of, or of the circumstances of, any trial or proceeding before [the Court]'.[75]

It is really only in relation to the right to silence that any significant modifications have been made to the applicable procedures for terrorism trials in Ireland. Section 52 of the OASA requires a person detained under section 30 to give 'a full account of [their] movements and actions during such specified period'.[76] It is a criminal offence carrying a maximum penalty of six months' imprisonment to refuse to give such an account or to provide false or misleading information. Contradictory decisions have been reached by the Supreme Court and the European Court of Human Rights in relation to the compatibility of section 52 with the Irish Constitution and international human rights law respectively.[77] In both instances, the issue was substantially the same, namely, whether the burden imposed upon the right to silence and freedom from self-incrimination was

[74] Special Criminal Court No 1 Rules 2016, s 7.

[75] Ibid.

[76] A person may also be required to provide 'all information in [their] possession in relation to the commission or intended commission *by another person* of any offence under [the 1939 Act] or any scheduled offence'. However, this does not give rise to the potential for *self*-incrimination.

[77] A detailed discussion of these decisions is provided by Y Daly, Chapter 11, this volume.

greater than what was necessary to protect the state and its population. The Supreme Court held in *Heaney v Ireland* that 'there is a proper proportionality between any infringement of the citizen's rights [by s 52] with the entitlement of the State to protect itself'.[78] In contrast, in *Heaney v Ireland; Quinn v Ireland*, the European Court held that the 'the security and public order concerns of the Government cannot justify a provision which extinguishes the very essence of the applicant's right to silence and against self-incrimination guaranteed by Article 6(1) of the Convention'.[79] Notably, the events at issue in this case occurred prior to the Supreme Court's ruling in *Re National Irish Banks* that evidence obtained pursuant to a statutory demand could not constitutionally be admitted in a subsequent criminal trial.[80] The European Court expressly referred in its judgment to the 'uncertainty [which the defendants faced] … as regards the later admission into evidence of section 52 statements'.[81] In light of the Supreme Court's subsequent recognition of a use immunity in *Re National Irish Banks*, it is unclear whether the European Court would take the same position today.

V. EVIDENTIARY RULES

A. Comparative Overview

Insofar as modifications to the rules of evidence are concerned, it is difficult to identify global trends. This is because there are as many different types of modifications to the rules of evidence as there are countries themselves. What these modifications do have in common, however, is that they are typically underpinned by one (or both) of two rationales.

The first rationale is the necessity of protecting the confidentiality of national security information. This is particularly significant in respect of terrorism prosecutions because of the proliferation of preparatory offences after the 11 September 2001 terrorist attacks.[82] These criminalise activities well before any substantive offence has been committed and even, in some cases, before the intent to do so has been formed. For example, in Australia, it is an offence to do (or to attempt, conspire or incite another person to do) any act in preparation for, or planning, a terrorist act.[83] Such offences blur the traditional distinction between intelligence and evidence, and therefore require intelligence officers to play a more integral role in the gathering of evidence for trial. To maintain the veil of secrecy under which the activities of these agencies have traditionally been shrouded has arguably necessitated modifications to the rules of evidence.

There is a clear relationship between this rationale and the discussion in the previous Part of this chapter about open justice. However, the critical point of distinction is that

[78] [1996] 1 IR 580, 590.
[79] [2001] Crim LR 481, para 58.
[80] [1999] 1 ILRM 191.
[81] [2001] Crim LR 481, para 54.
[82] See K Roach, 'The Eroding Distinction Between Intelligence and Evidence in Terrorism Investigations' in N McGarrity, A Lynch and G Williams, *Counter-Terrorism and Beyond: The Culture of Law and Justice after 9/11* (Abingdon, Routledge, 2010) 48–68.
[83] Criminal Code Act 1995 (Commonwealth) s 101.6.

this rationale goes beyond merely denying access to the public. It also goes to the restriction of access by the defendant and their legal representatives to information which is relevant to the proceedings but the disclosure of which may prejudice national security. It is common for jurisdictions to restrict access by a party or their legal representative to information in non-criminal judicial proceedings. This is so even amongst Western democracies. In the UK, for example, the state is permitted to rely upon 'closed material procedures' in a range of non-criminal judicial proceedings, including in relation to immigration matters and applications for control orders.[84] However, a clear line has been drawn between civil and criminal proceedings. Thus, a proposal by the UK Home Secretary in early February 2004 to allow secret evidence to be presented in criminal trials, with state-appointed special advocates appointed to protect the rights of defendants, did not progress any further.[85]

Australia represents something of an outlier amongst Western democracies insofar as this issue is concerned. The National Security Information (Criminal and Civil Proceedings) Act 2004 (Commonwealth) was enacted to get around the difficulty in obtaining a conviction where critical evidence was excluded based on the state's claim of public interest immunity.[86] Prior to this legislation, the only options available to the state were either to permit evidence to be disclosed to the defendant and admitted in full at trial or, alternatively, to claim that the evidence was covered by the immunity and therefore could not be admitted. The 'middle ground' established by the National Security Information (Criminal and Civil Proceedings) Act 2004 (Commonwealth) was that an application could be made by the relevant Minister for information to be disclosed in a summary form, as a statement of the facts proven, or with sensitive information redacted. At a hearing to determine whether this was appropriate, the defendant and their legal counsel could be excluded at the discretion of the court, and the factor to which the court must give greatest weight was any prejudice to national security which might be caused by disclosure.[87]

The second rationale for modifying the rules of evidence is to facilitate convictions where evidence, especially as to the state of mind of the defendant, is likely to be difficult to obtain. It is here that modifications to the prohibition upon the admission of evidence obtained through torture may be situated. Whilst the most obvious manifestation of this would be a legislative provision explicitly permitting evidence obtained through torture to be admitted at trial, this is virtually unheard of in the modern era. There are, however, a range of other modifications which arguably achieve a similar result, including narrowing the definition of what constitutes 'torture'[88] and putting the onus on the defendant to prove duress and ill-treatment.[89] These are amongst the most controversial modifications

[84] Justice and Security Act 2013 (UK) Pt 2.

[85] C Dyer, 'Lawyers Attack Blunkett Plan for Secret Trials', *The Guardian*, http://politics.guardian.co.uk/homeaffairs/story/0,11026,1137494,00.html (accessed 27 July 2020).

[86] The approach to privilege in Ireland is discussed by A Harrison, Chapter 7, this volume.

[87] National Security Information (Criminal and Civil Proceedings) Act 2004 (Commonwealth) ss 29 and 31(8).

[88] See, eg, Military Commissions Act of 2006 (US) s 6(b).

[89] See, eg, United Nations Special Rapporteur on the Promotion and Protection of Fundamental Human Rights while Countering Terrorism, *Mission to Sri Lanka* (2018) https://documents-dds-ny.un.org/doc/UNDOC/GEN/G18/365/92/PDF/G1836592.pdf?OpenElement (accessed 27 July 2020) 6–7.

to the rules of evidence made in response to the threat of terrorism. However, there are a plethora of other ways in which these rules have been modified in order to facilitate convictions.

The primary effect of many of the modifications to the rules of evidence is to permit relatively weak evidence to be relied upon, and even given considerable weight, at trial. For example, Indonesian criminal law only allows a conviction where a judge has a strong belief that the defendant committed a criminal offence.[90] This belief must be supported by at least two valid pieces of evidence (or '*alat bukti*') falling within a narrow list of categories. These categories were considerably expanded by the Anti-Terrorism Law of 2002 to include writing, sounds, symbols and pictures (whether accessible in physical form or through use of electronic device). This is a relatively unknown example of modifications to the rules of evidence in order to facilitate convictions. More notorious, however, is that the US military commission rules provide for the use of hearsay evidence.[91] Whilst it is possible that evidence adduced in this way *may* be both reliable and credible, the inability of the defendant's legal representative to cross-examine the original witness means that this is unable to be tested. Furthermore, unlike in many civil law systems, such as Germany, there is no requirement that hearsay evidence must be corroborated by non-hearsay evidence if it is to form the basis for a conviction.[92] Instead, it is possible for a military commission to find a person guilty entirely on the basis of uncorroborated hearsay evidence.

B. The Irish Experience

For the most part, the Special Criminal Court is required to comply with the ordinary rules of evidence. As noted above, section 41 of the OASA states that 'the rules of evidence applicable upon such trial in the Central Criminal Court shall apply to every trial by a Special Criminal Court'. However, there are rare instances of modifications being made to these rules in order to facilitate convictions.

Section 24 of the OASA provides that 'an incriminating document relating to [an unlawful] organisation' which is found in the possession of, or on property owned or occupied by, a person will 'be evidence until the contrary is proved that such person was a member of the organisation'. In *O'Leary v Attorney General*, the applicant challenged this provision on the basis that it unconstitutionally reversed the onus of proof.[93] As explained by the Hederman Committee, the Supreme Court held that the section means that 'the fact of possession of incriminating documents shall be evidence of membership

[90] S Butt, 'Anti-Terrorism Law and Process in Indonesia' https://law.unimelb.edu.au/__data/assets/pdf_file/0010/1546327/AntiTerrorismLawandProcessInIndonesia2.pdf (accessed 27 July 2020).

[91] S Turner and S Schulhofer, *The Secrecy Problem in Terrorism Trials* (Brennan Centre for Justice, 2005) www.brennancenter.org/sites/default/files/2019-08/Report_The_Secrecy_Problem_Terrorism_Trials.pdf (accessed 27 July 2020) 68.

[92] United Kingdom Law Commission, *Evidence in Criminal Proceedings: Hearsay and Related Topics: A Consultation Paper* (1995) www.lawcom.gov.uk/app/uploads/2016/08/No.138-Criminal-Law-Evidence-in-Criminal-Proceedings-Hearsay-and-Related-Topics-A-Consultation-Paper.pdf (accessed 27 July 2020) Appendix B [5.34].

[93] [1995] 1 IR 254.

of an illegal organisation unless it is shown not to constitute such evidence'.[94] In other words, at most, an evidential burden is placed on the defendant. It is ultimately for the trial court to weigh and evaluate any evidence, and then determine whether an inference of membership should be drawn. In spite of this, the Hederman Committee took issue with the breadth of 'incriminatory document', suggesting that the section could have the effect of declaring one thing (possession of a particular document) to be evidence of another quite unrelated thing (membership of an organisation). A majority of the Committee therefore recommended that the section be recast such that possession of documents 'could only be evidence of membership … where the possession was of such a kind as to give rise to a reasonable suspicion that the accused was a member of an unlawful organisation'.[95]

The other provision which deserves specific attention is section 3 of the Offences Against the State (Amendment) Act 1972. This provides that the opinion of an officer of the Garda Síochána of the rank of Chief Superintendent or above that a person was a member of an unlawful organisation shall be evidence of this fact.[96] This section is a response to 'the practical difficulties in proving membership of a clandestine and illegal organisation'.[97] However, the manner in which it goes about this has been the subject of strong criticism. The first basis for this criticism, which was raised by the applicant in *O'Leary v Attorney-General*, is that it violates the presumption of innocence. This argument was rejected by the High Court (and by the Supreme Court on appeal). The Court stated that '[l]ike other evidence it has to be weighed and considered and the section cannot be construed as meaning that the court of trial *must* convict the accused in the absence of exculpatory evidence'.[98] At most, an evidential burden is transferred to the defendant.[99]

The Hederman Committee accepted this conclusion in relation to the presumption of innocence. However, it then went on to express concerns about the appropriateness of the Oireachtas giving 'evidential status to an expression of opinion which may not merit that status'.[100] It suggested that to do so violated long-standing principles which underpinned the rules of evidence, namely, that the expertise of experts must be clearly established, expert evidence cannot go to the ultimate issue, and, finally, the opinion cannot be based on information which, in itself, would be inadmissible. Ultimately, however, the Hederman Committee (which was irreparably divided) recommended either no or minimal changes to the section. It noted that '[i]n practice, … the effect of this section was largely emasculated when the Court of Criminal Appeal subsequently indicated [in *The People (DPP) v Ferguson*, 31 October 1975] that the weight to be given to such opinion would be considerably undermined if the accused denied the membership

[94] Hederman Report (n 28) 6.57.
[95] Ibid, 6.64.
[96] This is discussed by L Heffernan and E O'Connor, Chapter 6, this volume.
[97] Ibid, 6.93.
[98] [1993] 1 IR 102, 112.
[99] The ability of a defendant to fulfil this burden is disputed by L Heffernan and E O'Connor, Chapter 6, this volume.
[100] Hederman Report (n 28) 6.90.

charge on oath'.[101] The only change of any substance which was proposed by members of the Committee was that 'no person should be convicted *solely* on the basis of such opinion, but that such opinion might be treated by the courts as corroborative evidence in appropriate cases'.[102]

VI. CONCLUSION

It is not this author's position that modifications to the ordinary criminal justice process are always unnecessary or inappropriate in response to the threat of terrorism. That would be to ignore the very different circumstances that countries find themselves in and the specific challenges they face. Rather, the core lesson is that caution must be exercised to ensure that countries don't stray too far in the opposite direction. The Hederman Committee regarded it as 'mistaken to assume that, simply because conduct damaging to the administration of justice was inspired by some political motive, it has to be dealt with by some distinctive process, involving unique restrictions on the rights of the accused'.[103]

In many instances, modifications have been justified on the basis that they will increase the efficiency of prosecuting alleged terrorists and, in turn, result in a higher rate of convictions. Not only may the validity of such justifications be doubted in and of themselves, but, in any event, they are substantially outweighed by the adverse effects upon the criminal justice system. Modifications to this system in response to the threat of terrorism should only be permitted where there is a clear body of evidence demonstrating that the specific proposal is necessary in order to protect the security of individuals, the state or the international community.

The suspension of the normal legal order in emergency situations may be characterised as an affront to the rule of law. Less frequently commented upon, but arguably bearing a more direct relationship to the rule of law, is the modification of the law in respect of one particular category of criminal offences. Emanuel Gross writes that 'a democratic state derives its court structure from the principle of equality, namely, a single body and not separate bodies adjusted to different types of offenders/offenses'.[104] There may be cases in which a meaningful distinction can be drawn between categories on the basis of either the conduct which they capture or the circumstances relating to their prosecution. For example, in relation to the latter, if laypeople are unlikely to be impartial when asked to determine the guilt or innocence of an alleged terrorist, either because they are sympathetic to their political goals or have been intimidated by their associates, this may justify a shift from trial by jury to trial by judge alone. However, the onus should be upon those seeking to justify modifications to the criminal justice system to present not only this body of evidence but also to clearly relate the proposed solution to the identified problem.

[101] Ibid, 4.33.

[102] Ibid, 6.93 (emphasis in original). See the discussion of *Redmond v Ireland* [2015] 4 IR 84 by L Heffernan and E O'Connor, Chapter 6, this volume.

[103] Hederman Report (n 28) 2.7.

[104] E Gross, 'Trying Terrorists – Justification for Differing Trial Rules: The Balance Between Security Considerations and Human Rights' (2002) 13(1) *Indiana International and Comparative Law Review* 1–97, 19.

It is essential to the proper workings of the criminal justice system that it is perceived as legitimate both by the public and also those who are directly subject to the process. Inconsistent treatment of alleged terrorists versus ordinary suspects is not only a violation of the rule of law, but it also has the potential to exacerbate claims on behalf of minority groups that they cannot work within mainstream processes. This, in turn, may operate as a rallying cry for further radicalisation.

In many cases, modifications to the criminal justice system in response to the threat of terrorism have resulted in considerable intrusions into fundamental human rights. Implicit in much of the political rhetoric surrounding these modifications is the assertion that the exceptional nature of terrorism means that it is acceptable – and even appropriate – for convictions to be achieved at a greater cost to civil liberties than would be tolerated for ordinary criminal offences. The human rights engaged by terrorism trials are not only those relating to its outcome, such as the right to life and the right to liberty, but also rights relating to the procedures to be followed. These include: the freedom from torture, and cruel, inhuman or degrading treatment; the right to a fair and public hearing by a competent, independent and impartial tribunal established by law; the right to be presumed innocent until proved guilty according to law; the right to know the nature and cause of the case against them; the right to adequate time and resources to prepare their defence; the right to be tried without undue delay; the right to legal counsel; and, finally, the freedom from self-incrimination. Of course, most of these rights are not absolute. To use the words of Article 4 of the International Covenant on Civil and Political Rights, countries may derogate from them '[i]n time of public emergency which threatens the life of the nation'. However, such derogations must be limited to what is 'strictly required by the exigencies of the situation'.

It is not only the impact upon the trial of an individual defendant which is of concern. In addition to the undermining of fundamental human rights, the other common thread which underpins modifications to the criminal justice system in response to the threat of terrorism is a shift in the balance of power from the judiciary to the executive branch of government. The consequence of this is a loss of true independence and impartiality on the part of the decision-makers. The most obvious example of this is the use of military courts which are composed (either wholly or in part) of members of the armed forces. For the reasons discussed earlier in this chapter, there are very real concerns about the ability of such people to bring an open mind to the proceedings. More insidious are changes to the applicable procedures and the rules of evidence which allow the executive branch of government and its agents to control the form in which evidence is admitted and which give weight to their assertions at trial. A further risk to which these modifications give rise is that of tainting ordinary criminal trials. For example, increasing the level of secrecy in terrorism trials in order to protect national security information from disclosure may result in less openness in criminal trials at large. This risk is not merely hypothetical. It is well documented that counter-terrorism measures, whilst generally justified at the point of enactment as extraordinary and temporary measures, often become permanent, in the sense of no longer being regarded as exceptional in nature,[105] and even 'seep' into the

[105] N McGarrity and G Williams, 'When Extraordinary Measures Become Normal: Pre-emption in Counter-Terrorism and Other Laws' in N McGarrity, A Lynch and G Williams (eds), *Counter-Terrorism and Beyond: The Culture of Law and Justice after 9/11* (Abingdon, Routledge, 2010) 131–149, 132.

ordinary law.[106] In Ireland, for example, the jurisdiction of the Special Criminal Court was substantially expanded by the Criminal Justice (Amendment) Act 2009 to cover a range of organised crime offences.[107] Despite the presentation of the Act as an emergency measure, and the requirement that it be assessed and renewed annually, it was not until 2015 that it was relied upon for the first time by Irish prosecutors.

[106] The Eminent Jurists Panel on Terrorism, Counter-Terrorism and Human Rights notes that '[t]here is a risk of seepage of special laws into normal legal procedures and practices': *Assessing Damage, Urging Action* (2009) 6 www.refworld.org/docid/499e76822.html (accessed 27 July 2020). The Irish experience of the migration of extraordinary counter-terrorism measures to the ordinary criminal justice system is discussed by C Hamilton, Chapter 14, this volume.

[107] This is paralleled by developments in Australia: see R Ananian-Welsh and G Williams, 'The New Terrorists: The Normalisation and Spread of Anti-Terror Laws in Australia' (2014) 38 *Melbourne University Law Review* 362–408. See the discussion by L Campbell, Chapter 8, this volume, of the use of the Offences Against the State Act 1939 in respect of non-subversive offences.

6

Threats to Security and Risks to Rights: 'Belief Evidence' under the Offences Against the State Act

LIZ HEFFERNAN AND EOIN O'CONNOR

I. INTRODUCTION

THE OFFENCES AGAINST the State Act 1939 (OASA) has left an indelible imprint on policing and criminal justice in Ireland over the course of its turbulent 80-year history. Although the OASA regime is habitually wrapped in the cloak of extraordinary or unconventional language, it is a truism that the powers exercised under the legislation have been prominent for decades if not generations. OASA functions might not be 'normal' but paradoxically they have become routine; and while state practice under the OASA is undoubtedly special, its influence has seeped into the mainstream of criminal justice.[1] The longevity and durability of the OASA is also indicative of an inherent co-mingling of the concepts of crime and security in Irish law. Against this backdrop of unusual features, it is not surprising that a tension between the societal imperatives of safeguarding state security and protecting human rights is a recurrent theme in discourse on the OASA. Reporting in 2002, the Committee to Review the Offences Against the State Acts 1939–1998 opened its substantive analysis with the following astute observation:

> Emergency legislation, special courts and distinctive restrictions on liberty, are features of the response of many legal systems to threats to the security of the State. They are so widespread that it may be easy to proceed on the unreflective premise that there is a compelling moral argument in their support. Yet it is plain that great dangers for human rights arise in this area. Emergency legislation may be abused for pragmatic political purposes; special powers, introduced for special reasons, may continue to be used when those reasons no longer justify this, or for purposes extending beyond those that warranted their original introduction; and powers of detention or interrogation may be used cruelly or inhumanly upon innocent (or even guilty) people.[2]

Although the history of the OASA is replete with examples of the dangers that special powers pose for the protection of human rights, ironically a majority of the Committee

[1] See C Hamilton, Chapter 14, this volume.

[2] *Report of the Committee to Review the Offences Against the State Acts 1939–1998 and Related Matters* (Dublin, 2002) 2.1 (hereinafter, Hederman Report).

concluded ultimately that the legislation should be retained in substance and adapted only in form.[3]

The present chapter explores the use of evidentiary props to support the prosecution of terrorist offences before the Special Criminal Court and exemplifies the tension between national security and human rights. The specific focus is the provision in section 3(2) of the Offences Against the State (Amendment) Act 1972 for the admissibility at a trial for the offence of membership of an unlawful organisation of the statement of a senior Garda officer of his/her belief that the accused is guilty.[4] So-called 'belief evidence', is similar to evidentiary shortcuts that are used in other jurisdictions in the prosecution of terrorist offences but its operation in Irish criminal trial practice has raised unique legal questions.[5] Drawing on the extensive case law that belief evidence has generated over the past 45 years, this chapter analyses the key issues that have emerged through judicial scrutiny of section 3(2) and offers some reflections on the implications for the broader OASA regime.

II. SECTION 3(2) OF THE 1972 ACT

Membership of an unlawful organisation, contrary to section 21 of the OASA, is the charge mostly commonly brought under the OASA and belief evidence plays a key role in supporting prosecutions.[6] Section 3(2) of the 1972 Act lays the statutory foundation in the following terms:

> Where an officer of the Garda Síochána, not below the rank of Chief Superintendent, in giving evidence in proceedings relating to an offence under the said section 21, states that he believes that the accused was at a material time a member of an unlawful organisation, the statement shall be evidence that he was then such a member.

At first glance, provision for belief evidence seems relatively clear and unvarnished yet the subsection is deceptively ambiguous on closer inspection. The Irish courts generally adhere to the common law rule against opinion evidence which constrains a witness from offering an opinion and, in particular, from opining on the ultimate issue in the case.[7] Section 3(2) constitutes a far-reaching exception to that rule: the Chief Superintendent's belief is admissible, without judicial imprimatur, as proof of the very offence for which the accused is being tried and, indeed, it has the potential to determine the outcome of the trial. Belief evidence also threatens other rules of evidence. For example, because it necessarily comprises information gleaned from second-hand sources, it may potentially

[3] The Committee were divided as to whether belief evidence, the mechanism discussed in this chapter, should be retained and, if so, reformed. Ibid, 6.93, 6.95 and 6.196.

[4] For previous discussion see L Heffernan, 'Evidence and National Security: 'Belief Evidence' in the Irish Special Criminal Court' (2009) 15(1) *European Public Law* 65; E O'Connor, *National Security Law in Ireland* (Dublin, Bloomsbury Professional, 2019) ch 4. On belief evidence, see generally, A Harrison, *The Special Criminal Court: Practice and Procedure* (Dublin, Bloomsbury Professional, 2019) 106–113 and 396–426.

[5] See, eg, the executive's hearsay affidavit evidence of 'enemy combatant' status criticised by the United States Supreme Court in *Hamdi v Rumsfeld* 542 US 507 (2004).

[6] By virtue of the Criminal Justice (Terrorist Offences) Act 2005, s 5, a terrorist group operating inside or outside the state is an unlawful organisation for purposes of the OASA.

[7] See, eg, *AG (Ruddy) v Kenny* (1960) 94 ILTR 185, 190; *People (DPP) v Kehoe* [1992] ILRM 481, 485.

infringe the rule against hearsay, although this argument has not found favour with the Irish courts.

Section 3(2) was enacted in response to perceived difficulties in adducing admissible evidence to prove that an accused was guilty of membership of an unlawful organisation beyond reasonable doubt. As the Minister for Justice put it, when introducing the Bill at the second stage in the Dáil: 'Section 3 is designed to facilitate the proof of a charge of being a member of an unlawful organisation contrary to section 21 of the Offences Against the State Act, 1939.'[8] By way of contrast, it is interesting to note that the Diplock Commission Report published in December 1972 considered whether a similar 'belief evidence' provision should be introduced in Northern Ireland.[9] The Report recommended against such a change in the rules of evidence because of the need to protect the lives of those who would provide the information upon which the police officer's belief would be based.[10]

Bearing in mind the inroads that section 3(2) makes on these common law rules of evidence, one might have expected the Oireachtas to temper the provision with a requirement that belief evidence be supported by some form of independent evidence. However, the subsection lacks an express corroboration requirement as a condition for the admissibility of belief evidence and does not rule out the possibility that a conviction for the offence of membership of an unlawful organisation might rest on belief evidence alone. As recently as 2015, however, the Supreme Court acknowledged that the existence in any given case of evidence that can corroborate the belief of the Chief Superintendent is necessary if the subsection is to operate in conformity with the Constitution.[11]

The relationship between belief evidence and the doctrine of privilege has been a particular source of difficulty in practice before the SCC. The conundrum derives from the interaction between section 3(2) and informer privilege, a vibrant constitutional and common law doctrine that is designed to protect informers' lives and safety and to preserve their valued contribution to law enforcement.[12] Over the years, the courts have afforded Garda witnesses considerable leeway when asserting informer privilege and have tended to accept at face value prosecutorial claims that maintaining the anonymity of informers and the confidentiality of their relationships with the Gardaí is essential.[13] Where a Chief Superintendent gives belief evidence pursuant to section 3(2), informer privilege is often invoked by the prosecution to conceal the identity of the source of the information grounding the belief. A successful assertion of privilege effectively deprives the accused of knowledge of the original source and, consequently, of an opportunity to confront the informer in open court. It also shields the Chief Superintendent him/herself from cross-examination on at least some issues. Defence counsel is precluded from asking any question that would tend to reveal the identity of the original source and is further

[8] *Dáil Deb* 29 Nov 1972, vol 264, col 267.

[9] Diplock Commission *Report of the Commission to Consider Legal Procedures to Deal with Terrorist Activities in Northern Ireland* (Cmnd 5185, 1972).

[10] Ibid, 22.

[11] *Redmond v Ireland* [2015] 4 IR 84.

[12] *Director of Consumer Affairs v Sugar Distributors Ltd* [1991] 1 IR 225; *Ward v Special Criminal Court* [1999] 1 IR 60; *People (DPP) v Kelly* [1990] 3 IR 115.

[13] See, eg, *People (DPP) v Eccles, Phillips and McShane* (19860 3 Frewen 36; *People (DPP) v Reddan* [1995] 3 IR 560.

stymied by the deference courts show to Garda witnesses when privilege is invoked, often without further explanation, as a justification for refusing to answer. In short, 'the provisions of s. 3(2) represent a very serious diminution in the protections ordinarily afforded to an accused person by the law of evidence'.[14]

The obstacles created by these two evidentiary mechanisms operating together test the boundaries of the accused's rights under the Constitution and international human rights law. Perhaps recognising an inherent threat to the accused's right to fair trial, the SCC has maintained the practice of requiring some form of independent evidence that would corroborate belief evidence, such as evidence of an accused's participation in the activities of an unlawful organisation obtained through Garda surveillance or evidence of possession by an accused of subversive material.[15] Geoghegan J, writing for a majority of the Supreme Court in 2006, had opined that this practice, though 'commendable', is not 'absolutely required' by the legislation with the consequence that '[t]here may be exceptional cases where the Special Criminal Court in its wisdom would be entitled to convict on belief evidence alone'.[16] In a concurring judgment, Fennelly J took the more principled view that an accused would have a 'powerful argument' based on the denial of his/her rights where belief evidence constituted the 'sole plank' in the prosecution's case.[17] Almost a decade later, in *Redmond v Ireland*[18] the Supreme Court squarely examined the issue of corroboration from a constitutional perspective and elevated the practice of the SCC not convicting on belief evidence alone to a rule of law. Hardiman J explained:

> I do not consider that s. 3(2) would be consistent with the Constitution if it permitted the conviction of a person solely on the basis of the opinion evidence. This is even more obviously the case if privilege is successfully asserted over the material which led to the formation of the opinion. This is because these matters in combination tend to exclude any 'examinable reality' from the case and thereby undermine any potential avenue to effectively challenge the opinion evidence. The effect of this is wholly to subvert the prospects of useful cross-examination and to exclude even the theoretical possibility of undermining the opinion by cross-examination. This creates scope for the possibility of a conviction on opinion evidence only, which evidence is effectively unchallengeable.[19]

The acknowledgement in *Redmond* that a conviction may not rest on belief evidence alone is an important legal qualification on the operation of section 3(2). Nevertheless, corroboration is a complex and malleable concept in the law of evidence and the effect

[14] *Redmond v Ireland* [2015] 4 IR 84, 88 (per Hardiman J). See also *People (DPP) v Kelly* [2006] 3 IR 115, 135 (per Fennelly J recognising that without knowledge of the basis of the belief, the accused is powerless to challenge the information provided by informers).

[15] Seemingly the Director of Public Prosecutions has adopted a corresponding policy of not seeking a conviction on the basis of uncorroborated belief evidence. *Redmond v Ireland* [2015] 4 IR 84, 96–97 & 120.

[16] *People (DPP) v Kelly* [2006] 3 IR 115, 122.

[17] Ibid, 147.

[18] *Redmond v Ireland* [2015] 4 IR 84.

[19] Ibid, 97. Denham CJ and McKechnie and MacMenamin JJ concurring. Agreeing with the result but writing separately, Charleton J outlined a plethora of safeguards which he viewed as affirming the admissibility of belief evidence and the constitutionality of s 3(2). Among those safeguards is that 'the belief evidence should not stand alone but that the charge should otherwise be supported by some other piece of evidence, or some admissible circumstance, which supports the charge'. [2015] 4 IR 84, 129. It follows in Charleton J's view that s 3(2) does not offend the constitutional right to a trial in due course of law under Art 38.1 'where such belief evidence is part of a body of evidence' as had occurred in *Redmond's* case. [2015] 4 IR 84, 131.

of the ruling may be undermined in practice by the possibility that corroboration may be found in a slight form of evidence such as an inference drawn from an accused's silence in response to a material question posed at a custodial interview.[20]

Belief evidence has been litigated extensively during the lifetime of the 1972 Act and consequently has generated a rich body of case law. Challenges have been mounted in various fora, through diverse procedural routes, and on a multiplicity of substantive grounds. The common thread woven through decisions spanning over several decades, is the consistent upholding by the courts of the legality of section 3(2) in principle and in practice. Although the case law might be catalogued in different ways, it is instructive to consider some of the leading cases by reference to three aspects of the rights of the defence: the presumption of innocence, the right to cross-examination, and the right to disclosure.

III. THE PRESUMPTION OF INNOCENCE

One of the first of the prominent legal attacks on section 3(2) of the 1972 Act came before the High Court in the 1990 case of *O'Leary v Attorney General*.[21] At issue was the compatibility of section 3(2) with the presumption of innocence, a fundamental principle that is safeguarded by the Constitution, the common law and international human rights law. The presumption manifests in several criminal protections including the corollary that the prosecution bears the burden of establishing the guilt of an accused beyond a reasonable doubt.[22] There are exceptions to this canon and they principally comprise of statutory clauses that purport to reverse the burden by requiring the defence to prove or disprove some fact relevant to a statutory offence.[23]

The plaintiff was convicted by the Special Criminal Court of offences under the OASA including membership of the IRA and leave to appeal the convictions was subsequently refused by the Court of Criminal Appeal. Before the High Court, the plaintiff contested the constitutionality of section 3(2) on the ground that it required him to disprove his guilt at trial. In a landmark judgment, Costello J acknowledged that the presumption of innocence is enshrined in the constitutional right of an accused to a trial in due course of law. It is not an absolute right, however, and Article 38.1 does not invariably prohibit the Oireachtas from restricting the presumption through the enactment of reverse onus clauses, which can take a myriad of forms.[24] Costello J famously distinguished between two types of proof. A legal or persuasive burden rests on the prosecution throughout the trial to prove each element of the offence beyond a reasonable doubt. The prosecution also bears a lesser burden of adducing sufficient evidence to raise a prima facie case; once that threshold has been crossed, the evidential burden shifts to the accused without disturbing the prosecution's legal burden. Whereas the removal of the legal burden by

[20] *DPP v Donnelly, McGarrigle and Murphy* [2012] IECCA 78 (30 July 2012).

[21] *O'Leary v AG* [1993] 1 IR 102.

[22] *Woolmington v DPP* [1935] AC 462, 481–82; *McGowan v Carville* [1960] IR 330, 345; *People (AG) v McMahon* [1946] IR 267, 273; *People (AG) v Quinn* [1965] IR 366, 382.

[23] *People (DPP) v Smyth* [2010] 3 IR 688 (CCA); *People (DPP) v Heffernan* [2017] 1 IR 82 (SC); *DPP v Forsey* [2018] IESC 55 (8 November 2018).

[24] *O'Leary v AG* [1993] 1 IR 102, 108.

statute may involve a breach of the accused's constitutional right, a mere shifting of the evidential burden will not result in a constitutional infringement.[25]

The High Court dismissed the plaintiff's claim on the basis that section 3(2) neither disturbed the allocation of the legal burden of proof nor affected the plaintiff's right to be presumed innocent. Costello J explained:

> What this section does is to make admissible in evidence in certain trials statements of belief which would otherwise be inadmissible. The statement of belief if proffered at the trial becomes 'evidence' by virtue of this section in the prosecution case against the accused. Like other evidence it has to be weighed and considered and the section cannot be construed as meaning that the court of trial *must* convict the accused in the absence of exculpatory evidence. The accused need not give evidence, and he may ask the court to hold that the evidence does not establish beyond a reasonable doubt that he is a member of an unlawful organisation. Should the court agree he must be acquitted.[26]

The High Court decision was appealed unsuccessfully on other grounds but the challenge to section 3(2) formed no part of that appeal.[27]

The decision in *O'Leary* set a pattern for an approach to reverse onus clauses that the Superior Courts would adhere to for several decades. Indeed, Costello J's judgment remains to this day the starting point for judicial and academic discourse on burdens of proof. Even so, the failure of the judgment to capture the subject in all its complexity arguably set the doctrine on statutory presumptions affecting the burden of proof on an uncertain path. *O'Leary* set a high bar on the creation of a statutory legal presumption and encouraged a trend of courts 'reading-down' reverse burdens as mere evidential presumptions.[28] This has had the undesirable effect of deflecting the need for a full-blown analysis of the relationship between reverse onus clauses and the presumption of innocence; if a court can discount entirely the possibility that an evidential burden may be constitutionally problematic, it need never reach the question of whether a statutory provision embodies a justified and proportionate interference in the rights of the accused. The Supreme Court has recently accepted and applied a more sophisticated approach to the classification of burdens of proof that recognises that some variation in the standard of proof which may attach to an evidential burden.[29] However, this approach itself involves a 'reading-down' of statutory clauses as imposing mere evidential probative burdens on the defence.

[25] Ibid, 109.

[26] Ibid, 112. See also *People (DPP) v Kelly* [2006] 3 IR 115, *Redmond v Ireland* [2015] 4 IR 84, 100 et seq (judgment of Charleton J).

[27] The case also involved a challenge to the constitutionality of s 24 of the OASA which provided that, on a charge of membership of an unlawful organisation, proof that an incriminating document was found on the person of the accused or in his/her possession or control would be evidence of membership of an unlawful organisation 'until the contrary is proved'. This claim was also rejected by the High Court but, unlike s 3(2), it formed the basis of an appeal by the plaintiff. The Supreme Court ultimately affirmed the High Court's ruling that s 24 did not infringe the constitutional protection of the presumption of innocence.

[28] The courts have been aided in this regard by the double construction rule whereby a statutory provision will not be declared invalid where it is open to be construed in a manner consistent with the Constitution. *McDonald v Bord nag Con* [1965] IR 217; *East Donegal Co-operative Livestock Marts Ltd v AG* [1970] IR 317; *O'Leary v AG* [1995] 2 ILRM 259 (SC).

[29] *DPP v Forsey* [2019] IESC 55 drawing on the earlier development of the doctrine in *People (DPP) v Smyth* [2010] 3 IR 688 (CCA); *People (DPP) v Heffernan* [2017] 1 IR 82 (SC).

Turning to section 3(2), the conclusion in *O'Leary* that its effect was to place a mere evidential burden on the accused is questionable when one considers the practical realities of proof in a trial for the offence of membership contrary to section 21. The defence is at an obvious strategic disadvantage not knowing in advance the basis for the Chief Superintendent's belief. The legislation does not expressly condition the belief, for example, with a requirement that it be reasonable or based on objective criteria. The defence can proceed on the premise that such conditions are implicit and seek to shake the belief in cross-examination but, as noted above, the Chief Superintendent can escape any rigorous testing of the basis for his/her belief by invoking informer privilege.[30] Whereas an alibi witness might present the court with testimony that would counter an allegation that an accused was at a particular location or involved in a specific activity, the value of such testimony would be limited given the generalised nature of an allegation of membership. Rules limiting opinion and character evidence combine to preclude the defence from tendering witnesses that might offer their own beliefs to contradict the testimony of the Chief Superintendent. An accused can opt to take the stand and offer testimony in the form of a denial of the allegation of membership; this would of course expose him/her to cross-examination on any matter the court deems relevant to the proceedings. Where he/she does testify, the issue may ultimately turn on which of the witnesses the court considers more credible, a possibly uneven contest between the belief of the Chief Superintendent and the explanation presented by the accused.

IV. THE RIGHT TO CROSS-EXAMINATION

The right of an accused person to cross-examine adverse witnesses is a cornerstone of the broader entitlement to present a defence to a charge of criminality. Although not expressly guaranteed in the Irish Constitution, it has been classified by the courts as an essential derivative of the right to a trial in due course of law under Article 38.1.[31] Famously described by Wigmore as 'the greatest legal engine ever invented for the discovery of truth', cross-examination enables the accused to challenge and contradict the prosecution's evidence and to impeach the credit of the prosecution's witnesses. The Supreme Court cited cross-examination as a core procedural right in *Re Haughey*[32] and time and again has reiterated its fundamental importance as a safeguard of fair procedure.[33] Article 6(3)(d) of the European Convention on Human Rights (ECHR) expressly acknowledges the 'minimum' right of the defence 'to examine or have examined witnesses against him' as part of the umbrella right to a fair trial under Article 6(1). The jurisprudence of the European Court of Human Rights (ECtHR) on point affirms the principle that national procedures must accord an accused an adequate and proper opportunity to question and challenge a witness giving evidence against him/her.[34] Bearing this in mind, it is perhaps

[30] *People (DPP) v Kelly* [2006] 3 IR 115, 135 (Fennelly J); *Redmond v Ireland* [2015] 4 IR 84, 88 (Hardiman J).

[31] *State (Healy) v Donoghue* [1976] IR 325.

[32] *Re Haughey* [1971] IR 217.

[33] *Donnelly v Ireland* [1998] 1 IR 321; *Maguire v Ardagh* [2002] 1 IR 385; *O'Callaghan v Mahon* [2006] 2 IR 32.

[34] *Kostovski v The Netherlands* (1990) 12 EHRR 647 at 447 (para 41); *Van Mechelen & Others v The Netherlands* (1997) 25 EHRR 647, 674 (para 60).

not surprising that the bulk of challenges to section 3(2) of the 1972 Act have focused on the implications of the accused's right to cross-examine the Chief Superintendent whose belief comprises the evidence that the accused was a member of an unlawful organisation at the material time.

The leading case is *People (DPP) v Kelly*[35] in which a unanimous Supreme Court rejected a claim that the restriction on the ability of the defence to cross-examine the Chief Superintendent in that case prejudiced the fairness of the appellant's trial. Geoghegan J, writing for a majority of the Court,[36] noted the legislative intent behind the subsection, which was passed in the context of preserving the security of the state, and reflected the difficulty that the prosecution faced in adducing direct evidence of membership of an unlawful organisation from lay witnesses who fear reprisal. His judgment continued:

> It is a reasonable inference to draw that the subsection was enacted out of bitter experience. It is carefully crafted ensuring that the belief evidence must come from an officer of an Garda Síochána not below the rank of Chief Superintendent. This is with a view to ensuring trust and credibility as far as possible. Counsel for the appellant accepts the concept of informer confidentiality but any extensive probing in relation to the basis of the information irrespective of whether names are requested or not may inevitably undermine the protection of the informer by affording clues as to his identity … I have no doubt that in so far as [counsel for the defence] was limited in his cross-examination … this limitation was inherent in the subsection itself which enjoys the presumption of constitutionality.[37]

These dicta are an instructive reminder of the turbulence of the times in which the subsection was enacted and of the perception by the Oireachtas of the need to strengthen the special powers in the OASA by dint of the 1972 amendments. The majority judgment in *Kelly* exemplified a willingness on the part of courts to defer to the judgment of the other branches of government when responding to threats to national security.[38] In a separate concurring judgment, Fennelly J acknowledged that the issue raised in the appeal was 'both important and difficult' because it set the policy of suppressing dangerous unlawful organisations against the fair trial rights of the accused.[39] Drawing on domestic and comparative rights jurisprudence, he concluded that the evidentiary prop in section 3(2) was proportionate provided that the restrictions on the defence's right to cross-examine did not stray beyond strict necessity and did not imperil the overall fairness of a particular trial.[40]

The comments of Geoghegan J in the passage quoted above also reflect the enormous dependency on testimony as a source of evidence in an era that pre-dated technological advances such as DNA profiling, surveillance technology, mobile phones and social media. However cogent the rationale of compensating the prosecution for difficulties in procuring witnesses in membership trials may have seemed in 1972, evidentiary

[35] *People (DPP) v Kelly* [2006] 3 IR 115.

[36] Murray CJ, Denham and Kearns JJ concurring.

[37] [2006] 3 IR 115, 121. See also *Remond v Ireland* [2015] 4 IR 84, 129 per Charleton J: 'Prosecutions are dependent upon the evidence of a chief superintendent in order to make the charge of membership of a proscribed organisation viable for prosecution. This charge is vital to the maintenance of the democratic polity of this country.'

[38] But see, eg, *Ambiorix Ltd v Minister for the Environment (No 1)* [1992] 1 IR 277; *Gormley v Ireland* [1993] 2 IR 75.

[39] *People (DPP) v Kelly* [2006] 3 IR 115, 129.

[40] Ibid, 146. The need for a narrow reading of s 3(2) was echoed by Geoghegan J. Ibid, 121.

conditions had arguably evolved by 2006, when the decision in *Kelly* was reported, and have continued to change rapidly in the years since. Trials no longer turn exclusively on direct testimony and the prosecution have at their disposal the evidentiary fruits of sophisticated investigative and scientific technologies. The threat and actuality of dissident paramilitary activity remain, albeit at a diminished level, but the capability of law enforcement to detect and prosecute offences has perhaps enhanced to the point where it is reasonable to revisit the question of the ongoing relevancy of the original justification for the subsection.[41] Nevertheless, it is noteworthy that as recently as 2015, the Supreme Court confirmed that the principles enunciated in *People (DPP) v Kelly* are 'still applicable' and, moreover, that the constitutional position chimes with the approach under the ECHR.[42]

V. THE RIGHT TO DISCLOSURE

Disclosure is an area where the common law adversarial trial process has been adapted in order to redress the imbalance in power between the parties and to vindicate the constitutional rights of the defence. The prosecution is obliged to disclose the details of the case that they intend to make at trial and the evidence on which they will rely.[43] Beyond this, the prosecution must also disclose any material in their possession or control that may assist the defence.[44] The substantial duty resting on the prosecution is an essential ingredient in a fair trial[45] and a tangible manifestation of the prosecutorial responsibility to assist the court in ensuring that justice is administered fairly and effectively.[46] Because the right to disclosure affords access to information relevant to the conduct of an effective defence, it serves as an essential prop to the right to cross-examination.[47]

Whereas the Irish courts have the authority in principle to exclude prosecution evidence that has been obtained by the state through a breach of the accused's constitutional rights,[48] the circumstances in which the courts can and must compel production of evidence in order to vindicate the accused's constitutional rights is less clear. Arguably the emphasis within Irish law on the exclusion of prejudicial prosecution evidence has inhibited the crystallisation of a robust, positive right on the part of the defence to adduce potentially exculpatory evidence, notably through the mechanism of disclosure.[49]

[41] The various issues and themes raised in *Kelly* have been revisited by the Superior Courts. See, eg, *People (DPP) v Binead and Donoghue* [2007] 1 IR 374; *Redmond v Ireland* [2009] 2 ILRM 419; *DPP v Donnelly, McGarrigle and Murphy* [2012] IECCA 78.

[42] *Sean Connolly v DPP* [2015] 4 IR 60, 46 (referring in particular to *DPP v Donnelly, McGarrigle and Murphy* [2012] IECCA 78); and *Donohoe v Ireland* App no 19165/08 (ECtHR, 5th Section, 12 December 2013).

[43] Criminal Procedure Act 1967, ss 4B and 4C as amended. See also Directive 2012/13/EU of the European Parliament and of the Council of 22 May 2013 on the right to information in criminal proceedings [2012] OJ L142/1.

[44] *Traynor v Judge Delahunt* [2009] 1 IR 605, 610; *DPP v Conmey* [2010] IECCA 105 (22 Nov 2010) 15; *DPP v Special Criminal Court* [1999] 1 IR 60, 76; *People (DPP) v Tuite* [2003] 2 Frewen 175, 180.

[45] Irish Constitution 1937, Art 38.1; ECHR, Art 6; EU Charter, Art 47.

[46] Director of Public Prosecutions, *Guidelines for Prosecutors* 4th edn (2016) ch 9.

[47] *O'Callaghan v Mahon* [2006] 2 IR 32, 66–67; *Redmond v Ireland* [2015] 4 IR 84, 93. See also *DPP v Banks* [2019] IECA 319, 78.

[48] *DPP v JC* [2015] IESC 31; *People (DPP) v Kenny* [1990] 2 IR 110; *People (AG) v O'Brien* [1965] IR 142.

[49] L Heffernan and EJ Imwinkelried, 'The Constitutional Right of the Accused to Introduce Demonstrably Exculpatory Evidence' (2005) 40 *Irish Jurist* 142.

As noted above, much of the controversy surrounding belief evidence stems from the invocation of informer privilege in order to restrict defence cross-examination of the Chief Superintendent.[50] There is no uniform procedure to which the trial courts must adhere when dealing with claims of privilege[51] and the law on informers has developed in an ad hoc fashion. The right of the accused to adversarial due process generally prevents a court from receiving contested evidence on an ex parte basis in a proceeding from which the defence is excluded. A practical conundrum arises because the lives and safety of an informer may be endangered if the information is revealed to the defence. Moreover, the Irish courts have rejected any compromise whereby material might be disclosed to an accused's lawyers but not to the accused him/herself.[52] The issue remains, therefore, of how belief evidence can be used in trials in a manner that respects the accused's constitutional and internationally protected right to disclosure.

The compatibility of belief evidence with the ECHR's protection against non-disclosure was tested before the European Court of Human Rights in *Donohoe v Ireland*.[53] The applicant, who had been convicted of membership of the IRA, contended that his right to fair trial under Article 6 had been infringed because the sources of evidence which comprised the Chief Superintendent's belief had been withheld at his trial. He further contended that Irish law lacked adequate measures to counterbalance the detriment that the procedure surrounding privilege and belief evidence caused to the defence. A particular focus of the applicant's challenge was the perceived procedural deficiency of the SCC's review of the material upon which the belief evidence had been based in the applicant's case: the SCC had reviewed it in private and for the purpose of deciding both the issue of disclosure and the ultimate decision to convict.[54]

Applying the general principles that govern the evidence of absent witnesses,[55] the Fifth Section of the ECtHR first considered whether it had been necessary for the SCC to uphold the claim of privilege. It recalled the strong public interest in ensuring that organised and subversive crime is prosecuted and observed that belief evidence, coupled with privilege, provides 'a crucial tool to overcome the evidential difficulties' in prosecuting the charge of membership of the IRA.[56] Thus the justifications for the grant of privilege were 'compelling and substantiated'.[57] The second tenet in the ECHR doctrine eschews interference with rights where the impugned evidence constitutes the sole or decisive basis for a conviction. Having reviewed the extensive and varied body of evidence that the prosecution had adduced at trial, the Fifth Section had little difficulty in concluding that the Chief Superintendent's evidence could not be considered to have reached

[50] *Redmond v Ireland* [2015] 4 IR 84, 89 per Hardiman J: 'It must also be said that the cross-examination of a chief superintendent giving evidence pursuant to s. 3(2) is fraught with danger because it will almost invariably open the door to the tendering by an adept and experience witness of prejudicial material, without any notice to the defence.'

[51] *Murphy v Dublin Corporation* [1972] IR 215.

[52] *Ward v Special Criminal Court* [1999] 1 IR 60, 84; *Redmond v Ireland* [2015] 4 IR 84, 95 and 127–128. Thus, the Supreme Court has also discounted the possibility of a role for 'special advocates' under Irish law. See A Harrison, Chapter 7, this volume.

[53] *Donohoe v Ireland* App no 19165/08 (ECtHR, 5th Section, 12 December 2013).

[54] Ibid, 66.

[55] *Al-Khawaja and Tahery v United Kingdom* (2012) 54 EHRR 23.

[56] *Donohoe v Ireland* App no 19165/08 (ECtHR, 5th Section, 12 December 2013) 80–81.

[57] Ibid, 81.

these thresholds.[58] At the same time, the belief evidence had not been negligible and because it 'clearly carried some weight' in establishing the applicant's guilt, the Fifth Section went on to consider the third question of whether there were sufficient procedures in place to counterbalance the detriment caused to the defence.

The Fifth Section noted that the SCC had been alert to the need to approach the Chief Superintendent's evidence with caution. It had reviewed the documentary material upon which the belief evidence was based, monitored the privilege issue throughout the trial, and excluded from consideration the material that it had reviewed on the question of disclosure.[59] Other strong counterbalancing factors cited by the ECtHR included the fact that the witness could be questioned 'on all matters collateral and accessory to the content of the privileged information'.[60] Ultimately, it held that the weight of the other evidence in the case, combined with the various counterbalancing measures, had been adequate to safeguard the fairness of the applicant's trial.[61]

In a persuasive concurring opinion, Judge Lemmens argued that the real issue in *Donohoe* was the role of the trial court with respect to privileged material. The crux of the applicant's complaint was that the same court (the SCC) had reviewed the material underlying the Chief Superintendent's belief *and* decided the applicant's guilt or innocence. By failing to address the SCC's dual role, the majority had neglected to answer the applicant's specific complaint.[62] Notwithstanding this criticism, Judge Lemmens ultimately concluded that 'despite the examination of some undisclosed, potentially damaging material' by the SCC, the applicant had not been deprived of a fair trial.[63] The concurring opinion highlighted the importance of robust, flexible procedures to govern decisions on disclosure. The absence of a dedicated mechanism in Irish law whereby undisclosed material can be reviewed by a court other than the trial court is a particular concern.[64] Irish policymakers and legislators might constructively review existing arrangements with a view to devising a principled scheme for adjudicating issues of non-disclosure.[65]

Concerns about the non-disclosure of the basis for belief evidence have been considered directly or indirectly by the Superior Courts on a number of occasions[66] including the recent case before the Court of Appeal of *DPP v Michael Connolly*.[67] The multiple grounds on which the conviction for membership of the IRA was challenged included claims relating to the trial judge's refusal to review privileged documentation that supported the belief evidence that had been adduced at trial. The appellant contended

[58] Ibid, 87.

[59] Ibid, 88.

[60] Ibid, 92.

[61] Ibid, 93. The ECtHR's analysis in *Donohoe* has been discussed favourably in subsequent Irish cases. See *People (DPP) v Donnelly, McGarrigle and Murphy* [2012] IECCA 78 (30 July 2012); *Sean Connolly v DPP* [2015] 4 IR 60 (SC); *Redmond v Ireland* [2015] 4 IR 84 (SC) (judgment of Charleton J).

[62] *Donohoe v Ireland* App no 19165/08 (ECtHR, 5th Section, 12 December 2013) concurring opinion of Judge Lemmens, 3.

[63] Ibid, 12.

[64] See O'Connor *National Security* (n 4) 108–110; Harrison *The Special Criminal Court* (n 4) 569–73.

[65] See A Harrison, Chapter 7, this volume.

[66] *Ward v Special Criminal Court* [1999] 1 IR 60; *DPP v Binead and Donohue* [2007] 1 IR 374; *DPP v Fitzpatrick and McConnell* [2013] 3 IR 656; *Redmond v Ireland* [2015] 4 IR 84; *DPP v Palmer* [2015] IECA 153.

[67] *DPP v Michael Connolly* [2018] IECA 201.

that the Chief Superintendent's invocation of privilege at trial had amounted to a bland and general refusal to answer questions and, as such, had unfairly restricted the defence's right to cross-examination.[68] It had been the defence's position that in circumstances where the Gardaí have not afforded the prosecution access to the material underlying the Chief Superintendent's belief, the SCC should either direct the prosecution to read and evaluate the material or alternatively review the material itself.[69] The SCC had refused to follow either suggestion, pointing out that the judges and lawyers are far less experienced than police officers in evaluating such information.[70]

Having conducted an extensive review of legal authorities on point,[71] the Court of Appeal acknowledged that the defence is entitled to request the trial court to review documentation but the trial court is not bound to do so.[72] Although the decision whether to review the material is within the trial court's discretion, McMahon J added the qualification that the discretion must be exercised 'judicially'.[73] In the present case, the reasons the SCC had given for declining to review the source material in the case were not persuasive; specifically, the Court of Appeal held that the reasons were insufficient to justify the SCC's refusal of the defence request.[74] Recognising that the belief evidence had contributed significantly to the guilty verdict, the Court allowed the appeal and set aside the conviction.[75]

The outcome in *Connolly* is unusual in so far as it constitutes an example of a superior court overturning a conviction for membership of an unlawful organisation because of a flaw in the process surrounding belief evidence. While the decision of the Court of Appeal affirms the importance of judicial rigour in respecting the defence's procedural rights, *Connolly* has not put to rest entirely concerns about the process whereby assertions of privilege are evaluated. The case ultimately turned on the relatively narrow point of the stated reasons for the SCC's refusal to review the supporting material and the Court of Appeal did not address other questions surrounding disclosure.

On a previous occasion, the Court considered the possible role of the prosecution in viewing the material which supports the Chief Superintendent's belief evidence. Under current practice, the prosecution does not have sight of the underlying material on security grounds and consequently does not conduct any independent review. In *DPP v Palmer*,[76]

[68] Ibid, 7–10.
[69] Ibid, 15–19.
[70] Ibid, 18–21.
[71] Such as *Ward v Special Criminal Court* [1999] 1 IR 60; *DPP v Binead* [2006] IECCA 147; *Donohoe v Ireland* App no 19165/08 (ECtHR, 5th Section, 12 December 2013).
[72] [2018] IECA 201, 50.
[73] Ibid, 50.
[74] Ibid, 52. The stated reasons included that the trial court had little experience in evaluating and assessing such information; that it was less equipped than a senior, experienced police officer in this regard; and that it did not feel that 'an inexpert and out of context analysis of intelligence material' was likely to add anything to the ultimate requirement that the belief evidence be substantiated by independent evidence. Ibid, 48. In contrast, the Court of Appeal viewed the trial court as having a wealth of relevant experience. It noted that '[j]udges are frequently, both on the civil and criminal side called upon to evaluate, analyse and assess information and evidence relating to the most complex of subjects and often in circumstances where their past experience or exposure in dealing with such issues is very limited or indeed non-existent.' Thus, 'a perceived or suspected lack of expertise' was not in itself a justification for 'a refusal to embark on the task'. Ibid, 49.
[75] Ibid, 52–53.
[76] *DPP v Palmer* [2015] IECA 153.

the Court of Appeal rejected the suggestion that this review would be an appropriate function for the DPP under section 3(2). Having emphasised that the evidence at issue in any such case comprises the belief of the Chief Superintendent and not the information in which it is grounded,[77] Birmingham P stated:

> There is no provision in the sub-section for the consideration of the material on which the Officer's belief is based by the Director of Public Prosecutions or another agency. It is not the belief of the Director of Public Prosecutions. Neither is it the Chief Superintendent's belief as approved or authorised or evaluated by the Director. The Director's functions in regard to prosecutions do not include consideration of the confidential material on which the Chief Superintendent's belief is based.[78]

The absence of a role for the DPP renders all the more significant the trial court's discretion to review the material itself. While it may be a rare case in which the defence requests the SCC to conduct such a review, it is surely an important safeguard that goes some way towards counterbalancing the lack of disclosure and its impact on the defence's right to cross-examination. The evolving case law of the Court of Appeal has clarified aspects of the operation of section 3(2) but uncertainty is likely to persist over the adequacy of procedures for disclosing the informational basis for belief evidence.[79]

VI. OTHER EVIDENTIARY ISSUES

Exploring belief evidence through the prism of a rights-based analysis runs the risk of overlooking some of the more ordinary but nevertheless potentially significant evidentiary aspects of this subject. As noted at the outset, belief evidence cuts across several rules of evidence including the general exclusion of opinion evidence. Some of the recent case law has touched upon these more mainstream evidentiary questions.

The decision of the Court of Criminal Appeal in *DPP v Donnelly, McGarrigle and Murphy*[80] raised the intriguing question of whether belief evidence can be properly characterised as a form of hearsay. The appellants challenged the compatibility of belief evidence with Article 6 of the ECHR, a question that has been considered only occasionally by the Irish courts.[81] They sought to rely, in particular, on the general antipathy in the ECtHR case law to the use in criminal trials of the hearsay statements of absent or anonymous witnesses.[82]

Writing for the Court of Criminal Appeal, O'Donnell J distinguished between belief evidence and scenarios involving the admission of the hearsay evidence of absent or anonymous witnesses on the basis that 'it is the belief of the Chief Superintendent which

[77] Ibid, 40.

[78] Ibid, 43.

[79] The practice of the Gardaí withholding access to supporting material from the prosecution was criticised recently by the SCC. 'Two on IRA charges found not guilty', *The Irish Times* (6 December 2019) 4.

[80] *DPP v Donnelly, McGarrigle and Murphy* [2012] IECCA 78 (30 July 2012).

[81] *People (DPP) v Kelly* [1990] 3 IR 115 (judgment of Charleton J); *People (DPP) v Binead and Donoghue* [2007] 1 IR 374; *People (DPP) v Matthews* [2007] 2 IR 169; *DPP v Vincent Kelly* [2007] IECCA 110 (6 December 2007).

[82] See, eg, *Doorson v The Netherlands* (1992) 22 EHRR 330; *Al-Khawaja and Tahery v United Kingdom* (2012) 54 EHRR 23.

is evidence, and not the material upon which that belief is based'.[83] This 'structural distinction' was endorsed by the ECtHR's Fifth Section in *Donohoe v Ireland;* ironically, although the Fifth Section reasoned that the evidence comprised the testimony of the Chief Superintendent and not the undisclosed sources that informed his belief, it went on, nevertheless, to apply the principles governing the evidence of absent witnesses in order to determine whether the applicant had received a fair trial under Article 6.[84]

O'Donnell J noted in *Donnelly, McGarrigle and Murphy* that a Chief Superintendent's belief may be based on 'a variety of sources: technological, electronic and human'.[85] However, it is also true that it may rest on the word of an informer alone; section 3(2) of the 1972 Act allows for the possibility that an informer is the direct and even exclusive source of the evidence.[86] Where this occurs, and belief evidence plays a decisive role in the outcome of the case, the cogency of the distinction between belief evidence and the ECHR case law on absent witnesses may be difficult to sustain. Though arguably a plausible characterisation in such cases, the idea of belief evidence as hearsay has not found traction in the Irish case law. The judgment in *Donnelly* was reinforced by the Court of Appeal in *DPP v Palmer*[87] quoted with approval by the Supreme Court in *DPP v Connolly*.[88]

Another evidentiary issue of considerable significance is the weight that the Special Criminal Court attributes to belief evidence. The legislation is silent in this regard and in the early years the SCC tackled the question on a case-by-case basis.[89] In some instances, belief evidence constituted the sole plank in the prosecution's case and, initially at least, the SCC was willing in principle to convict on belief evidence alone.[90] The cogency of the witness's belief could vary enormously from one case to the next and the Court placed particular store in the willingness of the accused to take the stand and challenge the belief evidence.[91] There remains some variation in the contemporary practice of the SCC regarding the weight it attaches to belief evidence: the issue is sometimes addressed in detail and at other times in a perfunctory fashion.[92]

The mercurial quality of belief evidence was captured in Geoghegan J's remark in *People (DPP) v Kelly* that '[t]he Chief Superintendent's evidence has no special status but is merely a piece of admissible evidence'. The majority of the Court thus endorsed the view that the balancing of the conflicting rights and interests caught up in belief evidence

[83] *DPP v Donnelly, McGarrigle and Murphy* [2012] IECCA 78, 27 (drawing on the Supreme Court's decision in *People (DPP) v Kelly* [2006] 3 IR 115).

[84] *Donohoe v Ireland*, App no 19165/08 (ECtHR, 5th Section, 12 December 2013) 78. See the judgment of Charleton J in *Redmond v Ireland* [2015] 4 IR 84, 125–127 (referring to the judgments of the CCA in *Donnelly* and the ECtHR in *Donohoe* with approval).

[85] *DPP v Donnelly, McGarrigle and Murphy* [2012] IECCA 78, 27.

[86] Hardiman J seemed to recognise as much in *Redmond v Ireland* [2015] 4 IR 84, 95–96 when he spoke of 'a prosecution which relies for evidence, wholly or mainly, on a hearsay statement of the contents of such a third party'.

[87] *DPP v Palmer* [2015] IECA 153, 40–41.

[88] *Sean Connolly v DPP* [2015] 4 IR 60, 32 and 46. See also the judgment of Charleton J in *Redmond v Ireland* [2015] 4 IR 84, 126.

[89] GW Hogan and C Walker, *Political Violence and the Law in Ireland* (Manchester, Manchester University Press, 1989) 249 (discussing *People (DPP) v Ferguson*, unreported, Court of Criminal Appeal, 27 Oct 1975).

[90] M Robinson, *The Special Criminal Court* (Dublin, Dublin University Press, 1974) 32.

[91] Heffernan, 'Evidence and National Security' (n 4) 72–73.

[92] See, eg, *People (DPP) v Binead and Donohue*, unreported, SCC, 18 Nov 2004; *People (DPP) v McGurk* [1994] 2 IR 579.

was a matter for the trial court.[93] Fennelly J espoused a more exacting standard of appellate review and commented that the SCC should have explained the weight, if any, which it had attached to the Chief Superintendent's evidence.[94]

In his concurring judgment in *Redmond v Ireland*, Charleton J drew on the judgment in *Kelly* when discussing the weight of belief evidence. He emphasised that 'there is no special status to such evidence' and rejected the idea that section 3(2) had created 'any presumption, evidential or substantive'.[95] Having observed that where belief evidence is supported by some other form of evidence no constitutional concern arises,[96] Charleton J remarked: 'The assessment of and the weight to be attached to evidence is a matter for the judges at trial. There is no legal formula in that regard.'[97]

VII. CONCLUSION

Belief evidence has been an effective tool in the prosecution of terrorist crime but its continued prominence is perhaps surprising when one considers the dramatic changes that have occurred in the investigation, prosecution and trial of offences over the past 45 years. Today, law enforcement agencies have at their disposal the full gamut of technological evidence, extended powers of investigation and detention, and measures to protect and support witnesses. Even so, belief evidence continues to play a key role in prosecutions for membership under section 21 of the 1939 Act. Moreover, the influence of belief evidence can be seen in legislation on organised crime which renders admissible the opinion of current or former members of the Gardaí as to the existence of criminal organisations.[98]

The history of the OASA reflects the risks that preserving national security can pose for the protection of rights: specifically, belief evidence embodies an inherent tension between the need for secrecy in matters relating to national security and the imperative of safeguarding the accused's constitutional and internationally protected right to a fair trial. The challenge of reconciling these competing societal interests is compounded in an Irish setting by the use of non-jury trials and the conflation of the roles of finder of law and finder of fact within the trial process. The case can be made that at least some of the dangers identified by the Committee to Review the OASA in their introductory comments

[93] *People (DPP) v Kelly* [2006] 3 IR 115, 122.

[94] Ibid, 146–47. But see *DPP v Vincent Kelly* [2007] IECCA 110, 6 (Finnegan J construing Fennelly J's remarks as stopping short of requiring the trial court to express the weight it attaches to belief evidence 'in the form of a mathematical notation or other scale of values …'.)

[95] *Redmond v Ireland* [2015] 4 IR 84, 124. He went on to observe that, nevertheless, 'courts of trial are alert to the need for caution', a point that had been acknowledged by the Supreme Court in *Connolly v DPP* [2015] 4 IR 60 and the ECtHR in *Donohoe v Ireland*, App no 19165/08 (ECtHR, 5th Section, 12 December 2013).

[96] *Redmond v Ireland* [2015] 4 IR 84, 129.

[97] [2015] 4 IR 84, 130. Thus, the weight of the belief evidence and the other evidence is a matter for the trial court and 'there is no order in which each such piece of evidence is to be assessed'. Ibid, 129.

[98] Criminal Justice Act 2006, s 71B(1) (as inserted by s 7 of the Criminal Justice (Amendment) Act 2009). The offences created by the 2006 Act include participation in or contribution to the activities of a criminal organisation directed towards the commission of serious offences in Ireland or abroad (s 72). The opinion evidence is admissible where the current or former Garda officer appears to the trial court to possess 'appropriate expertise' (s 71B(1)). Seemingly the impact of this legislative development has yet to be felt in case law and practice.

(quoted at the beginning of this chapter) have come to fruition in the continued application of belief evidence.

The Committee was itself divided in its recommendation regarding belief evidence. A majority surmised that section 3(2) violated canons of evidence but nevertheless recommended that the subsection be retained subject to the amendment that no person should be convicted on belief evidence alone.[99] A minority of the Committee favoured the repeal of section 3(2) taking the view that it violates rules of evidence and is likely to be incompatible with Article 6 of the ECHR.[100] Case law developments have broadened discourse about belief evidence in the 15 years since the Committee reported its findings but have not dispelled concerns about the protection of rights and the integrity of evidence. The time is surely ripe for renewed reflection, review and, ultimately, reform.

[99] Committee to Review the OASA Acts, 6.93. Beyond this recommendation, the majority was itself divided.

[100] Ibid, 6.196 (views and recommendations of Hederman J, Professor William Binchy and Professor Dermot Walsh). Professor Gerard Hogan also disagreed with the majority's pragmatic defence of s 3(2) which he considered insufficient to overcome constitutional and evidential objections. Ibid, 6.95.

7

Disclosure and Privilege: The Dual Role of the Special Criminal Court in Relation to Belief Evidence

ALICE HARRISON

I. INTRODUCTION

LIKE ANY OTHER trial court, the Special Criminal Court has full discretion to adjudicate issues of disclosure and privilege. In the ordinary courts, where such a dispute arises, the trial judge will be able to consider the evidence and make a ruling, ensuring that the jury does not have access to any inadmissible or prejudicial evidence. In the non-jury Special Criminal Court, the court is both arbiter of law and fact and the same three judges determine issues relating to admissibility or privilege and subsequently decide upon the guilt or innocence of the accused, notwithstanding that they have heard the impugned evidence. The issue is particularly acute in a trial for membership of an unlawful organisation where belief evidence of a Chief Superintendent is relied upon by the prosecution as one of the central strands of evidence grounding a conviction. In order to settle a dispute relating to privilege, the court may inspect the material upon which the Chief Superintendent's belief is based and may be exposed to material which – by its very nature – is extremely prejudicial to the accused, without the accused being able to challenge it in any meaningful way. The court will then have to attempt to remove any prejudicial information from its mind prior to deciding on the ultimate issue in the case.

This chapter examines the jurisprudence on the issue in order to demonstrate the dilemma faced by an accused charged with membership in the Special Criminal Court where a dispute over disclosure and privilege arises. The question of whether inspection by the court can actually be a safeguard for an accused is considered. The chapter also addresses how various solutions to this problem have been considered and dismissed at different times and finally concludes that consideration of the material in question by a differently constituted court, in conjunction with a prosecution obligation to review the material, might improve matters for the defence in a membership trial where such a dispute arises.[1]

[1] This chapter draws upon the author's book, A Harrison, *The Special Criminal Court: Practice and Procedure* (Dublin, Bloomsbury Professional, 2019), ch 8.

II. NON-DISCLOSURE ON THE GROUNDS OF PRIVILEGE AND THE DISCRETION TO INSPECT

Where privilege is claimed by the state over certain material during a criminal trial, it may become necessary for a court to hold a *voir dire* in order to determine a controversy over its disclosure. For example, if the defence challenges a claim of public interest privilege, it is for the court to balance the public interest in the administration of justice with the particular public interest claimed by the state.[2] In this way, the court can determine whether the claim of privilege should be upheld. Similarly, where the state resists disclosure in order to protect the lives of informers, there is a strict principle of non-disclosure unless the court finds that the innocence of the accused is at stake.[3] Disclosure must be ordered if the court finds the latter to be the case.

When a court is required to resolve a dispute over disclosure, it has full discretion in relation to whether to inspect documents in order to resolve the dispute.[4] It is clear from the dicta in *DPP v Special Criminal Court and Ward*[5] that there is no obligation on the courts to do so in every case and more recent case law suggests that the discretion to inspect material must be exercised judicially.[6] The Supreme Court in *Ward*,[7] which arose from the trial of the accused for the murder of journalist Veronica Guerin, stressed the fact that the trial court – in this case the Special Criminal Court – had full discretion to decide how a trial was conducted and, in particular, how a controversy about disclosure should be resolved.[8] As such, the Court removed a High Court direction to the Special Criminal Court to inspect certain statements from Garda informants – which were not contained in the book of evidence – over which the prosecution claimed privilege. In emphasising that the trial judge did not have to look at undisclosed evidence in every case, O'Flaherty J noted the 'critical role' of counsel for the prosecution in 'disclosing all relevant material to the defence'.[9] He noted, however, that: 'the duty that will devolve on the members of the court will be a continuing one as the trial develops and evolves. The members of the court will be astute, no doubt, to monitor the situation throughout.'[10]

Absent any unusual or particular circumstances, there does not appear to be any real concern where a trial judge in the ordinary courts chooses to inspect documents in order to determine a dispute over disclosure and privilege. If material is ruled inadmissible, the jury will not be exposed to it and can proceed with its role as the ultimate fact-finder without knowing anything of the prejudicial material. The difficulty arises where the Special Criminal Court inspects material over which privilege is claimed since the court is both arbiter of fact and law. Notwithstanding this, the Supreme Court in *Ward* was satisfied that the Special Criminal Court has a discretion to inspect material in order to determine a dispute over privilege. However, in *Ward*, privilege was claimed over 'unused

[2] *Murphy v Dublin Corporation* [1972] IR 215, 233–234.
[3] *DPP v Special Criminal Court and Ward* [1999] 1 IR 60, 87.
[4] *DPP v Special Criminal Court and Ward* [1999] 1 IR 60.
[5] Ibid, 88 (O'Flaherty J).
[6] *People (DPP) v Connolly* [2018] IECA 201.
[7] *DPP v Special Criminal Court and Ward* [1999] 1 IR 60.
[8] Ibid, 88 (O'Flaherty J).
[9] Ibid, 87. The role of the prosecution in relation to disclosure and privilege is discussed in further detail below.
[10] Ibid, 88. See also, *People (DPP) v Nevin* [2003] 3 IR 321.

material' or material that was not being used by the prosecution during trial. In other words, the issue for consideration by the Supreme Court was the inspection of material by the Special Criminal Court in circumstances where that material did not necessarily go toward the ultimate issue of guilt or innocence. The position is somewhat different where the prosecution relies on the 'belief evidence' of a Chief Superintendent that the accused is a member of an unlawful organisation, contrary to section 21 of the Offences Against the State Act 1939 (OASA). Since belief evidence goes toward the ultimate issue of the guilt or innocence of the accused, inspection by the Special Criminal Court of the material underlying the belief evidence in order to determine a dispute over privilege is objectionable for most accused persons.

III. BELIEF EVIDENCE AND THE PROBLEM WITH INSPECTION BY THE SPECIAL CRIMINAL COURT

In a trial for membership of an unlawful organisation, the Special Criminal Court may treat the opinion of a Chief Superintendent of An Garda Síochána that an accused was a member of an unlawful organisation as evidence of that fact.[11] In other words, where 'belief evidence' is used, it is proffered by the prosecution to the Special Criminal Court as inculpatory evidence of membership. Belief evidence is an important tool for the prosecution since the nebulous offence of membership would be extremely difficult to prove without it – there is no definition or specific criteria for membership contained in the OASA and there is no requirement for the physical manifestation of the offence. A Chief Superintendent's belief is generally based on a variety of sources, potentially including information furnished by informers or other persons and information gathered pursuant to different forms of surveillance.

A claim of privilege will generally accompany the use of belief evidence, ordinarily justified by the prosecuting authorities with reference to the dangers posed by subversive organisations, the reprisals an informer might face and the difficulties in proving the offence of membership of an unlawful organisation without the assistance of protected sources. It would appear that, in the past, some – albeit limited – information relating to the basis for the Chief Superintendent's belief was generally furnished to the defence. For example, information of the time period in which a Chief Superintendent formed his belief or whether the material which a Chief Superintendent considered was human or non-human has been disclosed in previous trials.[12] In more recent times, the state has often asserted a blanket claim of privilege over all of the materials relating to the basis for the Chief Superintendent's belief evidence and it seems as though the current trend in

[11] Pursuant to s 3(2) of the Offences Against the State (Amendment) Act 1972. See L Heffernan and E O'Connor, Chapter 6, this volume.

[12] See, eg, *People (DPP) v Maguire* [2008] IECCA 67; *People (DPP) v Kelly* [2006] 3 IR 115 and *Donohoe v Ireland* [2013] ECHR 1363. The Chief Superintendent in *People (DPP) v Maguire* [2008] IECCA 67 disclosed that '… He had received information about the applicant's status in the IRA at various times, and knew the identity of all the sources of the information, none of whom had been paid, so far as he knew, and none of whom had previous convictions, so far as he knew. Further he had checked the information, which came from both Garda and non-Garda origins, by assessing it with other information and by looking at the totality of the same emanating from different sources, verifying also whether the sources had been accurate in the giving of information in the past ….'

membership cases is to disclose little or no information relating to the basis for the Chief Superintendent's belief to the defence.[13] Where the disclosure furnished to the defence is limited, or non-existent, the defence is extremely hampered in its cross-examination of the Chief Superintendent and is not in a position to challenge his belief or the basis for his belief through cross-examination. Whilst the courts have pointed out that an accused's right of cross-examination is not entirely eliminated where belief evidence is relied upon,[14] this issue may need to be re-considered. It is arguable that the potential for cross-examination is in fact eliminated where such a sweeping claim of privilege is made.[15]

If the defence seeks disclosure of the material over which privilege is claimed in order to be able to conduct a more effective cross-examination, the Special Criminal Court will have to determine the controversy and decide whether or not to uphold the claim of privilege or to order disclosure. If a claim of privilege is ultimately upheld, a Chief Superintendent is not required to disclose any privileged documents to the defence or answer any questions in relation to the underlying facts, materials or sources which led to his belief on the basis that disclosure of this information could result in a credible threat to the life of persons or to the ongoing security of the state.[16]

During a dispute over disclosure and privilege, the defence must decide whether to ask the court to review the Chief Superintendent's file. Where the Special Criminal Court inspects the file, this necessarily involves the consideration of material which forms the basis for inculpatory evidence in the case. There is an inherent unfairness in a situation where the Special Criminal Court has both reviewed the Chief Superintendent's file – perhaps becoming exposed to prejudicial information which the accused has not had an opportunity to test or challenge – and is also the ultimate arbiter of fact as to the guilt or innocence of the accused. Given the risks involved, the occasions upon which the defence asks the Special Criminal Court to inspect the file are rare and a person accused of membership of an unlawful organisation is often left in a position where he is simply unable to challenge the belief evidence in a meaningful way. Even if the defence elects not to ask the court to review the file, the court has full discretion as to how to resolve a dispute over disclosure and may inspect the file of its own volition.[17] For the reasons already considered, this is an unpalatable situation for an accused before the Special Criminal Court charged with membership of an unlawful organisation.

IV. PRACTICE UPHELD BY THE SUPERIOR COURTS AND THE ECHR

Both the superior courts in this jurisdiction and the European Court of Human Rights (ECHR) have thus far refused challenges on the basis of fair trial rights in circumstances

[13] See, eg, *People (DPP) v Weldon* [2018] IECA 197 and *People (DPP) v Connolly* (Bill No 0009/2014, 24 June 2019) SCC).

[14] See *Donohoe v Ireland* [2013] ECHR 1363, para 92; *People (DPP) v Donnelly, McGarrigle and Murphy* [2012] IECCA 78, para 31.

[15] This issue was raised in the case of *People (DPP) v K and M* (Bill No 0012/2017, 5 December 2019), which is currently under appeal by the DPP following the acquittal of the accused by the Special Criminal Court at the direction stage.

[16] *People (DPP) v Binéad and Donohue* [2007] 1 IR 374, Macken J interpreting the *dicta* in *People (DPP) v Kelly* [2006] 3 IR 115.

[17] *DPP v Special Criminal Court and Ward* [1999] 1 IR 60, 88; *People (DPP) v Binéad and Donohue* [2007] 1 IR 374, 397. See, eg, *People (DPP) v Connolly* (Bill No 0009/2014, 24 June 2019) SCC).

where the Special Criminal Court inspected documents relating to belief evidence.[18] In fact, the ECHR has found that the inspection of material by the court is actually a safeguard which has the effect of neutralising any unfairness arising from the non-disclosure of such material to the defence.

In *People (DPP) v Binéad and Donohue*,[19] the Special Criminal Court inspected documents pertaining to the source for a Chief Superintendent's belief evidence and ruled that: (a) it was satisfied that the belief evidence was based on adequate and reliable information; and (b) nothing within the documentation would assist the accused in proving their innocence. The review of the material had been undertaken at the request of one of the accused only, and the second accused objected to the exercise. The Court of Criminal Appeal held that there was nothing unfair in the procedure – the trial court had followed the very full discretion to inspect the material, pursuant to the decision in *Ward*.[20] Macken J, in *Binéad and Donohue*, stated as follows:

> [J]udges sitting without a jury, such as in the Special Criminal Court, have long experience in removing from their consideration material or evidence which may have been admitted in error, or opened to them, even inadvertently, or which has otherwise come to their attention. A typical example exists every time a trial court, and not just the Special Criminal Court, conducts a *voir dire*, a trial within a trial.[21]

The Court also pointed out that the trial was not unfair in circumstances where the Special Criminal Court had ruled that it would not convict without supportive or corroborative evidence of that belief – thereby indicating that the belief evidence was not determinative of the guilt or innocence of the accused. The second accused, who had resisted the Court's viewing of the documents, applied to the Court of Criminal Appeal to obtain leave pursuant to section 29 of the Courts of Justice Act 1924 to appeal the decision to the Supreme Court as a matter of exceptional public importance but the Court refused to certify the matter.[22]

An application arising out of this case was subsequently made by the second accused to the ECHR. In that case, *Donohoe v Ireland*,[23] the applicant's central complaint focused on the trial court's review of the material upon which the belief evidence was based but the Court found that there had been no violation of the applicant's fair trial rights under Article 6 of the Convention. The Court made a number of observations in relation to the circumstances in which the belief evidence had been given and the counter-balances to the restriction imposed on the accused.[24] What is of particular relevance to the present discussion is the fact that the Court regarded the inspection of the non-disclosed material by the trial court as being one of a number of safeguards where belief evidence had been relied upon during the applicant's trial. The Court found that the fact that the trial court undertook a review, whilst not in itself a sufficient safeguard, did allow the trial court to monitor the fairness of the trial.

[18] *People (DPP) v Binéad and Donohue* [2007] 1 IR 374; *People (DPP) v Donohue* [2008] 2 IR 193; *Donohoe v Ireland* [2013] ECHR 1363.

[19] *People (DPP) v Binéad and Donohue* [2007] 1 IR 374.

[20] *DPP v Special Criminal Court and Ward* [1999] 1 IR 60.

[21] *People (DPP) v Binéad and Donohue* [2007] 1 IR 374, 397.

[22] *People (DPP) v Donohue* [2008] 2 IR 193.

[23] *Donohoe v Ireland* [2013] ECHR 1363.

[24] *Al-Khawaja and Tahery v United Kingdom* (Case 26766/05, 2012) 54 EHRR 23, para 147.

Amongst the other safeguards was the fact that the trial court was alive to the innocence at stake exception in relation to a claim of privilege and was vigilant in exploring whether the non-disclosed material was relevant or likely to be relevant to the defence. Furthermore, the Special Criminal Court had specifically stated that it had excluded any irrelevant material when coming to its conclusions on whether to convict the accused and that it would not convict the accused based on belief evidence alone.[25] It was also important for the ECHR that section 3(2) of the Offences Against the State (Amendment) Act 1972 allowed only Garda officers of a high rank to give belief evidence and that the belief evidence was proffered as opinion rather than fact and had no special status other than being a piece of admissible evidence to be considered by the trial court. Finally, the Court noted that the possibility to cross-examine the witness was not entirely eliminated.[26]

It is arguable that the judgment of the Court did not fully engage with the arguments made by the applicant in relation to the dual role of the Special Criminal Court and the question of inspection. In other words, the judgment of the majority placed more emphasis on the various safeguards employed where belief evidence was used, rather than analysing the fact that it was the same court which reviewed the privileged material and later decided on the issue of guilt. Interestingly, the opinion of Lemmens J, although ultimately concurring with the decision that there had been no violation of Article 6, lamented the reasoning adopted by the majority. He pointed out that the applicant did not take issue with the admissibility of the belief evidence nor the non-disclosure of underlying material, but instead objected to the inherent unfairness in the fact that the trial court reviewed the material upon which the belief was based, formed a view as to its reliability and later convicted the applicant, all the while denying the applicant an opportunity to challenge the evidence in any meaningful way. He stated that:

> [W]hile the majority correctly quote the applicant's complaint ... it seems to me that they do not focus their reasoning on the dual role of the trial court ... With all due respect, it seems to me that the majority thus fail to give an answer to the specific complaint made by the applicant.[27]

It would indeed appear to be the case that the majority of the Court did not focus on the arguments put before the Court in relation to the review of privileged material by the Special Criminal Court.[28] This may have left some scope for further argument before the ECHR on the issue and its re-consideration by that Court would be a welcome development. The current position – where the non-jury court, as the tribunal of law and

[25] *Donohoe v Ireland* [2013] ECHR 1363, para 88.

[26] Ibid, para 92 – a similar sentiment to that expressed by O'Donnell J in *People (DPP) v Donnelly, McGarrigle and Murphy* [2012] IECCA 78, para 31. It seems, however, that in recent times, the state has chosen to disclose practically no information relating to the basis for the Chief Superintendent's belief evidence to the defence and has often asserted a blanket claim of privilege over the file. It is arguable that the potential for meaningful cross-examination is restricted even more so where such a claim of privilege is made. One might consider the detail relating to the Chief Superintendent's belief that was furnished to the defendant in *People (DPP) v Maguire* [2008] IECCA 67 (see n 12 above) in contrast to the current trend in recent membership cases where a blanket claim of privilege is asserted over all materials relating to the basis for the belief evidence and the Chief Superintendent's file (See, eg, *People (DPP) v Weldon* [2018] IECA 197 and *People (DPP) v Connolly* (Bill No 0009/2014, 24 June 2019) SCC).

[27] *Donohoe v Ireland* [2013] ECHR 1363, Concurring Opinion of Lemmens J, para 3.

[28] See also, *People (DPP) v Fitzpatrick and McConnell* [2013] 3 IR 656, where the issue was not decided since it had been advanced on hypothetical grounds.

fact, must attempt to remove controversial and possibly prejudicial material from its mind prior to deciding on the ultimate issue in the case – is unsatisfactory and inherently unfair. Even in circumstances where the court succeeds in doing so, there still exists a very real issue where, objectively, the perception could be that it has not.

V. INSPECTION BY THE SPECIAL CRIMINAL COURT AS A SAFEGUARD?

As discussed, the Court in *Donohoe v Ireland*[29] specifically referred to the inspection of documents by the Special Criminal Court as one of the safeguards for an accused where belief evidence is used and it must be acknowledged that, despite the risk involved for an accused where the Special Criminal Court inspects a Chief Superintendent's file, inspection by the court can prevent an injustice.

In the case of *People (DPP) v Connolly*,[30] despite a request from the defence for the prosecution counsel to review the documentation and information grounding the belief evidence of an Assistant Commissioner of An Garda Síochána to ensure adequate disclosure had been made, the investigating authorities refused prosecution counsel access to the file. Consequently, the defence took the rare step of asking the trial court to review the documentation in order to determine a claim of privilege. The prosecution did not object to this course of action but the Special Criminal Court declined to do so. The Court was of the view that an 'inexpert and out of context analysis of intelligence material' would not be of assistance in assessing the belief evidence and that there was no necessity in any event, given the constitutional requirement for corroborating evidence where belief evidence is used.[31] The Court of Appeal subsequently allowed the appeal on the basis of the trial court's refusal to view the privileged documentation. Mahon J noted that a trial court is not bound to conduct a review of documentation simply because it is asked to do so and cited *Ward*,[32] where O'Flaherty J had highlighted the critical role of the prosecution in this context. However, Mahon J pointed out that the court must exercise its discretion judicially.[33] Allowing the appeal, he stated that the trial court consisted of criminal judges experienced in dealing with all aspects of information analysis in the context of criminal proceedings and the administration of justice. The Court found that 'a perceived or suspected lack of expertise … is not itself a reason for a refusal' to view documentation in order to determine a claim of privilege.[34] Whilst not explicitly stated in the judgment, it is reasonable to assume that, absent any particular and unusual circumstances, a refusal by a trial court to review material which has not been seen by counsel for the prosecution, following a request from the accused, would not be a judicial exercise of discretion.[35]

In the subsequent retrial in *Connolly*, the Court was asked by the defence to review the Garda file upon which the Assistant Commissioner's belief was based, in order to

[29] *Donohoe v Ireland* [2013] ECHR 1363.
[30] *People (DPP) v Connolly* [2018] IECA 201.
[31] *Redmond v Ireland* [2015] 4 IR 84, 97 (Hardiman J).
[32] *DPP v Special Criminal Court and Ward* [1999] 1 IR 60.
[33] *People (DPP) v Connolly* [2018] IECA 201, para 50.
[34] Ibid, para 49.
[35] Harrison, *The Special Criminal Court* (n 1) 570. A refusal would mean that neither the prosecution nor the trial court would have seen the material over which privilege had been claimed.

determine whether there were any documents on the file which ought to be disclosed under the innocence at stake exception to public interest privilege. The Court acceded to the request and, following a review of the file, ordered the disclosure of the extracts of two documents relating to the accused's movements on a certain date. The argument was subsequently made by the defence that this evidence was not independent evidence and fell foul of the rule against 'double counting'. This rule requires that the material which has been used by the Chief Superintendent as the basis for his belief is not used at trial by the prosecution and is not relied upon by the Special Criminal Court in considering the guilt or innocence of the accused.[36] It was described by the Court in *Connolly* as 'a corollary' of the requirement for corroboration and 'therefore an important safeguard which this Court must strictly uphold to counter balance the use of belief evidence.'[37] The Court held that, although the Assistant Commissioner had analysed the file in a careful and methodical way, he did not expressly address the issue of double counting or take any precautions to ensure that it did not occur. As such, the Court was not satisfied beyond reasonable doubt that he adhered to the rule. The Court could not be sure that the documents relating to the accused's movements on a particular day were not taken into account by the Assistant Commissioner and therefore could not be sure that it was evidence which was independent of that upon which the Assistant Commissioner relied in forming his belief. In those circumstances, the Court could not be satisfied beyond reasonable doubt of the guilt of the accused. His acquittal, therefore, was a direct result of the inspection of the Assistant Commissioner's file by the Special Criminal Court.

Notwithstanding this fact, the case of *Connolly* presented an atypical situation in that the defence had taken the rare step of asking the Special Criminal Court to review the file. This decision often creates a dilemma for the accused, and for most, it is simply not worth the risk.

VI. THE DILEMMA FOR AN ACCUSED IN RELATION TO INSPECTION

Whilst it is clear from the case law that there is no obligation on the courts to inspect documents in every case where a dispute over disclosure and privilege arises, it remains open to the Special Criminal Court to do so. The superior courts and the ECHR have found that there is no issue with inspection by the Special Criminal Court and, indeed, have held that the review of a Chief Superintendent's file by the court is one of a number of safeguards that exist where belief evidence is relied upon. It is true that inspection by the court can on occasion prevent an injustice, as in *Connolly*,[38] but the situation remains unsatisfactory.

In order to make a request of the Special Criminal Court to inspect the file of the Chief Superintendent – the tribunal which will ultimately decide on the guilt or innocence of the accused – the defence would have to approach the matter with very considerable

[36] *People (DPP) v Gannon* (2 April 2003) CCA.
[37] *People (DPP) v Connolly* (Bill No 0009/2014, 24 June 2019) SCC.
[38] *People (DPP) v Connolly* [2018] IECA 201.

caution and with an absolute certainty that there is nothing prejudicial contained within the material. In other words, in order to invoke the 'safeguard' of review by the Special Criminal Court, an accused is forced to speculate as to what may be contained within the Chief Superintendent's file. This is a difficult position for any accused charged with membership since the file will often contain information furnished by informers or gathered pursuant to different forms of surveillance and an accused is likely to be unaware of the nature or extent of the detail contained in the file. In those circumstances, the defence may not be willing to ask the Special Criminal Court to look at the file. Indeed, experience shows that the occasions upon which a person accused of membership before the Special Criminal Court will ask the court to review the file are extremely rare. Consequently, the viability of alternative options must be considered.

VII. THE VIABILITY OF ALTERNATIVE OPTIONS

The dual role of the Special Criminal Court as arbiter of law and fact is undesirable from the perspective of the defence but alternative options have consistently been considered and dismissed by the superior courts. These options include the inspection of materials by a differently constituted court, the recognition of an obligation on the prosecution to review the Chief Superintendent's file, the disclosure of material to legal representatives only and the use of 'special advocates'. As can be seen from the discussion below, each of the options for reform are not without their own difficulties and have, thus far, not been considered to be viable solutions to the contentious dual role of the Special Criminal Court.

A. Consideration and Inspection by a Differently Constituted Court

It is possible that matters of pre-trial disclosure could be settled in advance of a trial by means of a differently constituted panel of judges to the panel which ultimately conducts the trial. This would be especially beneficial in the context of the inevitable dispute over privilege associated with the use of belief evidence. These issues could be decided on the basis of a pre-trial hearing by a court which is not ultimately accepting belief evidence as evidence to ground a conviction for membership of an unlawful organisation. In the UK, where the prosecution intends to withhold evidence on the grounds that it would be damaging to the public interest to disclose that evidence, a 'public interest immunity application' must be made by the prosecution to the court. This can be done on an ex parte basis or on notice to the defence – in the latter situation, the defence is entitled to make submissions to the court. If the court decides to uphold the claim of privilege, the defence can apply for a review of the non-disclosure order at any time prior to conviction or acquittal.

The approach in the UK has a number of issues, however, especially if the application is heard ex parte.[39] For example, if there is a failure on the part of investigators to

[39] C Taylor, 'What next for Public Interest Immunity?', (2005) 69(1) *Journal of Criminal Law*, 75, 79.

examine the material in their possession adequately or to put all relevant material before the court, this may result in an injustice to an accused who is absent at the time of the application.[40] Neither the prosecution nor the court may be able to estimate the significance of a particular piece of information to the conduct of the defence if the application is made at a time when the nature of the defence is unclear.[41] Another difficulty arises from the fact that the court cannot look behind a ministerial certificate declaring that the disclosure of material would result in a risk to national security.[42]

The principal issue with pre-trial disclosure hearings is apparent when one considers the nature of disclosure as a continuing obligation on the prosecution and the duty of the trial judge to keep the matter under constant review as the trial proceeds. The obvious benefit of the current system in Ireland is that trial court has the ability to monitor and review the question of privilege throughout the trial and similarly, to monitor and review the fairness of the trial throughout. Similarly, a court in the UK which has dealt with a public interest immunity application can itself keep the matter under review during the trial.

Nonetheless, the approach in the UK does provide a model of sorts for a pre-trial disclosure hearing in this jurisdiction. Although Carney J in the High Court in *DPP v Special Criminal Court and Ward*[43] rejected the idea of a different chamber of the court dealing with the matter, he gave no reasons for this conclusion. In *People (DPP) v Fitzpatrick and McConnell*,[44] O'Donnell J stated that if matters of disclosure and privilege are agitated well in advance of the trial, 'it also might allow a differently constituted court to address the issue if that was thought necessary or desirable'.[45] This option is something that has not yet been utilised by the Special Criminal Court and may be more viable since the introduction of the second Special Criminal Court in 2016. The Law Reform Commission published a report in December 2014 recommending the introduction of legislation to clarify the prosecution duty to disclose in criminal trials, which would cover non-party disclosure and pre-trial hearings for determining issues of disclosure and privilege.[46] Indeed, the Director of Public Prosecutions has recently advocated the use of pre-trial procedures in criminal trials generally.[47] This proposal, though not specific to the Special Criminal Court, is a welcome one and would be particularly beneficial in the context of that court since it would go some way to alleviate the problem created by the dual role of the court as arbiter of law and fact.

[40] See, eg, *R v West (Ricky)* [2005] EWCA Crim 517, para 10 (Mance LJ) where the Court of Appeal found that all relevant material had not been placed before the trial judge. See also, C Taylor, 'Case Commentary, Public Interest Immunity: *R v West (Ricky)* [2005] EWCA Crim 517', (2005) 69(4) *Journal of Criminal Law*, 306, 310.

[41] *R v West (Ricky)* [2005] EWCA Crim 517, paras 8–9 (Mance LJ).

[42] Although, it should be noted that in *R (Al-Sweady) v Secretary of State for Defence* [2009] EWHC 1687 (Admin), the ministerial certificate claimed privilege over material that had been previously disclosed in other open court hearings and the Court held that the courts should approach the contents of such a certificate with caution until the Ministry of Defence had demonstrated that such errors would not recur.

[43] *DPP v Special Criminal Court and Ward* [1999] 1 IR 60.

[44] *People (DPP) v Fitzpatrick and McConnell* [2013] 3 IR 656.

[45] Ibid, 663.

[46] Law Reform Commission, 'Report on Disclosure and Discovery in Criminal Cases' 112/2014 (December 2014).

[47] A Hardiman, 'As Justice Requires' (2019) 24(2) *Bar Review* 40.

B. Recognising an Obligation on Prosecution Counsel to Review Material

It has been explicitly stated by the courts that prosecution counsel – who have an overall responsibility to assist in ensuring a fair trial – have a 'critical' role in relation to documents over which privilege is claimed.[48] The prosecution is also under an ongoing obligation to keep the question of disclosure of relevant material under review as the trial progresses. It might therefore be expected that the prosecution would engage in this role where the claim of privilege is made in respect of material underlying a Chief Superintendent's belief evidence.[49] If the prosecution took the opportunity to examine the Chief Superintendent's file in order to ensure that proper disclosure had been made, this may reduce the risk of the court inspecting the disputed material.

Indeed, Charleton J, in his minority judgment in the Supreme Court case of *Redmond v Ireland*[50] appears to suggest that the prosecution would examine the information underlying 'belief' evidence:

> [D]ocuments would not be given to the accused in the event of their pointing to the innocence of the accused. Rather, prosecution counsel would, in the role which O'Flaherty J characterises as being that of 'ministers of justice', scrutinise the documents as to the innocence at stake exception and report their findings to the defence … There are basically only two possible reports of such scrutiny: firstly, that innocence has not been imperilled by anything within the materials; and, secondly, if it is that the prosecution will not proceed with the charge because the privilege of the informer is not theirs to waive. The defence are, in addition to scrutiny by the prosecution, within their rights to seek to ask the court of three judges sitting as the Special Criminal Court to look at the documents themselves, and to rule if innocence is anywhere supported therein.[51]

However, a number of months before *Redmond* was decided, the Court of Appeal refused to accept that the Director of Public Prosecutions was under any obligation to review materials in order to assess the reliability of the belief evidence of a Chief Superintendent and the suitability of the claim of privilege over it. It was held that the Special Criminal Court had correctly relied upon the belief evidence to the effect that the accused were members of the IRA notwithstanding that the prosecution had not seen the underlying material. In *People (DPP) v Palmer*,[52] it was held that:

> There is no provision in [s 3(2) of the 1972 Act] for consideration of the material on which the Officer's belief is based by the Director of Public Prosecutions or another agency. It is not the belief of the Director of Public Prosecutions. Neither is it the Chief Superintendent's belief as approved or authorised or evaluated by the Director. The Director's functions in regard to prosecutions do not include consideration of the confidential material on which the Chief Superintendent's belief is based. This ground of appeal and the submissions supporting it suffer from the misunderstanding that the evidence before the Court is of the Officer passing on hearsay information. The distinction may at first sight appear to be a fine one between a belief based

[48] *DPP v Special Criminal Court and Ward* [1999] 1 IR 60, 88.
[49] Harrison, *The Special Criminal Court* (n 1) 574.
[50] *Redmond v Ireland* [2015] 4 IR 84.
[51] Ibid, 108–109. See also, 316 and 329. In *People (DPP) v Billings* (Bill No SCC6/2011, 5 October 2016) SCC, the Court declined to consult the privileged material, having regard to the 'ministerial role' of the prosecution.
[52] *People (DPP) v Palmer* [2015] IECA 153.

> on confidential information from a variety of sources, on one hand, and reporting information provided by others, on the other hand. However, as the case of *Donnelly & Ors* makes clear, the distinction is an important one for a proper understanding of the section and how it operates. The Court in that case also highlighted the evaluative role of the officer giving the evidence and the fact that it is a person of very senior rank in the Garda Síochána who has particular and relevant experience.[53]

The extent to which this reasoning addresses the central concerns of the accused in *Palmer* is questionable. Belief evidence is based on a variety of sources and materials which cannot be challenged by the defence in any meaningful way and the argument of the defence was that if the Director took the opportunity to scrutinise or assess the sources for the belief evidence, this could potentially provide a valuable safeguard which would reduce the risk of the Court inspecting the disputed material. Indeed, it is difficult to reconcile the conclusion of the Court of Appeal in *Palmer* with the comments of Charleton J in *Redmond*. One possible distinction between the two cases is that the Court in *Palmer* considered whether the prosecution was under an obligation to look at the file in order make a qualitative assessment of the basis for the Chief Superintendent's belief, whereas Charleton J in *Redmond* appears to have focused on the prosecution's obligation to assess claims of privilege and ensure adequate disclosure has been made. Therefore, it appears that the comments made by Charleton J are more relevant to the present discussion and there may be scope for the superior courts to recognise a prosecution obligation to review the Chief Superintendent's file.

In fact, in a recent case, *People (DPP) v K and M*,[54] the Special Criminal Court itself concluded that the prosecution counsel in that case were under a duty to consider the underlying material where belief evidence is relied upon. In the Court's view, this exercise was a safeguard in terms of the operation of section 3(2) of the 1972 Act. The Court held that the duty may not arise in every case but that, where a Chief Superintendent has based his belief on underlying material in relation to which a claim of privilege is made, the prosecution counsel have a duty 'to view the material to ensure that the disclosure process has been properly attended to'.[55] Despite this ruling, the investigating authorities refused to provide the relevant material to the Director, citing security concerns. Neither of the accused consented to the Court viewing the file and, following an attempt to cross-examine the Chief Superintendent, they argued against the admissibility of the belief evidence on grounds of fairness and on the grounds that it had little probative value or weight. The Court ultimately held that the blanket claim of privilege maintained by the prosecuting authorities effectively meant that the accused were not permitted to cross-examine the Chief Superintendent in any meaningful way. On grounds of fairness,[56] the Court found the belief evidence to be inadmissible and ultimately acquitted both accused. This case has subsequently been appealed by the Director and the outcome is awaited. The appeal might provide the superior courts with the opportunity to clarify the role of prosecution counsel in relation to belief evidence in the future. Clarification would be welcome on such an important practical matter.[57]

[53] Ibid, paras 43–44, citing *People (DPP) v Donnelly, McGarrigle and Murphy* [2012] IECCA 78.
[54] *People (DPP) v K and M* (Bill No 0012/2017, 5 December 2019).
[55] Ibid.
[56] The Court cited *People (DPP) v Donnelly, McGarrigle and Murphy* [2012] IECCA 78 in this regard.
[57] Harrison, *The Special Criminal Court* (n 1) 576.

Even if the role of the prosecution as described in *Redmond* were to prevail, it is of course arguable that the inspection of privileged material by prosecution counsel would still not provide a sufficient safeguard for accused persons. It may also have the effect of putting counsel for the prosecution in a compromised position. In any event, it appears from the cases of *People (DPP) v Connolly*[58] and *People (DPP) v K and M*,[59] discussed above, that investigating authorities are not prepared to furnish the prosecution with the relevant material for counsel's consideration. This leaves an accused before the Special Criminal Court in the extremely difficult position of having to either ask the Court to look at the Chief Superintendent's file, with all the risk that course entails, or accept the word of the investigating authorities that there is nothing in the Chief Superintendent's file that would show his innocence. The investigating authorities – who are members of the police, rather than experienced lawyers – are not on notice of the accused's defence nor the intricacies of his instructions and cannot assess the material in light of this information.[60] In the retrial in *Connolly*, it emerged that there was in fact something within the undisclosed material which was helpful to the accused and which, when disclosure was ultimately ordered by the Special Criminal Court, led to his acquittal.

If the courts see fit to recognise a prosecution obligation to review the file, it would certainly improve matters for the defence. However, it would not exactly be a panacea – the problem remains that the prosecution counsel will also be unaware of the nature of the defence or the accused's instructions and may not be in a position to assess the significance of a particular piece of information. A prosecution obligation of this nature should, therefore, be considered as giving supplementary protection to an accused where belief evidence is relied upon, rather than providing a complete solution.

C. Disclosure to Legal Representatives Only

It is possible that disclosure of privileged material could be made to a person's legal representatives only and on the undertaking that they would disclose the contents of the documents only with the leave of the court. The Court in *Ambiorix Ltd v Minister for the Environment (No 1)*[61] was receptive to this compromise in terms of resolving a dispute regarding a claim of public interest privilege. However, while this approach may be viable in the context of civil proceedings, the notion of disclosing disputed documents to the legal team of an accused in a criminal case and not the accused himself is undesirable. It would interfere with the ability of counsel to defend an accused person effectively, which is dependent upon taking full and frank instructions from that person in light of all the

[58] *People (DPP) v Connolly* (Bill No 0009/2014, 24 June 2019) SCC.

[59] *People (DPP) v K and M* (Bill No 0012/2017, 5 December 2019).

[60] A review in the UK revealed that investigators and prosecutors were 'interpreting the disclosure test too narrowly or placing too much focus on what the defence asserts to be its case, disregarding other matters unknown to the defence that would be part of the defence case if only they were made aware of them or other possible defences which the facts might support'. (Rt Hon Geoffrey Cox QC, MP, Attorney General, *Review of the Efficiency and Effectiveness of Disclosure in the Criminal Justice System* (November 2018) 12, www.gov.uk/government/publications/review-of-the-efficiency-and-effectiveness-of-disclosure-in-the-criminal-justice-system (accessed 20 October 2019). Where such issues have been unearthed in the UK, it is reasonable to assume that similar problems might also occur in the Irish criminal justice system.

[61] *Ambiorix Ltd v Minister for the Environment (No 1)* [1992] 1 IR 277. See also, L Heffernan and U Ní Raifeartaigh, *Evidence in Criminal Trials* (Bloomsbury Professional, 2014) 741.

evidence. It would also interfere generally with the relationship between legal representatives and their criminal clients by undermining the trust and confidence between them.

This solution was proposed by the Special Criminal Court itself in *DPP v Special Criminal Court and Ward*,[62] but was ultimately rejected by both the High Court and the Supreme Court. The Special Criminal Court, seeking to achieve a compromise between disclosure and privilege, held that it would order disclosure of the documents to the accused's legal representatives if he waived his right to personal inspection and being informed of the contents. The Court envisaged that if it transpired that there was material relevant to the defence, a further application could be made to divulge that material to the accused. The Director of Public Prosecutions obtained leave to judicially review this proposal and the matter was heard before Carney J in the High Court who granted *certiorari*. He stated:

> I have come to the view that the Special Criminal Court exceeded its jurisdiction in fundamentally altering the established relationship between defence lawyers and their client. It does not seem to be any answer that the notice party has consented to his legal team having sight of the statements on the terms that they are not disclosed to him without leave of the court. His present legal team could be discharged at any time and it does not seem to me that there would be a trial in accordance with constitutional justice if any subsequent legal representatives did not enjoy the full lawyer-client relationship with their client but were under an obligation to keep secrets from him.[63]

This decision was upheld by the Supreme Court on appeal, which also concluded that the proposal of the Special Criminal Court was 'not a feasible compromise solution'.[64]

Interestingly, in the civil case of *Burke v Central Independent Television plc*,[65] the Supreme Court also took the opposite view to that expressed in *Ambiorix* and Finlay CJ noted the procedure would result in a 'wholly undesirable breach' in the duty which counsel owes to his client.[66] Certainly in criminal proceedings before the Special Criminal Court, the disclosure of privileged information to legal representatives only would be an inappropriate solution for this reason.

D. Inspection of Documents by Lawyers or 'Special Advocates'

An alternative route, which has been utilised in other jurisdictions,[67] is the use of 'special counsel' or 'special advocates' to represent the interests of the accused in disclosure hearings. This procedure is increasingly used in other jurisdictions in the context of 'closed material proceedings', in which the state can apply to the court to rule on disclosure issues on an ex parte basis if matters of national security or intelligence sources need to

[62] *DPP v Special Criminal Court and Ward* [1999] 1 IR 60.
[63] Ibid, 75.
[64] Ibid, 88.
[65] *Burke v Central Independent Television plc* [1994] 2 IR 61.
[66] Ibid, 80.
[67] For eg, special advocates have been utilised in the UK, Canada, New Zealand and Hong Kong. See generally B Emerson, A Ashworth, A McDonald et al, *Human Rights and Criminal Justice* (London, Sweet & Maxwell, 2012) 488–99; J Jackson, 'The Role of Special Advocates: Advocacy, Due Process and the Adversarial Tradition' (2016) 20(4) *International Journal of Engineering Pedagogy* 343; J Ip, 'The Rise and Spread of the Special Advocate' (2008) *Public Law* 717.

be protected. A special advocate is an independent advocate who is appointed to represent the interests of non-governmental parties excluded from such hearings. Though not instructed by those parties nor acting for them, the role of the special advocate is to examine sensitive material and to make representations to the court on their behalf.[68]

This mechanism has been considered by the ECHR[69] and a general trend in favour of appointing special counsel is apparent in a number of cases in the UK.[70] It should be noted, however, that in the UK, special advocates are mainly utilised in immigration proceedings and very rarely in criminal proceedings. The House of Lords in *R v H and C*[71] did approve the use of special counsel in a criminal context, but only in exceptional circumstances. The Lords noted a number of difficulties inherent in the special counsel system, including the fact that counsel would not be instructed by the defendant nor could they report to their client, as well as the possible practical difficulties such as delay, added expense and a continuing duty as proceedings progress. However, it was pointed out that:

> None of these problems should deter the court from appointing special counsel where the interests of justice are shown to require it. But the need must be shown. Such an appointment will always be exceptional, never automatic; a course of last and never first resort. It should not be ordered unless and until the trial judge is satisfied that no other course will adequately meet the overriding requirement of fairness to the defendant.[72]

The use of 'special counsel' could provide another option for the Special Criminal Court, in the light of its dual role as arbiter of law and fact. The Irish courts have rejected proposals to introduce the system on several occasions and have expressly stated that it is a matter for consideration by the legislature. Fennelly J in *People (DPP) v Kelly*[73] stated that '[o]ur courts have preferred to resolve conflicts between the conflicting imperatives of a fair trial and the protection of public confidential information by asking the responsible court itself to examine the material'.[74] In *People (DPP) v Binéad and Donohue*,[75] the Court of Criminal Appeal held that, since the Special Criminal Court is a creature of statute and cannot operate outside the scope of its statutory mandate, the appointment of a

[68] J Jackson, 'The Role of Special Advocates: Advocacy, Due Process and the Adversarial Tradition' (2016) 20(4) *International Journal of Engineering Pedagogy* 343, 343 & 351.

[69] See, eg, *Rowe and Davis v United Kingdom* (2000) 30 *Essex Human Rights Review* 1, *Jasper v United Kingdom* (2000) 30 *Essex Human Rights Review* 441 and *A v United Kingdom* (2009) 49 *Essex Human Rights Review* 29.

[70] See Emerson et al, *Human Rights and Criminal Justice* (n 67) 489–90, fn 405–411. Special advocates were introduced following the case of *Chahal v United Kingdom* (1997) 23 *Essex Human Rights Review* 413. The Special Immigration Appeals Commission Act 1997 and Northern Ireland Act 1998 allow for 'special counsel' on the grounds of 'national security'. In *Roberts v Parole Board* [2005] UKHL 45, the House of Lords recognised that in principle there was nothing inherently wrong in having a special advocate appointed by the Parole Board to determine a key issue in a parole hearing in the absence of the prisoner. See also, *R v Botmeh* [2002] 1 WLR 531; *Secretary of State for the Home Department v Rehman* [2003] 1 AC 153 and *R v Shayler* [2003] 1 AC 247. See also, Auld, *Review of the Criminal Courts of England and Wales* (Stationery Office Books, 2001) ch 10, 478 and *Review of the Criminal Courts (Auld): The Bar Council Response*.

[71] *R v H and C* [2004] 2 AC 134.

[72] Ibid, 150–151.

[73] *People (DPP) v Kelly* [2006] 3 IR 115.

[74] Ibid, 145. See also, *People (DPP) v Binéad and Donohue* [2007] 1 IR 374.

[75] *People (DPP) v Binéad and Donohue* [2007] 1 IR 374.

special advocate was not within its powers nor implied from its statutory jurisdiction.[76] After the decision of the Court of Criminal Appeal was handed down in *People (DPP) v Fitzpatrick and McConnell*,[77] the second accused unsuccessfully sought leave to appeal to the Supreme Court on the ground that the Irish system involved the trial court viewing documents underlying the claim of privilege instead of a system involving the use of a special advocate. The Court found that the accused did not have grounds to make this argument since the trial court had not undertaken a review of the documents and the argument was purely hypothetical.[78] In *Redmond v Ireland*,[79] Hardiman J discussed the notion of using special advocates and held, obiter, that the implementation of such a system was for the legislature and not the courts. He stated:

> I do not consider that this Court has the power, even if it were inclined to do so, to order the use of some sort of 'special advocate', as they are dubbed in other jurisdictions, to secretly examine the papers which point to the concerns of the authorities and to make representations on behalf of an accused person, though not on his instructions.[80]

Interestingly, in *People (DPP) v McKevitt*,[81] the prosecution relied upon the evidence of an agent of the FBI and the British Secret Service and disclosure documentation was largely in the hands of overseas agencies. The British Security Service employed a Treasury barrister of considerable experience to make assessments as to relevance and voluntary disclosure was made subject to certain redactions. The Supreme Court pointed out that, the concept of relevance in Irish law having been clearly explained to agencies at a high level, the approach of the special counsel engaged by the British was 'clearly impressive'.[82] It should be noted that the appeal did not challenge the use of special counsel per se, but it is noteworthy that the Supreme Court, while it acknowledged the difficulties presented to the defence by the fact that material was in the possession of foreign intelligence agencies, stated that the engagement of the special counsel seemed 'wholly appropriate' in the circumstances.[83] The Court concluded that, having regard to the manner in which the difficulties had been addressed both pre-trial and during the trial, it was difficult to see how the accused would have a legitimate complaint with regard to disclosure.[84]

The system in the UK can be distinguished from that in Ireland since it is not the practice of the courts in this jurisdiction to engage in ex parte applications in the context of disclosure or disputes over privilege. Indeed, there are both practical and ethical difficulties associated with the procedure since, having seen the sensitive material, a special advocate cannot generally consult with the accused in order to determine the intricacies of the defence or the relevance of the material.[85] There is the added issue that they would

[76] Ibid, 396.
[77] *People (DPP) v Fitzpatrick and McConnell* [2013] 3 IR 656.
[78] *People (DPP) v McConnell* [2013] IECCA 45, para 4.
[79] *Redmond v Ireland* [2015] 4 IR 84.
[80] Ibid, 95.
[81] *People (DPP) v McKevitt* [2009] 1 IR 525.
[82] *People (DPP) v McKevitt* [2009] 1 IR 525, 535.
[83] Ibid, 538.
[84] Ibid, 533.
[85] See J Jackson, 'The Role of Special Advocates: Advocacy, Due Process and the Adversarial Tradition' (2016) 20(4) *International Journal of Engineering Pedagogy* 343, 343, 353; J Jackson, 'The Use of Special Advocates in Countering Terrorism: Human Rights, Best Practice and Procedural Tradition' in G Lennon, C King and

need to sit in on the trial in order to keep abreast of the evolving issues in the trial and assess any impact on the disclosure obligation.[86]

VIII. CONCLUSION

It is a regrettable aspect of trials before the Special Criminal Court that the same tribunal hears a *voir dire* as determines the facts. The accused faces the difficulty that the same court is ruling on the issue of admissibility or privilege and later deciding the ultimate issue of guilt or innocence. Indeed, the very notion of a *voir dire* before the Special Criminal Court seems artificial because, in practice, where evidence is called for the purposes of a *voir dire*, the prosecution will ask the court to treat the evidence as having been heard for the purpose of the substantive trial. As discussed throughout this chapter, the issue is particularly apparent in the context of belief evidence where the court chooses to review the Chief Superintendent's file. The court, as the tribunal of law and fact, is obliged to embark on the exercise of removing such material from its mind prior to deciding on the ultimate issue in the case. Even if the court succeeds in doing so, the perception could be that it has not.

Although the defence may be assured by investigating and prosecuting authorities that adequate disclosure has been made, there are cases – such as those where a blanket claim of privilege is made – where the defence is so hampered in its cross-examination that the accused has to consider asking the court to inspect the Chief Superintendent's file. For most accused persons, exposing the court to unknown and possibly prejudicial material is not a risk worth taking.

In light of the establishment of the second Special Criminal Court in 2016 – as well as the increasing use of the Special Criminal Court for the trial of organised crime – this issue needs to be addressed. The Special Criminal Court is a creature of statute and, consequently, it is for the legislature to provide a solution. The most viable option appears to be the inspection of materials by a differently constituted court in advance of a trial in the Special Criminal Court. This would allow disputes over disclosure and privilege to be dealt with in advance of the trial, permitting the trial to proceed without delay. Indeed, as noted above, the Director of Public Prosecutions has recently advocated for the use of pre-trial procedures in criminal trials. This solution is not without its difficulties since new issues may arise as the trial proceeds. An added safeguard would be for the superior courts to recognise that the prosecution counsel has an obligation to consider the Chief Superintendent's file in order to ensure that proper disclosure has been made. Neither of these options provide the perfect solution but they would, in tandem, certainly ameliorate the situation for a person standing accused of membership of an unlawful organisation before the Special Criminal Court. Given the high status formally accorded to trial by jury in the Irish Constitution, alternative solutions warrant further consideration in the context of the non-jury court.

C McCartney (eds), *Counter-Terrorism, Constitutionalism and Miscarriages of Justice: A Festschrift for Professor Clive Walker* (Oxford, Hart Publishing, 2019) 99, 107–109.

[86] Harrison, *The Special Criminal Court* (n 1) 576.

8

The Offences Against the State Acts and Non-Subversive Offences

LIZ CAMPBELL*

I. INTRODUCTION

THE HISTORY OF paramilitary activity and the associated threats to the security of the Irish state were instrumental in shaping Bunreacht na hÉireann (the Constitution of Ireland), and ensured the inclusion of extraordinary protective measures in the Constitution and subsequent legislation. Any law 'expressed to be for the purpose of securing the public safety and the preservation of the State in time of war or armed rebellion' enjoys constitutional immunity;[1] special non-jury courts may hear cases when the ordinary courts are deemed to be inadequate to secure the administration of justice and the preservation of public peace and order;[2] and at a time of armed conflict, the Houses of Parliament may declare that a national emergency exists which affects the vital interests of the state, thereby facilitating restrictions on constitutional rights and liberties.[3] Crucially, the Offences Against the State Act 1939 (OASA) is framed in sufficiently broad terms to enable deployment in respect of non-subversive offences, in both the pre-trial and trial contexts. Concerns have been raised about the normative legitimacy, constitutionality, and compliance with human rights of provisions in the OASA that enable suspected and charged individuals to be treated in an extraordinary fashion, through the abrogation of standard rights relating to arrest and detention and the mode of trial, for instance.[4]

Building on this existing commentary and critique, which is comprehensive and persuasive, the novelty of this chapter lies in an updated analysis of the challenges to the OASA in respect of its use for non-subversive matters, and more significantly in examining more closely the impact of trials on members of the jury, as well as considering the

* Thanks to Mark Coen, Rebecca Coen, and Jacqui Horan, as well as the participants at the Society of Legal Scholars Annual Seminar 2019, UCD, for comments and guidance on the first draft of this chapter. Any errors are my own.

[1] Bunreacht na hÉireann, Art 28.3.3°.

[2] Ibid, Art 38.3.

[3] Ibid, Art 28.3.3°.

[4] See, eg, M Robinson, *The Special Criminal Court* (Dublin, Dublin University Press 1974) and F Davies, *The History and Development of the Special Criminal Court 1922–2014*, 2nd edn, (Oxford, Hart Publishing, 2014).

implications of the so-called 'digital age' on the criminal trial of serious offences in the orthodox way. These two elements add a contemporary complexion to this critique of the use of the OASA against non-subversive offences, and reframe the debate to look at the problem that is sought to be resolved by use of the OASA in this manner.

The chapter begins with a description and consideration of how certain non-subversive offences are captured doctrinally within the OASA, and what this means for the criminal suspect. I then turn to focus on the use of judge-only trials in the Special Criminal Court (SCC) for non-subversive offences. While not neglecting the implications of this for the accused person, I shift focus somewhat to consider the potential ramifications for the members of the jury of maintaining trial by jury. As the SCC is being used in an effort to protect the jury, alternative protective measures should be contemplated. In this analysis, I draw particularly on reforms in my new home, Australia, and more specifically, the State of Victoria. Consideration of such mechanisms allows us to envisage a move away from the use of the SCC, and present us with pragmatic and workable alternatives to the status quo.

II. THE 'SCHEDULING' OF NON-SUBVERSIVE OFFENCES

Certain substantive offences, which are not paramilitary or subversive in nature, fall legislatively within the scope of the OASA. Firearms offences and explosives offences are included in a Schedule to the OASA,[5] and so persons suspected of such crimes may be searched and arrested under section 30(1) of the Act (as amended). Section 30(1) permits a Garda to stop, search, interrogate and arrest without warrant any individual whom he suspects of having committed or being about to commit an offence under the Act or a scheduled offence. In contrast to other powers of stop and search, the suspicion of the Garda in this respect need not be reasonable. Section 30 also permits the arrest of persons 'having been concerned in the commission' of a relevant offence. This is a low threshold.

Murder and armed robbery investigations, for instance, may involve arrest under the 1939 Act even if the suspect does not have subversive links or does not threaten the security of the state, as long as there is a nexus with a scheduled offence.[6] Though these are not scheduled offences and so do not fall automatically within the 1939 Act, the Gardaí may arrest the individual in question for a related scheduled offence. In other words, someone suspected of robbery by firearm could be arrested for an offence contrary to section 27B of the Firearms Act 1964 as amended, which would encapsulate both acts. That said, this convenient tactic is only permissible if the scheduled offence is not a mere 'colourable device' which the Gardaí have no real interest in pursuing.[7] Crucially, an individual arrested and detained under the 1939 Act may be held for up to 72 hours, rather than the standard 24 hours under section 9 of the Criminal Justice Act 2006.

[5] Offences Against the State Act 1939 Pt V; Offences Against the State (Scheduled Offences) (No 3) Order 1940, No 334 of 1940.

[6] P McDermott, 'Criminal Procedure and Evidence' in P O'Mahony (ed), *Criminal Justice in Ireland* (Dublin, Institute of Public Administration, 2002) 49.

[7] *State (Bowes) v Fitzpatrick* [1978] ILRM 195, 196. See also *People (DPP) v Walsh* [1986] IR 729; *People (DPP) v Howley* [1989] ILRM 629.

The OASA also impacts on the right to silence of a person accused of a scheduled offence. Under section 52(1), a Garda may demand a full account of the movements and actions of a suspect detained under the Act during a specified period of time, in addition to all information known to him regarding the commission or intended commission by another person of an offence under the Act. Failing to give such information or giving false information is an offence for which a person may be imprisoned for up to six months.[8] The constitutionality of section 52 was upheld in *Heaney v Ireland*, where the restriction of the right was deemed to be proportionate with respect to the section's aims of investigating and punishing serious, subversive crime.[9] The Supreme Court adjudged that the right of the citizen to remain silent was of lesser importance than the right of the state to protect itself and to maintain public peace and order. This reasoning was not accepted by the European Court of Human Rights (ECHR) in *Quinn v Ireland*, on the basis that the 'degree of compulsion … destroyed the very essence of his privilege against self-incrimination and his right to remain silent' and could not be justified by the security and public order concerns of the Irish state.[10]

The cognate but distinct provision of section 9(1)(b) of the Offences Against the State (Amendment) Act 1998 requires those who have information about the commission of a serious offence, who know or believe that disclosing this information might be of material assistance to securing the apprehension, prosecution or conviction of any other person are obliged to disclose that information to the police. This extends to non-subversive offences. Section 9 was upheld by the Supreme Court in *Sweeney v Ireland*,[11] reversing of the order of the High Court whereby section 9(1)(b) was declared to be incompatible with Bunreacht na hÉireann.

III. TRIALS WITHOUT JURY IN THE SPECIAL CRIMINAL COURT

The clearest and most controversial manifestation of the use of the OASA in the context of non-subversive offences is in the holding of non-jury or judge-only trials for certain suspects. Trial by jury is guaranteed expressly in Bunreacht na hEireann,[12] but may be restricted by the establishment of 'special' courts where the ordinary courts are deemed to be inadequate.[13] This limitation of trial by jury is not confined to proceedings for subversive offences.

Part V of the OASA regulates the establishment and operation of special judge-only courts: 'Special Criminal Courts'. Unlike the first four parts of the Act which are permanently in force,[14] this Part comes into force only 'if and whenever and so often as the

[8] OASA, s 52(2).

[9] *Heaney v Ireland* [1996] IR 580.

[10] *Quinn v Ireland* (2001) 33 EHRR 264. See Y Daly, Chapter 11, this volume.

[11] *Sweeney v Ireland* [2019] IESC 39.

[12] Bunreacht na hÉireann, Art 38.5.

[13] Ibid, Art 38.3.

[14] Part I concerns the interpretation of terms in the Act and other general matters; Pt II concerns, inter alia, offences against the state such as the obstruction or usurpation of government or the President, unauthorised military exercises, and the possession of treasonable and seditious documents; Pt III deals with membership of unlawful organisations; and Pt IV concerns miscellaneous matters, including the prohibition of meetings in the vicinity of the Oireachtas, search warrants, and the re-capture of escaped prisoners.

Government is satisfied that the ordinary courts are inadequate to secure the effective administration of justice and the preservation of public peace and order'.[15] The necessary proclamations under Part V, which do not require any explanation or justification on the part of the government, have been made for the periods 1939 to 1946, 1961 to 1962, and 1972 to date.[16] This declaration can be annulled only by a resolution of the Dáil or when the government declares that Part V is no longer in force.[17]

While there is a qualified constitutional right to a jury trial for criminal charges,[18] Article 38.3.1° of Bunreacht na hÉireann provides that:

> Special courts may be established by law for the trial of offences in cases where it may be determined in accordance with such law that the ordinary courts are inadequate to secure the effective administration of justice, and the preservation of public peace and order.

Persons charged with scheduled offences may be tried before the Special Criminal Court.[19] Indeed, they will be tried before the SCC, unless the DPP directs otherwise. That said, all firearms charges are scheduled but most frequently are disposed of in the ordinary courts. In addition, the DPP may request that a person charged with a non-scheduled offence be tried before that court on the basis that she believes that the ordinary courts are inadequate to secure the administration of justice and the preservation of public peace and order.[20] The judge must send the case to the Special Criminal Court on such a request of the DPP. The case could also commence in the Special Criminal Court, without the District judge sending it there.

Although the creation of the Special Criminal Court was to address the threat of subversion, the Supreme Court has stressed that Part V concerns the adequacy of the ordinary courts rather than subversion per se.[21] Cases which have been heard in the Special Criminal Court include the murder of journalist Veronica Guerin;[22] the murder of Roy Collins in Limerick;[23] possession of 15 guns and over 1,300 bullets;[24] conspiring to murder;[25]

[15] OASA, s 35.

[16] *Report of the Committee to Review the Offences Against The State Acts 1939–1998 and Related Matters* (Dublin: Stationery Office, 2002) hereinafter Hederman Report, 9.8.

[17] OASA, ss 35(4)–(5).

[18] Bunreacht na hÉireann, Art 38.5: 'Save in the case of the trial of offences under section 2, section 3 or section 4 of this Article no person shall be tried on any criminal charge without a jury.'

[19] Under s 45(1) of the OASA, the DPP may request that a person charged with a scheduled offence which may be dealt with summarily in the District Court be tried before the Special Criminal Court. Section 45(2) provides that if the accused is to be tried on indictment, he will be sent before the Special Criminal Court unless the DPP issues directions to the contrary.

[20] Section 46 applies to non-scheduled summary and indictable offences where an individual is charged in the District Court, s 47 provides for the direct charge and trial of an individual before the Special Criminal Court for non-scheduled offences, while s 48 permits the transferral of a trial on indictment to the Special Criminal Court where the accused has been returned for trial to the Central Criminal Court or the Circuit Court. These sections require the written certification of the DPP.

[21] *People* v *Quilligan* [1986] IR 495.

[22] See *People (DPP)* v *Ward*, unreported, Special Criminal Court, 27 November 1998; *People (DPP)* v *Meehan*, unreported, Special Criminal Court, 29 July 1999.

[23] *DPP v Dundon* [2017] IECA 265.

[24] 'Man who admitted gun possession 'took orders from criminals abroad'', *Irish Times*, 24 June 2019, www.irishtimes.com/news/crime-and-law/courts/man-who-admitted-gun-possession-took-orders-from-criminals-abroad-1.3935946.

[25] A O'Riordan, 'Gangland criminal Alan Wilson pleads guilty to conspiring to murder Dublin man' (30 May 2019) www.thejournal.ie/gangland-criminal-alan-wilson-pleads-guilty-to-conspiring-to-murder-dublin-man-4661109-May2019/.

the murder of a number of individuals allegedly involved in organised crime in Dublin;[26] and Thomas Murphy's tax evasion.[27]

Indeed, a second Special Criminal Court was established in 2016 in order to deal with a backlog of cases and to expedite the hearing of cases,[28] thought it appears that this will be suspended due to falling case numbers.[29] The 2019 Courts Service of Ireland report indicates that there were eight trials in the Special Criminal Court involving 10 defendants in 2019.[30] In 2019, the Special Criminal Court dealt with 70 incoming offences compared to 51 in 2018, and it resolved 80 in 2019, and 74 in 2018. The DPP's Annual Report of 2019 indicated the notably and consistently high conviction rate in the Special Criminal Court.[31]

	TOTAL			Percentage of Convictions		
	2018	2017	2016	2018	2017	2016
Assisting an Offender	0	3	0	N/A	100%	N/A
Attempted Murder	0	0	0	N/A	N/A	N/A
Conspiracy to Murder	5	3	0	100%	N/A	N/A
Criminal Damage	0	0	0	N/A	N/A	N/A
False Imprisonment	0	0	3	N/A	N/A	67%
Firearms and Explosives Offences	8	10	5	100%	100%	100%
Membership of Unlawful Organisation	0	3	13	N/A	100%	85%
Moneylaundering	0	0	0	N/A	N/A	N/A
Murder	0	1	7	N/A	100%	100%
Offences Against the State	0	0	1	N/A	N/A	100%
Participating in Organised Crime	0	0	0	N/A	N/A	N/A
TOTAL	13	20	29	100%	100%	90%

Total Cases Finalised in the Special Criminal Court and Percentage of Convictions.
Source: DPP Annual Report 2019, Chart 2.2.3c.

SPECIAL CRIMINAL COURT						
	INCOMING		RESOLVED: OFFENCES			
				Trials		
Categories	Offences*	Defendants	Guilty pleas	Convicted	Acquitted	Nolle prosequi
Membership of illegal organisation	2	2	0	4	4	4

(continued)

[26] A O'Riordan, 'Man pleads guilty to helping a criminal gang carry out a murder on a Dublin street' (22 Nov 2018) www.thejournal.ie/daithi-douglas-guilty-nathan-foley-4354464-Nov2018/; 'The funeral of Gareth Hutch in Dublin in June 2016' (2 Nov 2018).

[27] *Murphy v Ireland & ors* [2014] 1 IR 198.

[28] Statutory Instrument nos 182 and 183 of 2016; 'Minister Fitzgerald signs rules of court for the second Special Criminal Court' www.justice.ie/en/JELR/Pages/PR16000088.

[29] C Gallagher, 'Second Special Criminal Court to suspend operation amid falling case numbers' *The Irish Times* (August 2019) www.irishtimes.com/news/crime-and-law/second-special-criminal-court-to-suspend-operation-amid-falling-case-numbers-1.3995590.

[30] Courts Service, *Annual Report 2019* (Dublin, Courts Service, 2020), 88.

[31] Director of Public Prosecutions, *Annual Report 2019* (Dublin, Director of Public Prosecutions, 2020) chart 2.2.3c.

(Continued)

SPECIAL CRIMINAL COURT							
	INCOMING		RESOLVED: OFFENCES				
				Trials			
Categories	Offences*	Defendants	Guilty pleas	Convicted	Acquitted	Nolle prosequi
Possession of firearms/ ammunition/explosive substance	16	8	18	4	2	18
Murder	3	3	0	1	0	1
Threaten to kill	0	0	0	0	0	0
Other	49	11	13	1	7	13
Total	70	24	31	10	13	36

* there may be more than one offence brought against a defendant.
Source: Courts Service Annual Report 2019. p88.

Court Service data indicate that of the 70 offences dealt with by the SCC in 2019, around half were resolved by guilty pleas, though there is no indication as to which charges these pleas relate.

In addition to the requesting power of the DPP, some non-subversive offences may be heard without a jury due to the inclusion of substantive offences within the scope of the OASA by virtue of section 8 of the Criminal Justice (Amendment) Act 2009. This means that the ordinary courts are deemed automatically to be inadequate in relation to certain offences.

Section 8 provides that:

> It is hereby declared that the ordinary courts are inadequate to secure the effective administration of justice and the preservation of public peace and order in relation to an offence under each of the following provisions of Part 7 of the Act of 2006, namely, sections 71A, 72, 73 and 76.

Generally speaking, these are organised crime offences.[32] Section 71A concerns the offence of directing a criminal organisation; section 72: organised crime; section 73: commission of an offence for a criminal organisation, and section 76: liability for offences by bodies corporate. This section has a 'sunset clause' of 12 months, but has been renewed each year since enactment, most recently in June 2020.[33] 2018 was the first time that convictions in respect of offences under section 72 were secured in the Special Criminal Court. This was described as:

> highlight[ing] the considered approach of the DPP in using her discretion to direct that cases would be tried in the ordinary courts where it is possible to do so. The Garda authorities have

[32] See L Campbell, *Organised Crime and the Law: A Comparative Analysis* (Oxford, Hart Publishing, 2013) ch 5.
[33] See Criminal Justice (Amendment) Act 2009: Motion Seanad Éireann, 19 June 2020.

> made clear that this provision continues to be required. As Minister, I must at all times have the utmost regard for the views of the Garda authorities.[34]

There has been consistent international criticism of the retention and use of the Special Criminal Court. In 1993 the United Nations Human Rights Committee stated that it did not consider that 'the continued existence of that court is justified in the present circumstances'.[35] In 2014 the Committee reiterated its concern at the continuing operation of the Special Criminal Court, expressed further concern at the expansion of the Court's remit to include organised crime, and ultimately recommended consideration of its abolition.[36] Oddly, and rather inconsistently, it appears that terrorist financing offences are not scheduled.[37]

Judge-only trials raise concerns about equality as protected by Article 40.1 of Bunreacht na hÉireann. This argument has been raised unsuccessfully before the Irish courts.[38] Moreover, the DPP's request is reviewable only on the grounds of *mala fides.*[39] While the decision is not beyond the scope of judicial review, that review, and any consequent obligation to provide reasons, is limited.[40]

The Supreme Court in *Murphy v Ireland & ors*[41] considered the constitutionality of section 46(2) in respect of a non-subversive, triable either way offence, which was directed to be heard before the Special Criminal Court. The plaintiff Thomas Murphy, a suspected IRA member, had been charged with failing without reasonable excuse to make an income return as required by section 951 and section 1078 of the Taxes Consolidation Act 1997. The section offence is triable either way, and could be tried before the District Court, but the DPP had issued a certificate pursuant to section 46(2) for trial in the Special Criminal Court. Murphy sought declarations, inter alia, that section 46(2) was unconstitutional and not in compliance with the European Convention on Human Rights in failing to guarantee his right to be held equal before the law and his right to a fair trial. He also challenged the DPP's policy of refusing to give reasons for the decision, arguing that it rendered the decision to deprive him of his right to trial by jury effectively non-justiciable.

After recounting the context in which the OASA was enacted, the Supreme Court emphasised that 'trial by jury is not just a fundamental right of the citizen, it is a vital constitutional obligation on the State',[42] and that the exception to this right 'is itself constitutional in its nature'.[43] Murphy had claimed that his right to equality under Article 40.1 had been breached. While the court held that plainly he was treated differently from other persons charged with offences against the Taxes Consolidation Act, he is 'not only different to such persons in an important respect, but is legally distinct', on the basis that he is a person in respect of whom the ordinary courts are deemed inadequate

[34] C Flanagan TD, 'Speech by the Minister for Justice and Equality' (12 June 2019, Dáil Éireann) www.justice.ie/en/JELR/Pages/SP19000150.

[35] United Nations Human Rights Committee, *Report of the Human Rights Committee*, Official Records of the General Assembly, 48 Session, Supplement no 40, 1993, (A/48/40), Pt 1, 125–128.

[36] Human Rights Committee, *Concluding observations on the fourth periodic report of Ireland* (Aug 2014).

[37] Criminal Justice (Terrorist Offences) Act 2005 (revised and updated to 28 September 2019).

[38] *Kavanagh v Ireland* [1996] 1 IR 321. See Y Daly, Chapter 11, this volume.

[39] *Savage and Owen* v *DPP* [1982] ILRM 385.

[40] *Murphy v Ireland & ors* [2014] 1 IR 198, 226–227.

[41] ibid.

[42] Ibid, 215.

[43] Ibid.

to secure the administration of justice in this case. As such a differentiation is permitted to be made according to the Constitution, it could not offend Article 40.1.[44]

In terms of Murphy's claim that he had a right to receive reasons for the decision, the Supreme Court concluded that he had a limited right of procedural fairness which imposed a duty on the DPP to give reasons for sending him to a non-jury trial at the Special Criminal Court on various taxation offences. Where the DPP's decision is not subject to appeal or review, then fair procedures require that the accused be provided with the reasons for considering that the ordinary courts are not sufficient in the particular case.[45] That said, the Court held that a statement of reasons indicating that the DPP believes the accused to be a member of an organisation that is prepared to interfere with the administration of justice, or even justifying the non-delivery of such reasons, will suffice, unless the accused challenges the decision and provides information undermining these reasons.[46] In this case, Murphy had not challenged the certificate in a timely manner, and so even if his right to procedural fairness were violated, by then it was too late.

Though ostensibly a positive move towards the provision of reasons, the impact of this decision is narrow. While the Supreme Court emphasised the importance of reasons it also indicated a willingness to accept the non-provision of reasons if the DPP asserts that reasons could not be provided on national security grounds, for instance. Moreover, the Supreme Court requires the accused to provide 'sufficient information to the court, to presumptively undermine the Director's reasons',[47] which can be a high bar to reach.

A. Comparative Approaches to Judge-only Trials

Few other common law jurisdictions with comparable legal systems to Ireland have contemplated and introduced measures to enable judge-only trials.[48] Closest to home, trial by judge alone has existed in Northern Ireland since 1973, due to the political violence, fears of intimidation and undue acquittals.[49] The Emergency Provisions Act 1973 allowed trials on indictment of scheduled offences in single-judge 'Diplock' courts. This Act was introduced in an attempt by the UK Government to deal with juror intimidation by paramilitary organisations as well as perverse acquittals along religious or sectarian lines.[50] Trials on indictment may still be held in Northern Ireland without a jury where the DPP

[44] Ibid, 288.
[45] Ibid, 229.
[46] Ibid, 233.
[47] Ibid.
[48] J Horan and J Goodman-Delahunty, 'The legal landscape in terrorism trials' in D Tait and J Goodman-Delahunty (eds), *Juries, Science and Popular Culture in the Age of Terror* (London, Palgrave MacMillan, 2017) 11–35.
[49] Northern Ireland (Emergency Provisions) Act 1973. See J Jackson and S Doran, *Judge Without Jury* (Oxford, Oxford University Press, 1996).
[50] See Report of the Commission to Consider Legal Procedures to Deal with Terrorist Activities in Northern Ireland, Cmnd 5185 (London, HMSO, 1972) and the Northern Ireland (Emergency Provisions) Act 1973. See S Greer and A White, 'A Return to Trial by Jury' in A Jennings (ed), *Justice under Fire: The Abuse of Civil Liberties in Northern Ireland* (London, Pluto Press, 1988) 58; S Greer and A White, 'Restoring Jury Trial to Terrorist Offences in Northern Ireland' in M Findlay and P Duff (eds), *The Jury under Attack* (London, Butterworths, 1988) 186.

for Northern Ireland suspects that there is a link to a proscribed organisation or political or religious hostility, and that in view of this there is a risk to the administration of justice if the trial were conducted with a jury.[51] The legislation was due to expire on 31 July 2011, but has been extended for numerous consecutive two-year periods, most recently by the Justice and Security (Northern Ireland) Act 2007 (Extension of Duration of Non-Jury Trial Provisions) Order 2019.[52]

The Criminal Justice Act 2003 enables jury-less trials across England, Wales, and Northern Ireland,[53] though this scheme is more limited than the Irish approach. Such trials may be held where there is evidence of a real and present danger that jury tampering would take place and that despite any reasonable preventative steps there is such a substantial risk that tampering would occur as to make it necessary in the interests of justice to hold a jury-less trial.[54] It appears this this mode is little used: in 2017, 0.6 per cent of all Crown Court cases heard in Northern Ireland were conducted without a jury, and this figure has been less than 2 per cent for the last decade.[55]

The significance of the right to jury trial was emphasised in *J, S, M v R*, which concerned a successful appeal against an order to conduct the trial by judge alone. While the Court of Appeal agreed that there was and continued to be a real and present danger of jury tampering,[56] it disagreed with the trial judge that the necessary protective measures would either impose an unacceptable burden on the jurors, or that the jury would be inhibited from giving the case proper attention and returning a true verdict.[57] The Court of Appeal stressed that ordering the trial of a serious criminal offence without a jury must be the decision of last resort.[58] The Court spoke of 'extreme cases, where the necessary protective measures constitute an unreasonable intrusion into the lives of the jurors' such as those involving a constant police presence in or near their homes, or police protection at all times. This sets the bar very high in terms of the level of protection and intervention that will be deployed to ensure a trial by jury, and underestimates the burden and potential anxiety placed on the members of the jury.

Moreover, the Criminal Justice Act 2003 permits a jury to be discharged during a trial and the trial to be continued without one.[59] The English Court of Appeal approved such a situation in *R v McManaman*, where the jury was discharged and a rape trial continued without a jury, after a third party who was in the gallery sent a Facebook friend request to one of the jurors.[60] The Court of Appeal endorsed the trial judge proceeding alone, on the basis that the necessary statutory conditions were fulfilled, and that it was fair and in the interests of justice to have a judge-only trial. The Court observed that it did not have

[51] Justice and Security (Northern Ireland) Act 2007, s 1.

[52] SI 2019/1097.

[53] Notably there is no option for judge-only trials in Scotland, perhaps due to the fact that an 8:7 split in jury decisions will suffice.

[54] Criminal Justice Act 2003, ss 43 and 44. I am not keen on the terms 'tampering' or 'nobbling', as they run the risk of de-humanising what is going on – this is intimidation of jurors.

[55] Northern Ireland Office, *Consultation Response Non-Jury Trials Justice and Security (Northern Ireland) Act 2007* https://assets.publishing.service.gov.uk/government/uploads/system/uploads/attachment_data/file/798532/NJT_Consultation_Response_-_Final_29.04.19__1_.pdf.

[56] Ibid, [4].

[57] Ibid, [7].

[58] Ibid, [8].

[59] Criminal Justice Act 2003, s 46; see, eg, *R v Clarke and McStravick* [2010] NICA 34.

[60] *R v McManaman* [2016] EWCA Crim 3 [30].

to be shown that a defendant had instigated jury tampering; fundamentally the concern is to protect the integrity of a jury.[61]

Shifting jurisdictional focus, the Australian Constitution stipulates that all Commonwealth proceedings must be tried by a jury.[62] Legislation has been passed at the State level in Queensland and Western Australia permitting a court to take into account conduct constituting intimidation, corruption or threatening of a juror in determining whether to proceed by judge alone. In Western Australia, section 118 of the Criminal Procedure Act 2004 (WA) provides that the prosecutor or the accused may apply to the court for an order that the trial be by a judge alone without a jury. The court may make the order if it considers it is in the interests of justice to do so but, if the application is by the prosecutor, it must not do so unless the accused consents. This of course is in contrast to the Irish scheme under the OASA. Likewise, in Queensland, section 615 of the Criminal Code Act 1899 (Qld) allows for the making of a 'no jury order' if the court considers it is in the interests of justice to do so. Again, like in WA, if the prosecutor applies for the no jury order, the court may only make the no jury order if the accused person consents to it. Of course, this means that the process for judge alone trial could be stymied where associates of the accused are involved in jury intimidation, that is where the accused wants the jury to be influenced and so won't consent to judge-only trial.

In New Zealand, a court may proceed to a trial by judge alone where it is satisfied that there are reasonable grounds to believe: (a) that intimidation of any person or persons who may be selected as a juror or jurors has occurred, is occurring, or may occur; and (b) that the effects of intimidation can be avoided effectively only by making (such) an order.[63] A recent case in New Zealand, *R v Cameron*, exemplifies the potential threat to juries, though still the trial was not held by judge alone.[64] Here the defendant had gone to the opening day of the trial by jury of a man who was apparently the 'vice president' of a gang to which the defendant belonged, and was seen using his phone to film candidates for jury selection. This resulted in the trial being abandoned. The defendant was convicted of wilfully attempting to pervert the course of justice, and was sentenced to three years' imprisonment.

This brief comparative exercise brings to the fore two arguments that could be made in the Special Criminal Court's favour, namely the number of judges involved, and the provision of a written judgment. In contrast to the three judges that constitute the Special Criminal Court,[65] the equivalent schemes overseas comprise of a judge sitting alone. This raises concerns regarding the single judge's role as arbiter of both fact and law,[66] especially given the 'adversarial deficit' for defendants and judicial case-hardening that John Jackson and Seán Doran identified in studying trials in Northern Ireland.[67] And of

[61] Ibid, [22].

[62] Commonwealth of Australia Constitution Act (The Constitution), s 80; see *Brown v The Queen* (1986) 160 CLR 171.

[63] Criminal Procedure Act 2011, s 103.

[64] *R v Cameron* [2019] NZDC 10953.

[65] OASA, s 39.

[66] L Campbell, 'The Prosecution of Organised Crime: Removing the Jury' (2014) 18 *The International Journal of Evidence & Proof*, 83–100, 95. See A Harrison, Chapter 7, this volume.

[67] J Jackson and S Doran, *Judge without Jury: Diplock Trials in the Adversary* System (Oxford, Clarendon Press, 1995) 293.

course, the provision of the written judgment articulating the court's basis for its factual conclusion, which does not occur in jury trials,[68] is another potential safeguard for the accused.

B. Impact on Jurors

The continuing rationale for the use of the Special Criminal Court and other judge-only trials is that juries in the trial of organised and other suspected criminals could be subject to threats or intimidation, impacting on their safety and/or the verdict, and that it is better to seek to prevent this by removal of the jury entirely, rather than seeking to respond after the event. Indeed, the Irish Government sought to justify the re-introduction of the Special Criminal Court in 1972 on the ground that juries were likely to be intimidated by paramilitaries.[69] And as for the extension to organised crime in 2009, the logic behind such a legislative approach is that such criminality is distinct from 'ordinary' crime in the threat it poses to jurors in particular, and so warrants equivalent automatic measures to those used against suspected terrorists. Though conceptually problematic and contested, organised crime can be characterised by the nature and level of the offending, the group perpetration and dynamics involved, the motivating factor of profit or benefit, with the presence or threat of violence and/or corruption.[70] Moreover, there is sometimes overlap in personnel as well as strategy with paramilitaries.[71] All of this ratchets up the potential for and likelihood of jurors being threatened.

As Walsh J noted in *People (DPP)* v *Quilligan*:

> There could well be a grave situation in dealing with ordinary gangsterism or well-financed and well-organised large scale drug dealing, or other situations where it might be believed or established that juries were for some corrupt reason, or by virtue of threats, or of illegal interference, being prevented from doing justice.[72]

Similarly, in *Kavanagh* v *Ireland* Keane J endorsed the trial of persons engaged in non-paramilitary crime before a special court where there appeared to be a significant risk of intimidation or corruption of the jury.[73]

There is little empirical work on jury interference and intimidation in Ireland, and on the implications of the criminal trial for the lay participants. That said, the Committee to Review the Offences Against The State Acts 1939–1998 asserted in 2002 that juries are 'distinctly uncomfortable' in cases involving organised crime, and that attempts have been made to tamper with juries in high-profile criminal trials in the ordinary courts.[74]

[68] See *Taxquet v Belgium* [2010] ECHR 1806.

[69] See the submission of the Irish Government in *Eccles, McPhillips and McShane* v *Ireland* (App no 12839/87, 9 December 1988).

[70] Campbell, *Organised Crime* (n 32), ch 2.

[71] T Makarenko, 'The Crime-Terror Continuum: Tracing the Interplay between Transnational Organised Crime and Terrorism' (2004) 6 *Global Crime* 129–145; 6 Organised Crime Task Force, *Annual Report & Threat Assessment* 2017–18.

[72] *People* v *Quilligan* [1986] IR 495, 509.

[73] *Kavanagh v Ireland* [1996] 1 IR 321, 364.

[74] Hederman Report, (n 16) 9.33, 9.36. For an examination of Court of Appeal case law in which interference has been an issue see M Coen, 'Interference with Jurors and its Potential Legal Consequences' [2011] *Criminal Law and Procedure Review* 142–154.

A comparable concern was raised in 2003 by the DPP at the time to an Oireachtas Committee.[75] Mark Coen, Niamh Howlin, Colette Barry and John Lynch, in *Judges and Juries in Ireland: An Empirical Study*, found that while there was no sense of widespread jury interference, it was nevertheless regarded by interviewed judges and practitioners as a known feature of a small number of Irish trials by jury.[76] Notably, a number of judges interviewed for their research project referred to the issue without being prompted to do so. Three judges referred to the need for the judge to be alert to the possibility of jury intimidation and interference.[77]

From the point of view of jurors themselves, while there is considerable anecdotal evidence of anxiety and fear in respect of certain types of trials and defendants,[78] there is no existing research in Ireland on this dimension of the issue. A UK Home Office Report in 2004 found that juror stress and intimidation in the courtroom was a significant component of their experience, with 36 per cent of jurors reporting that they felt 'very uncomfortable, or intimidated' in court.[79] Factors causing this included the possibility of meeting the accused on the street (17 per cent); the prospect of meeting families of the accused coming in and out of court (14 per cent); the gaze of the accused in the courtroom (11 per cent); stares from the public gallery (10 per cent); the general atmosphere of the court (8 per cent); the manner of counsel (6 per cent); and/or from the witnesses (6 per cent).

Concerns have been expressed in Western Australia, comparable to those raised in Ireland, about the possibility of intimidation influencing jury verdicts, often in cases of alleged organised crime or outlaw motorcycle gang members on trial for serious criminal offences. This has prompted calls for legislative reform. Nonetheless, a 2010 Report found in fact that the incidence of intimidation was relatively unusual, and it was rare that intimidation by those outside the jury room affected the verdict.[80] An unexpected finding was that some verdicts were affected by intimidation in the jury room.

The vulnerability of jurors may be compounded by the extent to which identifying material is now widely available online. While much has been written on the use of search engines and social media by jurors during the trial and deliberation process, ranging from intentional online research of legal terms through to inadvertent exposure to prejudicial material,[81] there is less focus on the extent to which social media could impact negatively on the jury itself. Technology has facilitated certain forms and levels of intimate partner

[75] Presentation by J Hamilton, then Director of Public Prosecutions, to Joint Committee on Justice, Equality, Defence and Women's Rights, 8 December 2003, www.oireachtas.ie/en/debates/debate/joint_committee_on_justice_equality_defence_and_womens_rights/2003-12-08/2/.

[76] M Coen, N Howlin, C Barry and J Lynch, *Judges and Juries in Ireland: An Empirical Study* (UCD, 2020) ch 8.

[77] Ibid, 114.

[78] T Brady, 'Most jurors too scared to turn up or gangster trials' *News Irish Times* (December 2019) www.independent.ie/irish-news/most-jurors-too-scared-to-turn-up-for-gangster-trials-26548258.html.

[79] R Matthews, L Hancock and D Briggs, 'Jurors Perceptions, Understanding, Confidence and Satisfaction in the Jury System: A Study in Six Courts' (2004) Home Office Online Report 05/04.

[80] J Fordham, *An investigation into the prevalence and nature of juror intimidation in Western Australia* (2010) www.law.uwa.edu.au/__data/assets/pdf_file/0005/836906/jury_intimidation_report.pdf.

[81] D Harvey, 'The Googling Juror: The Fate of the Jury Trial in the Digital Paradigm' [2014] *New Zealand Law Review* 203; J Johnston et al, *Juries and Social Media – A Report Prepared for the Victorian Department of Justice* (Report, Victorian Department of Justice, 1 June 2013) 9; P Keyzer et al, 'The Courts and Social Media: What Do Judges and Court Workers Think?' (2013) 25 *Judicial Officers' Bulletin* 47.

and family violence.[82] So, it is not inconceivable that accused persons would also google or would have online investigations carried out on their behalf to identify and target particular jurors. This is an issue in Ireland where the use of social media is widespread,[83] enabling instant sharing of information through text posts, photos, and videos, but also identification and locating of people.

Beyond this, though there is a limited and unclear evidence base in respect of the prevalence and nature of juror intimidation, what is clear is that the trauma that is experienced by various parties in and throughout the criminal justice process has long been overlooked.[84] In certain instances the trauma which is a feasible consequence of jury service for some would be compounded by the prospect of juror intimidation,[85] and that whatever could be done to mitigate this should be done. If the DPP does regard the ordinary courts as adequate to secure the administration of justice and the preservation of public peace and order,[86] then this could be seen to convey some belief in the ability of the state to safeguard jurors, and vice versa. This is not insignificant.

C. Responding to Concerns about Jury Safety

Concerns about juror safety and possible intimidation could be addressed through alternative mechanisms in court proceedings. Currently jurors are selected from the Register of Electors, and on the first day of jury service all names of the summoned potential jurors are called out. Names are drawn out of a ballot box in order to select a panel of 12 jurors for a particular case. Section 16(1) of the Juries Act 1976 provides that:

> Every person shall be entitled to reasonable facilities to inspect a panel of jurors free of charge and a party to any proceedings, civil or criminal, to be tried with a jury shall be entitled to a copy free of charge on application to the county registrar.

As the Law Reform Commission noted in its 2013 Report on Jury Service, section 16 does not confer a right to be provided with the names of jurors selected, rather it only confers an entitlement to access the names of persons summoned for service.[87] Nevertheless, the openness in the 'standard' criminal proceedings may render the jurors vulnerable. As noted above, this is particularly pronounced in the digital era, where publication means something different than was the case in the past. While of course Ireland has always been

[82] H Douglas, BA Harris and M Dragiewicz, 'Technology-facilitated Domestic and Family Violence: Women's Experiences' (2019) 59 *The British Journal of Criminology* 551–570.

[83] Figures from IPSOS, 2017 indicate that 65% have a Facebook account; 27% have a Linkedin account; 32% have an Instagram account; 29% have a Twitter account, and 40% use WhatsApp. See www.ipsos.com/en-ie/social-networking-nov-17.

[84] Eg, L Ellison and VE Munro, 'Taking trauma seriously: Critical reflections on the criminal justice process' (2017) 21(3) *The International Journal of Evidence & Proof* 183–208.

[85] N Robertson, GM Davies and A Nettleingham, 'Vicarious traumatisation as a consequence of jury service' (2009) 48 *Howard Journal of Criminal Justice* 1–12.

[86] Section 46 applies to non-scheduled summary and indictable offences where an individual is charged in the District Court, s 47 provides for the direct charge and trial of an individual before the Special Criminal Court for non-scheduled offences, while s 48 permits the transferral of a trial on indictment to the Special Criminal Court where the accused has been returned for trial to the Central Criminal Court or the Circuit Court. These sections require the written certification of the DPP.

[87] Law Reform Commission, (LRC 107-2013) *Report on Jury Service*, 7.29.

small and well-connected, there is another dimension in terms of identifying and tracking someone online. Personal information is easily accessible online,[88] and with social media and facial recognition technology it is reasonably straightforward to ascertain a detailed account of someone's life, family and personal connections, and movements.

One alternative to judge-only trials could lie in the closing of the court, such as was ordered by Spigelman CJ in the New South Wales Court of Criminal Appeal in *R v Richards & Bijkerk*.[89] The closing of the court was held to be necessary for the administration of justice to prevent tampering with jurors. This raises concerns about the presumption of innocence of the accused, however, as well as open justice.

Altering the law relating to access to jury lists might also mitigate the possibility of juror intimidation. Indeed, the Justice and Security (Northern Ireland) Act 2007 places restrictions on disclosure of juror information, so that jury lists are no longer available for examination in criminal trials and jury members are now identified by number alone.[90] A challenge to this on the ground it breached Article 6 of the ECHR was rejected in *In Re McParland*.[91]

I endorse the recommendation of the Law Reform Commission that access to jury lists should be possible only by the parties' legal advisors (or the parties if they are not legally represented) and only for a period of four days prior to the trial in which the parties have an interest.[92] This enables the accused to challenge juror selection while maintaining the privacy of the jury members. Similarly, the LRC recommendation that the daily roll call of the jury after empanelment should be abolished is a sensible one,[93] and one which is also endorsed by Coen et al.[94] Indeed, Coen's study reports that in one instance a request for the roll call to be discontinued on the ground of jury fear was refused by the relevant judge.[95]

Comparable changes have been made elsewhere with no evidence of problematic issues arising. At the federal level in Australia a 'confidentiality direction' may be given requiring a juror(s) to be identified by number if the Federal Court thinks it 'necessary in order to protect the security of a juror or potential juror'.[96] This approach was adopted in Victoria by the Justice Legislation Amendment (Court Security, Juries and Other Matters) Act 2017, amending section 31 of the Juries Act 2000 which had a default position that panel members were identified by name, unless the judge ordered that names not be read out. Now the presumption is that panel members will be identified in court by number, rather than name.[97] A court may, if it considers that it is in the interests of justice to do so,

[88] A juror's address may yield a juror's 'family relationships, employment details, and general background information [all] immediately obtained at the courthouse'. *People v Flores*, 153 AD 3d 182 (NY App Div 2017) at 206 (Dillon JP, dissenting).

[89] *R v Richards & Bijkerk* [1999] NSWCCA 114.

[90] Justice and Security (Northern Ireland) Act 2007, s 10; see *In Re McParland* [2008] NIQB 1.

[91] *In Re McParland* [2008] NIQB 1.

[92] Law Reform Commission, (n 87), 7.51.

[93] Ibid, 7.52.

[94] See Coen et al, *Judges and Juries* (n 76), 114–115.

[95] Ibid.

[96] Federal Court of Australia Act 1976 (Cth), s 23EB.

[97] See Juries Act 2000, s 30A(1). There was a similar provision in Ireland in s 4(d) of the temporary Juries (Protection) Act 1929.

direct that members of the panel be identified by name.[98] Moreover, the Jury Directions and Other Acts Amendment Act 2017 amends the Juries Act 2000 in Victoria to the effect that it is no longer necessary for jurors to 'parade' in front of an accused during the empanelment process.

These changes followed the Victorian Law Reform Commission *Jury Empanelment Report* in 2014. In its work the Commission carried out a juror survey with 367 respondents, of whom 71.4 per cent indicated a preference for identification in court by number in criminal trials.[99] It also consulted with 42 jurors and prospective jurors from regional areas who had attended empanelments. Almost all of these expressed a preference for being identified in court by number, on the basis that there is no reason for the accused or parties to know one's name, and the ease with which someone could find out where someone lived from their name, particularly in regional areas.[100] This echoed some of the observations in a contemporaneous academic empirical study on juror stress: one juror described the stress in court as coming from the witnesses, who 'sometimes looked at the jury very hard (almost intimidating)', while another juror expressed concerns linked to preconceived notions of the danger of being a juror and noted that he 'felt protected by not having my name revealed'.[101]

Such identification of prospective jurors by numbers in Australia is compatible with the constitutional guarantee to a trial by jury in Commonwealth matters. Moreover, the New South Wales Court of Criminal Appeal held in *R v Ronen* that failure to disclose the names of jurors does not place an improper fetter on the exercise of the right to make peremptory challenges.[102] So there is no legal obstacle to this legislative development in Australia, which serves to safeguard the privacy and safety of the jurors without impacting on the rights of the accused. Likewise, I would suggest that the reasoning in *Ronen* is sensible. However, there is a body of opinion that says that depriving the defence of access to the jury names would interfere with the right to peremptory challenge.[103] I argue that this limitation is permissible and desirable in the interests of protecting jurors, and does not compromise the rights of the accused.

IV. CONCLUSION

This chapter has provided a contemporary critique of the 'scheduling' of non-subversive offences and the use of the Special Criminal Court for non-subversive offences. The threats to juries and the integrity of the criminal process more widely are significant concerns that must be confronted, not least given the pervasiveness of social media and other mechanisms that enable ready identification and tracking of individuals. While a

[98] Juries Act 2000, s 30A(2)).

[99] Victorian Law Reform Commission, 'Jury Empanelment Report' (2014), Table 2.

[100] Ibid, 4.62.

[101] J Hunter, *Jurors' Notions of Justice: An Empirical Study of Motivations to Investigate & Obedience to Judicial Directions* (Sydney, University of New South Wales, 2014), 16.

[102] *R v Ronen* [2004] NSWCCA 176.

[103] Law Reform Commission, (n 87), 103.

case-by-case, risk-based scheme such as in England and Wales seems preferable in this respect,[104] the use of a single judge is not to be advocated.

In terms of suggestions for reform, firstly and most fundamentally the category of 'scheduled offences' should be removed from the OASA, as has been argued elsewhere previously.[105] Cases should be heard before the Special Criminal Court only where the DPP can establish on reasonable and objective grounds that the ordinary courts are inadequate to deal with the administration of justice in the particular case under consideration.

Then, in foregrounding jury welfare, protective alternatives to the current framework have been mooted, such as holding the trial where the jury views the proceedings by means of closed-circuit television,[106] or by transporting juries to the court from a distance so that they could not be followed or could be sworn in anonymously.[107] Given the logistical issues with this, and the implications of 'anonymous' juries,[108] the easiest way of mitigating potential harm to jurors while retaining judge-only trials for the rarest cases, would be to empanel jurors using numbers, and to ensure a separate entrance to court from that used by the lawyers, the public and the defendant.[109] This is constitutionally compliant, and practically achievable.

[104] Campbell, 'The Prosecution of Organised Crime' (n 66), 100; LRC, *Report on Jury Service* (n 7), 7.42.

[105] Hederman Report, (n 16), 9.57. See also Irish Human Rights Commission Press Releases, 'IHRC says blanket extension of Special Criminal Court powers to deal with organised crime not human rights compliant' (30/06/2009).

[106] Bar Council, *Oral Submissions of the Bar Council to the Joint Committee on Justice, Equality, Defence and Women's Rights*, 2 December 2003, 31 per Mr Birmingham SC.

[107] Irish Human Rights Commission, *Oral Submissions of the Irish Human Rights Commission to the Joint Committee on Justice, Equality, Defence and Women's Rights*, 2 December 2003, 9, per Mr Farrell.

[108] *US v Krout* 66 F.3d 1420 (5th Cir 1995) at 1427: anonymity 'rais[es] the specter that the defendant is a dangerous person from whom the jurors must be protected'. Also, there is evidence that anonymous juries are more likely than identifiable juries to convict: D Hazelwood and J Brigham, 'The effects of juror anonymity on jury verdicts' (1998) 22 *Law and Human Behavior* 695.

[109] J Goodman-Delahunty, N Brewer, J Clough, J Horan, JRP Ogloff, D Tait, and J Pratley, *Practices, Policies and Procedures That Influence Juror Satisfaction in Australia* (2008) (Canberra, ACT: Australian Institute of Criminology Research and Public Policy Series 87), 103.

9

The Proscription of Organisations in the Republic of Ireland

JAMIE McLOUGHLIN AND CLIVE WALKER

I. BACKGROUND AND HISTORY OF PROSCRIPTION

THE POWER TO proscribe 'tumultuous', 'dangerous', 'unlawful', or 'terrorist' (in contemporary parlance) organisations[1] has existed almost continuously in Ireland since the mid-eighteenth century. It is tempting to dwell upon this history,[2] but this book marks the 80 years of the Offences against the State Act 1939 (OASA), and so this chapter's span should be more contemporary. Nevertheless, some sense of background will be conveyed, starting with the Criminal Law and Procedure (Ireland) Act 1887 by which the modern contours of proscription emerged.

Unlike its more transient predecessors which it otherwise reflected as an executive-based device,[3] the 1887 Act laid down a permanent code of coercive powers. Thus, by section 6, the Lord Lieutenant, if satisfied that any association was formed for the commission of crime, or promoting or inciting to acts of violence or intimidation or interfering with the administration of the law or disturbing law and order maintenance, could proclaim it to be 'dangerous'. On the same day as the Act received its assent, the Irish National (Land) League was proclaimed.[4] That legislation persisted for several decades,

[1] The epithet has changed with political stances over time from 'tumultuous' (Whiteboy Act 1765 (5 Geo III c 8 (Ir)) to 'dangerous' (Criminal Law and Procedure (Ireland) Act 1887, s 6, (50 & 51 Vict c 20)) to 'unlawful' (Offences against the State Act 1939, s 18) and finally to 'terrorist' (Criminal Justice (Terrorist Offences) Act 2005, s 4).

[2] For accounts, see LP Curtis, *Coercion and Conciliation in Ireland 1880–1892* (New Haven, Princeton UP, 1963); TD Williams, *Secret Societies in Ireland* (Dublin, Gill & MacMillan, 1973); C Townshend, *The British Campaign in Ireland 1919–1921* (Oxford, Oxford University Press, 1975); V Crossman, 'Emergency Legislation and Agrarian Disorder in Ireland, 1821–41' (1991) 27 *Irish Historical Studies* 309; C Campbell, *Emergency Law in Ireland 1918–1925* (Oxford, Clarendon Press, 1994); S Clark and JS Donnelly, *Irish Peasants: Violence and Political Unrest, 1780–1914* (Madison, University of Wisconsin Press, 2003); B Kissane, 'Defending Democracy? The Legislative Response to Political Extremism in the Irish Free State, 1922–39' (2004) 34 *Irish Historical Studies* 156; N Howlin, Chapter 1, this volume.

[3] See Unlawful Assemblies (Ireland) Act 1793 (33 Geo III c 29 (Ir)); Aliens and Gunpowder Act 1799 (39 Geo III c 4 (Ir)); Unlawful Societies (Ireland) Act 1825 (6 Geo IV c 4); Dangerous Assemblies (Ireland) Act 1829 (10 Geo IV c 1); Peace Preservation (Ireland) Act 1881 (44 & 45 Vict c 5).

[4] Hansard (House of Commons) vol 320 col 33, 26 August 1887.

and, during the War of Independence, most major 'nationalist' organisations, including Dáil Éireann and Sinn Féin, as well as sporting and cultural organisations,[5] were banned. However, the tactics of legislative coercion and military repression failed to maintain British rule. Indeed, the senior British military officer in Ireland during the height of the War of Independence, General Nevil McCready, later admitted that proscription had backfired as a tactic because it had turned moderate politicians into extremists.[6]

Following the War of Independence, the outbreak of civil war in the Irish Free State made it 'almost inevitable' that the use of proscription did not cease with British rule.[7] The Irish Free State enacted successive laws to suppress groups deemed to be treasonous or unlawful.[8] It even adopted the Constitution (Amendment No 17) Act 1931, which, despite its title, was regular legislation but which imported Article 2A as a constitutional amendment so as to avoid challenge to this 'new form of martial law'.[9] Within Part IV, section 19(1) defined what constituted an unlawful association, while section 19(2) empowered the governmental Executive Council to declare by order that an association was unlawful. Section 20 made it an offence to be a member of an unlawful association. Accordingly, the Executive Council issued the Constitution (Declaration of Unlawful Associations) Order 1931[10] which banned 12 organisations, including the IRA, and some allied and communist groups. Article 2A was suspended on 18 March 1932 by the incoming Fianna Fáil Government but was revived in 1933 to deal with the 'Blueshirts' (the Army Comrades Association and later the National Guard) and other Fascist-leaning factions.[11] The renewed proscription of the IRA on 18 June 1936 followed two murders and other serious attacks,[12] though alternative tactics such as the provision of pensions and employment were also deployed.[13] This 1931 proscription power was explored in the High Court in 1936 in *Blythe v Attorney General (No 2)*.[14] The plaintiffs (who included the former President of the Executive Council, William T Cosgrave, and the leader of the Blueshirt organisation, Eoin O'Duffy, as members of the political opposition party Fine Gael) sought a pre-emptive declaration that their newly formed organisation (a youth wing of Fine Gael called the 'League of Youth') was not an unlawful organisation. However, Johnston J declined to make the declaration since the right to form the body had not been impugned or threatened.

[5] C Billings, 'Speaking Irish with Hurley Sticks: Gaelic Sports, the Irish Language and National Identity in Revival Ireland' (2017) 37(1) *Sport in History* 25.

[6] M Coleman, *The Irish Revolution, 1916–1923* (Abingdon, Routledge, 2014) 68.

[7] *Report of the Committee to Review the Offences Against the State Acts 1939–1998 and Related Matters* (Dublin, Government Publications, 2002), hereinafter Hederman Report, 4.1.

[8] See Treasonable Offences Act 1925; Public Safety Act 1927, ss 4–9; G Hogan, G Whyte, D Kenny, and R Walsh, *Kelly: The Irish Constitution* 5th edn (London, Bloomsbury, 2018) 7.6.210; T Mohr, Chapter 2, this volume.

[9] L Cohn, *The Constitution of the Irish Free State* (London, Allen & Unwin, 1932) 156. A challenge failed in *State (Ryan) v Lennon* [1935] IR 170.

[10] Constitution (Declaration of Unlawful Associations) Order 1931, SR&O 73/1931.

[11] Constitution (Declaration of Unlawful Associations) Orders 1933, SR&O 91/1933, SR&O 95/1933, SR&O 97/1933.

[12] Constitution (Declaration of Unlawful Association) Order 1936, SR&O 172/1936; Hederman Report (n 7) 4.7.

[13] See JA Murphy, 'The New IRA 1925–62' in TD Williams, *Secret Societies in Ireland*, 156.

[14] [1936] IR 549. See also *Blythe v Attorney-General of the Irish Free State* [1934] IR 266.

A new constitutional order was unveiled in 1937,[15] but proscription was soon revived and has since endured. In this and other respects, the current Constitution (*Bunreacht na hÉireann*) bears pronounced resonances with past arrangements,[16] including the establishment of special courts[17] and the declaration of a state of emergency in a time of war or armed rebellion.[18] At the same time, compared to its 1922 predecessor,[19] fundamental individual rights are accorded greater prominence and enforceability,[20] and less malleability is allowed than evident with Article 2A.[21] However, the 1937 Constitution was soon sorely tested by the combined destabilising effects of, first, the international turmoil caused by mounting German aggression and, second, the IRA's wish to exploit this instability. Through its 'S' Plan at the end of 1938, the IRA declared that its Army Council represented the legitimate government of Ireland and issued an ultimatum to the British Government to withdraw from Northern Ireland.[22] These declarations were followed up with a campaign of bombings in England in early 1939[23] and with collusion with the German authorities.[24] Both actions put in jeopardy the Irish Government's policy of international neutrality.

As a result of these dire circumstances, and even before a national emergency was declared on the 3 September 1939,[25] the Irish Government decided to revive many of the old coercive powers, including proscription. The Taoiseach, Éamon de Valera commented that 'it is a very serious responsibility for a Government to find that all the powers which it needs to preserve order are not available to it …'.[26] Consequently, the OASA was passed on the 14 June 1939.[27] It has been contended that the 1939 Act embodied a 'somewhat more liberal' instrument than its Free State antecedents.[28] In reality, there were more echoes than cleavages from the past, and the revived proscription model drew

[15] Art 2A and other parts of the 1922 Constitution were terminated by Art 48 of the new Constitution.

[16] Section 3 of the Tumultuous Risings (Ireland) Act 1831 (1 & 2 Will IV c 44) was upheld as constitutional long after 1937: *State (O'Connor) v O'Caomhanaigh* [1963] IR 112. The Criminal Law and Procedure (Ireland) Act 1887 (50 & 51 Vict c 20) was not repealed until the Statute Law Revision Act 1983.

[17] Art 38.

[18] Art 28.3.3. See A Greene, Chapter 13, this volume.

[19] See Cohn, *The Constitution of the Irish Free State* (n 9) 109; B Farrell, 'The Drafting of the Irish Free State Constitution' (1970) 5 *Irish Jurist (NS)* 115, 343; MB Crowe, 'Human Rights, the Irish Constitution and the Courts' (1971) 47 *Notre Dame Lawyer* 280; G Hogan, *The Origins of the Irish Constitution 1928–1941* (Dublin, Royal Irish Academy, 2012); DK Coffey, *Drafting the Irish Constitution 1935–1937* (Cham, Palgrave Macmillan, 2018).

[20] Primarily, Arts. 40–44.

[21] Hederman Report (n 7) 4.14.

[22] See P McMahon, *British Spies and Irish Rebels* (Woodbridge, Boydell, 2008) 262–75.

[23] OG Lomas, 'The Executive and the Anti-Terrorist Legislation of 1939' [1980] *Public Law* 16; J McKenna, *The IRA Bombing Campaign Against Britain, 1939–1940* (Jefferson, McFarland, 2016).

[24] MM Hull, *Irish Secrets: German Espionage in Wartime Ireland, 1939–1945* (Dublin, Irish Academic Press, 2004); D O'Donoghue, *The Devil's Deal: The IRA, Nazi Germany and the Double Life of Jim O Donovan* (Dublin, New Island Books, 2010).

[25] See *In re Article 26 and the Emergency Powers Bill 1976* [1977] IR 159. The internal security situation was said to be 'comparatively quiet': *Dáil Debates*, vol 74, col 1285, 2 March 1939 (PJ Ruttledge).

[26] *Dáil Debates*, vol 74, col 1385, 2 March 1939.

[27] G Hogan and C Walker, *Political Violence and the Law in Ireland* (Manchester, Manchester University Press 1989) ch 8; Hederman Report, (n 7) 4.15; G Hogan, 'The Supreme Court and the Reference of the Offences Against the State (Amendment) Bill 1940' (2000) (35) *Irish Jurist* 238, 239; S Ó Longaigh *Emergency Law in Independent Ireland 1922–1948* (Dublin, Four Courts Press, 2006).

[28] Hederman Report, (n 7) 4.16.

from Part IV of Article 2A.[29] The relevant details of the OASA are examined next. The analysis will consider: the powers to proscribe and the selection of impugned organisations; and the consequences of proscription, mainly involving criminal offences. In both aspects, the normative performance in terms of constitutionality, oversight and accountability will be assessed. Many aspects of proscription are shared with Northern Ireland laws,[30] but the confines of this chapter mean that comparisons must be curtailed.

II. POWERS TO PROSCRIBE AND THE SELECTION OF IMPUGNED ORGANISATIONS

The OASA (as amended) remains the principal legal instrument behind the proscription (or 'suppression' in the language of Part III) of 'unlawful organisations' in the Republic of Ireland. However, the 1939 Act has been supplemented by the Criminal Justice (Terrorist Offences) Act 2005 (as amended), Part II of which tackles the suppression of 'terrorist groups'.[31] This duality reflects the terminologies and attitudes of different eras. As outlined above, the chief concern of the 1939 Act was domestic subversion carried out by the IRA, a group steeped in Irish history which became viewed as deviant but towards which a 'policy of patience' was applied decade after decade.[32] By contrast, the 2005 Act, adopted after the 9/11 attacks, responded to international groups, like Al-Qaida, which are depicted as responsible for alien and 'barbarous acts of terrorism'.[33] The two sources incorporate different modes of empowerment and selection, which will now be examined.[34]

A. Proscription by Definition

Part III of the 1939 Act addresses 'Unlawful Organisations' by a definitional approach. Under section 2, 'the word "organisation" includes associations, societies, and other organisations or combinations of persons of whatsoever nature or kind, whether known or not known by a distinctive name'. This formula ensures breadth of coverage by avoiding explicit reference to particular formats (such as associations)[35] or to particular causes

[29] Ibid, 4.19. The 1939 Act, s 5 repealed the Treasonable Offences Act 1925.

[30] See Hogan and Walker, *Political Violence and the Law in Ireland* (n 27) ch 5; C Walker, '"They haven't gone away you know": The Persistence of Proscription and the Problems of Deproscription' (2018) 30 *Terrorism & Political Violence* 236.

[31] N Neligan, 'Criminalising International Terrorism: The Criminal Justice (Terrorist Offences) Bill 2002' (2004) 9(4) *Bar Review* 152.

[32] *Dáil Debates*, vol 153, col 1349, 30 November 1955 (JA Costello). Even UK authorities in that era avoided reference to 'terrorism': Prevention of Violence (Temporary Provisions) Act 1939; *R v Dacey* (1940) 27 Cr App R 86; *R v Barnes* (1940) 27 Cr App R 154.

[33] *Dáil Debates*, vol 541, col 4, 18 September 2001 (B Ahern).

[34] Terrorist organisations are also countered by targeting their financial operations. The extensive and complex Criminal Justice (Money Laundering and Terrorist Financing) Acts 2010–2018 give domestic effect to EU Directives. However, a consideration of this framework is beyond the remit of this chapter.

[35] By contrast under Art 2A, the emphasis was on associations, defined as 'any combination of persons whether such combination is or is not known by a distinctive name'. Constitution (Amendment no 17) Act 1931, Sch, Pt 1, Art 3.

(whether political, religious or cultural).[36] But a 'lone wolf' or even a coincidence of fellow travellers are ruled out.

'In order to regulate and control in the public interest the exercise of the constitutional right of citizens to form associations', an organisation can be condemned as 'unlawful' under section 18 whenever it:

(a) engages in, promotes, encourages, or advocates the commission of treason or any activity of a treasonable nature, or
(b) advocates, encourages, or attempts the procuring by force, violence, or other unconstitutional means of an alteration of the Constitution, or
(c) raises or maintains or attempts to raise or maintain a military or armed force in contravention of the Constitution or without constitutional authority, or
(d) engages in, promotes, encourages, or advocates the commission of any criminal offence or the obstruction of or interference with the administration of justice or the enforcement of the law, or
(e) engages in, promotes, encourages, or advocates the attainment of any particular object, lawful or unlawful, by violent, criminal, or other unlawful means, or
(f) promotes, encourages, or advocates the non-payment of moneys payable to the Central Fund or any other public fund or the non-payment of local taxation.

It should be emphasised here that the offence of membership of an unlawful organisation under section 21 (described later) can apply to membership of terrorism organisations which meet any of the foregoing statutory criteria. It is not necessary for the further step of the issuance of a suppression order under section 19 (the second means of proscription which is considered in detail below under the heading of 'proscription by declaration'). This bifurcated approach to proscription contrasts with the position prior to 1939, whereby proscription by declaration was always necessary to trigger the membership offence.

Returning to the proscription by definition approach, is the extensive list in section 18, which draws heavily from section 18 of Article 2A and goes beyond 'treasonable',[37] consistent with Article 40.6.1(iii) of the Constitution which guarantees liberty for the right to form associations? Presaging Article 11 of the European Convention on Human Rights,[38] Article 40.6.1(iii) recognises that freedom of association is not absolute but is subject to 'public order and morality'. It has been argued that the prefatory language of section 18 'echoes, and thus claims authority from, Article 40.6.1°.iii, and is the foundation on which much of the law against subversion rests …'.[39] Bolstering further the constitutionality of section 18 is the dictum of Walsh J in *Aughey v Ireland*,[40] whereby considerations of 'public order and morality', could justify a total ban on an organisation, though one might ask whether a total ban would be proportionate if only a minor amount of organisational effort is devoted to section 18 objectives.[41] Nonetheless, some

[36] See further Lord Carlisle, *The Definition of Terrorism* (London, Cm.7052, 2007) 54.
[37] *Finucane v McMahon* [1990] I IR 165, 209.
[38] For relevant case law on proscription, see CP Walker, *The Anti-Terrorism Legislation* 3rd edn (Oxford, Oxford University Press, 2014) ch 2.
[39] Hogan et al, *Kelly: The Irish Constitution* (n 8) 7.6.212.
[40] [1989] ILRM 87, 92.
[41] See M Forde, *Constitutional Law* 2nd edn (Dublin, First Law, 2004) 576.

aspects are arguably excessive. Thus, under paragraph (f), advocacy in favour of the non-payment of taxes could attach to various social and political movements which emerged during budgetary austerity in Ireland (2008–2015) and which called for a boycott of the payment of water charges and local property taxes.[42] The Committee to Review the Offences Against the State Acts 1939–1998 (the 'Hederman Report') also expressed disquiet about the suppression of legitimate political expression and trade union activity.[43] The Committee recommended the abolition of paragraph (f) and also the replacement of paragraphs (d) and (e) with a new paragraph requiring that the purpose of the impugned activity be designed to undermine the authority of the state by way of promoting, encouraging or advocating any criminal offence or the obstruction of, or interference with, the administration or enforcement of the law. These recommendations remain unimplemented.

Another criticism of the Hederman Report went in the opposite direction. The Committee feared that foreign terrorist organisations (such as Al-Qaida) would not fall within the domestically oriented milieu of section 18 since they have no interest in localised constitutional upheaval, and so a new power to proscribe should be added.[44] This idea was powerfully reinforced by the EU's Framework Decision on Combating Terrorism[45] which required Member States to ensure that a range of 'terrorist offences' are available in domestic law. In response, Part II of the Criminal Justice (Terrorist Offences) Act 2005 deals with the suppression of terrorist groups and terrorist offences, thereby amending the 1939 Act. Pursuant to section 5, the concept of 'unlawful organisation' in section 18 is extended so as to encompass 'terrorist groups':

> (1) A terrorist group that engages in, promotes, encourages or advocates the commission, in or outside the State, of a terrorist activity is an unlawful organisation within the meaning and for the purposes of the Offences against the State Acts 1939 to 1998 and section 3 of the Criminal Law Act 1976.[46]
>
> (2) For the purposes of this Act, the Offences against the State Acts 1939 to 1998 and section 3 of the Criminal Law Act 1976 apply with any necessary modifications and have effect in relation to a terrorist group referred to in subsection (1) as if that group were an organisation referred to in section 18 of the Act of 1939.

The 2005 Act embraces the definition of 'terrorist group' contained in the EU's Framework Decision which is replicated in Schedule 1 to the Act. Thus, a terrorist group is defined as:

> … a structured group of more than two persons, established over a period of time and acting in concert to commit terrorist offences. 'Structured group' shall mean a group that is not randomly formed for the immediate commission of an offence and that does not need to

[42] R Dunphy, 'Beyond Nationalism? The Anti-Austerity Social Movement in Ireland: Between Domestic Constraints and Lessons from Abroad' (2017) 13 *Journal of Civil Society* 267.

[43] Hederman Report, (n 7) 6.12, 6.13.

[44] Ibid, 6.27, 6.31.

[45] Council Framework Decision 2002/475/JHA of 13 June 2002 on combating terrorism [2002] OJ L164. See also Directive (EU) 2017/541. See C Harte, 'The Offence of Membership of an Unlawful Organization and the Evidential Provisions Relating to It, under the Offences against the State Acts, 1939–1998' (2010) 17 *Irish Student Law Review* 51, 71.

[46] Section 3 makes it an offence to recruit, incite, or invite a person to join an unlawful organisation, or to support or assist its activities.

have formally defined roles for its members, continuity of its membership or a developed structure.[47]

Furthermore, section 5(4) establishes that a terrorist group will be an 'unlawful organisation' provided it meets the definition in section 5(1), irrespective of whether it is based within Ireland. In effect, the 2005 Act thereby accords extraterritorial reach to the 1939 Act.[48] This is followed up by related extraterritorial offences in section 6, including membership of an unlawful organisation, as described below.

The 'proscription by definition' approach embodies flexibility and so is arguably more efficient than the 'proscription by order' approach (discussed next). The point might be illustrated by the pending prosecution of Lisa Smith.[49] Smith, an Irish citizen and former member of the Irish Defence Forces, is alleged to have travelled from Ireland to Syria in order to join the Islamic State ('ISIS') and was repatriated with governmental aid in 2019.[50] She is now awaiting trial for the offence of membership of an unlawful organisation contrary to section 21 of the 1939 Act as applied by the 2005 Act.[51] 'ISIS' is treated as an 'unlawful organisation' by definition, without the need for any specific suppression order (under section 19 of the 1939 Act). This flexibility can be helpful in the context of the range of armed groups in Iraq and Syria which have operated, with considerable fluidity in membership and formations. To pin down allegiance to one group has drawbacks, though it might be argued that ISIS has been the leading non-state armed actor and the UN Security Council has displayed no compunction in singling it out for international and state attention.[52]

[47] Sch 1, Pt 2, Art 2.1.

[48] The case of *Department of Justice and Equality v Gleeson* [2019] IEHC 562 concerned an objection to surrender to Northern Ireland via a European Arrest Warrant on *ne bis in idem* grounds. The core argument was that having been convicted of membership of the IRA in the Republic of Ireland, the applicant could not be surrendered to face a charge of membership of the IRA in Northern Ireland. Owens J rejected this argument, stating that the applicant's conviction in the Republic of Ireland was under the 1939 Act only because it related to activities carried on by him in the Republic of Ireland. He had not been prosecuted under the 2005 Act with its extra-territoriality provisions applying the 1939 Act against him in respect of acts committed outside the state (in Northern Ireland, for example) and so he could be surrendered to face charges in Northern Ireland without *ne bis in idem* concerns arising as the facts giving rise to that charge were different to those that had given rise to his conviction in the Republic of Ireland.

[49] See A Speckhard, 'Perspective: Ireland's Lisa Smith Is a Test Run on Repatriation of ISIS Women' (*Homeland Security Today*, www.hstoday.us/subject-matter-areas/counterterrorism/perspective-irelands-lisa-smith-is-a-test-run-on-repatriation-of-isis-women/, 14 January 2020); A Speckhard and M Ellenberg, 'Is Internet Recruitment Enough to Seduce a Vulnerable Individual into Terrorism?' (*Homeland Security Today*, www.hstoday.us/subject-matter-areas/counterterrorism/is-internet-recruitment-enough-to-seduce-a-vulnerable-individual-into-terrorism/, 15 April 2020).

[50] *Dáil Debates*, vol 989, col 48, 12 November 2019 (S Coveney).

[51] C Lally, 'Lisa Smith signs on at Garda Station as part of bail conditions', (*Irish Times* 1 January 2020) www.irishtimes.com/news/crime-and-law/lisa-smith-signs-on-at-garda-station-as-part-of-bail-conditions-1.4128236 (accessed 25 June 2020); T Tuite, 'ISIS membership suspect Lisa Smith pleads with DPP to discontinue terror charge', (*Irish Examiner* 8 January 2020) www.irishexaminer.com/breakingnews/ireland/isis-membership-suspect-lisa-smith-pleads-with-dpp-to-discontinue-terror-charge-974255.html (accessed 25 June 2020). Prior to trial, Smith was also charged with the offence of 'financing terrorism' contrary to s 13 of the 2005 Act. T Tuite, 'Isis suspect Lisa Smith charged with financing terrorism', (*Irish Times* 26 July 2020) www.irishtimes.com/news/crime-and-law/courts/district-court/isis-suspect-lisa-smith-charged-with-financing-terrorism-1.4312732 (accessed 26 July 2020).

[52] See UNSCR 2170 (2014), 2178 (2014), 2199 (2015), 2242 (2015), 2249 (2015), 2253 (2015), 2322 (2016), 2331 (2016), 2341 (2017), 2347 (2017), 2354 (2017), 2367 (2017), 2368 (2017), 2370 (2017).

B. Proscription by Declaration

The second pathway to proscription involves direct declaration via a suppression order under section 19 of the 1939 Act. Section 19(1) empowers the government, by order, to declare unlawful any organisation based on its 'opinion' of unlawfulness and 'the public interest'. Section 19(2) allows the government to revoke or amend a suppression order whenever 'they so think proper'. Extensive subjectively formulated discretion is thus placed in the hands of the executive. A suppression order renders an organisation unlawful without proof before a court of any activities listed in section 18. Under section 19(4), a suppression order is 'conclusive evidence' that the organisation is unlawful. The order results in its property being forfeit to the state under section 22. In addition, under section 21, proof of membership of a section 19 unlawful organisation is short-circuited; evidence is not required that the organisation is unlawful by design or activity, only that an order has been made and has been published in *Iris Oifigiúil* (Official Gazette) under section 19(4). However, a suppression order against an organisation is not necessary to prosecute for the offence of membership (described below). This point has not been judicially confirmed but was 'clear' to the Hederman Committee.[53] Furthermore, in debates on the Criminal Law Act 1976, the then Minister for Justice stated that a suppression order was unnecessary for conviction under section 18; in the absence of a suppression order, the question of whether or not an organisation was unlawful within the meaning of section 18 was to be established through prosecution evidence.[54] The Hederman Committee considered that the section 19 power should rest with the executive (but subject to appeal to the High Court) since the government is best placed to make the necessary security and intelligence assessments.[55]

Just two suppression orders have been made under section 19. One was made in 1939 against the 'Irish Republican Army';[56] the other was made in 1983 against the 'Irish National Liberation Army'.[57] There has also been no instance of de-proscription. The dearth of suppression orders under section 19 reflects several factors. One is the fact that a suppression order is not a necessary pre-requisite for prosecution for the offence of membership and that the alternative pathway of proscription by definition can be followed. Thus, a stark contrast can be drawn with the position under the UK's Terrorism Act 2000, Part II, whereby 14 organisations have been subject to proscription orders in Northern Ireland (in place since the commencement of the legislation) in addition to 75 international terrorist organisations (plus four such groups now de-proscribed).[58] Crucially, UK law does not allow for proscription by definition. A second reason is that international terrorism has largely bypassed the Irish Republic which, according to police assessments, is 'not in the same league' as the UK, France or Belgium.[59] The same point

[53] Hederman Report, (n 7) 6.44.
[54] See *Dáil Debates*, vol 292, col 1004, 10 September 1976, (PM Cooney).
[55] Hederman Report, (n 7) 6.24.
[56] Unlawful Organisation (Suppression) Order 1939, SR&O 162/1939.
[57] Unlawful Organisation (Suppression) Order 1983, SI 7/1983.
[58] Home Office, *Proscribed Terrorist Organisations* (London, 28 February 2020).
[59] C O'Keefe, 'What is the reality of the threat posed by Islamic extremists in Ireland?' *Irish Examiner*, 2 May 2016, www.irishexaminer.com/viewpoints/analysis/what-is-the-reality-of-the-threat-posed-by-islamic-extremists-in-ireland-396021.html. See also M Mulqueen, 'A Weak Link? Irish National Security Policy on International Terrorism' (2007) 28 *Contemporary Security Policy* 330.

even applies, though with much less force, to Loyalist terrorist groups which have sporadically been active south of the border.[60] Consequently, it is untrue that 'a wide variety of subversive organisations on both sides of the Northern Ireland conflict have been the subject of suppression orders'.[61] A third reason is that the Irish courts have adopted an interpretation whereby the 'IRA' and its various mutations, dissident or otherwise, are treated as being the same organisation and therefore within the scope of the 1939 suppression order. This approach was challenged in *DPP v Campbell*.[62] The accused had been convicted of membership based on involvement in the 'Real IRA', a Republican faction which rejected the ongoing 'Peace Process'. The 'Real IRA' was founded in 1997 and so could not have been in the mind of the Minister at the time of the suppression order made in 1939. However, McGuiness J, in the Court of Criminal Appeal, held that subsequently added labels like 'Real', 'Continuity', 'Official' and 'Provisional' did not necessarily exclude successor organisations from the ambit of the original suppression order so long as those various off-shoots were 'on all-fours' in terms of philosophy and aims with the organisation identified by the 1939 Order.[63] A similar interpretation has been adopted by the UK courts (also in relation to the Real IRA),[64] though misgivings exist in Northern Ireland about whether the group, Arm na Poblachta, whose targets include other Republican factions ought to be explicitly and separately proscribed.[65]

Overall, these three factors (the ability to prosecute the membership offence without prior suppression, the relative absence of international terrorism in Ireland, and apparent judicial willingness to apply existing suppression orders to off-shoot organisations) make it unlikely that suppression orders will proliferate. However, two possibilities might alter the situation. One would be the shock of attacks from international sources, though returning foreign terrorist fighters from Iraq and Syria have not yet perpetrated any major outrage in Ireland. Second would be a decisive change of political policy at home whereby it became important to signal for symbolic purposes Irish society's terminal disdain for paramilitarism, perhaps associated with the need for political assurance in a new arrangement. However, the policy in Northern Ireland in those circumstances since 1998, as shown by the absence of proscription or de-proscription orders after 2001, has been slanted towards 'letting sleeping dogs lie' in the sense that there has been no changes to the proscription list since 1998, even though most listed groups have solemnly renounced violence.[66]

[60] The Dublin and Monaghan bombings were allegedly carried out by the UVF on 17 May 1974: *(Barron) Report of the Independent Commission of Inquiry into the Dublin and Monaghan Bombings* (Dublin, 2003); Joint Committee on Justice, Equality, Defence and Women's Rights, *Final Report on the Report of the Independent Commission of Inquiry into the Dublin and Monaghan Bombings* (Dublin, 2004) and *Final Report on the Report of the Independent Commission of Inquiry into the Dublin Bombings of 1972 and 1973* (Dublin, 2005); P MacEntee, *Commission of Investigation into The Dublin and Monaghan Bombings of 1974, Final Report* (Dublin, 2007).

[61] J Hamilton, 'The Interplay Between EU and Irish Domestic Counter-Terrorism Laws' (2007) 8 *ERA Forum* 549, 553. A much wider range was subject to the ban of 1987: see *State (Lynch) v Cooney* [1982] IR 337.

[62] Unreported, Court of Criminal Appeal, 19 December 2003. Paragraph numbers are not provided in the judgment. See also *Ó Bradaigh v Fanning*, unreported, High Court, 25 November 1972.

[63] Unreported, Court of Criminal Appeal, 19 December 2003. Paragraph numbers are not provided in the judgment.

[64] *R v Z* [2005] UKHL 35. See Walker, *The Anti-Terrorism Legislation* (n 38) 2.05–2.07.

[65] J Hall, *The Terrorism Acts in 2018* (London, Home Office, 2020) 9.23.

[66] For an assessment of practice, see Independent Reporting Commission, Second Report (2017–19 HC 131). The Commission operates under the Northern Ireland (Stormont Agreement and Implementation Plan) Act 2016, ss 1–5 (UK), and the Independent Reporting Commission Act 2017 (Ireland).

A 'declaration of legality' is the appeal mechanism against suppression orders afforded by section 20(1) of the 1939 Act:

> Any person (in this section referred to as the applicant) who claims to be a member of an organisation in respect of which a suppression order has been made may, at any time within thirty days after the publication of such order in the *Iris Oifigiúil*, apply to the High Court in a summary manner on notice to the [Director of Public Prosecutions][67] for a declaration (in this Act referred to as a declaration of legality) that such organisation is not an unlawful organisation.

If, under section 20(2), evidence presented by the applicant or the state leaves the High Court 'satisfied' that the organisation is not an unlawful organisation, then 'it shall be lawful for the High Court to make a declaration of legality'. If issued, the suppression order is rendered null and void under section 20(4).[68] Amongst the consequences, section 23 requires the release from custody of persons detained on a charge of membership of a previously unlawful organisation and provides for the return of forfeited property.

The odds are stacked against the applicant seeking a declaration of legality. Some discouragement is applied by section 20(3) which prevents the High Court from making a declaration of legality unless the applicant gives evidence in support of the application and submits to cross-examination by counsel for the state. Thus, someone must have considerable courage (and financial wherewithal) to become the public champion of an unlawful organisation, albeit that subsection (6) prohibits the use of evidence tendered by an applicant for a declaration of legality in any subsequent criminal proceedings relating to the offence of membership.[69] Relatedly, section 21(4) prevents persons from being brought to trial in respect of a charge of membership while they have an unresolved application for a declaration of legality in relation to the same organisation. However, they may still be detained while this appeal process plays out, and criminal proceedings relating to non-membership offences may still draw on tendered evidence.

This appeal mechanism is a solitary device, since, unlike in the UK, there is no form of regular independent review under the 1939 Act.[70] As for its fairness and effectiveness, no application for a declaration of legality has ever been reported. Of course, only two narrow opportunities to challenge have ever arisen, namely, within 30 days of the publication of either suppression order made to date in 1939 or 1983. The fleeting timeframe and meagre oversight mechanisms have been criticised:

> It is important that there should be regular, objective and public determination that the organisation has been involved in subversive crime. While the proscription of organisations such as the IRA and the INLA is entirely justified in view of the commitment of such organisations to paramilitary crime, similar powers have been abused in the past. Section 20, by vesting the High

[67] See Prosecution of Offences Act 1974, s 3.

[68] Appeal under s 20(4) is now to the Court of Appeal, rather than the Supreme Court: Court of Appeal Act 2014, s 74. Subsection (5) allows the High Court on the application of the state to suspend the nullifying effects of a declaration of legality, pending a final resolution on appeal.

[69] The Hederman Report, (n 7) 6.38 recommended the abolition of s 20(3). See A Harrison, *The Special Criminal Court: Practice and Procedure* (Dublin, Bloomsbury Professional, 2019) 6.102.

[70] Compare the work of the Independent Reviewer of Terrorism Legislation, as described in Walker, '"They haven't gone away you know"' (n 30).

> Court with power to review suppression orders, does provide some safeguards, but it is regrettable that s 20(1) puts a time limit of thirty days for the making of such an application from the date of publication in Iris Oifigiúil. This time limit precludes judicial review in circumstances where the nature of the organisation has changed and has lost its paramilitary character, but where the original suppression order has not been revoked.[71]

The short window of opportunity might even be unconstitutional, the view taken about a two-month time limit to appeal a planning decision in *Brady v Donegal County Council*.[72] Other procedural shortcomings identified by the Hederman Committee relate to the absence of any advance notice of a suppression order or chance to make representation before it is issued, though the Committee ultimately concluded that it would be inappropriate, given the nature of the organisations involved, to require the state to give advance notice.[73] Instead, it concluded that due process concerns could be addressed by an amendment to section 20 which stipulated that a suppression order would not take effect until the impugned organisation had had a chance to appeal.[74]

Another problem with section 20 is the burden and standard of proof. According to the Hederman Committee, 'the onus remains on the applicant to establish the legality of the organisation' and the grounds for overturning an order are confined 'to the judicial review grounds of reasonableness, irrationality or error of law' rather than a full appeal on the facts.[75] The latter assertion may be disputed; Hogan and Walker[76] argue that when a court is given a statutory power of appeal, it must be presumed to have a wider jurisdiction than when exercising its inherent jurisdiction of judicial review and that therefore the section would seem to allow for an appeal on the merits. The safeguards for freedom of association could be further augmented by shifting the onus of proof under section 20, perhaps after the issue has been raised, from the applicant onto the government to establish that the organisation subject to the suppression order under challenge is unlawful. At the very least, 'intense and detailed scrutiny' should be applied to the demand to suppress.[77] The judges and legislators should also assert that regular review is required by administrative law and fairness.[78]

As for more general arguments of fairness, the constitutionality of section 19(4) of the OASA was tested in *Sloan v Special Criminal Court*.[79] The accused, who had been charged with membership of an unlawful organisation, argued that, by providing under section 19(4) that a suppression order is 'conclusive evidence' of unlawfulness, the Oireachtas had invaded the judicial domain under Article 34 of the Constitution and

[71] Hogan and Walker, *Political Violence and the Law in Ireland* (n 27) 247.
[72] HC, 6 November 1987. The Hederman Report, (n 7) 6.38 recommended the removal of the time limit.
[73] Ibid, 6.32, 6.33.
[74] Ibid, 6.34.
[75] Ibid, 6.36. It sought a reformulation: 6.38.
[76] Hogan and Walker, *Political Violence and the Law in Ireland* (n 27) 246, citing *Dunne v Minister for Fisheries* [1984] IR 230.
[77] Compare *Secretary of State for the Home Department v Lord Alton of Liverpool* [2008] EWCA Civ 443, 43.
[78] Compare *Lord Alton of Liverpool & others (In the Matter of The People's Mojahadeen Organisation of Iran) v Secretary of State for the Home Department* PC/02/2006, 30 November 2007, 73; *Council of the European Union v Liberation Tigers of Tamil Eelam (LTTE)*, Case C-599/14 P, 26 July 2017, 51, 54.
[79] [1993] 3 IR 528.

improperly removed a justiciable controversy from the purview of the courts. Costello J disagreed:

> It seems to me that the Oireachtas, by the Act of 1939, established procedures by which an organisation could be declared an illegal organisation. Instead of declaring that membership of named organisations would be illegal, the Oireachtas provided that membership of an illegal organisation which had been designated by the Government would be illegal. This provision of the Act is not, in my judgment, an impermissible infringement of the judicial power. If an order is made under the section, then the justiciable dispute which may be before the court is whether an accused is a member of an illegal organisation and not whether the organisation itself is illegal.[80]

This decision has been questioned by the Hederman Committee[81] and by leading constitutional commentators.[82] Their argument is that it is at odds with the judgment of the Supreme Court in *Maher v Attorney General*[83] wherein section 49(1) of the Road Traffic Act 1961, which stipulated that a certain certificate should be 'conclusive' evidence of the blood-alcohol level of a person for the purposes of prosecution for the offence of drink-driving, was found to be unconstitutional.[84] The *Sloan* interpretation precludes arguments that the activities of the defendant were not of a harmful nature and perhaps also that the organisation concerned cannot realistically be characterised as unlawful. As such, objections might arise not only under Article 34 of the Constitution but also under Article 6 of the European Convention on Human Rights (not considered at all in *Sloan*) since section 19 imposes an absolute finding rather than an evidential burden.[85] In this way, the suppression order should be treated as proffering no more than 'prima facie' evidence of unlawfulness, but this more balanced approach was rejected in debates on the 1939 Act.[86]

Despite shortcomings within the section 19 pathway of proscription by declaration, this mode offers better legal certainty compared to proscription by definition. A declaration is a public act which can be observed and disputed in equal measure. By contrast, proscription by definition carries with it the potential for a chilling effect, on the activities of protest groups such as the opponents of economic austerity (as discussed previously in relation to section 18(f)) and Extinction Rebellion (whose UK adherents have been depicted as extremists who could be candidates for terrorism preventive responses).[87] Nevertheless, a condemnatory declaration must be fair, which means it must be carefully scrutinised at the time of issuance, and its continuance should be periodically reviewed on the basis of a presumption in favour of expiration, regardless of whether any challenger steps forward. Those features are currently lacking.

[80] Ibid, 532.
[81] Hederman Report, (n 7) 6.17.
[82] G Hogan et al, *Kelly: The Irish Constitution* (n 8) 6.1.214, fn 549.
[83] [1973] IR 140.
[84] See Harrison, *The Special Criminal Court* (n 69) 6.07.
[85] See *Sheldrake v Director of Public Prosecutions; Attorney General's Reference (No 4 of 2002)* [2004] UKHL 43.
[86] *Dáil Debates*, vol 75, col 668, 19 April 1939 (JA Costello).
[87] Its depiction as 'extremist' was an error of judgment by the police (*Hansard Debates*, vol 670, col 303, 22 January 2020 (B Lewis)), but compare T Wilson and R Walton, *Extremism Rebellion* (Policy Exchange, 2019).

C. Consequences of Proscription

A litany of 'Offences against the State' abounds in Part II of the 1939 Act. The 'usurpation of functions of government' (section 6), the possession of 'treasonable, seditious, or incriminating documents' (section 12), unauthorised military exercises (section 15), the formation of secret societies (section 16) and unlawful oaths (section 17) could readily form part of the activities of an unlawful organisation, though the offences are general in nature and are not confined to that context.[88] Therefore, for reasons of space, this chapter focuses on the offence of membership of an unlawful organisation and closely related offences,[89] as well as other sanctions within Part III of the 1939 Act.

The most prolific criminal offences relevant to proscription are those relating to membership of, and/or assisting, and/or directing, an unlawful organisation. The Hederman Committee considered it 'imprudent' to confine the offence of membership by making it consequent upon a suppression order; in its opinion, a dangerous 'lacuna' might arise whereby a suppressed organisation could simply 'reinvent' itself, thus making subsequent prosecutions for membership impossible without a *de novo* suppression order.[90] However, this risk is much reduced by the doctrine in *DPP v Campbell*.[91]

Most prominent of the offences in the 1939 Act is section 21(1) which creates the offence of 'membership': 'It shall not be lawful for any person to be a member of an unlawful organisation.' What constitutes 'membership' is not defined, but prosecution is aided by several evidential devices.[92] One is that, under section 24, if a person is found in possession, or has on their property, an 'incriminating document', then this shall be evidence until the contrary is proved that such person is a member of the unlawful organisation to which the document relates.[93] Second, the Offences Against the State (Amendment) Act 1972, section 3(1) (as amended by section 4 of the Offences Against the State (Amendment) Act 1998), allows for statements or conduct (which might include an omission to issue denials) 'implying or leading to a reasonable inference' of membership to be admissible in evidence. Third, even more controversial but still a frequently invoked 'key provision',[94] by section 3(2), a Garda Síochána officer not below the rank of Chief Superintendent can offer opinion evidence of membership. Fourth, adverse inferences may be drawn from silence in response to police questioning in the circumstances specified by section 2 of the Offences Against the State (Amendment) Act 1998. By contrast,

[88] See Hogan and Walker, *Political Violence and the Law in Ireland* (n 27) 251; Hederman Report, (n 7) 6.5–6.9.

[89] See Hogan and Walker, *Political Violence and the Law in Ireland* (n 27) 248; Harte, 'The Offence of Membership' (n 45).

[90] Hederman Report, (n 7) 6.46, 6.49. Professor Walsh dissented (6.50). The offence may fail constitutional standards elsewhere: G Hogan and G Whyte, *J.M. Kelly: The Irish Constitution* 4th edn (Dublin, Butterworth, 2002) 1072.

[91] Unreported, Court of Criminal Appeal, 19 December 2003. Paragraph numbers are not provided in the judgment. Some details are related in [2004] IESC 26.

[92] See Hederman Report, (n 7) 6.51; Harte, 'The Offence of Membership' (n 45) 60; see L Heffernan and E O'Connor, Chapter 6, this volume.

[93] By s 26, a Chief Superintendent may provide evidence on oath that he believes that such document was published by the accused. For application, see *People (DPP) v O'Leary* (1988) 3 Frewen 163. Eamonn MacThomais (editor of *An Phoblacht*) was repeatedly convicted of membership between 1972 and 1974: *An Phoblacht* 29 August 2002, https://republican-news.org/archive/2002/August29/29eamm.html.

[94] Hamilton, 'The Interplay Between EU and Irish' (n 61) 553.

section 21(3) affords a defence for a person to show that either they did not know the organisation in question was an unlawful organisation, or that as soon as reasonably possible after they became aware of the true nature or after the making of a suppression order, they ceased their membership of, and dissociated from attachment. Given the venerable and prominent nature of the two suppression orders against the IRA and INLA, section 21(3) will realistically most relate to international groups proscribed by definition, save that the operation of the interpretation in *DPP v Campbell* might catch out some Dissident Republicans.[95]

The core membership offence in section 21 is directly complemented by four further offences. First, recruiting, inciting, or inviting another person to join, or to take part in, support or assist an unlawful organisation is an offence under section 3 of the Criminal Law Act 1976.[96] Second, directing at any level the activities of an organisation which is subject to a suppression order under section 19 is an offence under section 6 of the Offences Against the State (Amendment) Act 1998.[97] It is noteworthy that, unlike the membership offence under section 21, a suppression order is a condition precedent for this offence. This qualification reflects the aetiology of the directing offence. Thus, the offence was aimed against the 'Godfathers' of the Republican paramilitary groups,[98] such as the prime suspects of the Omagh bombing which had prompted the legislation,[99] namely, the Real IRA, which already conveniently fell within the terms of the IRA 1939 suppression order. Reflecting the high-ranking targets, section 6 carries the penalty of imprisonment for life compared to up to eight years'[100] imprisonment (raised in 1976 from just two years to seven years, and then raised again by section 48 of the 2005 Act) for section 21.[101]

Third, also under the 1998 Act, section 8 creates the offence of the unlawful collection or possession of information which is of such a nature that it is likely to be useful in the commission by members of an unlawful organisation of serious offences. This formula bears some resemblance to the UK Terrorism Act 2000, section 58, but that offence is wider since it is not confined to the work of organisations nor to serious offences of terrorism. Despite these limits, a majority of the Hederman Committee called for repeal.[102] By comparison, the Hederman Committee was content with section 7, an offence which is confined to the possession or control of articles connected with the preparation of

[95] [2005] IECCA 27.

[96] See Hogan and Walker, *Political Violence and the Law in Ireland* (n 27) 253.

[97] See Hederman Report, (n 7) 6.147–6.149.

[98] There is some mention of the term during the passage of the Bill, eg, *Dáil Debates*, vol 494, cols 90, 95, 119 and 120, 2 September 1998. The notion had also affected UK law: Walker, *The Anti-Terrorism Legislation* (n 38) 6.22.

[99] See C Walker, 'The Bombs in Omagh and their Aftermath: the Criminal Justice (Terrorism and Conspiracy Act 1998)' (1999) 62 *Modern Law Review* 879; SR Elsbernd, 'Draconian Yet Constitutional: The Republic of Ireland's Offences against the State Act (1998)' (2000) 23 *Hastings International & Comparative Law Review* 261; Hederman Report, (n 7) 4.43

[100] However, where someone is convicted of the membership offence under s 21 of the 1939 Act as applied by section 6(1)(b) of the 2005 Act, ie they commit an act outside of the state which if committed in the state, would contravene s 21, they may be sentenced to up to 10 years' imprisonment by virtue of s 7 of the 2005 Act as amended by s 8 of the Criminal Justice (Terrorist Offences) (Amendment) Act 2015.

[101] Criminal Law Act 1976, s 2. Following the increase, IRA defendants less commonly refused to recognise the court: Hamilton, 'The Interplay Between EU and Irish' (n 61) 553.

[102] Hederman Report, (n 7) 6.171.

explosives or firearms offences; it was said to be 'relatively limited' and is much narrower than the UK Terrorism Act 2000, section 57.[103]

Fourth, under section 21A (imported by the 2005 Act),[104] it is an offence knowingly to render assistance (including financial assistance) to an unlawful organisation, whether directly or indirectly, in the performance or furtherance of an unlawful object. This supplement reflects a recommendation made by the Hederman Committee which had argued that active assistance to an unlawful organisation might be easier to prove than passive membership.[105] Alongside section 21A, the 2005 Act also implemented the general offence of financing terrorism (in section 13) so as to ensure domestic implementation of the United Nations Convention for the Suppression of the Financing of Terrorism 1999.[106]

Extra-territorial effect for membership-type offences in certain circumstances is accorded by section 6 of the 2005 Act which mainly has the effect of establishing a further terrorism offence which is chiefly related to activity but, contrary to the ethos of the Framework Directive, also extends the offences based on group affiliation.[107] Section 6(1)(a) states that a person is guilty of an offence if, in or outside the state, they engage in a 'terrorist activity'[108] or 'terrorist-linked activity'[109] or, under section 6(1)(b), commit outside the state an act that, if committed in the state, would constitute: (i) an offence under section 21 or 21A of the Act of 1939; or (ii) an offence under section 6 of the Act of 1998. Section 6(2) sets out the circumstances in which acts committed outside the state will be offences for the purpose of subsection (1).[110] Furthermore, where a section 6 offence is committed outside the state and a request for extradition or a European Arrest Warrant is received and refused, section 43(3) of the 2005 Act affords jurisdiction to try the case in Ireland.

These membership offences have not been constitutionally challenged per se, unlike their evidential appurtenances. The principal section 21 membership offence has been regularly prosecuted as a key tool to suppress domestic terrorist and subversive activity. The offences have often provided the most frequent charges in the Special Criminal Court; there were 72 convictions from 2002–17.[111]

[103] Ibid, 6.150.

[104] Criminal Justice (Terrorist Offences) Act 2005, s 49. See also ss 50, 51 relating to property. For indirect assistance, see *People (DPP) v Hannaway* [2020] IECA 38; *People (DPP) v Metcalfe* [2020] IECA 176.

[105] Hederman Report, (n 7) 6.48.

[106] A/RES/54/109, as specified in the 2005 Act, Sch 7. Implementation is required by UNSCR 1373 (2001).

[107] See Hamilton, 'The Interplay Between EU and Irish' (n 61) 556–557; Harte, 'The Offence of Membership' (n 45) 72.

[108] As defined by s 4 of the 2005 Act and reproducing the Council Framework Decision of 13 June 2002 on combating terrorism (2002/475/JHA) Art 1.1.

[109] 'Terrorist-linked activity' is defined in s 4 of the 2005 Act as relating to a range of offences in Sch 2 if committed with a view to engaging in a terrorist activity, or would constitute an offence under s 21 or 21A of the Act of 1939, as well as public provocation, recruitment for terrorism, or training.

[110] These circumstances apply if the act is committed: (a) on board an Irish ship; (b) on an Irish aircraft; (c) by an Irish citizen or person resident in the state; (d) for the benefit of a legal person established in the state; (e) against thestate or an Irish citizen; or (f) against (i) an EU institution based in the state or (ii) a body that is based in the state and is set up under a European Union Treaty.

[111] See Office of the Director of Public Prosecutions, *Annual Reports 2003–18* (www.dppireland.ie/publication-category/annual-reports). During 1974–1986, there were 226: Hogan and Walker, *Political Violence and the Law in Ireland* (n 27) 260. The totals are much smaller for s 3 of the Criminal Law Act 1976 (ibid, 261) and the 2005 Act, s 6 (Harrison, *The Special Criminal Court* (n 69) 6.76).

Moving from criminal offences, other legal consequences are specified by sections 22 and 25. First, section 22 of the 1939 Act[112] provides for the forfeiture to the Minister for Justice of all property of the suppressed organisation; the Minister can then dispose of the property in consultation with the Minister for Finance. This mechanism was extended by section 2 of the Offences Against the State (Amendment) Act 1985.[113] The Minister for Justice may direct a bank to lodge in the High Court, funds which stand in a bank account and which are in the opinion of the Minister liable to forfeiture under section 22, without having to provide notice to those affected. A further extension is made by the Criminal Justice (Terrorist Offences) Act 2005, section 51, which imports sections 22A to 22I into the 1939 Act. They concern a further procedure for the recovery of the property of unlawful organisations, other than moneys held in a bank, which should be forfeited to the Minister by virtue of section 22. The constitutionality of the financial pre-emptive strike allowed by the 1985 Act was challenged in *Clancy v Ireland*.[114] The plaintiffs argued that the Minister's exercise of this power amounted to a confiscation of property in violation of the right to the peaceful enjoyment of property under Articles 40.3 and 43 of the Constitution. Barrington J rejected their arguments, holding that section 2 of the 1985 Act did not effect a confiscation of funds, but rather constituted a temporary freezing of funds, which the plaintiff was entitled to challenge in the High Court (under section 3) and to receive compensation if in error (under section 4). As a result, Barrington J concluded that the provision represented a permissible delimitation of private property rights in the interests of the common good. This reasoning was endorsed by the Supreme Court in *Murphy v GM* in relation to the Proceeds of Crime Act 1996,[115] and the freezing and confiscation of illicit assets has become a mainstream feature within the anti-money laundering regimes. However, the Hederman Committee noted that the safeguards of challenge under the 1985 Act are not present in section 22 which it also found to be 'ineffective' and 'unworkable' and so worthy of abolition.[116] The broader consideration of whether these quasi criminal approaches are fair goes beyond the confines of this chapter.[117]

The final non-criminal sanction is that, under section 25 of the 1939 Act as amended by section 4 of the Criminal Law Act 1976, a Garda Chief Superintendent may order the closure of a building for 12 months (extendable to three years in total) if satisfied of its use, directly or indirectly, for the purposes of an unlawful organisation.[118] The invocation of this power is very rare, with just one recorded case,[119] and the Hederman Committee favoured its repeal.[120]

[112] The meaning of 'property' is expanded by the Criminal Justice (Terrorist Offences) Act 2005, s 50 to cover not only real, chattel real or personal property, but also 'funds' as defined by s 12 of the 2005 Act.

[113] See Hogan and Walker, *Political Violence and the Law in Ireland* (n 27) 271–273.

[114] [1988] IR 326

[115] [2001] 4 IR 113.

[116] Hederman Report, (n 7) 6.97, 6.98 (with a dissent at 6.99).

[117] See C King, 'Civil Forfeiture and Article 6 of the ECHR: Due Process Implications for England and Wales and Ireland' (2014) 34 *Legal Studies* 371; C King, C Walker, and J Gurulé (eds), *The Palgrave Handbook of Criminal and Terrorism Financing Law* (London, Palgrave MacMillan, 2018).

[118] See Hogan and Walker, *Political Violence and the Law in Ireland* (n 27) 250–251.

[119] *Ó'Brádaigh v Fanning*, *The Irish Times*, 25 November 1972, High Court.

[120] Hederman Report, (n 7) 6.124–6.129.

III. CONCLUSION

Proscription has retained vitality in Ireland. Its functions go beyond the presentational or symbolic purposes which are often achieved by proscription,[121] and it seeks to deliver more transactional outcomes in terms of deterrence and prosecutions. Several reasons may invest this energy. One is that its focus remains domestic and so involves relatively organised groups compared to the decentred and heterarchical groups common in international (foreign) terrorism, where central organisation and discipline is relatively weak and so any organisational ban seems futile. Second, the Irish legal system has been prepared to invest an extraordinary level of trust in senior police officers who are allowed to present untrammelled opinion evidence, which is regularly the key to conviction for proscription crimes.[122] Leaving aside ongoing doubts about whether the device is fair, experiences of miscarriages of justice in terrorism cases in other jurisdictions, especially the UK,[123] seem to rule out such heavy evidential reliance on police opinion.[124] Third, alternatives to proscription and membership offences are limited. By comparison, the UK Terrorism Act 2000, sections 57 and 58 (discussed above), plus the Terrorism Act 2006, sections 1, 2 (terrorist messages online) and (above all) section 5 (the offence of preparation of terrorism) have left membership offences as marginal and less attractive options.[125]

This depiction of vitality might be contrasted with the position said earlier to prevail in Northern Ireland – 'let sleeping dogs lie'. However, while prosecution convictions are being racked up south of the Border, the Republic's proscription structure does evince similar traits of somnolence. The need for reform in regard to powers and review represents unfinished business at least from the time of the Hederman Committee over two decades ago, with many recommendations ignored. The shelving of radical reform[126] is testament to the emotions and divisions roused by proscription. For now, Ireland persists with its apprehensions about subversive organisations (arguably more acute than its fear of 'terrorism') and maintains in full working order[127] its 80-year-old superstructure, including proscription. Yet, the gap between 'a perpetual state of emergency'[128] and sharply directed, fully accountable counter terrorism laws is broad and should not be allowed to persist for another 80 years.

[121] See (Baker) *Review of the Operation of the Northern Ireland (Emergency Provisions) Act 1978* (London, Cmnd.9222, 1984) 414

[122] See L Heffernan and E O'Connor, Chapter 6 and F Ní Aoláin, Chapter 4, this volume.

[123] See C Walker and K Starmer (eds), *Miscarriages of Justice* (London, Blackstone Press, 1999).

[124] Comparable provisions were introduced after the Omagh bombing by the Criminal Justice (Terrorism and Conspiracy) Act 1998, ss 1–2, but were never used and were repealed by the Terrorism Act 2000.

[125] Some difficulties were illustrated by *Choudary and Rahman v R* [2016] EWCA Crim 61.

[126] The Offences Against the State Acts Repeal Bill 2008 did not proceed past First Reading: *Dáil Debates* vol 657, 18 June 2008.

[127] Expiration became a legal crisis in *Bacik v An Taoiseach* [2020] IEHC 313. Compare *R (Murphy) v Military Governor, Mountjoy Prison* (1924) 58 ILTR 1.

[128] S Kilcommins and B Vaughan, 'A Perpetual State of Emergency: Subverting the Rule of Law in Ireland' (2004) 35 *Cambrian Law Review* 55.

10

New Media, Free Expression, and the Offences Against the State Acts

LAURA K DONOHUE*

I. INTRODUCTION

SOCIAL MEDIA HAS become an integral part of modern human interaction. As of October 2019, Facebook reported 2.414 billion active users worldwide.[1] YouTube, WhatsApp, and Instagram were not far behind, with 2 billion, 1.6 billion, and 1 billion users respectively.[2] In Ireland, 3.2 million people (66 per cent of the population) use social media for an average of nearly two hours per day.[3] By 2022, the number of domestic Facebook users is expected to reach 2.92 million.[4] Forty-one per cent of the population uses Instagram (65 per cent daily); 30 per cent uses Twitter (40 per cent daily), and another 30 per cent uses LinkedIn.[5] With social media prevalent amongst the younger generation, these numbers will only rise.

New media facilitates communication and creates a common, lived experience. It also carries the potential for great harm on an individual and societal scale. Posting integrates information and emotion, with study after study finding that fear and anger transfer most

* Thanks to Mark Coen, Fergal Davis, and the Sutherland School of Law for hosting the Offences Against the State Act Seminar in October 2019, and to Dr Coen for his thoughtful suggestions on the manuscript. I am further indebted to Mr Jeremy McCabe at the Georgetown Law library for his help in obtaining materials used in the chapter.

[1] S Kemp, 'Digital 2019: Q4 Global Digital Statshot' (*DataReportal*, 23 October 2019) slide 24 https://datareportal.com/reports/digital-2019-q4-global-digital-statshot. See also 'Most Popular Social Networks Worldwide as of January 2020, Ranked by Number of Active Users' (*Statista*, 25 January 2020) www.statista.com/statistics/272014/global-social-networks-ranked-by-number-of-users/.

[2] Ibid.

[3] S Kemp, 'Digital 2019: Ireland' (*DataReportal*, 31 January 2019) slides 19 and 31 https://datareportal.com/reports/digital-2019-ireland.

[4] S O'Dea, 'Forecast of the Facebook User Penetration Rate in Ireland from 2015–2022' (*Statista*, July 2017), www.statista.com/statistics/566781/predicted-facebook-user-penetration-rate-ireland/. See also K Twomey, 'Social Media Stats Ireland 2019' (*Communications Hub*, 12 August 2019) http://communicationshub.ie/blog/2019/08/12/social-media-statistics-ireland-2019/.

[5] Ibid.

readily online.[6] Isolation follows, with insular groups forming. The result is an increasing bifurcation of society. Scholars also write about rising levels of depression and suicide that stem from online dependence and replacing analogical experience with digital interaction, as well as escalating levels of anxiety that are rooted in the validation expectation of the 'like' function.[7] These changes generate instability and contribute to a volatile social environment. Significant political risks also accompany this novel genre. Hostile actors can use social media platforms to deepen political schisms, to promote certain candidates, and, as demonstrated by the recent Cambridge Analytica debacle, to swing elections.[8] Extremist groups and terrorist organisations can use online interactions to build sympathetic audiences and to recruit adherents.[9]

In Ireland, since 1939, the Offences Against the State Act (OASA) has served as the primary vehicle for confronting political violence and challenges to state authority. How effective is it in light of new media? The challenges are legion. Terrorist recruitment is just the tip of the iceberg. Social networking sites allow for targeted and global fundraising, international direction and control, anonymous power structures, and access to expertise. These platforms create spaces within which extreme ideologies can prosper, targeting individuals likely to be sympathetic to the cause, 24 hours a day, seven days a week, ad infinitum. They offer an alternative reality, subject to factual manipulation and direction – a problem exacerbated by the risk of so-called deep fakes: autonomously-generated content that makes it appear that people acted, or that certain circumstances occurred, which never did.[10]

In November 2019, the Irish Government indicated an intention to introduce a law targeting social media.[11] The proposed legislation would regulate political advertising to ensure that voters would not be misled by inaccurate information.[12] However, the measure, which has not been enacted, would not have addressed the myriad further risks. This chapter, accordingly, focuses on ways in which the OASA and related laws have historically treated free expression as a prelude to understanding how and whether the existing provisions are adequate for challenges from new media.

[6] PW Singer and ET Brooking, *Like War: The Weaponization of Social Media* (Boston, Houghton Mifflin Harcourt, 2018).

[7] See, eg, C Newport, *Digital Minimalism: Choosing a Focused Life in a Noisy World* (New York, Portfolio/ Penguin, 2019); JM Twenge et al, 'Increases in Depressive Symptoms, Suicide-Related Outcomes, and Suicide Rates Among U.S. Adolescents After 2010 and Links to Increased New Media Screen Time' (2018) 6 *Clinical Psychological Science* 3; H Clelland Woods and H Scott, '#Sleepyteens: Social Media Use in Adolescence Is Associated with Poor Sleep Quality, Anxiety, Depression and Low Self-Esteem' (2016) 51 *Journal of Adolescence* 41; H Sampasa-Kanyinga and RF Lewis, 'Frequent Use of Social Networking Sites Is Associated with Poor Psychological Functioning among Children and Adolescents' (2015) 18 *Cyberpsychology, Behavior, and Social Networking*; J Fox and JJ Moreland, 'The Dark Side of Social Networking Sites: An Exploration of the Relational and Psychological Stressors Associated with Facebook Use and Affordances' (2015) 45 *Computers in Human Behavior* 168; JD Elhai et al, 'Fear of Missing Out, Need for Touch, Anxiety and Depression Are Related to Problematic Smartphone Use' (2016) 63 *Computers in Human Behavior* 509.

[8] C Cadwalladr, 'Fresh Cambridge Analytica Leak 'Shows Global Manipulation Is Out of Control'' *The Guardian* (London, 4 January 2020) www.theguardian.com/uk-news/2020/jan/04/cambridge-analytica-data-leak-global-election-manipulation.

[9] Singer & Brooking, *Like War* (n 6).

[10] B Chesney and D Keats Citron, 'Deep Fakes: A Looming Challenge for Privacy, Democracy, and National Security' (2019) 107 *California Law Review* 1753.

[11] H McGee, 'New Legislation will Regulate Political Advertising on Social Media' *Irish Times* (Dublin, 5 November 2019).

[12] Ibid.

II. ORIGINS

Like the Irish Free State Constitution, the Treasonable Offences Act and the Public Safety Acts were forged in the fires of Irish Republicanism. Mohr, in his chapter on precursors to the OASA,[13] discusses these Acts and the conditions accompanying their introduction. This chapter focuses on the statutory provisions that restricted free speech and association. It argues that the 1937 Constitution cemented many of these legislative measures into the state structure, which laid the groundwork for their further expansion in the OASA and its progeny.

A. 1925 Treasonable Offences Act

Outside of a narrow exception for public morality, the 1922 Free State Constitution protected free expression.[14] The guarantee, though, proved unable to withstand the challenges posed by violent skirmishes, hunger strikes, and continued sympathy for anti-Treatyites. High unemployment and food shortages exacerbated political tension. Cuman na nGaedheal, which came into power in the August 1923 election, took steps to protect the fledgling state.

Under the Treasonable Offences Act of 1925, it became an offence to conspire with or to incite others to attempt to overthrow the government of Saorstát Eireann.[15] The statute forbade the administration or taking of any oath pledging to commit, promote, or conceal the commission of any crime.[16] It made it illegal to incite any member of the military or police force to mutiny, leave service, or refuse to obey orders, or to incite any member of the civil service to refuse, neglect, or omit to perform their duty.[17] The Act further outlawed refusing to speak when requested for information about any crime or breach of the peace.[18]

Although the government did use the law to prosecute members of the Irish Republican Army (IRA), recourse to its provisions proved problematic. During the 1916 Rising, almost identical measures had been used by the British Crown.[19] They had been designed to obtain a higher rate of conviction – not necessarily to ascertain guilt. Their purpose was to counter jury intimidation, but the result was a statutory framework that had been largely discredited. The re-enactment of parts of the Treason Felony Act 1848 in the 1925 statute did little to demonstrate a break with the past.[20] Ministers' consequent reluctance to use such provisions against their former

[13] See T Mohr, Chapter 2, this volume.

[14] Constitution of the Irish Free State 1922, Art 9. See also Censorship of Publications Act 1929, ss 6, 17; Censorship of Publications Act 1946; Censorship of Films Act 1923. For further discussion of censorship in Ireland for reasons of public morality see K Rockett, *Irish Film Censorship: A Cultural Journey from Silent Cinema to Internet Pornography* (Dublin, Four Courts Press, 2004).

[15] Treasonable Offences Act 1925, s 1(c), (e).

[16] Ibid, s 9(1)(a).

[17] Ibid, s 13.1(c); 3.1(e); 3.1(f).

[18] Ibid, s 9(1)(c)–(d).

[19] M Head, *Crimes against the State: from Treason to Terrorism* (Farnham, Ashgate, 2011) 99; Treason Act 1795 (36 Geo 3 c 7) (Eng); Treason Act 1817 (57 Geo 3 c 6) (Eng); Treason Felony Act 1848 (11 & 12 Vict c 12) (Eng).

[20] Compare Treasonable Offences Act 1925, s 3(1) and Treason Felony Act 1848 (11 & 12 Vict. c 12) s 3 (Eng). On pre-Independence emergency law, see N Howlin, Chapter 1, this volume.

comrades shifted the government's emphasis to the Public Safety Acts and, thence, to the OASA.

B. 1923–31 Public Safety Acts and Article 2A

The 1923 Public Safety Act (PSA) was born of Civil War. It provided for broad powers of detention and internment for anyone considered a threat to public safety.[21] It forbade threatening or coercing others to a revolt against the government.[22] Punishment for crimes committed under the Act ranged from property seizure to flogging, imprisonment, and death.[23] The following year, a second Public Safety Act targeted speech, making it illegal to incite others to engage in rebellion.[24] It outlawed any effort 'to induce any officer of the Government of Saorstát Eireann to refuse, neglect, or omit to discharge his duty' as an officer.[25] Even encouraging individuals not to serve in government could result in imprisonment. In 1926, a third PSA made allowance for the proclamation of a public emergency during which the Executive Minister could assume extraordinary powers related to arrest and detention.[26] These powers were premised in part on the foregoing crimes of incitement and inducement, as well as those detailed in the 1925 Treasonable Offences Act.[27]

Throughout this time, violence propagated by the IRA, Fianna Eireann, and Cumann na mBan continued. In 1931, Cumann na nGaedheal, under WT Cosgrave's leadership, responded by pushing the Constitution (Amendment No 17) Act (referred to as the Public Safety Act 1931) through the Oireachtas, resulting in the incorporation of Article 2A into the Irish Free State Constitution.[28] Cosgrave set aside two days in the Dáil and a day and a half in the Seanad for the Bill to go through all of its stages.[29]

In the Dáil, Cosgrave promoted suspending rights as a way of safeguarding them.[30] The Minister for Defence, Desmond FitzGerald, took a more philosophical stance: 'Why have we a Constitution at all? Why have we a Government? Why have we a State?'[31]

[21] Public Safety (Emergency Powers) Act 1923, ss 1, 3. See also Public Safety (Emergency Powers) (No 2) Act 1923; B Vaughan and S Kilcommins, *Terrorism, Rights and the Rule of Law: Negotiating Justice in Ireland* (Cullompton, Willan Publishing, 2008) 70.

[22] Public Safety (Emergency Powers) Act 1923, Sch, Pt I, para 2.

[23] Public Safety (Emergency Powers) Act 1923, s 5.

[24] Public Safety (Punishment of Offences) Temporary Act 1924, Sch, Pt I.

[25] Ibid, Sch, Pt II, para 1.

[26] Public Safety (Emergency Powers) Act 1926, Sch, paras 1, 2, and 14. Legislation passed by the Parliament of Northern Ireland paralleled this statute. See Emergency Powers Act (NI) 1926 (16 & 17 Geo 5 c 8) (empowering the Governor of Northern Ireland to declare a state of emergency).

[27] Public Safety (Emergency Powers) Act of 1926, Sch, paras 1, 2.

[28] Constitution (Amendment No 17) Act 1931. See also *Ryan and Others (The State) v Lennon and Others* [1935] IR 170 (HC), 69 ILTR 125 (determining that the Oireachtas did not act ultra vires in passing the legislation).

[29] WT Cosgrave, *Dáil Debates* 14 October 1931, vol 40, col 29; T O'Connell (Labour Party), *Dáil Debates* 14 October 1931, vol 40, col 61. Constitution of the Irish Free State 1922, Art 50 provided an eight-year grace period for the Oireachtas to amend the Constitution without returning to the people for a referendum. The Oireachtas subsequently amended that article to extend the time period, with the result that from 1922 to 1937, the Constitution could be amended by statute, which it was, on 27 occasions. See G Hogan, *The Origins of the Irish Constitution, 1928–1941* (Dublin, Royal Irish Academy, 2012) 4–8.

[30] WT Cosgrave, *Dáil Debates* 14 October 1931, vol 40, col 31.

[31] D FitzGerald, *Dáil Debates* 14 October 1931, vol 40, col 69.

To his mind, 'we have a Government and a State because we were made to live in society that man, being subject to the performance of evil, requires to be controlled by law'.[32] FitzGerald argued that the fact that the measures were coercive did not make them any different from the Egg Grading Act or the Live Stock Bill.[33] They were just directed at a serious threat.[34] In his view, the failure to augment state power would result in the dissolution of the state.[35]

Fianna Fáil and Labour objected to the measures' breadth and the speed with which they were being introduced.[36] The statute's impact could hardly be ignored: 'The Constitution', Seán Lemass argued, 'may be the most glorious Constitution in the world, but it will be a dead letter before Friday evening if the Minister and his Party get their way'.[37] The exceptions would abrogate constitutional rights. Lemass called out Cosgrave on the contradiction in stating that because rights were secure, they could be suspended to prevent violence, citing particular concern about the impact of the provisions on 'the right of free speech, the right of free assembly, [and] freedom of the Press'.[38]

Article 2A had a profound effect on constitutional rights. As Mohr observes, its primary purpose was to establish an emergency court with extraordinary powers.[39] Freedom of expression did not escape the net. The statute made it illegal to possess any treasonable or seditious documents, defined in terms of unlawful associations: ie, a document related to any group that promoted, encouraged, or advocated: (a) any act of a treasonable or seditious character; (b) the commission of any offence; (c) the obstruction of justice; or (d) non-payment of taxes.[40] The burden was on the person on whose property or person such documents were found to demonstrate to the satisfaction of the Court (or the Special Tribunal) either that he did not know that the material was in his possession, or was unaware of the contents.[41] Otherwise, possession demonstrated membership.[42] The statute made further inroads into free expression. It prohibited printing, publishing, selling, or distributing 'any book, newspaper, magazine, periodical, pamphlet, leaflet, circular, or other document' on behalf of unlawful associations, regardless of their content.[43] 'Print' was construed broadly to mean any mode of representing or reproducing words in visible form.[44] It captured any notes made at a meeting; letters or invitations sent by members of the group; or announcements of planned events. The Special Tribunal could

[32] Ibid.

[33] Ibid, col 70. See, eg, Agricultural Produce (Eggs) Act 1924, No 35, s 14; Agricultural Produce (Eggs) Act 1930, No 36, s 11.

[34] Ibid.

[35] Ibid, col 78.

[36] See, eg, E de Valera, *Dáil Debates* 14 October 1931, vol 40, cols 58, 61; T O'Connell (Labour Party), *Dáil Debates* 14 October 1931, vol 40, col 62.

[37] S Lemass, *Dáil Debates* 14 October 1931. vol 40, col 81.

[38] Ibid, cols 85–86. For a direct response to Lemass, see Minister for Justice, J Fitzzgerald-Kenney, *Dáil Debates* 14 October 1931, vol 40, col 110.

[39] See T Mohr, Chapter 2, this volume. Article 2A empowered the Executive Council to declare a state of emergency suspending certain constitutional clauses; created a Special Powers Tribunal for political crimes; introduced new arrest powers; and provided for proscription. See Constitution (Amendment No 17) Act 1931. See also Constitution (Operation of Article 2A) Order 1931, SR&O 1931/72 (bringing in the provision).

[40] Constitution (Amendment No 17) Act 1931, s 19(1), s 21 and Sch, para 3(1).

[41] Ibid.

[42] Ibid, s 22(1).

[43] See ibid, s 23(1)–(2).

[44] See ibid, s 23(3).

declare any periodical seditious and order the Garda Síochána to search for and seize it.[45] Treasonable documents also became a trigger for extraordinary stop, search, and arrest powers.[46] The statement by any member of the Gardaí that he suspected an individual to be carrying seditious material was treated as 'conclusive and final evidence, incapable of being rebutted or questioned by cross-examination' as a rationale for arrest.[47] For home searches, the presence of treasonous documents became sufficient for the reasonableness determination.[48] Any documents seized could be destroyed.[49]

Fianna Fáil, which had bitterly opposed the statute, ended the emergency when it came to power in 1932, leaving the Gardaí with ordinary criminal law to counter the IRA.[50] The suspension of Parts II to V of Article 2A, however, did not revoke the Constitution (Amendment No 17) Act of 1931, leaving the underlying powers in place. Following almost nightly confrontations between the Blueshirts and the IRA, in 1933 Éamon de Valera re-activated Article 2A and banned the Blueshirts.[51] Three years later, he extended the prohibition to the IRA.[52]

C. The 1937 Irish Constitution

In 1934, Fianna Fáil began to prepare a new Constitution. Foremost in the Committee's mind was the concentration of power in Article 2A.[53] Following intense debate and multiple amendments, the new Constitution passed by national plebiscite, coming into force in December 1937. Bunreacht na hÉireann repealed section 2A and placed more restrictions on the use of emergency powers.[54] Simultaneously, it limited the right of free expression, dividing the speech clause from the earlier Constitution into three sections: freedom of expression, assembly, and association. In each, it augmented the prior concerns about public morality with an assurance that freedoms would not be used to undermine the state – in essence, constitutionalising the exceptions in the Public Safety Acts.[55]

The new speech clause established '[t]he right of the citizens to express freely their convictions and opinions', while placing controls on the radio, press, and film industry to ensure that communication could not be used to undermine public order or morality, or

[45] Ibid, s 26.
[46] Ibid, s 29(1).
[47] Ibid, s 29(2).
[48] Ibid, s 30(1).
[49] Ibid, s 32.
[50] Constitution (Suspension of Article 2A) Order 1932, SR&O 1932/11 (suspending Ps II–V of Art 2A as permitted by Constitution (Amendment No 17) Act 1931, s 1(3)).
[51] Constitution (Operation of Article 2A) Order 1933, SR&O 1933/91; Constitution (Declaration of Unlawful Association) Order 1933, SR&O 1933/95; Constitution (Declaration of Unlawful Association) (No 2) Order 1933, SR&O 1933/189.
[52] Constitution (Declaration of Unlawful Association) Order 1936, SR&O 1936/172 (banning the Irish Republican Army / IRA / Óglaigh na hÉireann under Constitution (Amendment No 17) Act 1931, s 19(2)).
[53] DK Coffey, *Drafting the Irish Constitution 1935–1937: Transnational Influences in Interwar Europe* (Cham, Palgrave Macmillan, 2018) 188, 193. See also G Hogan, 'The Constitution Review Committee of 1934' in F Ó Muircheartaigh (ed), *Ireland in the Coming Times: Essays to Celebrate T.K. Whitaker's 80 Years* (Dublin, Institute of Public Administration, 1997).
[54] Constitution of Ireland (Bunreacht na hÉireann) 1937.
[55] Compare above n 1 and Constitution of Ireland 1937, Art 40.6.1.i–iii.

the authority of the state.[56] The Constitution echoed the 1925 Treasonable Offences Act, prohibiting '[t]he publication or utterance of seditious' (as well as indecent) matter.[57]

The 1937 Constitution separated out the right of assembly, allowing for peaceable congregation, while empowering the government to prevent or control meetings 'calculated to cause a breach of the peace or to be a danger or nuisance to the general public'.[58] The addition of this section reflected the Article 2A approach, with unlawful associations premised on the marshalling of force against the government.[59] It weighed the exception to the right against the communal interest in protecting the state.

The Constitution forbade laws regulating associations from discriminating based on political, religious, or class distinctions.[60] Nevertheless, treasonous, anti-constitutional associations could not rely on Article 40 for protection. Since Article 2A of the prior Constitution had not been continued, the new document superseded the earlier provisions. Article 40 thus functioned to fold in press and publication elements as a basis for considerations related to speech and the associative rights. Despite the incorporation of elements of the Treasonable Offences Act into the new Constitution, the 1925 statute, as well as the 1926 Public Safety (Emergency Powers) Act remained in place until the adoption, two years later, of the OASA.[61]

III. THE OFFENCES AGAINST THE STATE ACT

The 1939 OASA passed amidst heightened global political tension. Democracies across the globe were under siege.[62] In 1932, following the assassination of Prime Minister Inukai Tsuyoshi, the Japanese military assumed control. In Spain, a coup by right-wing military leaders in 1936 led to Civil War. In Germany, Adolf Hitler and the Third Reich abolished the presidency and introduced extraordinary powers.[63] In 1938, the country annexed Austria and, the following year, asserted dominion over parts of Czechoslovakia. Benito Mussolini, having established an authoritarian regime in Italy, invaded Albania.

Concern about the international backdrop wove its way into OASA debates. In some ways, it made restrictions more palatable, as the issue was how to protect democracy – not, more narrowly, whether to incorporate the six counties or respond to those willing to use violence to do so. Nevertheless, the immediate rationale offered by the government followed the familiar line, justifying new restrictions on speech, publication, and association by reference to Republican dissidents.

[56] Constitution of Ireland 1937, Art 40.6.1.i.
[57] Ibid.
[58] Ibid, Art 40.6.1.ii.
[59] See ibid, Art 40.6.1.iii.
[60] Ibid, Art 40.6.2.
[61] Offences Against the State Act of 1939, s. 5.
[62] Offences Against the State Act 1939.
[63] See, eg, Law for the Prevention of Offspring with Hereditary Diseases (*Gesetz zur Verhütung erbkranken Nachwuchses*) s 1, 1933 RGBl I, 529 (creating a Genetic Health Court (*Erbgesundheitsgericht*) and mandating forced sterilisation for persons with certain physical and mental disabilities or chronic alcoholism); Law against Dangerous Habitual Criminals and on Measures for Security and Improvement (*Gesetz über die gefährliche Gewohnheitsverbrecher und über Massregeln zur Sicherung und Besserung*), 1933 RGBl I, 995 (providing for indefinite detention, inter alia); Law on Treason, 1934 RGBl I, 341 (Ger) (making most activities of opposition groups punishable by death).

A. Broader Context and Supporting Arguments

In 1939, the spectre of WWII loomed large. In the Seanad, Professor Helena Concannon pronounced, 'It is because ours is a democratic State – and most of us wish it to remain such – that the Government we have chosen for ourselves must be provided by us with the powers necessary to protect the State.'[64] She highlighted the 'many examples in recent years of the dangers to democratic governments if they are left defenceless and if they have not those necessary powers'.[65] The Fianna Fáil leader in the Seanad (and a senior member of the IRA in County Tipperary during the War of Independence), William Quirke, underscored the importance of restricting freedom to protect democracy in light of the changed circumstances.[66]

Members of Dáil Éireann similarly recognised the new kind of threat. James Matthew Dillon argued that 'in recent years, the technique of potential tyranny has completely changed'.[67] Rights made democratic states vulnerable, as those seeking 'to destroy democratic government' could 'use the very privileges conferred by the Constitution for the purpose of destroying the Constitution itself'.[68] He warned that 'while democracy is shivering on the brink' authoritarian adherents could 'give democracy the felon's blow, destroy it and grab power and after they have grabbed power then proceed to subjugate the people'.[69]

While some members of the Oireachtas argued that the threat facing democracy internationally required extraordinary measures, the government cited the IRA's resumption of its violent campaign in Britain and the continued challenge of Republicanism in justification.[70] Numerous members oppugned this rationale, citing the absence of evidence that such a campaign was underway.[71] They expressed alarm about normalising extraordinary powers at a time of relative peace.[72] Without evidence, it was hard to justify the restrictions on freedom of expression and of the press.[73] General Seán MacEoin doubted that a sub-constitutional instrument could deprive citizens of their fundamental rights.[74] Fine Gael politician and future Attorney General Patrick McGilligan noted:

> We have a series of Articles in our Constitution which state fundamental principles and rights. It has stated them with so many reservations that the rights and liberties have almost disappeared. The law may change, and if it does change the fundamental rights under the Constitution are gone.[75]

[64] Prof H Concannon, *Seanad Debates* 3 May 1939, vol 22, col 1540. See also, ibid, col 1539–40.
[65] Ibid.
[66] See, eg, W Quirke, *Seanad Debates* 4 May 1939, vol 22, col 1557.
[67] JM Dillon, *Dáil Debates* 3 March 1939, vol 74, col 1440.
[68] Ibid.
[69] Ibid.
[70] See S Goulding, *Seanad Debates* 4 May 1939, vol 22, col 1551; W Davin, *Dáil Debates* 7 March 1939, vol 74, col 1565; PJ Ruttledge, *Dáil Debates* 8 Feb 1939, vol 74, col 90. See also W Quirke, *Seanad Debates* 4 May 1939, vol 22, cols 1554–55.
[71] See, eg, J McLoughlin, *Seanad Deb* 3 May 1939, vol 22, col 1526; P Hogan, *Seanad Debates* 3 May 1939, vol 22, col 1534; W Davin, *Dáil Debates* 7 March 1939, vol 74, col 1564; W Davin, *Dáil* Debates 3 March 1939, vol 74, col 1476; General S MacEoin, *Dáil Debates* 7 March 1939, vol 74, cols 1565–66; P Belton, *Dáil Debates* 3 March 1939, vol 74, col 1459; Captain P Giles, *Dáil Debates* 2 March 1939, vol 74, cols 1356–57; ibid, col 1358.
[72] See, eg, S Brodrick, *Dáil Debates* 2 March 1939, vol 74, col 1375.
[73] See, eg, P Hogan, *Seanad Debates* 3 May 1939, vol 22, cols 1536–37.
[74] General S MacEoin, *Dáil Debates* 7 March 1939, vol 74, col 1566.
[75] P McGilligan, *Dáil Debates* 2 March 1939, vol 74, cols 1399–1400.

He despaired of the impact of the OASA on '[m]atters affecting conscience', 'freedom of the Press, and freedom to speak one's thoughts'.[76]

Foremost in the Opposition's mind was the potential for abuse.[77] The same objections had been brought forward during the debates on Article 2A, eliciting guarantees that the powers would be used appropriately. Nevertheless, they had been misapplied.[78] Backbenchers observed that while Fianna Fáil might be in power now, in the future, they too could become subject to a different government wielding the measures against them. In the Seanad, Cumann na nGaedheal politician John McLoughlin made dire predictions, quoting Shelley: 'I met Murder on the way,/ He wore the mask of Castlereagh,/ Very smooth he looked, yet grim,/ Seven bloodhounds followed him.'[79] Despite such misgivings, the OASA was passed in the Dáil by 53 votes to 8 and in the Seanad by 28 votes to 9.[80] International concerns might have loomed large; but the language continued to be redolent of anti-Treaty challenges to the state. The restrictions on freedom of expression, in particular, targeted Republican activities.

B. Impact of the 1939 OASA on Speech, Expression, and the Associative Rights

The OASA had immediate implications for freedom of expression. The statute made it illegal to advocate the usurpation or unlawful exercise of government functions (section 6); to obstruct legislative, executive, or judicial functions (section 7); or to incite or encourage any government employee to refuse, neglect or omit to perform their duties (section 9). It created new strictures to deal with printed matter. The Act prohibited printing, publishing, selling, or distributing incriminating material (books, newspapers, magazines, publications, pamphlets, circulars, or advertisements).[81] Like section 2A, content did not matter. Instead, it defined such material as anything issued by or 'emanating from an unlawful organisation' or 'appearing to aid or abet any such' entity.[82] The statute forbade treasonable, as well as seditious documents, the latter being understood in particularly broad terms, ie:

(a) a document consisting of or containing matter calculated or tending to undermine the public order or the authority of the State, and
(b) a document which alleges, implies, or suggests or is calculated to suggest that the government functioning under the Constitution is not the lawful government of the State or that there is in existence in the State any body or organisation not functioning under the Constitution which is entitled to be recognised as being the government of the country, and
(c) a document which alleges, implies, or suggests or is calculated to suggest that the military forces maintained under the Constitution are not the lawful military forces of the

[76] Ibid, col 1400.
[77] See, eg, P Cogan, *Dáil Debates* 2 March 1939, vol 74, col, 1300.
[78] Ibid ('[T]he people who introduced that measure and sponsored it and succeeded in getting it passed were the very people who were penalised afterwards by the Act.').
[79] J McLoughlin, *Seanad Debates* 3 May 1939, vol 22, col 1531.
[80] *Dáil Debates* 27 April 1939, vol 74, col 1274; *Seanad Debates* 31 May 1929, vol 22, col 1634.
[81] OASA, s 2.
[82] Ibid.

State, or that there is in existence in the State a body or organisation not established and maintained by virtue of the Constitution which is entitled to be recognised as a military force, and

(d) a document in which words, abbreviations, or symbols referable to a military body are used in referring to an unlawful organisation.[83]

The OASA thus outlawed any effort to undermine the legitimacy of the Irish Government as a political entity. It did not draw attention to what form that government ought to take (eg, an autocracy, oligarchy, democracy, or republic) – a consideration already addressed in Article 5 of the Constitution. It forbade documents related to paramilitary organisations as an alternative to the existing military – again reflecting the Republican challenge. The statute made it illegal to send or to publish any incriminating, treasonous, or seditious document, with penalties ranging from a fine and imprisonment to forfeiture.[84] Parliamentarians expressed alarm at the potential use of the measure to stifle political dissent.[85] Even if the 'truth' could be published, political critique might not escape. The government swept aside these objections.

With restrictions focused on domestic publications, some politicians raised concerns about foreign manipulation and control.[86] The government responded that the situation was already covered by the Bill.[87] This explanation did not satisfy the Irish press, which underscored the risk of unfair competition.[88] The Seanad, accordingly, brought in an additional measure targeting foreign newspapers.[89] It provided for the Minister of Justice to prevent foreign papers from entering the country and to seize them within domestic bounds.[90] Introducing the measure in Dáil Éireann, the Minister for Justice, Patrick Joseph Ruttledge, further raised the importance of not putting distributors in the position of censor.[91]

The OASA made possession of incriminating, treasonable, or seditious documents illegal.[92] Like Article 2A, the burden was on the defendant to demonstrate that he did not know that he had the document, or that he did not know the nature of its contents.[93] Where publishers found themselves in possession of such material and the Garda Síochána requested it, they had the option of either turning it over to the police or destroying the document.[94] This clause had been put forward at the request of Dublin newspapers to ensure the continued protection of their sources.[95] During the Committee stage, the government added a provision to require printers to retain copies of the documents, as

[83] Ibid.
[84] Ibid, s 10(2)–(3).
[85] See, eg, W Davin and R Corish, *Dáil Debates* 7 March 1939, vol 74, cols 1562–63.
[86] See, eg, F Aiken, Minister for Defence, *Dáil* Debates 3 March 1939, vol 74, cols 1436–37.
[87] See, eg, D Fitzgerald, *Seanad Debates* 31 May 1939, vol 22, col 1624.
[88] W Quirke, *Seanad Debates* 17 May 1939, vol 22, col 1594.
[89] The measure was adopted as Amendment 2 in the Seanad. See OASA, s 11.
[90] Ibid, s 11(1).
[91] PJ Ruttledge, *Dáil Debates* 6 June 1939, vol 76, col 581.
[92] OASA, s 12(1).
[93] Ibid, s 12(3).
[94] Ibid, s 12(5).
[95] PJ Ruttledge, *Dáil Debates* 6 June 1939, vol 76, cols 581–82 (Amendment 3 in the Seanad).

well as particulars of the person for whom the work was done, for six months following publication, to be turned over to the Gardaí on request.[96] Publishers were also required to put their name and address on every document.[97]

The government quickly used its new power. On 23 June 23 1939, it issued an order, citing sections 18 and 19 of the OASA, and stating that 'the Government are of opinion that the organisation styling itself the Irish Republican Army (also the I.R.A. and Oglaigh na hÉireann) is an unlawful organisation'.[98] Depending upon the level of Republican agitation, the government exercised its authority under the order. In 1955, for instance, the Taoiseach, John A Costello, met with the editors of Irish newspapers to remind them that the IRA was an unlawful organisation in respect of which an OASA Suppression Order had been issued.[99] The order prohibited the media from printing or publishing information publicising the organisation. Failure to abide by the suppression order would result in seizure and destruction of the edition in which the information appeared, and up to three months' ban on any future publication.[100]

In 1957, ten men were sent to prison for, alternately, failing to give an account of their movements and actions over a specified period, being a member of a proscribed organisations, and being in possession of incriminating documents.[101] That same year, charges were brought against two men in Cork for membership of an illegal organisation, possession of incriminating documents, and failing to answer questions in connection with the commission of an offence by others. The documents related to the purchase of sleeping bags, ground sheets, haversacks, uniforms and spirit lamps, and the payment of money. One of the documents contained the heading, 'Irish Resistance to British Aggression.'[102] During the trial the public galleries were full. Some 300 people gathered in the streets outside on the final day, alternately cheering and booing the authorities for use of the power.[103]

C. Evolution of the OASA

The OASA underwent four amendments, three of which implicated free speech and expression.[104] Like the initial provisions, the new clauses reflected the Republican challenge.

[96] OASA, s 13(1)(b). See also PJ Ruttledge, *Seanad Debates* 31 May 1939, vol 22, cols 1624–25 (inserting s 13(1)(a)–(c)).

[97] OASA, s 14(1).

[98] Unlawful Organisations (Suppression) Order 1939, 23 June 1939. See also 'Suppression Order Still In Force', *Irish Times*, 3 December 1955 1, 8.

[99] 'Suppression Order Still In Force', *Irish Times*, 3 December 1955 1, 8; 'Ban on News of I.R.A.' *The Times*, 3 December 1955, 6.

[100] 'Ban on News of I.R.A.' *The Times*, 3 December 1955, 6.

[101] 'Charges Under Offences Against State Act: Ten Men Sent to Prison' *Irish Times*, 26 January 1957 9.

[102] 'Crowd Boohs After Cork Court Case', *Irish Times*, 28 January 1957 3.

[103] Ibid.

[104] Offences Against the State (Amendment) Act 1940 (OASA 1940), Offences Against the State (Amendment) Act 1972 (OASA 1972), [Offences Against the State (Amendment) Act 1985 (nothing on speech/press/publication; focused on banks)], and Offences Against the State (Amendment) Act 1998 (OASA 1998).

The first change, the Offences Against the State (Amendment) Act 1940, expanded the government's authority to determine what statements undermined public order.[105] Section 4(1) contained an internment power and permitted a government minister to order the arrest and detention of anyone 'engaged in activities which, in his opinion, are prejudicial to the preservation of public peace and order or the security of the State'.[106] Reminiscent of the provision in the 1922 Civil Authorities (Special Powers) Act granting the Northern Ireland Prime Minister the power 'to take all such steps and issue all such orders as may be necessary for preserving the peace and maintaining order', designation in the Republic could be based entirely on speech, expression, or associations considered by the Minister to be a threat.[107]

History has not treated section 4(1) kindly. In 1999, the government established the Committee to Review the Offences Against the State Acts 1939 to 1998 under the chairmanship of Hederman J (Hederman Report). In its final report, the committee wrote:

> [O]ne must ... regard the [provision] as constituting a draconian interference with fundamental rights to liberty, due process, freedom of expression and freedom of association .... [T]he powers in question are inconsistent with the basic tenets of democracy and the rule of law, and it is inappropriate that a liberal democracy should retain them on its statute book in the twenty-first century.[108]

The provision, nevertheless, remains in force.

In 1972, the Oireachtas again amended the OASA, adding a clause that allowed for membership of an unlawful organisation to be predicated upon any oral or written statement.[109] The statute outlawed any statement or meeting that interfered with the 'course of justice' – ie, anything intended, or likely (directly or indirectly) 'to influence any court, person or authority' concerned in criminal proceedings – including as a party or witness.[110] The statute amended the definition of 'document' to incorporate any map, plan, graph, or drawing; photograph; digital media; and film, microfilm, or tape.[111]

During the mid-1970s, political leaders, referencing the OASA, again reminded journalists that the law prohibited them from publishing statements by proscribed organisations.[112] The government went on to make direct use of the power. In 1973, for example, printers from Drogheda were charged under the OASA for printing the book *Freedom Struggle*.[113] The cover of the publication featured a person dressed in military-type uniform with a sub-machine gun. The Gardaí seized the printed books, the plates, and other information related to publication.[114] The following year the editor of

[105] See OASA 1940.

[106] Ibid, s 4(1). See A Greene, Chapter 13, this volume.

[107] Civil Authorities (Special Powers) Act (Northern Ireland) 1922, s 1(1).

[108] Committee to Review the Offences against the State Acts 1939 to 1998, *Report of the Committee to Review the Offences Against the State Acts, 1939–1998 and Related Matters* (Dublin, Stationery Office, 2002) hereinafter, Hederman Report, 5.67.

[109] Offences Against the State (Amendment) Act 1972, s 3(1)(a). See L Heffernan and E O'Connor, Chapter 6, this volume.

[110] Ibid, s 4(1).

[111] Ibid, s 5(a)–(d).

[112] 'Kelly Critical of Journalists', *Irish Times*, 14 November 1975, 13.

[113] 'Company and Two Employees Are Charged with Printing Seditious Document Booklet by the Provisional I.R.A.' *Irish Times*, 6 November 1973, 13.

[114] Ibid.

An Phoblacht, Eamonn MacThomais, was sentenced to 15 months' imprisonment under the OASA for IRA membership and possession of an incriminating document.[115] The 1972 amendment generated significant concern among journalists, spurring the National Union of Journalists (NUJ) to make numerous representations to the government.[116]

Following a series of high-level IRA operations, in 1976 the Fine Gael-Labour coalition introduced an Emergency Powers Act that increased detention from 48 hours to seven days.[117] In concert with the measure, a new Criminal Law Act sought to strengthen section 10 of the 1939 OASA, which prohibited publishing, distributing, or possessing any seditious or treasonable document.[118]

The new provision, which forbade inciting others to join an unlawful association or to assist in its activities, was initially drafted broadly enough to encompass the print media – essentially creating an OASA corollary to section 31 of the Broadcasting Authority Act 1960, which provided for the minister to 'direct the Authority in writing to refrain from broadcasting any particular matter or matter of any particular class'.[119] Conor Cruise O'Brien, Labour Minister for Posts and Telegraphs, explained that the OASA provision would be used to prosecute editors of newspapers who published readers' letters to which the government objected.[120] The Attorney General confirmed the government's intent to a reporter from the *Irish Press*.[121] A bitter fight ensued, in the course of which the then Bill was amended to exclude the media provisions.

Following the Omagh bombing, the Oireachtas further curtailed the right to silence for individuals accused of membership of a proscribed entity, providing in the Offences Against the State (Amendment) Act of 1998 for an inference of guilt to be drawn from the failure to respond to questions.[122] The statute also allowed for the failure to provide a full account of one's 'movements, actions, activities, or associations during any specified

[115] D Walsh, 'Journalists Concerned at Jailing of Editor', *Irish Times*, 10 October 1974, 1.

[116] Ibid; 'Kelly Critical of Journalists', *Irish Times*, 14 November 1975, 13.

[117] Emergency Powers Act 1976, s 2(3).

[118] Criminal Law Act 1976, s 3.

[119] Broadcasting Authority Act 1960, s 31(1). In October 1971, RTÉ aired interviews with members of the IRA. The Fianna Fáil Minister for Posts and Telegraphs, issued the first order under s 31, directing RTÉ not to broadcast, 'any matter that could be calculated to promote the aims or activities of any organisation which engages in, promotes, encourages or advocates the attaining of any particular objectives by violent means'. See *Dáil Debates*, 4 November 1971, vol 256, col 1361 (Gerry Collins); M O'Brien, *The Fourth Estate: Journalism in Twentieth-Century Ireland* (Manchester, Manchester University Press, 2017), 138. In 1976, the government amended s 31 of the 1960 Act to prohibit material likely 'to promote, or incite to, crime or [that] would tend to undermine the authority of the State': Broadcasting Authority (Amendment) Act 1976, s 16. Conor Cruise O'Brien followed the legislation with an order forbidding RTÉ from carrying any interview, or report of an interview, with a spokesperson for the IRA/Oglaigh na hÉireann, Provisional Sinn Féin or any organisation proscribed by the British Government under the Northern Ireland (Emergency Provisions) Act 1973: Broadcasting Authority Act 1960 (Section 31) Order 1977, SI 1977/7. This brought Cumann na mBan, Na Fianna Éireann; Saor Éire, the Ulster Volunteer Force, Ulster Freedom Fighters and the Red Hand Commandoes within the reach of the Act. See LK Donohue, *Counterterrorist Law and Emergency Powers in Northern Ireland 1922–2000* (Dublin, Irish Academic Press 2007).

[120] M O'Brien, *The Fourth Estate: Journalism in Twentieth-Century Ireland* (Manchester, Manchester University Press, 2017), 145.

[121] Ibid.

[122] OASA 1998, s 2(1). See also M Melaugh, 'Main Events Surrounding the Bomb in Omagh' (*CAIN Web Service*) https://cain.ulster.ac.uk/events/omagh/events.htm (accessed 20 February 2020).

period' to be treated as corroborating evidence.[123] The law further amended the prior definition of conduct to include failure to deny published reports of membership.[124] It also made it a crime to collect, record or possess information that 'is likely to be useful' in the commission of serious offences by unlawful organisations.[125] The burden lay on the defendant to demonstrate that they were not collecting the information for such a purpose.[126] Constitutional challenges to the OASA provisions governing speech have been relatively few and far between. None have succeeded. In *People (DPP) v O'Leary*, for instance, a poster depicting a man in paramilitary gear and the slogan 'IRA calls the shots,' constituted incriminating material within the meaning of section 10 of the OASA.[127]

IV. NEW MEDIA, NEW THREATS

The OASA is not the only statute employed to censor free expression.[128] But the general trend, acknowledged decades ago in the Hederman Report, has been to extend greater protections to speech.[129] To some extent, the shift has had to do with the democratisation of the production and dissemination of information, as well as access: it is far easier to control a handful of domestic newspapers and radio and television networks than to monitor everything written and disseminated online, worldwide – and accessible to anyone with a mobile device.[130]

The change also relates to a shift in perspective. As the review committee explained:

> political philosophy in the broad sense is not the same today as it was in 1939. Freedom of speech, even hurtful, untrue and dangerous speech, is regarded more positively. Hierarchical deference has given way to egalitarian norms, which are not sympathetic to the notion that those in positions of political power and responsibility should be immunised from harsh attack.[131]

While violence continues in regard to the political status of Northern Ireland, the existential threat to the existence of the state from Republican dissidents has dissipated. As a result, legal constructs aimed at constraining that specific challenge can no longer rely on the immediate threat to the state for justification. To the extent that the threat is one of violence to persons or property, then a similar rationale to that underlying criminal provisions holds. Even if augmented based on the aims of the groups and individuals engaged in such activities, the impetus for Republican violence is not to undermine the political legitimacy of the Irish Government.

[123] Ibid, s 2(4)(a).
[124] Ibid, s 4 (amending OASA 1972, s 3).
[125] OASA 1998, s 8(1).
[126] Ibid, s 8(2).
[127] *People (DPP) v O'Leary* (1988) 3 Frewen 163.
[128] See, eg, Broadcasting Authority Act 1960 (BAA 1960); Broadcasting Authority (Amendment) Act 1976 (BAAA 1976), Radio and Television Act 1988, Broadcasting Act 1990, Broadcasting Authority (Amendment) Act 1993, and Broadcasting Act 2001.
[129] Hederman Report (108) 6.3.
[130] See also ibid, 6.2.
[131] Ibid, 6.3.

Different types of threats, however, now challenge the stability of the state. Is the OASA sufficient to respond? The provisions in the statute relating to speech were designed with a specific organisation, or set of associations, in mind. These groups operated in a particular manner and used certain instruments to accomplish their goals. The world in which we live has fundamentally altered. New media, in particular, can be used and manipulated by foreign governments, foreign movements, and others to create domestic social and political unrest – and to accomplish violent ends. While a full consideration of these threats is beyond the scope of this chapter, a brief discussion of two aspects – extremist ideology and terrorist recruitment, and the magnification of acts of terrorism – illustrate the point. For these, the OASA appears ill-suited to the task at hand.

A. Extremist Ideology and Terrorist Recruitment

One of the most serious consequences of social media is the way in which it alienates individuals and increases societal levels of isolation, depression and anxiety. Part of the problem is the structure itself: algorithms that preference similar views and trending material, the swift proliferation of emotionally-imbued information, and the 'like' function privilege extreme emotions. Of these, fear and anger fly most readily through the networks. Sophisticated algorithms pre-select what material users see, with the result that individuals become not just more entrenched in their world views, but more extreme.

The fact that other people are articulating outlying ideas, particularly when an algorithm feeds multiple such articulations into an individual's feed, creates a skewed world view: ie, that they are mainstream, when in fact, they are not. The situation becomes even more pronounced when botnets amplify certain messages, making it seem like 'trending' news, when it is not. The situation is ripe for organisations committed to violence to create greater sympathy for their cause and to recruit potential members. Because of the global nature of new media, they can do it from half a world away – anonymously. This is a very different situation than that which the Irish state has historically confronted.

Consider the role of social media as a recruitment platform. It runs 24 hours a day, seven days a week. It 'allows terrorists to reach out to their target audiences and virtually "knock on their doors" – in contrast to older models of websites in which terrorists had to wait for visitors to come to them'.[132] Because of the massive amounts of data now available, the process can be highly individualised and difficult to detect. A group may seek out disenfranchised or disaffected people by tweeting, retweeting, or using popular hashtags related to divisive current events. By creating an online micro-community around the target, the individual develops a sense of comradery and belonging. The micro-community can then nudge the person to become increasingly isolated from others, before shifting the conversation to private social media platforms that have encryption, such as WhatsApp, Kik, or Telegram.

[132] G Weimann, 'New Terrorism and New Media' (Wilson Center Commons Lab, 2014) 3 www.wilsoncenter.org/sites/default/files/media/documents/publication/STIP_140501_new_terrorism_F.pdf.

Global movements are taking advantage of these structures. The Islamic State (ISIS) has proven particularly savvy: at its height in 2015, the network produced 38 daily batches of propaganda (ie, videos, photos, photo essays, articles and audio programs).[133] During the Islamic month of Shawwal, 17 July to 15 August 2015, the organisation released 1,146 batches of online propaganda.[134] It was not disseminated through official online accounts (from 2014, ISIS had stopped making use of these on Twitter). Instead, the information was carried on accounts sympathetic to the organisation – which on Twitter number upwards of 46,000 accounts with an average of 1,000 followers each.[135] ISIS also uses other social media sites, like YouTube, Google Drive, JustPaste.It, Google Photos, SendVid, and the Internet Archive.[136] The aim of using these platforms is to generate sympathy for the cause and to increase the number of individuals willing to take up arms.

The ISIS campaign has proven incredibly effective. Scholars estimate that by 2017 ISIS had recruited more than 16,000 foreign fighters through this means.[137] The network does not just use social media to recruit foreign fighters. It uses the platforms to encourage individuals to engage in violent acts in their own country as well.[138] Subsequent action may be directed, or it may simply arise from a particularly insidious form of crowd sourcing: inspiring individuals, through their ideology, to undertake destructive acts.[139]

Social media, in turn, can provide resources for individuals to develop the knowledge and information necessary to mount attacks.[140] A 2017 study of 223 terrorist offenders in the UK found, for instance, that in 61 per cent of the cases there was evidence of online activities – ie, radicalisation and/or attack planning.[141] Forty-four per cent of the perpetrators had found or downloaded extremist media, while more than half (54 per cent) went online to investigate some aspect of their intended attack – including whom to target and where to find them. The scholars who designed the study concluded: 'The Internet is largely a facilitative tool that affords greater opportunities for violent radicalization and attack planning.'[142] The use of new media was particularly pronounced for right-wing extremists, which do not have a large presence in the UK.[143] This suggested that online social interactions – at the heart of

[133] C Winter, *Documenting the Virtual 'Caliphate'* (London, Quilliam, 2015) 3, www.quilliaminternational.com/wp-content/uploads/2015/10/FINAL-documenting-the-virtual-caliphate.pdf. For a detailed discussion of ISIS's online activities, see *Special Issue: Islamic State's Online Activity and Responses*, 2014–2017, Studies in Conflict & Terrorism 2019, vol 42, Nos 1-2, 1-4.

[134] Winter, *Documenting the Virtual 'Caliphate'* (n 133) 4.

[135] Ibid, 11; JM Berger and Morgan, The ISIS Twitter Consensus: Defining and Describing the Population of ISIS Supporters on Twitter, Washington, DC, Brookings, 2015, at 3, available at www.brookings.edu/wp-content/uploads/2016/06/isis_twitter_census_berger_morgan.pdf.

[136] M Conway et al, 'Disrupting Daesh: Measuring Takedown of Online Terrorist Material and Its Impacts' (2019) 42 *Studies in Conflict & Terrorism* 141.

[137] S Klein and C Flinn, 'Social Media Compliance Programs and the War against Terrorism' (2017) 8 *Harvard National Security Journal* 53, 65.

[138] Ibid.

[139] M Conway, 'Is Cyberterrorism a Real Threat? Yes: Why We Should Start from This Assumption' in R Jackson and D Pisoiu (eds), *Contemporary Debates on Terrorism*, 2nd edn (Abingdon, Routledge, 2018) 102.

[140] P Gill et al, 'Terrorist Use of the Internet by the Numbers: Quantifying Behaviors, Patterns, and Processes' (2017) 16 *Criminology and Public Policy* 99.

[141] Ibid, 107.

[142] Ibid.

[143] Ibid, 110–111.

new media – provide a way for individuals to find others of like mind, similarly bent on harming others.[144]

What does the 1939 OASA and its progeny have to say about this kind of challenge? Very little. Its prohibition on treasonable, seditious, or incriminating documents turns on proscribed, mostly Republican, organisations – not political views or opinions about recent events.[145] Granted, unlike section 31 of the Broadcasting Authority Act 1960, associations do not have to be known by distinctive names in order to be unlawful – making, perhaps, those recruiting subject to prohibition.[146] The Criminal Justice (Terrorist Offences) Act 2005 does make provision for international groups to be considered terrorist organisations.[147] But in relation to the types of individuals targeted by groups like ISIS, the relevant posts may be news articles reporting on government actions, or growing social or economic concerns – not direct engagement in terrorist activity or threats to do so.[148] Here, the law explicitly protects persons engaged 'in any protest, advocacy, or dissent'.[149] The intent of disseminating such information is not to intimidate or to compel a government to act.[150] It is to persuade.

The Criminal Justice (Terrorist Offences) (Amendment) Act 2015 altered the prior statute to try to target provocation, recruitment, and training.[151] The statute broadened the understanding of public provocation to include 'making available, by whatever means of communication by a person of a message to the public, with the intent of encouraging, directly or indirectly, the commission by a person of a terrorist activity'.[152] At first glance, this language seems broad enough to include political commentary or propaganda. But what happens when the distribution is undertaken by members of the general public, with no ties whatsoever to particular organisations or individuals? Or by algorithms developed by social media companies? Or bots intended to drive increased revenues? The same intent element required in relation to recruitment or training is similarly not met merely by how new media works.[153]

As for the OASA, a rant about recent events may fall well short of material 'calculated to promote the formation' of an unlawful group, as forbidden by the statute. This type of communication falls within the core of free speech – precisely the type of ideas whose exchange is considered essential to modern democratic states. Even if the Irish Government were to revert to prohibiting the types of violent materials outlawed under the censorship acts, much of the propaganda would still stand.[154] ISIS and others are

[144] Ibid, 113.
[145] OASA 1939, ss 2(a)–(d), 10(1)–(2).
[146] Ibid. See n 119 for further discussion of s 31.
[147] Criminal Justice (Terrorist Offences) Act 2005, s 5.
[148] Ibid, s 6(1).
[149] Ibid, s 6(5).
[150] See ibid, s 6(7).
[151] Criminal Justice (Terrorist Offences) (Amendment) Act 2015, ss 4, 5, 6.
[152] Ibid, s 4.
[153] See ibid, ss 5, 6.
[154] See Censorship of Films Act 1923, Censorship of Films (Amendment) Act 1925, Censorship of Films (Amendment) Act 1930, Censorship of Films (Amendment) Act 1970, Video Recordings Act 1989, Censorship of Films (Amendment) Act 1992, and Blasphemy (Abolition of Offences and Related Matters) Act 2019. From the 1920s until the 1980s, the Censorship Board banned more than 2,500 films and cut over 11,000 more. 'Irish Film Censors' Records 1923–38' (*Trinity College Dublin*) www.tcd.ie/irishfilm/censor/ (accessed 25 February 2020). Prominent stars and films, and work by well-known directors, such as Humphrey Bogart and Lauren

using messaging, and the structure of social media platforms – which drive individuals to more extreme views – to generate support and recruits.

There are further problems with applying the OASA and associated laws to the new media environment. First, *is* social media the equivalent of a newspaper? Or is it merely a form of communication? Posting is *not* the same as publishing. Individuals online may operate in their private capacity, limiting their communications to 'friends' – putting their thoughts and ideas at the core of how we think about free speech and freedom of association.

Second, material swiftly proliferates. So as soon as a comment is posted, it may almost immediately be picked up and re-posted by hundreds, or even thousands of people, making the prosecution of all of those involved in the circulation of such material preposterous.[155] Nor can such material, in any way, be 'given up' to the Garda Síochána.[156] Even erasing it online will fail to eradicate it from online caches. These are not documents that can be 'seized' or 'destroyed'.[157]

Third, the law makes it unlawful to possess certain documents.[158] But the way new media works, users do not have control over material on their accounts. Sophisticated algorithms pick material for their feed. Those purchasing ads gain access without the user's permission. Where a user employs a particular hashtag, any number of comments may be generated on the same topic and be forwarded to their account.

Fourth, anonymity may make it almost impossible to ascertain *who* is posting the materials. In fact, it could be bots circulating information and adding content. Those pulling the strings need be nowhere near the country. A newspaper can be stopped at the border. Global communication systems cannot.

B. Heightened Impact

In 1974, Brian Jenkins famously observed, 'Terrorism is theater'.[159] If an entity gets enough attention, it does not matter how big or small it is. It is being *seen* that creates

Bacall in *The Big Sleep* (1946); Stanley Kubrick's *Clockwork Orange* (1971); *Monty Python's Life of Brian* (1979); *Monty Python's The Meaning of Life* (1983); and Oliver Stone's *Natural Born Killers* (1994) failed to pass muster. See 'The Land of Saints, Scholars and Censorship' (*Independent.ie*, 31 July 2012) www.independent.ie/lifestyle/the-land-of-saints-scholars-and-censorship-26882364.html; Irish Central Staff, 'Top Ten Movies Banned in Ireland' (*Irish Central*, 11 May 2017) www.irishcentral.com/roots/top-ten-movies-banned-in-ireland-124842519-237396851. Although the Board rejected most films on religious and moral grounds, some fell under the knife because of the level of violence or the manner in which they portrayed crime. See, eg, 'Irish Film Censors' Records, Scarface' (*Trinity College Dublin*) www.tcd.ie/irishfilm/censor/show.php?fid=4765 (accessed 25 February 2020). Others were banned because of their political content. See, eg, 'Irish Film Censors' Records, One Day in Soviet Russia' (*Trinity College Dublin*) www.tcd.ie/irishfilm/censor/show.php?fid=5949 (accessed 25 February 2020). In 2008, the Irish Film Censor's Office was re-cast as the Irish Film Classification Office (*Oifig Aicmithe Scannán na hÉireann*). The office now rates films according to their appropriateness for different age levels and only occasionally prohibits certain films on the grounds that they are indecent or obscene.

[155] See OASA 1939, s 10(3).

[156] Ibid, s 10(4).

[157] See ibid, ss 11(a), 12(4).

[158] Ibid, s 12.

[159] BM Jenkins, 'International Terrorism: A New Kind of Warfare' (P-5261, RAND Corporation, 1974) 4 www.rand.org/content/dam/rand/pubs/papers/2008/P5261.pdf.

fear and facilitates manipulation. New media presents a prime opportunity to do just that and, accordingly, it has become a platform for those engaged in violence to magnify their actions. In 2014, for instance, ISIS branded their offensive #AllEyesOnISIS to ensure that the world was watching. Unlike in the past, where violent organisations have been dependent on the news media (which could be regulated), on the new platforms, they convey their own messages. They control the narrative and communicate directly with their audience. The more extreme the actions, the more emotions they generate, ensuring that the news moves even more swiftly through online communications. Violent extremists and terrorist organisations harness the power of others – including ordinary citizens – to get their message across. Thus, when Brenton Tarrant, a white supremacist, went on a rampage in Christchurch, New Zealand, killing 51 people, he announced that he was going to do it via 8Chan.[160] He then broadcast the shooting on Facebook Live, YouTube, Twitter, and Instagram.[161] During the attack, Tarrant shouted, 'Remember, lads, subscribe to PewDiePie' – a reference to an anti-Semitic YouTube channel with 89 million followers – the highest number on YouTube.[162] These actions ensured maximum publicity.

Such incidents point to associated concerns. Posts circumnavigate Earth at the speed of light. The alternative legal structure on which the Irish Government has previously depended to restrict terrorist publicity (section 31 of the Broadcasting Authority Act 1960), was premised on prior identification of paramilitaries, as were many of the OASA measures. It is impossible to do this in relation to anyone (worldwide) with violent potential. Nor does Ireland control the platforms; almost all of the top social media companies are foreign-owned, and some are foreign state controlled. Putting information up on a foreign server is not the same as printed material crossing the border. Organisations, additionally, can use social media not just to promote their own actions and 'brand', but to undermine the opponent's (or state's) narrative.[163] This can become particularly insidious when paired with false information, much less deep fakes.

V. CONCLUSION

Throughout the twentieth and early twenty-first centuries, numerous provisions in the OASA and associated laws restricted speech with the aim of countering Republican violence. Some of these measures have since been relinquished or discredited. The threat posed by Republicanism has abated. The trend is towards fewer direct restrictions on expression. Many of the provisions, moreover, such as those based on associational ties,

[160] See Associated Press, 'Death Toll from Christchurch Mosque Attack Grows to 51 After Turkish Man Dies' (*NBC News*, 2 May 2 2019) www.nbcnews.com/news/world/death-toll-christchurch-mosque-attacks-grows-51-after-turkish-man-n1001476; E Lopatto, 'The Mass Shooting in New Zealand Was Designed to Spread on Social Media' (*The Verge*, 15 March 2019) www.theverge.com/2019/3/15/18266859/new-zealand-shooting-video-social-media-manipulation.

[161] Lopatto, 'Mass Shooting' (n 160).

[162] Ibid; 'Social Media's Role in Mosque Attack' (*CBS News*, 15 March 2019) www.cbsnews.com/video/disturbing-role-of-social-media-in-new-zealand-mosque-shooting/.

[163] M Borkowski, 'Isis and the Propaganda War: How the Social-Savvy Extremist Are Dominating the Headlines' (*The Drum*, 25 June 2014) www.thedrum.com/opinion/2014/06/25/isis-and-propaganda-war-how-social-savvy-extremists-are-qdominating-headlines.

or treasonous materials, are inapposite to the types of challenges encapsulated in new media. Efforts to modify the OASA to address novel threats, though, may themselves fall foul of Ireland's obligations under international law.

Article 10 of the European Convention of Human Rights (ECHR), protects free expression, meaning the right to hold opinions and 'to receive and impart information and ideas without interference'.[164] The Convention recognises that states *can* license broadcast, television, or cinema enterprises. It protects restrictions 'necessary in a democratic society', introduced 'in the interests of national security', or adopted to prevent 'disorder or crime'.[165] But disrupting online communities may trigger claims under Article 11, which protects peaceable assembly and association.[166]

In 2010, for instance, the European Court of Human Rights considered a case in which Turkish magazine editors had been convicted for publishing statements made by members of illegal Marxist-Leninist groups.[167] The Court rejected the country's effort to criminalise publication of statements by terrorist organisations, absent contextual consideration. According to the Court, should identity be sufficient to preclude speech, Article 10 would fail to afford protection. Since the statements in question did not threaten or perpetuate violence, the national security justification failed to overcome Article 10 protections. The case raises the question as to whether, under the Convention, Ireland could prohibit individuals from using social media purely on the basis of their identity.

The International Covenant on Civil and Political Rights (ICCPR) similarly guarantees the 'freedom to seek, receive and impart information and ideas of all kinds, regardless of frontiers, either orally, in writing or in print, in the form of art, or through any other media of his choice'.[168] While national security may allow for some restrictions, freedom of opinion and expression are considered central to self-realisation and democratic governance – 'the foundation stone for every free and democratic society'.[169] They are integral to the right to vote.[170] Freedom of opinion is so important that even in an emergency, states cannot derogate from it.[171] Individuals have the right to obtain all forms of audio-visual as well as electronic and internet-based modes of expression.[172] The Covenant requires states 'to ensure universal access'.[173]

[164] Convention for the Protection of Human Rights and Fundamental Freedoms (ECHR), Art 10. Like the ECHR, the Universal Declaration of Human Rights protects the right to freedom of opinion and expression. See Universal Declaration of Human Rights (UDHR) (1948), UN Doc A/810 (1948) 71, Art 19.

[165] ECHR, Art 8.

[166] Ibid, Art 11.

[167] *Gözel and Özer v Turkey* App nos 43453/04 and 31098/05 (ECtHR, 6 July 2010).

[168] International Covenant on Civil and Political Rights (ICCPR) (1966) 999 UNTS 171, Art 19.

[169] Human Rights Committee General Comment 34 (General Comment 34), CCPR/C/GC/34 (2011) para 2 (citing communication no 1173/2003, *Benhadj v Algeria*, Views adopted on 20 July 2007; No 628/1995, *Park v Republic of Korea*, Views adopted on 5 July 1996).

[170] See, eg, ICCPR Arts. 18, 25, 27 (freedom of expression integral to enjoyment of other rights (eg, assembly, association, right to vote)).

[171] ICCPR General Comment 34 (2011), para 9; ibid, para 5, fn 3.

[172] Ibid, paras 11, 12.

[173] 'Freedom of Expression Everywhere, Including Cyberspace, Office of the High Commissioner' (*UN Human Rights, Office of the High Commissioner*, 4 November 2011) www.ohchr.org/EN/NewsEvents/Pages/Freedomofexpressioneverywhere.aspx.

Under the ICCPR, protecting online expression matters because other rights rely on the free press, making it 'one of the cornerstones of a democratic society'.[174] Without it, and the ability 'to comment on public issues without censorship or restraint' is compromised.[175] The media, in turn, must be able to produce *and to receive* information.[176] Social media, if anything, underscores the importance of the right.[177] Statutes related to treason, sedition, or public order therefore must be drawn as narrowly as possible.[178]

With both the inadequacies of the OASA and the requirements of Ireland's international obligations in mind, the challenges posed by extremist manipulation of social media appear all the more pronounced. More work needs to be done to determine how best to mitigate the risks posed by this new medium, consistent with the liberal, democratic structure of the state.

[174] ICCPR General Comment 34, para 13 (citing communication no 1128/2002, *Marques v Angola*, views adopted on 29 March 2005).

[175] ICCPR General Comment 34 (citing the Committee's general comment no 25, CCPR/C/GC/25 (1996) on Article 25 (Participation in public affairs and the right to vote) para 25).

[176] ICCPR General Comment 34, para 13 (citing communication no 633/95, *Gauthier v Canada*).

[177] ICCPR General Comment 34, para 15.

[178] See ibid paras 21, 29–31; Human Rights Committee, Consideration of Reports Submitted by States Parties under Article 40 of the Covenant Concluding Observations of the Human Rights Committee Hong Kong Special Administrative Region (HKSAR), CCPR/C/HKG/CO/2 (2006).

11

The Offences Against the State Acts and International Human Rights

YVONNE MARIE DALY

I. INTRODUCTION

THIS CHAPTER FOCUSES primarily on the international courts and bodies which have examined the Offences Against the State Acts through the lens of international human rights covenants and conventions. As criminal statutes which, inter alia, enhance police powers of investigation and make bespoke arrangements for trial in specific circumstances, these Acts clearly engage important rights. Some of the most obvious rights affected are those which protect liberty, fair trial, equality before the law, and the privilege against self-incrimination. These are recognised in domestic law, but also in international documents such as the International Covenant on Civil and Political Rights (ICCPR) and the European Convention on Human Rights (ECHR). Arguments on the impact of the Offences Against the State Acts on these, and other related, rights have been made before the Irish courts, the European Court of Human Rights (ECtHR), and the UN Human Rights Committee, each of which occupies a different place in the hierarchy of influence on Irish law.

This chapter begins at the point furthest from the centre of gravity in terms of influence and impact on Irish law, and examines both the reporting requirements and the right of individual petition to the UN Human Rights Committee (UNHRC) pursuant to the ICCPR. The chapter then outlines the examination of certain aspects of the Offences Against the State Acts by the ECtHR, through its interpretation and application of the ECHR. After this, the impact of international human rights in the Irish courts and legislature is briefly considered. The conclusion draws together some themes from across the chapter and notes the increasing interest of the European Union in providing for suspect rights, which may be influential in the future.

II. THE OFFENCES AGAINST THE STATE ACTS BEFORE THE UN HUMAN RIGHTS COMMITTEE

Ireland operates a dualist system when it comes to international law:[1] an international covenant or treaty does not automatically become part of domestic law when it is ratified by the state. Separate incorporating legislation would be required to do so. This is the case with the ICCPR which was ratified by Ireland in December 1989 and entered into force in March 1990. No domestic legislation has been enacted to make the rights and obligations within the ICCPR justiciable in the Irish courts, and it is accordingly of persuasive value only therein. However, its ratification and entry into force means that the state is required to report to the UNHRC on its compliance with the ICCPR on a cyclical basis. Ireland also ratified the First Optional Protocol to the ICCPR in December 1989. This allows the UNHRC to receive and consider communications from individuals alleging violation of their rights under the ICCPR.

The UNHRC is a body created by the states parties to the ICCPR. While it is not a UN organ, per se, McGoldrick has suggested that its de facto position is that of a UN organ, due to its financing and its reporting activities, along with the serious manner in which its reports are considered by the Third Committee of the General Assembly.[2]

A. Reporting to the UNHRC

Ireland is currently in its fifth reporting cycle under the ICCPR, and submitted its state party report for this purpose on 23 September 2019. Since its First Periodic Report, in 1992 and the Concluding Observations thereon in 1993, the UNHRC has expressed concern about the existence and functioning of the Special Criminal Court. This is the three-judge non-jury court provided for under the Offences Against the State Act 1939 (OASA).[3] The current Court was established by way of governmental proclamation, in May 1972, declaring that the ordinary courts 'are inadequate to secure the effective administration of justice and the preservation of public peace and order'.[4] In the 1993 Concluding Observations, the UNHRC noted that Ireland ought to have informed other state parties to the ICCPR of a state of emergency, as required under Article 4(3) of the Covenant, if that was the justification for the establishment of a special court.[5]

[1] See Art 29.6 of the Irish Constitution. Hogan describes the Irish approach as 'ultra dualist': G Hogan, 'The Constitution and the Convention: Happily Married or a Loveless Co-existence?' in S Egan, L Thornton, J Walsh (eds), *Ireland and the European Convention on Human Rights: 60 Years and Beyond* (Dublin, Bloomsbury Professional, 2014) 73, 75.

[2] D McGoldrick, *The Human Rights Committee: Its role in the development of the International Covenant on Civil and Political Rights* (Oxford, Clarendon Press, 1991) 52–3.

[3] For detailed discussions of the Special Criminal Court see M Robinson, *The Special Criminal Court* (Dublin, Dublin University Press, 1974); F Davis, *The History and Development of the Special Criminal Court, 1922–2005* (Dublin, Four Courts Press, 2007) and A Harrison, *The Special Criminal Court: Practice and Procedure* (Dublin, Bloomsbury Professional, 2019).

[4] Pursuant to s 35(2) of the OASA.

[5] Concluding observations on the first periodic report of Ireland, UN Human Rights Committee, CCPR/C/79/Add.21, 3 August 1993, para 11, referencing also the Emergency Powers Act 1976.

In the third reporting cycle, in 2008, 10 years after the Belfast/Good Friday Agreement, which brought greater stability to Northern Ireland, the Committee stated that Ireland should 'carefully monitor, on an ongoing basis, whether the exigencies of the situation in Ireland continue to justify the continuation of a Special Criminal Court with a view to abolishing it'. Furthermore, Ireland was called upon in that set of concluding observations, to ensure that 'for each case that is certified by the Director of Public Prosecutions for Ireland as requiring a nonjury trial, objective and reasonable grounds are provided and that there is a right to challenge these grounds'.[6]

More recently, in its 2014 Concluding Observations on the Fourth Periodic Report of Ireland under the ICCPR, the UNHRC reiterated its concern about the continuing operation of the Special Criminal Court, and expressed further concern about the 'expansion of the remit of the Court to include organised crime'.[7] This was brought about by way of the Criminal Justice (Amendment) Act 2009, section 8 of which states that 'the ordinary courts are inadequate to secure the effective administration of justice and the preservation of public peace and order in relation to' a list of specific offences related to organised crime. While the Irish legislature has thus expanded the use of the Special Criminal Court, the UNHRC in these concluding observations advised the state to consider abolishing it.[8] Undeterred, expansion has continued with the creation, in 2015, of a second Special Criminal Court.[9]

In its most recent report to the UNHRC under the ICCPR, in 2019, the state addresses the issue of the Special Criminal Court in extremely truncated form, simply directing the reader to one paragraph of the Common Core Document where '[i]nformation pertaining to the creation and functioning of the Special Criminal Courts can be found'.[10] That information states, again in rather brief terms, that:

> … there are … two Special Criminal Courts, established pursuant to Article 38.3 of the Constitution for the trial of offences in cases where it is determined that the ordinary courts are inadequate to secure the effective administration of justice and the preservation of public peace and order. The Special Criminal Court was established in 1972 and sits without a jury. The Government is satisfied that there is a continuing need for this Court to deal with a range of offences arising from terrorism and organised crime and, due to the volume of cases, a Second Special Criminal Court was established in 2016. The establishment of the Second Special Criminal Court significantly reduced waiting times from 24 months to circa 10 months. The need for the Special Criminal Courts is kept under review.[11]

[6] Concluding observations on the third periodic report of Ireland, UN Human Rights Committee, CCPR/C/IRL/CO/3, 30 July 2008, para 20.

[7] Concluding observations on the fourth periodic report of Ireland, UN Human Rights Committee, CCPR/C/IRL/CO/4, 19 August 2014, para 18. See L Campbell, Chapter 8, this volume.

[8] Concluding observations on the fourth periodic report of Ireland, UN Human Rights Committee, Concluding observations on the third periodic report of Ireland, UN Human Rights Committee, CCPR/C/IRL/CO/3, 30 July 2008, para 20CCPR/C/IRL/CO/4, 18 August 2014, para 18.

[9] Provided for by s 53 of the Criminal Justice (Terrorist Offences) Act 2005, which amended s 49 of the OASA, so as to allow for the transfer of cases from a Special Criminal Court to another Special Criminal Court.

[10] Ireland: Fifth Periodic Report under the International Covenant on Civil and Political Rights, CCPR/C/IRL/5, submitted 23 September 2019, published 31 January 2020, para 222.

[11] Common Core Document forming part of the reports of States parties – Ireland, HRI/CORE/IRL/2019, Received 23 September 2019, published 4 December 2019, para 65.

While the UNHRC has expressed ongoing concern about the Special Criminal Court, in terms of its existence, functioning and expansion, within the reporting cycles dating right back to 1992, this appears to have had no impact.

Some interesting detail on the numbers of arrests, convictions and cases pending under the Offences Against the State Acts is included within the 2019 Irish report:[12]

Arrests, convictions and cases pending under the Offences against the State Acts			
Year ending	**Arrests**	**Convictions**	**Cases Pending**
31 May 2019	130	13	34
31 May 2018	194	23	84
31 May 2017	192	18	44
31 May 2016	226	16	58
31 May 2015	246	17	49

This table seems to show that arrest numbers are falling. However, it is unlikely that any great change in approach to the existence of the Special Criminal Court or indeed the Offences Against the State Acts will occur in the short to medium term, given the potential of Brexit to destabilise the situation in Northern Ireland, and the opportunities for organised crime which any new customs arrangements might create.

B. Individual Petition to the UNHRC

As well as the reporting requirements under the ICCPR processes, as noted above, Ireland permits the individual petition process, whereby a person can seek the views of the UNHRC on a possible breach of the ICCPR by a state party. In August 1998, Joseph Kavanagh wrote to the UNHRC alleging a breach of his rights under the ICCPR as a result of being sent for trial before the Special Criminal Court, pursuant to the OASA. Mr Kavanagh was suspected of involvement in an incident of the type that has since become known as a 'tiger kidnapping': on 2 November 1993 the chief executive of a banking company, his wife, their children, and a baby-sitter, were falsely imprisoned and assaulted at their home. This incident involved a gang of seven members who then forced the chief executive to steal a large amount of money from the bank. While Mr Kavanagh admitted being involved, he claimed that he was acting under duress and had been kidnapped by the gang prior to the incident.

In July 1994 Mr Kavanagh was charged before the Special Criminal Court with seven different charges, six of which were not scheduled offences under the Offences Against the State Acts. The DPP had ordered that the Special Criminal Court should be used for the trial of each of these charges, pursuant to sections 47(1)[13] and 47(2)[14] of the 1939 Act.

[12] Ireland: Fifth Periodic Report under the International Covenant on Civil and Political Rights, CCPR/C/IRL/5, submitted 23 September 2019, published 31 January 2020, para 224.

[13] Section 47(1) provides that a person may be charged with a scheduled offence before the Special Criminal Court, on the direction of the DPP.

[14] Section 47(2) provides that a person may be charged before the Special Criminal Court with an offence which is not a scheduled offence if the DPP certifies that the ordinary courts are, in his/her opinion, inadequate

Before both the High Court and the Supreme Court, Mr Kavanagh unsuccessfully challenged the decision to try him before the Special Criminal Court.[15] He argued, inter alia, that there was no subversive or paramilitary connection to the relevant offences and that the ordinary courts were adequate for his trial. He also contended that the decision to try him before the Special Criminal Court amounted to unfair discrimination. Having been unsuccessful in these claims, Mr Kavanagh was tried before the Special Criminal Court in October 1997, and convicted on a number of charges.

He brought his situation to the attention of the UNHRC in August 1998, and a decision was issued on 4 April 2001.[16] He argued that one of the main issues in his trial was his claim that he was acting under duress and was not a participant in the criminal gang. By sending him forward for trial before the Special Criminal Court, he contended that the DPP was prejudging this aspect of his case and impinging on his presumption of innocence.[17] He argued, in communication with the UNHRC, that:

> … the decision of the DPP involves a determination either that the author is a member of, or is associated with, a paramilitary or subversive group involved in the Northern Ireland conflict, or that he, or persons associated with him, are likely to attempt to interfere with or otherwise influence a jury if tried before an ordinary court.[18]

Kavanagh also claimed that he was unfairly discriminated against, contrary to Article 26 of the ICCPR as he had been '… deprived, without objective reason, of important legal safeguards available to other accused persons charged with similar offences'.[19] Furthermore, he argued that the situation of increasing violence in Northern Ireland which had led to the 1972 proclamation, which established the Special Criminal Court, had ceased and could 'no longer be characterised as a public emergency which threatens the life of the nation'. Accordingly, he argued, any derogation from parts of the ICCPR by the Irish state was no longer required. The state responded, making reference to the continuing threat to national security from the rise of organised crime and criminal gangs which could undermine the administration of justice and engage in jury intimidation.

Ultimately, the UNHRC concluded that a trial in a venue other than the ordinary courts was not, in and of itself, a violation of the rights protected under the ICCPR. However, it found that there had been a breach of Mr Kavanagh's ICCPR right to equality under Article 26, which provides that '[a]ll persons are equal before the law and are entitled without any discrimination to the equal protection of the law …'. The UNHRC's finding that the right to equality before the law had been breached was based on the fact that Mr Kavanagh could be said to have been treated differently from other persons who would be charged with similar offences before the ordinary courts.

The Committee stated:

> The DPP's decision to charge the author before the Special Criminal Court resulted in the author facing an extraordinary trial procedure before an extra-ordinarily constituted court.

to secure the effective administration of justice and the preservation of public peace and order in relation to the trial of such person on such charge.

[15] *Kavanagh v Ireland* [1996] 1 IR 321.

[16] Communication no 819/1998, Kavanagh v Ireland, CCPR/C/71/D/819/1998.

[17] Ibid, para 4.5.

[18] Ibid, para 4.4.

[19] Ibid, para 4.7.

> This distinction deprived the author of certain procedures under domestic law, distinguishing the author from others charged with similar offences in the ordinary courts.

Furthermore, it observed that:

> [w]ithin the jurisdiction of the State party, trial by jury in particular is considered an important protection, generally available to accused persons. Under article 26, the State party is therefore required to demonstrate that such a decision to try a person by another procedure was based upon reasonable and objective grounds.[20]

Part of the reasoning of the Committee was based on the absence of any requirement for the DPP to give reasons for the view that it would be 'proper' to try the accused before the Special Criminal Court, or that the ordinary courts are 'inadequate', and it noted that no reasons had been provided to it in relation to this particular case. The Committee also observed that 'judicial review of the Director of Public Prosecution's decisions is effectively restricted to the most exceptional and virtually undemonstrable circumstances'.[21] This left Mr Kavanagh with no effective remedy: 'With the Courts tying their own hands and restricting their scrutiny to exceptional, and almost impossible to demonstrate, reasons of mala fides, improper motives or considerations on the part of the DPP, it could not be said that an effective remedy existed.'[22]

Ultimately the UNHRC concluded that Ireland had failed to demonstrate that the decision to try Mr Kavanagh before the Special Criminal Court, and therefore treat him differently before the law, was based upon reasonable and objective grounds.[23] While a minority of the Committee would also have found a breach of Article 14(1) which relates to equality in the judicial system itself, the majority did not consider this, having already found a violation of Article 26.

Following the communication of the UNHRC's view, Mr Kavanagh sought to have his conviction quashed and sought a declaration to the effect that section 47(2) of the OASA was incompatible with the ICCPR and was accordingly repugnant to the Constitution.[24] He sought to rely directly on the ICCPR, with the view of the UNHRC illustrating the requirements of the guarantee of equality in the Covenant.[25] This was dismissed by both the High Court and the Supreme Court. The Supreme Court held that the views of the UNHRC could not be invoked to invalidate a conviction of a properly constituted domestic court.[26] Accordingly, his conviction stood, and the decision of the UNHRC has had no impact on the ongoing existence of the Special Criminal Court, or the referral of cases thereto.

All of the reporting, concluding observations, and the finding of a violation in the case of Joseph Kavanagh have had only the slightest impact on the procedure and functioning of the Special Criminal Court. Indeed, while the Office of the DPP now provides reasons, when requested, for the decision to try an accused before the Special Criminal Court, this did not arise as a direct result of Mr Kavanagh's experiences. In the unrelated

[20] Ibid, para 10.2.
[21] Ibid, para 10.2.
[22] Ibid, para 4.6. This is based on the Supreme Court decision in *H v DPP* [1994] 2 IR 589.
[23] Ibid, para 10.3.
[24] *Kavanagh v Governor of Mountjoy Prison* [2002] 3 IR 97.
[25] Ibid, 114.
[26] Ibid, 127.

2014 case, of *Murphy v Ireland*,[27] the Supreme Court held that, in order to ensure fair procedures, reasons should be given by the DPP for the decision to try an accused person before the Special Criminal Court. These should extend to stating why the DPP considers that the ordinary courts are not suitable for the trial of this particular accused, though in certain cases it might be acceptable to state that no reason can be given without impairing national security.[28] O'Donnell J, giving the unanimous decision of the Court, went on to say that:

> [a] statement of reasons that the Director of Public Prosecutions believes the accused to be a member of, or associated with, an organisation that is prepared to interfere with the administration of justice, or even justifying the non-delivery of such reasons, will be sufficient unless the accused challenges the decision and provides sufficient information to the court, to presumptively undermine the Director's reasons … it may be permissible at that stage for the Director to amplify and explain any reasons if thought desirable. It follows however that the entitlement to obtain such reasons does not carry with it any right … to obtain the gist of information grounding such a decision, or to have a hearing or to make submissions before a decision is made.[29]

While this is generally a welcome change to procedures, it appears from the foregoing that the new practice of providing reasons for the decision to try a case before the Special Criminal Court may be extremely circumscribed in its actual operation. Furthermore, there is little real prospect of challenging any such decision, as the courts have insisted that such a challenge could only be made on the basis of evidence of *mala fides* or evidence that the DPP had been influenced by an improper motive or policy, or other exceptional circumstances.[30]

The impact of the UNHRC on the existence and functioning of the Special Criminal Court accordingly seems quite limited. Indeed, it is interesting to note in the context of the *Murphy* case, that while the decision of the UNHRC in *Kavanagh* was mentioned in correspondence between Mr Murphy's solicitors and the Office of the DPP,[31] no mention of that decision was made in any substantive sense by either the High Court or the Supreme Court.

III. THE OFFENCES AGAINST THE STATE ACTS AND THE EUROPEAN COURT OF HUMAN RIGHTS

Ireland ratified the ECHR in 1953. It was the first state to accept the right of an individual to bring a petition against their own state, and the jurisdiction of the ECtHR. Indeed,

[27] [2014] 1 IR 198. The decision in the case is specifically reference in the Annual Report of the DPP's Office in 2014: *Office of the Director of Public Prosecutions Annual Report 2014*, 29, available at: www.dppireland.ie/app/uploads/2019/03/AR_2014_eng.pdf.

[28] [2014] 1 IR 198, 233.

[29] Ibid, 233–234.

[30] See, eg, *The State (McCormack) v Curran* [1987] ILRM 225; *Ward v The Government of Ireland & Ors* (Unreported, Supreme Court, 18 December 1987); *H v DPP* [1994] 2 IR 589; *Byrne and Dempsey v The Government of Ireland & Ors* (Unreported, Supreme Court, 11 March 1999); *Eviston v DPP* [2002] 3 IR 260; *Murphy v Ireland* [2014] 1 IR 198.

[31] This is referred to in the High Court judgment: *Murphy v Ireland Murphy v Ireland* [2011] IEHC 536; [2011] 11 JIC 1605, para 28.

the very first case decided by the ECtHR in respect of an individual petition related to the operation of the Offences Against the State (Amendment) Act 1940 in Ireland. This case, *Lawless v Ireland*,[32] addressed the issue of internment and the right to liberty under Article 5 of the ECHR. Other Offences Against the State Acts cases before the ECtHR have focused on the Article 6 right to a fair trial in the light of interference with the privilege against self-incrimination by the creation of offences based on pre-trial silence, and the use of belief evidence at trial. These are explored in turn below.

It is important to note that after 50 years of engagement with the ECHR as a ratified international agreement, it was incorporated into domestic Irish law under the European Convention on Human Rights Act 2003.

A. Liberty and Internment – Article 5 ECHR

In *Lawless v Ireland*, decided on 1 July 1961, the applicant claimed that his right to liberty, protected under Article 5, ECHR, had been breached by the use of an internment procedure provided for under Part II of the Offences Against the State (Amendment) Act 1940. Under section 4 of that Act,[33] the Minister for Justice had, on 12 July 1957, issued a warrant providing for the detention without trial of Gearóid Ó Laighléis (Lawless), who had been arrested the previous day on suspicion of membership of an unlawful organisation (an offence under section 21 of the 1939 Act). Mr Lawless was then detained without trial until 11 December 1957. He was released on that date, having agreed not to take part in any illegal activities under the Offences Against the State Acts 1939 and 1940.

During his detention without trial, the applicant had failed in his *habeas corpus* application to both the High Court and the Supreme Court.[34] The 1940 Act had been previously given an unreviewable constitutional seal of approval through an Article 26 reference to the Supreme Court prior to presidential signature[35] and, in *In Re Ó Laghléis*,[36] the Supreme Court refused to consider that the ECHR might trump domestic law, as it remained at the status of any other international agreement at that time, and had not been incorporated into the domestic legal order.

When the matter was brought before the ECtHR, it held that the internment procedure was in breach of the Article 5 protection for the right to liberty. However, derogation from Article 5 is possible under Article 15, 'to the extent strictly required by the exigencies of the situation' in 'time of war or other public emergency threatening the life of the nation'. The ECtHR accepted that Ireland had validly derogated from Article 5, given the level of violence and ongoing threat of terrorism associated with paramilitary activity in Ireland, and indeed outside of the state, at the time. Internment was therefore viewed by the ECtHR as an acceptable requirement in an attempt to deal with the situation. The Court also observed certain safeguards in the internment process, such as ongoing

[32] *Lawless v Ireland (No 3)* (1979–80) 1 EHRR 15.

[33] Which was operational due to the fact that a proclamation required under s 3 has been made by the government on 5 July 1957.

[34] [1960] IR 93.

[35] *In re Art 26 and the Offences Against the State (Amendment) Bill 1940* [1940] IR 470.

[36] [1960] IR 93.

parliamentary supervision, and the establishment of a Detention Commission to review the detention of internees.[37] Despite the finding in the state's favour in *Lawless*, the practice of internment was discontinued in 1959. A proclamation re-introducing the practice was issued again in December 1970, but in fact no-one was interned thereunder.[38]

Interestingly, the Irish Government was in something of a contradictory position in operating internment in the state, given its clear opposition to the practice in Northern Ireland. This, along with the ongoing use of specific interrogation techniques, saw Ireland take the UK before the ECtHR in *Ireland v UK*,[39] the first inter-state case of which the Court was seised. On internment, the Court accepted, as it had in *Lawless*, that the UK had properly derogated, under Article 15, ECHR, from the provisions of Article 5, which protect the right to liberty, on the basis of there being a 'public emergency threatening the life of the nation' in Northern Ireland.[40] Had the derogation gone beyond that which was 'strictly required by the exigencies of the situation' the Court would have found violations of Article 5 paragraphs 1 to 4.[41] However, it accepted that the laws providing for internment were strictly required in the circumstances.

On the 'five techniques' of interrogation, the Court held that these constituted 'inhuman and degrading treatment' contrary to Article 3, ECHR, from which no derogation is possible, though they did not amount to torture. Efforts to reopen this case on the basis of new evidence in 2015 and 2018 were unsuccessful.[42]

B. Fair Trial and Failure to Account for Movements – Art 6 ECHR

The ECtHR was called upon to consider the operation of section 52 of the OASA in the cases of *Heaney and McGuinness v Ireland*,[43] and *Quinn v Ireland*.[44] Section 52 provides that a person arrested and detained in custody under section 30 of the OASA may be required by a member of the Garda Síochána to account for his/her movements and actions during a specified period and to give all the information which s/he possesses in regard to the commission or intended commission by another person of any offence under the Act or any scheduled offence. Failure or refusal to give the required account or information, or the provision of false or misleading information or account is an offence punishable by a term of imprisonment not exceeding six months.

Heaney and McGuinness had been arrested under section 30 on suspicion of involvement in a bombing at a British Army/Royal Ulster Constabulary checkpoint in County Derry, and on suspicion of membership of an unlawful organisation, namely the IRA. During Garda interview both applicants refused to answer questions, including those put to them pursuant to section 52 of the OASA. Both were charged before the Special Criminal Court with the membership offence, and with the offence of failing to account

[37] See further Harrison, *The Special Criminal Court* (n 3) 67–70.
[38] Ibid, 69.
[39] Application no 5310/71, 18 January 1978.
[40] Ibid, paras 202–224.
[41] Ibid, para 201.
[42] See further Harrison, *The Special Criminal Court* (n 3) 70.
[43] *Heaney and McGuinness v Ireland* (Application no 34720/97), 21 December 2000, (2001) 33 EHRR 264.
[44] *Quinn v Ireland* (Application no 36887/97), 21 December 2000.

for their movements, contrary to section 52. While they were both acquitted on the first charge, they were convicted on the second. Constitutional challenges mounted by the applicants against section 52 were unsuccessful in both the High Court and the Supreme Court.[45]

In the High Court, Costello J held that the right to silence was a constituent part of the right to a fair trial within Article 38.1 of the Constitution. However, he accepted section 52 as a proportionate interference with the applicants' right to silence, given the objective of assisting police investigations into serious crimes of a subversive nature involving the security of the state. On further appeal to the Supreme Court, Article 40.6, which protects freedom of expression, was preferred as the location of the right to silence within the Constitution. On the basis of the proviso contained in Article 40.6 to the effect that the right to freedom of expression may be curtailed where the exigencies of public order or morality so require, the Supreme Court held that the incursion on the right to silence contained in section 52 was constitutionally permissible. In making that finding, the Court carried out a proportionality test and held that the state was entitled to encroach on the citizen's right to silence in pursuit of the legitimate aim of maintaining public peace and order, although the right must be affected as little as possible. The incursion on the right to silence contained in section 52 was held to be proportionate to the state's aim of protecting itself.[46]

The ECtHR took a different view, however. That Court located the right to silence within Article 6, the 'fair trial' provision of the ECHR. As in the earlier case of *Murray v UK*,[47] the ECtHR stated that the right to silence is a generally recognised international standard which lies at the heart of the notion of a fair procedure under Article 6.[48] While recognising that the right to silence and the privilege against self-incrimination are not absolute rights, the Court went on to hold that the degree of compulsion to provide information which was imposed on the applicants by virtue of section 52 in effect 'destroyed the very essence of their privilege against self-incrimination and their right to remain silent'.[49] The ECtHR referred to the Irish Government's argument that certain safeguards existed to minimise the risk that an individual may wrongly confess to a crime including, amongst others, the requirement that an arrest be based on bona fide suspicion; the obligation to inform the suspect of the reasons for arrest; the right to legal and medical assistance; the right of access to a court; and, the obligation not to subject a detainee to unfair or oppressive questioning. However, it held that even an entirely lawful application of section 52, in conformity with such safeguards, 'could not change the choice presented by section 52 of the 1939 Act: either the information requested was provided by the applicants or they faced potentially six months' imprisonment'.[50]

While taking judicial notice of the 'security and public order' concerns of the Irish Government, the ECtHR held that these could not justify 'a provision which extinguishes the very essence of the applicant's right to silence and against self-incrimination

[45] [1996] 1 IR 580.
[46] Ibid, 590.
[47] (1996) 22 EHRR 29.
[48] (2001) 33 EHRR 334, 40. See also *Saunders v United Kingdom* (1996) 23 EHRR 313.
[49] (2001) 33 EHRR 334, 55.
[50] Ibid, 51.

guaranteed by Art 6(1) of the Convention'.[51] Furthermore, given the close link between the rights contained in Article 6(1) and the presumption of innocence guaranteed by Article 6(2), a breach of the latter was also found. A virtually identical finding was made in *Quinn v Ireland*,[52] the judgment in which was handed down on the same day as *Heaney*.

Despite these ECtHR judgments, and the subsequent recommendation of the Committee to Review the Offences Against the State Acts 1939–1998 that section 52 be removed from the statute book,[53] it remains in place. Furthermore, a number of other provisions which create offences based on the pre-trial silence of a suspect have also been promulgated by the Oireachtas and applied by the courts. These include:

- section 2 of the Offences Against the State (Amendment) Act 1972 whereby a Garda may demand of a person found at or near the place at the time of the commission of a scheduled offence or soon afterwards his name, address and an account of his recent movements;
- section 15 of the Criminal Justice Act 1984 whereby a Garda may demand of a person found in possession of a firearm or ammunition any information which he has in relation to the possession of such firearm or ammunition; and
- section 16 of the Criminal Justice Act 1984 whereby a Garda may demand of a person found in possession of stolen property an account of how he came by the property.

Failure or refusal to provide the relevant information under each of these provisions amounts to an offence punishable by imprisonment, or fine, or both.[54]

However, the prosecutorial value of legislative provisions which criminalise a failure or refusal to provide certain information was diminished by the Supreme Court in *Re National Irish Bank (under investigation) (No.1)*, in 1999.[55] The Court held that the use at trial of any statement made under the compulsion of such a provision during a pre-trial stage of investigation might breach the constitutional right to a fair trial, under Article 38.1. Only voluntary statements can be admitted at trial, and the Court was concerned that voluntariness would be difficult to establish in such circumstances.

While the legislature has not removed section 52, or altered it in any way in the aftermath of the ECtHR findings in *Heaney* and *Quinn*, it seems to have fallen into disuse, perhaps as a result of those cases, or the decision in *Re National Irish Bank*, or both. Legislative interference with the right to silence has shifted to the design of provisions which allow inferences to be drawn at trial from the failure of a detained suspect to mention certain facts, provide certain information, or answer certain questions. The Irish

[51] Ibid, 59.

[52] (2001) 33 EHRR 264.

[53] *Report of the Committee to Review the Offences Against the State Acts 1939–1998 and Related Matters* (Dublin, Stationery Office, 2002) para 8.57.

[54] Other provisions also exist which criminalise failure to give one's name and address in particular circumstances, eg, s 30 of the OASA; s 107 of the Road Traffic Act 1961, and s 4 of the Criminal Justice Act 1984. Section 9(1) of the Offences Against the State (Amendment) Act 1998 makes it an offence to fail, without reasonable excuse, to disclose to Gardaí information which may be of 'material assistance' in: (a) preventing the commission by any other person of a serious offence; or (b) securing the apprehension, prosecution or conviction of any other person for a serious offence. The constitutionality of this section was upheld in *Sweeney v Ireland* [2019] 2 ILRM 457.

[55] [1999] 3 IR 145.

iterations of such provisions have not been tested before the ECtHR, but similar provisions in the UK have been accepted by the Court.[56] While the ECtHR accepts the notion of inference-drawing provisions, it has consistently linked the right of access to legal advice with the privilege against self-incrimination and found breaches of Article 6(3), ECHR where legal advice was not provided in a timely fashion to persons against whom inferences were later drawn.[57] The jurisprudence of the ECtHR on this appears to have been influential in policy and legislative decision-making in Ireland as specific safeguards have been attached to inference-drawing provisions requiring, for example, reasonable opportunity to consult a solicitor prior to relevant interviews.[58]

C. Fair Trial and Belief Evidence – Article 6 ECHR

A third issue arising from the Offences Against the State Acts which has come before the ECtHR for determination is belief evidence. Section 3(2) of the Offences Against the State (Amendment) Act 1972 provides that an officer of the Garda Síochána not below the rank of Chief Superintendent may give evidence in a trial for the offence of membership of an unlawful organisation contrary to section 21 of the OASA to the effect that 'he believes that the accused was at a material time a member of an unlawful organisation' and that statement shall be evidence that he was then such a member.[59]

Two Irish cases sought to bring this issue to the attention of the ECtHR. In the first, *Kelly v Ireland*,[60] the applicant claimed that the use of belief evidence before the Special Criminal Court had resulted in a violation of Article 6, ECHR. The ECtHR, however, found the complaint to be manifestly ill-founded and accordingly it was declared inadmissible. This was based on a finding that in *Kelly* there had been significant evidence other than the belief evidence to ground the conviction of membership of an unlawful organisation. The impugned belief evidence was, accordingly, viewed by the Court as insufficient to render the proceedings in their entirety unfair.

A second case, *Donohoe v Ireland*,[61] was deemed admissible, though ultimately no breach of Article 6 was found. The ECtHR set out in that case to consider the overall fairness of the trial proceedings, which included the admission and acceptance of belief evidence from a Chief Superintendent to the effect that the applicant was a member of an unlawful organisation, namely the IRA. In October 2002, the applicant, Kenneth Donohoe, had been arrested under section 30 of the OASA on suspicion of being a member of an unlawful organisation. He made no comment throughout various Garda interviews. He was ultimately charged with the membership offence, tried before the

[56] See *Murray v United Kingdom* (1996) 22 EHRR 29 and *Averill v United Kingdom* (2001) 31 EHRR 839 re the Northern Ireland Order 1988.

[57] Eg, in *Averill v United Kingdom* (2001) 31 EHRR 839.

[58] See, eg, s 2 of the Offences Against the State (Amendment) Act 1998, as amended by s 31 of the Criminal Justice Act 2007.

[59] See L Heffernan and E O'Connor, Chapter 6, this volume.

[60] Application no 41130/06, 14 December 2010.

[61] Application no 19165/08, 12 December 2013, [2013] ECHR 1363.

Special Criminal Court, and convicted. Four strands of evidence were identified by that Court as the basis of the conviction:

(1) belief evidence from a Chief Superintendent to the effect that the applicant was a member of the IRA;
(2) evidence linking the applicant with suspicious activity that had been observed, and was contended by the prosecution to be of a type usually associated with the IRA;
(3) evidence of documents found during a search of the applicant's house; and
(4) inferences from the applicant's failure to answer questions material to the investigation of the offence, pursuant to section 2 of the Offences Against the State (Amendment) Act 1998.

The Special Criminal Court expressly noted that none of the four strands of evidence, if taken in isolation, was sufficient to ground the applicant's conviction. However, collectively they were held to be supportive of the charge of membership of the IRA.[62] While the evidence of the Chief Superintendent was not the sole or decisive reason for the conviction, it certainly carried some weight in the establishment of the applicant's guilt.[63] The Chief Superintendent had claimed privilege over his sources and, while the Special Criminal Court examined the documentary material on which his belief was based, the applicant did not have access to this material.[64]

The ECtHR found that the reasons provided for the claim of privilege, ie the need for 'effective protection of persons and State security as well as effective prosecution of serious and complex crime',[65] were compelling and substantiated. In considering the overall fairness of the proceedings, the ECtHR sought to examine if there were counterbalancing factors and safeguards in place to ensure that the disadvantage caused to the applicant by the Chief Superintendent's claim of privilege did not restrict his defence rights to an extent incompatible with the requirements of Article 6, ECHR.

In that context, the ECtHR observed that the judges of the Special Criminal Court had found no material within the documentary evidence that they viewed which might assist the defence in terms of disclosure. They had also expressly stated that they were excluding anything that they had viewed in considering the claim of privilege from their consideration of the guilt of the accused. The ECtHR also noted further safeguarding factors such as the requirement that belief evidence be given by a Garda of very high rank, and the possibility that the Chief Superintendent could be cross-examined by the defence, at least on matters related to his belief, if not on the material over which privilege had been claimed.[66] Looking at the overall fairness of the trial, the ECtHR found that there had been no violation of the Article 6 right to a fair trial in this case.[67] It seems clear from

[62] Ibid, para 85.
[63] Ibid, para 87.
[64] See A Harrison, Chapter 7, in this volume.
[65] Application no 19165/08, 12 December 2013, [2013] ECHR 1363, para 81.
[66] Ibid, para 92.
[67] A concurring opinion was provided by Lemmens J, which drew attention to the potential difficulty caused by the same court examining the privileged material and then making the ultimate decision on the guilt or innocence of the applicant, without the applicant being in a position to challenge the privileged evidence in any meaningful way. In this case he held, with the majority, that no violation had occurred, though he considered that this issue had not been fully explored in the case.

the foregoing that the ECtHR does not find Garda belief evidence objectionable per se. Given its contemporary preference to view the fairness of trials in the round,[68] it seems unlikely, in the absence of a rather exceptional fact scenario, that a breach of Article 6 would be found by the ECtHR in relation to such evidence, as allowed under the Offences Against the State Acts.

IV. INTERNATIONAL HUMAN RIGHTS IN THE IRISH COURTS AND LEGISLATURE

So far, this chapter has outlined the examination of the Offences Against the State Acts by the UN Human Rights Committee and the European Court of Human Rights, further to Ireland's obligations under the ICCPR and the ECHR respectively. We turn now to consider matters at a domestic level.

The dualist nature of the Irish state, combined with an expressed judicial preference to decide constitutional matters first, even in the context of the now-incorporated European Convention on Human Rights,[69] has meant that very few, if any, domestic cases relating to the Offences Against the State Acts have turned on the interpretation or application of international human rights instruments. While such matters have been canvassed and considered in certain cases, the ultimate decision has rarely, if ever, been made on that basis.

The case of *Murphy v Ireland*,[70] discussed above, provides a useful illustration. The plaintiff was sent forward by the District Court for trial before the Special Criminal Court in relation to certain revenue offences, pursuant to the issuing of a certificate by the DPP under section 46(2) of the OASA. He sought a declaration, inter alia, that section 46(2) was repugnant to the Constitution and incompatible with the state's obligations under the ECHR. The ECHR arguments centred on the right to a fair trial under Article 6 and the prohibition on discrimination under Article 14. In his Supreme Court judgment, O'Donnell J stated that, in the circumstances 'it is not apparent that the claim of a breach of the Convention adds anything of substance to the plaintiff's claim under the Constitution'.[71] This demonstrates well the manner in which international human rights instruments are seen as peripheral, as compared with the centrality of the Constitution, within domestic judicial examination of the Offences Against the State Acts.

In the Court of Criminal Appeal case of *People (DPP) v Donnelly*,[72] the Court seemed to observe with bemusement, or possibly shock, that the appellant's claim of a breach of the right to a fair trial arising from his conviction for membership of an unlawful organisation on the basis of belief evidence and an inference from pre-trial silence, was 'advanced almost exclusively by reference to the European Convention on Human Rights and the case law of the ECtHR'.[73] The Court pointed to the 'rich jurisprudence' of the

[68] See, eg, *Ibrahim and Others v UK* (Application nos 50541/08, 50571/08, 50573/08 and 40351/09) 13 September 2016; *Beuze v Belgium* (Application no 71409/10) 9 November 2018; and *Doyle v Ireland* (Application no 51979/17) 23 May 2019.

[69] *Carmody v Minster for Justice* [2010] 1 IR 635.

[70] [2014] IESC 19; [2014] 1 IR 198.

[71] Ibid, para 37; 229–230.

[72] [2012] IECCA 78.

[73] Ibid, para 22.

Constitution, which 'has arisen from and is focussed on the Irish legal context', and the wider range of remedies available for a breach thereof as compared to the invocation of the ECHR in a domestic court.[74]

In the arena of Irish legislative policy, matters of both constitutionality and compatibility with international human rights obligations appear to have an influence. Coen has observed the 'generally receptive attitude of the Irish official and political classes to evolving human rights standards and their incorporation into the domestic legal order.'[75] While this is certainly true in and of itself, the more pragmatic observation can also be made, that when introducing measures which significantly impact on hitherto protected rights, the cushioning provided by rights-compliant safeguards can increase acceptability. When introducing the Bill which would become the Offences Against the State (Amendment) Act 1998 to the Dáil, just two weeks after the horrific Omagh bombing, for example, the then Minister for Justice, Equality and Law Reform, John O'Donoghue, assured the House that the proposals in the Bill represented a 'measured and balanced response proportionate to the threat which the activities of groups opposed to the [Belfast/Good Friday] Agreement pose[d]'. He went on: 'The Government is further satisfied on the advice available to it that the measures the Bill contains are consistent with the Constitution and its international human rights obligations.'[76] Later, discussing specifically the introduction of a new inference-drawing provision under section 2 of the 1998 Act, the Minister said 'I understand people's concerns in regard to the drawing of an inference in relation to an individual's silence. I am of the view that this provision is constitutional and within the parameters of the European Convention on Human Rights.'[77]

Other members of the Dáil expressed the need to ensure that the legislation would 'stand up to scrutiny'. Deputy Nora Owen (a former Minister for Justice herself) advocated for a review mechanism for the 1998 Act to be included in the legislation and she stated as follows:

> … we must ensure that if this legislation is put in place with the express purpose of taking monsters off our streets who continue to see bombings, killings and beatings as legitimate acts, it will stand up to scrutiny and will not be cast down by a Supreme Court judgment, the European Court of Human Rights or by any other court within this jurisdiction or outside it. We have a responsibility to ensure the legislation will stand up to scrutiny.[78]

There is a hint here that human rights compliance is necessary to ensure that new legislative provisions which push the boundaries of traditionally-protected rights do not push too far. While this is, on its face, a laudable thing, there is a risk that through ensuring a baseline of rights-compliance, extraordinary measures become accepted. Experience shows that once accepted, such measures become less extraordinary, and come to be

[74] Ibid.

[75] M Coen, 'International Human Rights Law: A Flavour of its Impact on the Irish Criminal Justice System' in S Egan (ed), *International Human Rights: Perspectives from Ireland* (London, Bloomsbury Professional, 2015) 333. See also F de Londras, 'Neither Herald nor Fanfare: The Limited Impact of the ECHR Act 2003 on Rights Infrastructure in Ireland' in S Egan, L Thornton and J Walsh (eds), *Ireland and the European Convention on Human Rights* (London, Bloomsbury Professional, 2014) 47.

[76] *Dáil Debates*, Second Stage, 2 Sept 1998 www.oireachtas.ie/en/debates/debate/dail/1998-09-02/5/.

[77] Ibid, www.oireachtas.ie/en/debates/debate/dail/1998-09-02/7/.

[78] Ibid.

replicated across other aspects of the criminal justice system.[79] The provisions of the Offences Against the State Act*s* have often been the ones to break the seal and allow for traditionally protected rights to be impinged in new ways. In fact, section 2 of the 1998 Act is the perfect example of this. Enacted as part of the very speedy legislative response to the Omagh bombing, this inference-drawing provision has been more recently replicated within section 72A of the Criminal Justice Act 2006, as inserted by the Criminal Justice (Amendment) Act 2009, which applies to specific organised crime offences.[80]

Legislative safeguards may be included so as to ensure that boundary-pushing statutes are not 'cast down' by domestic or external courts, and such safeguards may add valuable protections on the periphery of suspect rights in the context of broader interferences therewith. However, it is important to note that the Offences Against the State Acts allow for so many alterations to traditionally protected rights and procedures that their cumulative effect may be much greater than an analysis of individual provisions would expose. A person may be convicted, as in *Donnelly*, discussed above, of the offence of membership of an unlawful organisation before the non-jury Special Criminal Court on the basis of the belief evidence of a Chief Superintendent, based on privileged sources, in conjunction with an inference drawn from the failure of the accused to answer a specific question during Garda interrogation. While neither piece of evidence could ground a conviction alone, they can corroborate one another. The extraordinary nature of such evidence is sometimes forgotten. And, again, once the seal was broken by the Offences Against the State Acts in relation to belief evidence, this was replicated in the context of organised crime. Section 71B of the Criminal Justice Act 2006, as inserted by the Criminal Justice (Amendment) Act 2009, allows for any member or former member of the Garda Síochána who appears to the Court to possess the 'appropriate expertise' to give evidence in relation to the existence of a particular criminal organisation. The mould-breaking nature of the Offences Against the State Acts is clear.

V. CONCLUSION

The Irish state has shown an ability to turn a blind eye to certain findings of international courts or bodies against it in the context of the Offences Against the State Acts. This applies most obviously to the ongoing existence of the Special Criminal Court in light of sustained objections thereto on the part of the UNHRC. Coen has suggested that '[t]he continuing use of the Special Criminal Court in the face of long-running UN criticism … evinces a choice on the part of the Irish state to ignore its international obligations in the criminal justice sphere'.[81] In fact, as we have seen, despite this ongoing disapproval, the Special Criminal Court is now used for a broader range of offences than originally planned, and a second Court is operational.

[79] See further Y Daly and J Jackson, 'The Criminal Justice Process: From Questioning to Trial' in D Healy, C Hamilton, Y Daly, and M Butler (eds), *The Routledge Handbook of Irish Criminology* (London, Routledge, 2016). See also, C Hamilton, Chapter 14, this volume.

[80] An inference may be drawn at trial from a failure to answer any question material to the investigation of an offence of participating in or contributing to any activity of a criminal organisation.

[81] Coen, 'International Human Rights Law' (n 75) 350.

A second example of the state's ability to carry on regardless is the failure to remove section 52 from the statute book following the ECtHR decisions in *Heaney* and *Quinn*, and, indeed, the recommendation of the Hederman Committee. While this provision has fallen into disuse, either because of the ECtHR decisions or due to concerns about the voluntariness, and therefore the admissibility, of any statement which might be obtained as a result of its proposed invocation, the failure to repeal the provision is symptomatic of a lack of regard for a decision of the ECtHR.

Having said that, it seems clear that the jurisprudence of that Court is influential in a softer sense on the development of Irish criminal legislation. Members of the Oireachtas are conscious of the need for such legislation to be human rights compliant so as to be effective. It seems clear too that the judges of the Special Criminal Court, drawn as they invariably are nowadays, from the benches of the ordinary courts, are steeped in the culture of rights protection. This may, however, stem more from the constitutional tradition than from international human rights.

One final issue is worthy of note. The EU, in recent years, has taken an increasing interest in the rights of both suspects and victims of crime. Ireland has an 'opt-in' when it comes to EU Directives relating to justice and home affairs. While the state has opted in to some Directives, such as the Victims' Rights Directive,[82] the Directive on Information,[83] and the Directive on Interpretation and Translation,[84] it has not opted in to others, such as the Directive on Access to a Lawyer in Criminal Proceedings[85] and the Directive on the Presumption of Innocence.[86]

The status of inference-drawing provisions under the Directive on the Presumption of Innocence is somewhat unclear; they may arguably be prohibited, at least where an inference is used as evidence of guilt.[87] The Offences Against the State Acts, and other statutes which now include similar inference-drawing provisions, might possibly be incompatible with that Directive.

In relation to the Directive on Access to a Lawyer in Criminal Proceedings. it seems that a significant part of the reason for not opting in must relate to the Offences Against the State Acts and/or other legislation which mirrors their provisions. The costs of providing access to legal advice for impecunious suspects who might be detained in Garda custody for lengthy periods of time under the Offences Against the State Acts[88] might possibly be a reason for not opting in. Having said that, such access is currently granted at the

[82] Directive 2012/29/EU establishing minimum standards on the rights, support and protection of victims of crime [2012] OJ L315/57.

[83] Directive 2012/13/EU on the right to information in criminal proceedings [2012] OJ L142/1.

[84] Directive 2010/64/EU on the right to interpretation and translation in criminal proceedings [2010] OJ L280/1.

[85] Directive 2013/48/EU on the right of access to a lawyer in criminal proceedings [2013] OJ L294/1.

[86] Directive 2016/343/EU on the strengthening of certain aspects of the presumption of innocence [2016] OJL65/1.

[87] Article 7(5) of the Directive states that '[t]he exercise by suspects and accused persons of the right to remain silent or of the right not to incriminate oneself shall not be used against them and shall not be considered to be evidence that they have committed the criminal offence concerned.' Recital 28, however, adds that while the silence of the accused cannot in itself be considered incriminating evidence 'this should be without prejudice to national rules concerning the assessment of evidence by courts or judges, provided that the rights of the defence are respected.' The exact interaction between and impact of these two provisions is unclear.

[88] A potential total period of detention of up to 72 hours is possible under s 30 of the 1939 Act, as amended.

request of the detained suspect, and financed via the Garda Station Legal Advice Scheme. In that context, the reason for not opting in remains somewhat unclear, especially given the significant role of the Irish Presidency of the European Council in finalising the text of that Directive.[89] Perhaps it is felt that opting in would increase the numbers of suspects choosing to obtain legal advice in the Garda station,[90] and therefore increase the costs involved.

Ireland's engagement with international human rights bodies has served to highlight several problematic aspects of the Offences Against the State Acts, but the tangible effects of those interactions have been limited thus far. As with the jurisprudence of the ECtHR, the Procedural Roadmap Directives of the EU may have a soft influence on the Irish criminal justice system, showing the trajectory of our European counterparts on these issues, and highlighting where our system is out of line with them. If the peace of Northern Ireland is not disturbed by Brexit or other events, these developments may in time lead to changes in the Offences Against the State Acts, or the addition of further safeguards to diminish the adverse impact of extraordinary powers and procedures on human rights.

[89] S Cras 'The Directive on the right of access to a lawyer in criminal proceedings and in European arrest warrant proceedings' (2014) 1 *Eurocrim* 32, 35.

[90] Conway and Daly suggest that the percentage of detained suspects who have consultations with solicitors is in the region of 21%, while just 10% of detainees have their solicitor present during interview. See V Conway and Y Daly 'From Legal Advice to Legal Assistance: Recognising the Changing Role of the Solicitor in the Garda Station' (2019) *Irish Judicial Studies Journal* 103, 111.

12

The Offences Against the State Acts: Reflections from Practice and the Legislature

IVANA BACIK

I. INTRODUCTION

MY INTEREST IN the operation of the Offences Against the State Acts derives from my time in practice as a criminal barrister. Over several years prior to 2011, I acted as defence counsel in a series of eight or ten Special Criminal Court (SCC) cases, at a time when that Court was still sitting in the historic building on Green Street in Dublin's north inner city – just beside the Smithfield fruit market. During that time, I became very familiar with the complex and intricate statutory framework created by the Offences Against the State Acts, which governs the trial of offences before the SCC. In parallel, as an elected member of Seanad Eireann since 2007, I have also participated in the parliamentary debates held annually on renewal of various Offences Against the State Acts and related statutory provisions.

In this chapter, some reflections based on these varied experiences of working with the Offences Against the State Acts are offered. But by way of introduction, no discussion of SCC practice should omit reference to the built environment within which criminal trials under these Acts took place over many years, until 2010 when the SCC finally moved to the newly constructed Criminal Courts of Justice (CCJ) building on Parkgate Street. The SCC courtroom there, while much more suited to the efficient conduct of legal proceedings, is devoid of the highly charged atmosphere that prevailed in the old Green Street building.

II. PRACTICE IN GREEN STREET

Green Street Courthouse, which still stands today, was originally constructed in 1797. It was designed by Whitmore Davis as the Dublin City Sessions House, with prison buildings constructed alongside it. The curved wall to the right of the Green Street entrance is all that is left now of Newgate Gaol (where the eighteenth century revolutionary Lord Edward Fitzgerald died in custody, as a result of injuries caused when he was arrested during the 1798 Uprising). The building currently looks rather forlorn and neglected, although somewhat incongruously a children's playground has been developed since 2010 in the small green park behind it. It is difficult now for anyone who might walk past this pleasant open space to imagine that so many dramatic trials took place within the nearby walls over several centuries.

Shortly following its completion, the Green Street building was used for a number of high-profile trials of Republicans and Fenians; including the trial of Robert Emmet in 1803. All death sentences in the new Irish Free State after 1922 were handed down in Green Street, as it became the Central Criminal Court; it subsequently became the home of the re-constituted Special Criminal Court in 1972.[1] Those convicted there after that date included Martin McGuinness in 1973, Nicky Kelly and others for the Sallins train robbery after 1976;[2] and John Gilligan in 2001. The building was subjected to an IRA bombing in 1976.

In more recent decades, in my own experience it had become a very strange building within which to work. Tight security had been put in place both inside and outside the building, with uniformed and plainclothes Gardaí patrolling the perimeter. Security was especially tight for those who accessed the building through the public entrance. Those persons included defence counsel and solicitors, along with relatives of the accused and members of the public; all of whom were subjected to body searches by police before being permitted to enter. By contrast, Gardaí and prosecution teams could enter by the much grander front door on Halston Street.

Once inside, the building featured steeply tiered seating for members of the public in attendance. The dock within which the accused sat was, unusually, not at the side of the courtroom but placed in a reserved section at the front of the public seating area, facing the judges and at the same level of elevation as their bench (the SCC constitutes a three judge panel, with no jury). In front of the rows of seating, fine old wooden benches and desktops were reserved for prosecution and defence legal teams, with a raised witness box and the judicial bench both looming above them. The three judges presiding from above had a view out over the entire courtroom, often full of people with significant numbers in attendance for high-profile trials. Ancient dark passageways ran beneath the building and were used for bringing prisoners to and from the cells. The cells themselves were horrible, tiny and claustrophobic caves deep beneath the public spaces in the building. We Defence counsel routinely had to conduct hurried consultations with clients held in custody in these inappropriately dank caverns. Many of these clients were charged with offences related to membership of an unlawful organisation under section 21 of the Offences Against the State Act 1939 (OASA).

At one point, on a rainy afternoon just a few days into a trial in which I was acting for one of several men accused of charges relating to membership of a paramilitary organisation, part of the Green Street building roof suddenly collapsed and water

[1] For more on the history of the Special Criminal Court, see F Davis, *The History and Development of the Special Criminal Court 1922–2014* (Dublin, Bloomsbury, 2014); for more on the historical development of prisons in Ireland generally, see T Carey, *Mountjoy: the Story of a Prison* (Dublin, Collins Press, 2000).

[2] *People (DPP) v Kelly* [1983] IR 1. The story of the miscarriage of justice in Nicky Kelly's case has been comprehensively told in P McGarry, *While Justice Slept: The True Story of Nicky Kelly and the Sallins Train Robbery* (Dublin, Liffey Press, 2007). See also J Joyce and P Murtagh, *Blind Justice* (Dublin, Poolbeg Press, 1984).

poured in.[3] The trial had to adjourn for a few days as a result while temporary repairs were carried out, and a short time thereafter the building was finally closed as a courthouse, with all SCC proceedings moved to the ostentatiously contemporary surroundings of the CCJ on Parkgate Street. While some Courts Service business continued to be administered from there for a time, the building remains largely unused. Since 2010, I have been back once for a one-off arts performance event organised on the theme of 'justice'. On that occasion, I had the pleasure of being invited to speak to the audience from the highly elevated judges' platform alongside former SCC defendant Nicky Kelly, who spoke passionately about his time as an accused man standing in the dock of that very same building. His experience of being subjected to a miscarriage of justice before the special courts forms an appropriate context within which to consider how the operation of the SCC has been developed through case law and legislation.

III. DEVELOPMENT OF JURISPRUDENCE AND LEGISLATION ON THE SPECIAL CRIMINAL COURT

Article 38.3. 1° of the Constitution provides that 'Special courts may be established by law for the trial of offences in cases where it may be determined in accordance with such law that the ordinary courts are inadequate to secure the effective administration of justice, and the preservation of public peace and order.'[4] Part V of the OASA provides for the establishment of special (non-jury) criminal courts in accordance with this Article. Such courts, now referred to as the SCC, have operated in Ireland from 1939 to 1946, from 1961 to 1962 and from 1972 until the present date. Within Part V, section 36 provides for the creation of different classes of 'scheduled offences' to be tried before these non-jury courts.[5]

The intricate framework of 'special' laws and procedures emanating from the OASA and governing the conduct of trials before the SCC has been developed extensively over the years, accompanied in more recent years by the emergence of a welcome body of academic and practitioner-focused literature on the work of the SCC and the OASA.[6]

Significant amendments to the OASA were introduced in 1972 and 1976.[7] Following the Omagh bombing in August 1998, the Offences Against the State (Amendment) Act 1998 (the OAS(A)A) was passed to amend the earlier legislation. The 1998 Act contained new provisions on the rules of evidence concerning the offence of membership of an

[3] I was Junior Counsel, led by Deirdre Murphy (now a High Court judge, then Senior Counsel).

[4] For recent discussion on the juror intimidation campaign that preceded the adoption of provisions for non-jury trial in the Constitution (Amendment No 17) Act 1931, see M Coen, '"The Work of Some Irresponsible Women": Jurors, Ghosts and Embracery in the Irish Free State' (2020) 38(4) *Law and History Review* 777–810.

[5] The classes of scheduled offences include not only those created by the OASA (such as the s 21 offences of membership of an unlawful organisation); but also offences created under other legislation such as the Firearms Acts 1925–1990.

[6] This includes A Harrison, *The Special Criminal Court: Practice and Procedure* (Dublin, Bloomsbury, 2019); Davis, *The History and Development of the Special Criminal Court*(n 1); *Report of the Committee to Review the Offences Against the State Acts 1939–1998* (Dublin, Government Publications, 2002) hereinafter, Hederman Report; G Hogan and C Walker, *Political Violence and the Law in Ireland* (Manchester, Manchester University Press, 1989); and M Robinson, *The Special Criminal Court* (Dublin, Dublin University Press, 1974).

[7] These amendments were made through the Offences Against the State (Amendment) Act 1972 and the Criminal Law Act 1976.

unlawful organisation. It also created certain additional scheduled offences, while extending the maximum period of detention permitted under the 1939 Act. In 2009, the Criminal Justice (Amendment) Act (CJ(A)A) was passed with the aim of combatting organised crime, providing in section 8 that certain further offences would be regarded as scheduled offences for the purpose of the OASA.[8]

A panel of serving judges from the High Court, Circuit Court and District Court are appointed to the Special Criminal Courts.[9] Where the Court is dealing with scheduled offences, which tend to involve subversive or paramilitary crime, these will generally be sent automatically to the SCC. But the Court can also deal with certain non-scheduled offences, where such offences are referred to the Court by the Director of Public Prosecutions (DPP) under section 46 of the OASA. Such referral is made where the DPP is of the opinion that the ordinary courts are inadequate to secure the effective administration of justice and the preservation of public peace and order in relation to that particular trial. Challenges to the status of the SCC itself, and to the power of the DPP to refer non-scheduled cases there for trial, have been unsuccessful. In *Murphy v Ireland*, however, the Supreme Court held that the DPP may be obliged in some circumstances to provide reasons for her decision.[10]

The SCC may have originally been envisaged as a court exclusively for the trial of scheduled offences, but as Alice Harrison writes, even when it was first established in 1939, 'the cases heard before it were not limited to subversive crime and the Court spent much of the later years of the Emergency trying economic cases'.[11] Fergal Davis, referring to a governmental memorandum of 1942 concluding that the Circuit Court was unsuitable to hear cases involving 'deep seated conspiracy', suggests that the reason for using the SCC was rooted in a view that juror intimidation would be likely; or that convictions might be difficult to obtain before a jury given the growing unpopularity of rationing laws at the time.[12]

However, in more recent decades the Court has increasingly been used to try non-subversive organised crime (or so-called 'gangland' crime) alongside subversive crime, particularly since the enactment of the CJ(A)A 2009.

IV. CRITIQUES OF THE SCC: INSISTENCE ON 'DUE PROCESS'

The continued existence, development and entrenchment of the OASA structures and of the SCC itself have been condemned by human rights and civil liberties bodies, both nationally and internationally, over many years for their encroachment upon fundamental due process rights, particularly the right to trial by jury.[13] In the 2002 report of the

[8] These are the 'organised crime' offences provided for in Pt 7 of the Criminal Justice Act 2006.

[9] In 2016, a second SCC began to operate, in order to deal with a backlog of cases.

[10] [2014] 1 IR 198.

[11] Harrison, *The Special Criminal Court* (n 6) 583.

[12] Davis, *The History and Development of the Special Criminal Court* (n 1)104.

[13] See Y Daly, Chapter 11, this volume. The phasing out of the SCC was envisaged in the Belfast (Good Friday) Agreement; see text of *Good Friday Agreement*, at 25, under Security heading: '1. The participants note that the development of a peaceful environment on the basis of this agreement can and should mean a normalisation of security arrangements and practices.' Accessible at: www.dfa.ie/media/dfa/alldfawebsitemedia/ourrolesandpolicies/northernireland/good-friday-agreement-1.pdf.

government-appointed Committee to review the OASA, a minority view was expressed that 'the case in favour of the continued existence of the Special Criminal Court has not been made out'.[14] At international level, the UN Human Rights Committee has repeatedly identified the existence of the SCC as violating Ireland's legal obligations under international human rights treaties. In 2014, for example, in its *Concluding Observations on the Fourth Periodic Report of Ireland* under the International Covenant on Civil and Political Rights, the Committee reiterated its 'concern at the lack of a definition of terrorism under domestic legislation and the continuing operation of the Special Criminal Court … [and its] further concern at the expansion of the remit of the Court to include organized crime', and recommended that Ireland 'should introduce a definition of "terrorist acts" in its domestic legislation, limited to offences which can justifiably be equated with terrorism and its serious consequences. It should also consider abolishing the Special Criminal Court'.[15]

Similarly, the Irish Council for Civil Liberties (ICCL) has always been strongly critical of the continued application of the concept of 'extraordinary' courts in peacetime in Ireland; and of the effective normalisation of such courts. In 2015, when the government decided to establish the second juryless SCC, then ICCL Executive Director Mark Kelly observed that the establishment of extraordinary courts in peacetime is a violation of Ireland's international legal obligations, saying that:

> The Special Criminal Court was created as an extraordinary court in extraordinary times; however, no reasonable person could today claim that there is a public emergency threatening the life of the nation. It is therefore unjustified that this Court's procedures suspend fundamental fair trial guarantees, including the right to trial by jury.[16]

In November 2018, at a conference in Dublin jointly organised by the ICCL and the International Network of Civil Liberties Organisations (INCLO), the UN Special Rapporteur on the promotion and protection of human rights and fundamental freedoms while countering terrorism, Professor Fionnuala Ní Aoláin, commented on the 'consistent and trenchant concerns about the use of the Special Criminal Court and the Offences Against the State Act as a "work-around" the ordinary protection of the law'.[17] The same year, the Commission on the Future of Policing in Ireland recommended a 'comprehensive and robust review of the legislative framework within which police and other agencies operate in the area of national security' and called for 'the establishment of an Independent Examiner of terrorist and serious crime legislation'.[18] More recently, in June 2020 the ICCL again called for the abolition of the SCC on the basis that its continued use offends the constitutional rights of accused persons, notably the right to trial by jury;

[14] Hederman Report (n 6) 9.89. This review was established in the context of the Good Friday Agreement. The majority supported the retention of the SCC (9.38 et seq) but recommended three-yearly parliamentary reviews of the need for its retention (9.44); and abolition of the scheduled/non-scheduled offence distinction (9.57).

[15] UN, 19 August 2014, accessible at: http://docstore.ohchr.org/SelfServices/FilesHandler.ashx?enc=6QkG1d-%2FPPRiCAqhKb7yhsieXFSudRZs%2FX1ZaMqUUOS9yIqPEMRvxx26PpQFtwrk%2BhtvbJ1frkLE%2BCPVCm6lW%2BYjfrz7jxiC9GMVvGkvu2UIuUfSqikQb9KMVoAoKkgSG.

[16] ICCL, *Special Criminal Court Decision Flouts Rule of Law*, 29 October 2015, accessible at: www.iccl.ie/press-release/special-criminal-court-decision-flouts-rule-of-law-says-iccl/.

[17] ICCL, *UN Expert Criticises Special Criminal Court*, 21 November 2018, accessible at www.iccl.ie/news/un-expert-criticises-special-criminal-court/. See Ni Aolain, Chapter 4, this volume.

[18] Report of the Commission on the Future of Policing in Ireland, 2018, at 38: www.policereform.ie/en/POLREF/Pages/PB18000006.

and that alternative measures to protect against juror intimidation should be introduced instead.[19]

Much of the criticism to date has focused upon the way in which regular usage of the SCC has brought about a situation where the court now has 'de-facto permanency in our criminal justice system … emergency powers have become normalised'.[20] This has given rise to an acceptance of the extraordinary as ordinary, both by judges and practitioners. As Ms Justice Iseult O'Malley writes in her foreword to the same text, practitioners and the judiciary 'must always be aware of the risk that they will become overly habituated to the abnormal'.[21] She suggests that this risk is 'best countered by constant insistence upon constitutional due process'[22] – a vitally important principle.

A good example of the application of this principle may be found in the case law developed over the years concerning the application of section 3(2) of the Offences Against the State (Amendment) Act 1972; the 'belief evidence' provision which confers evidential status upon the statement by a Chief Superintendent that he or she believes the accused 'was at a material time a member of an unlawful organisation'.[23] In *Redmond v Ireland*,[24] the Supreme Court in 2016 read into this provision the requirement for supporting evidence, in other words evidence additional to that of the Chief Superintendant's belief. This decision followed from a line of earlier case law in which the Court of Criminal Appeal (CCA) and Supreme Court had set out the parameters within which the 'belief evidence' provision could be relied upon.[25]

Over several decades, therefore, the superior courts have effectively created a set of constitutionally derived parameters, within which the SCC has to navigate the operation of this 'extraordinary' belief evidence provision. Although in some other cases[26] the provisions of the OASA have been upheld as conforming to constitutional guarantees, the development of this jurisprudence may be seen as demonstrating the importance of 'constant insistence upon constitutional due process' as a curb against what would otherwise become over-habituation to the abnormal.[27]

This point is not just relevant to practitioners and judges, however; it is also essential when considering the role of legislators within the OASA framework, under those specific provisions conferring powers and responsibilities upon the Houses of the Oireachtas. The remainder of this chapter will focus upon the role of legislators in undertaking

[19] www.iccl.ie/wp-content/uploads/2020/06/ICCL-Review-of-the-Special-Criminal-Court-2020.pdf.

[20] Harrison, *The Special Criminal Court* (n 6) vii.

[21] I O'Malley, foreword to Harrison, ibid, v.

[22] Ibid.

[23] This statement is used to provide evidence of membership in prosecutions for the offence of membership under s 21 of the OASA (as amended by s 2 of the Criminal Law Act 1976). See L Heffernan and E O'Connor, Chapter 6, this volume.

[24] [2016] ILRM 301.

[25] These cases included: *AG v Desmond Ferguson*, CCA, 27 October 1975; *O'Leary v AG* [1993] 1 IR 102; *DPP v Dermot Gannon*, CCA, 2 April 2003; *DPP v Martin Kelly* [2006] 3 IR 115; *DPP v Birney, Brennan, Gilson, O'Donnell & Troy* [2007] 1 IR 337; *DPP v Binead* [2007] 1 IR 374; *DPP v Vincent Kelly*, CCA, 6 December 2007; *DPP v Colm Maguire*, CCA, 7 May 2008.

[26] See, eg, *Sweeney v Ireland* [2019] IESC 39, where the Supreme Court upheld the constitutionality of s 9(1)(b) of the OAS(A)A 1998, reversing the High Court decision; see also commentary by M Coen, 'Withholding the Right to Silence: *Sweeney v Ireland*', paper given at the Irish Supreme Court Review Conference, Trinity College Dublin, 12 October 2019.

[27] I O'Malley, foreword to Harrison, *The Special Criminal Court* (n 6) v.

consideration of the annual motions that come before both Dáil and Seanad regarding renewal of certain provisions of the OAS(A)A 1998 and the CJ(A)A 2009.

V. OVERSIGHT ROLE OF LEGISLATORS WITHIN OASA FRAMEWORK – 'SUNSET CLAUSES'

Originally, the scheduling of offences as provided for under the OASA had been envisaged as a matter for government, and not for the Oireachtas. Under Article 38.3.1, the inadequacy of the ordinary courts must be determined 'in accordance with law' in order to justify the existence of special courts. Section 36(1) of the OASA provides that when Part V of that Act is in force, and the government is satisfied that the ordinary courts are 'inadequate' as required under Article 38.3.1, then the government has the power by order to declare certain offences as scheduled offences under Part V.

However, in 2002 the Committee to Review the OASA (the Hederman Committee) expressed concern that this provision might be unconstitutional, since it could be interpreted as conferring a legislative role upon the government and usurping the functions of the Oireachtas under Article 15 of the Constitution.[28] The Committee took the view that the Oireachtas, and not the government, should in future determine whether an offence is scheduled, in other words that 'the offences that trigger the application of the section 30 arrest powers ought to be determined by the Oireachtas itself by means of primary legislation'.[29] The Committee further suggested that in such cases:

> the Oireachtas will have to consider factors such as the connection between the offence in question and paramilitary crime and (if thought appropriate) organised crime; the seriousness of the offence; the inherent complexity of the offence and whether or not extended detention is necessary for the proper investigation of that crime ... any such list of offences should be tightly drawn with these considerations in mind and ... the list of specified offences ought to be reviewed by the Oireachtas at regular intervals, preferably every three years.[30]

Even before the publication of the Hederman Report, however, the 1998 Act (OAS(A)A) had been passed, specifically conferring power upon the Oireachtas through section 18 to review the premise for the scheduling of certain identified offences. This approach was also taken in the subsequent 2009 Act (CJ(A)A), which like the 1998 Act incorporated in section 8 a mandatory parliamentary review to continue certain provisions in force. These provisions, and the role of Oireachtas oversight, are considered further below; it is now a matter for legislators to determine on an annual basis whether the relevant 1998 and 2009 Act provisions should remain in force.

A similar requirement for regular parliamentary oversight of criminal justice provisions had previously been provided for in the Criminal Justice (Drug Trafficking) Act 1996, albeit in respect of powers related to non-scheduled drugs offences. Section 11 of

[28] Hederman Report (n 6) 7.25–6. Article 15.2.1 of the Constitution provides that 'The sole and exclusive power of making laws for the State is hereby vested in the Oireachtas: no other legislative authority has power to make laws for the State.'

[29] Ibid, 7.26.

[30] Ibid; see Harrison, *The Special Criminal Court* (n 6) 133. This recommendation has not been implemented as scheduled offences are still generally not subject to parliamentary oversight, with the exception of the specific offences discussed below.

the 1996 Act had placed a 12-month time limit upon the continuance in force of certain sections of that Act which created new powers of detention and re-arrest, and which provided for related procedural matters, unless each House of the Oireachtas had passed a resolution continuing the provisions in force.[31] However, section 11 was itself repealed by section 22(4) of the CJ(A)A 2009, which provides instead that the sections of the 1996 Act to which section 11 related 'shall continue in operation indefinitely'. The requirement for parliamentary oversight thus no longer applies to drugs offences under the 1996 Act, but it remains in place in respect of the OAS(A)A and CJ(A)A provisions.

In recent years, regular provision has been made in specific statutes for the Oireachtas to engage in 'Post-enactment Scrutiny' (PeS).[32] Indeed, this concept (defined as 'the review of a piece of legislation which is in force') was considered in some detail by the Oireachtas Library and Research Service in 2017.[33] Their report noted that such scrutiny is generally required in order 'to ascertain whether the legislation … has achieved the original policy objectives'; many jurisdictions incorporate parliamentary oversight mechanisms into legislation, and the oversight itself may take a number of different forms.[34] Provision may be made, for example, for a general review of the operation of particular sections, but also for so-called 'sunset clauses', whereby continuance of specific provisions must be affirmed by Parliament. The provisions of section 18 of the OAS(A)A and section 8 of the CJ(A)A constitute just such sunset clauses; without the affirmation of each House of the Oireachtas at designated intervals, relevant sections in both Acts will 'cease to be in operation'.[35]

The requirement for annual parliamentary oversight under section 18 of the OAS(A)A 1998 applies to sections 2–4, 6–12, and 14–17 of that Act. The substantive offences created are: section 6 (directing an unlawful organisation); section 7 (possession of articles for certain purposes); section 8 ('unlawful collection of information'); section 9 (withholding information); and section 12 (training in the use of firearms and explosives).

The other provisions are procedural: section 2 enables inferences to be drawn from an accused's silence when questioned about membership of an unlawful organisation; section 3 concerns notification of witnesses; section 4 enables inferences to be drawn from certain conduct by an accused.[36] Section 10 allows for extension of detention under section 30 of the OASA. Section 11 provides for re-arrest under section 30 and section 14 states that the new offences created in the Act are scheduled. Section 17 provides for forfeiture of property.

[31] The relevant sections of the 1996 Act were ss 2, 3, 4, 5 and 6.

[32] Eg, s 7 of the Gender Recognition Act 2015 requires a review of the operation of the Act to begin two years after its commencement and a report made to the Houses of the Oireachtas no later than 12 months after the review begins; s 27 of the Criminal Law (Sexual Offences) Act 2017 requires a review of the operation of s 7A of the Criminal Law (Sexual Offences) Act 1993 to have taken place within three years of its commencement and a report laid before the Houses.

[33] Oireachtas Library and Research Service, *Spotlight: Post-Enactment Scrutiny by Parliament* (Oireachtas, 21 December 2017) 3; see https://data.oireachtas.ie/ie/oireachtas/libraryResearch/2018/2018-01-08_spotlight-post-enactment-scrutiny-in-parliament_en.pdf.

[34] Ibid, 4. The report notes that such provisions are used in a wide range of jurisdictions including Australia, Belgium, France, Sweden, Switzerland and the UK.

[35] OAS(A)A, s 18(1); CJ(A)A, s 8(4).

[36] Section 5, originally included in the list of offences subject to parliamentary review, also related to evidential matters (enabling inferences to be drawn from the failure of an accused to mention certain facts) but it was repealed by s 3 of the Criminal Justice Act 2007. Part 4 of that Act contains detailed provisions enabling inferences to be drawn in different circumstances.

The consequences of non-renewal are as follows. Even if the section 18 motion is not renewed in any year, the SCC would continue in operation and much of the OASA framework would remain in force. Non-renewal would not prevent the prosecution and trial of 1998 Act offences committed before the renewal deadline, but such offences would cease to be scheduled and instead would be tried in the ordinary jury courts, unless referred by the DPP to the Special Criminal Court under section 46 of the OASA. The offences would also cease to operate into the future but could be legislated back into existence by the Oireachtas – although not retrospectively. Thus, any relevant acts committed in the interim period following non-renewal and before passage of further legislation could not be prosecuted under the Act.

Significantly, non-renewal would also mean the ending in force of the procedural provisions used by Gardaí in investigating offences. Thus, inferences could not be drawn from the silence of accused persons under questioning (section 2); nor would extension of detention and re-arrest under sections 10 and 11 be permitted. Again, these powers could be re-introduced prospectively through primary legislation, but the lapse in their existence could create difficulties and impede ongoing investigations and prosecutions where the state seeks to rely upon evidence gained through application of the relevant provisions. Non-renewal of the 2009 CJ(A)A provisions would have less far-reaching consequences. Section 8 of that Act provides for the scheduling of certain 'organised crime' offences under Part 7 of the Criminal Justice Act 2006: section 71A (directing the activities of a criminal organisation); section 72 (participating in activities of a criminal organisation); section 73 (committing an offence for a criminal organisation) and section 76 (liability for offences by a body corporate). Non-renewal would mean that those offences would remain in force and could still be prosecuted in the ordinary courts; but they would cease to be scheduled. Again, they could instead be sent individually by the DPP to the SCC.[37]

The statutory oversight role for legislators provided for in the two sunset clauses has rarely been considered in Irish case law, although a related procedural issue did arise in one 2013 High Court judgment.[38] It was already well-established that the necessary Oireachtas resolutions would have to be provided to the court in any relevant criminal proceedings: where an accused was charged with an offence under one of the relevant sections; or where the prosecution sought to rely upon section 2 of the 1998 Act in order to invoke adverse inferences where the accused had remained silent on being questioned; or indeed where an application was made to a District Judge for an extension of detention under section 30(4) of the OASA as inserted by section 10 of the 1998 Act.[39] Ordinarily, as Harrison writes, the state had sought to prove the existence in force of the relevant sections on the date in question by handing in copies of the journals of both Houses of

[37] Harrison summarises the effect of non-renewal by saying that the offences under the 1998 Act and Pt 7 of the Criminal Justice Act 2006 'are only scheduled as long as both Houses of the Oireachtas pass a resolution that they should continue to be'. Harrison, *The Special Criminal Court* (n 6) 135. She notes further: 'The Government may also declare that certain offences shall cease to be scheduled offences, but this power does not appear to have been utilised thus far.' While the Oireachtas could in practice remove certain offences from the schedule by repealing the relevant legislation, this has only happened rarely, as when s 7 of the Conspiracy and Protection of Property Act 1875, which contained scheduled offences, was repealed and replaced by s 31 of the Non-Fatal Offences Against the Person Act 1997 (which is not scheduled); Harrison, *The Special Criminal Court* (n 6) 133; and D Walsh, *Walsh on Criminal Procedure* 2nd edn (Dublin, Round Hall, 2016) 1481.

[38] *Mitchell v Member in Charge of Terenure Garda Station* [2013] 1 IR 651.

[39] See Harrison, *The Special Criminal Court* (n 6) 134 and 188–9.

the Oireachtas. Indeed, this is still regarded as 'best practice'.[40] However, in 2013, Hogan J held that a District Court Judge was entitled to rely upon the website of the Houses of the Oireachtas in establishing that the appropriate resolutions had been passed to continue section 10 of the 1998 Act in force, thereby enabling the applicants' detention to be extended lawfully, even without the handing in of the journals.[41]

VI. ANNUAL RENEWAL MOTIONS BEFORE THE OIREACHTAS

This procedural point aside, the annual renewal motions before the Oireachtas under the OASA and CJ(A)A have tended not to be subject to academic analysis or judicial consideration. Yet it is clear that, in carrying out their mandated oversight role under these statutes, legislators must bring to bear the same 'constant insistence upon constitutional due process' that O'Malley J has noted is required more generally.[42] That principle must therefore apply where members of the Dáil and Seanad decide each year whether the ordinary courts remain inadequate for the trial of certain offences, in accordance with the procedures set out in both the 1998 Act and the 2009 Act.

Section 14 of the 1998 Act provides:

> (1) It is hereby declared that the ordinary courts are inadequate to secure the effective administration of justice and the preservation of public peace and order in relation to each offence under *sections* 6 to *9* and *12*.[43]

While this provision is retained in force, the offences created under sections 6 to 9 and 12 remain as scheduled offences, triable before the SCC. Section 14(3), however, contains the proviso that this does not affect or limit the exercise by the government of its powers under the OASA, including its powers under section 36 to declare certain offences as scheduled

Under section 18 of the 1998 Act, certain sections of that Act[44] would 'cease to be in operation on and from the 30th day of June, 2000',[45] unless each of the Houses of the Oireachtas has passed a resolution to continue them in force. Section 18(2) at its inception had provided that the relevant sections might be continued in operation 'from time to time' by a resolution passed by each House of the Oireachtas 'for such period as may

[40] Ibid, 189. Section 11 of the Criminal Evidence Act 1992 provides that 'In any criminal proceedings evidence of the passing of a resolution by either House of the Oireachtas … may be given by the production of a copy of the Journal of the proceedings of that House relating to the resolution.'

[41] [2013] 1 IR 651.

[42] I O'Malley, foreword to Harrison, *The Special Criminal Court* (n 6) v.

[43] As outlined above, s 6 creates an offence of 'directing an unlawful organisation'; s 7 creates an offence of possession of certain articles; s 8 creates an offence of unlawful collection of information; s 9 creates an offence of withholding information concerning the commission of a serious offence; and s 12 creates an offence of training a person in the use of firearms etc.

[44] Those sections as outlined above are: ss 2 to 12; and ss 14 and 17 of the 1998 Act. Sections 6 to 9 and 12 create the offences listed in the previous footnote; the other provisions are procedural. Section 2 concerns inferences that may be drawn from an accused's silence when questioned about membership of an unlawful organisation; s 3 concerns notification of witnesses; ss 4 and 5 concern evidential issues (s 5 was later repealed by s 3 of the Criminal Justice Act 2007). Section 10 allows for extension of detention under s 30 of the OASA; s 11 provides for re-arrest under s 30 of the OASA; and s 17 provides for forfeiture of property.

[45] The date originally specified in the Bill as introduced was that of 30 December 2000, later brought forward by amendment in the Dáil to 30 June 2000 following the raising of Opposition concerns.

be specified in the resolutions'. However, some restriction was placed upon this widely-drawn parliamentary power through the subsequent passage of section 37 of the Criminal Justice Act 1999, which substituted a new section 18(2) stipulating that the period for which the provisions might be maintained in force by the Oireachtas could not exceed 12 months. This change was made in 1999 because the then Minister for Justice, John O'Donoghue, had given a commitment during Oireachtas debates on the 1998 Act that he would introduce an annual review provision.[46] Section 18(3) further provides that before those resolutions may be passed, the Minister for Justice and Equality must lay a report before each of the Houses of the Oireachtas on the operation of the sections in question over the previous period; meaning that this report is now required to be laid annually before both Dáil and Seanad. Section 18(3) also provides that the report must cover the period starting on the last day covered by the previous report and ending not later than 21 days before the date of the moving of the resolution in each House.

During the debates on the introduction of section 18 in 1998, Minister O'Donoghue had described the OAS(A)A provisions as 'harsh' and expressed the hope that, once the specified end date of 30 June 2000 was reached, 'violence for political ends will have ended completely and … it will be possible to reform the Offences against the State Acts and dispense with those elements no longer required'.[47] Two decades later, that hope has not been borne out by events. Section 14 of the 1998 Act has continued in force by way of resolution passed annually by the Houses of the Oireachtas. For as long as these resolutions continue to be passed annually, the relevant offences set out in sections 6 to 9 and 12 of the 1998 Act will remain scheduled.

In a similar way to the 1998 Act, the Criminal Justice (Amendment) Act 2009 provides in section 8 that certain offences under Part 7 of the Criminal Justice Act 2006 ('organised crime') are scheduled offences for the purposes of Part V of the OASA 1939.[48] Section 8(1) outlines the basis for this, again in keeping with the constitutional formula used in Article 38.3.1, that the ordinary (jury) courts must be deemed 'inadequate to secure the effective administration of justice and the preservation of public peace and order' in relation to these offences. Section 8(4) provided that the entire section was to lapse after 12 months, unless continued in force by a resolution passed by each House of the Oireachtas; and section 8(5) provides that thereafter, the section 'may be continued in operation from time to time by a resolution passed by each House of the Oireachtas before its expiry for such period as may be specified in the resolutions'.

Interestingly, unlike the sunset clause in the 1998 Act, the parliamentary review period in section 8 is not limited to 12 months. Section 8 could thus be continued in force for longer periods and only subject to Oireachtas scrutiny 'from time to time'. However, in

[46] See closing statement in this regard made during Report Stage debate on the 1999 Act by Mary Wallace TD, Minister of State at the Department of Justice, Equality and Law Reform, *Seanad Debates*, 20 May 1999, at www.oireachtas.ie/en/debates/debate/seanad/1999-05-20/4/. She refers to comments made by Minister O'Donoghue during the Seanad Committee Stage debate on the 1998 Act, where he stated his view that an annual review was already possible under the original wording of s 18(2), but that he would commit to amending the provision in later legislation to specify that the review would be made annually: *Seanad Debates*, 3 September 1998, www.oireachtas.ie/en/debates/debate/seanad/1998-09-03/6/.

[47] *Dáil Debates*, 2 September 1998, at www.oireachtas.ie/en/debates/debate/dail/1998-09-02/5/.

[48] The relevant offences in Pt 7 of the 2006 Act are: s 71A, directing the activities of a criminal organisation; s 72, participating in or contributing to certain activities of a criminal organisation; s 73, committing an offence for a criminal organisation and s 76, liability for offences by a body corporate.

practice the renewal motions in respect of both the 1998 and the 2009 provisions are now considered together by the Oireachtas on an annual basis, on or around the same date each year.

The first occasion on which a resolution for renewal of the 1998 Act provisions came before the Oireachtas was on 20 June 2000, on which date Minister O'Donoghue informed the Houses that the report on the operation of the section disclosed that no court proceedings under sections 2 to 9 or section 12 had yet arisen, but that 'the provisions in question have been utilised where appropriate by the Garda during the investigation of offences'.[49] He further referred to 'immediate security concerns' as justifying the continuance in force of the provisions despite their lack of usage. While a small number of Deputies contested the basis for the continuance of the sections in force, insufficient members objected to enable a vote to be put, and so their continuance was assured for a further 12 months. This debate was to set a decade-long pattern for the annual decision-making process on renewal of the 1998 provisions. On 17 June 2010, for example, then Minister for Justice Dermot Ahern referred extensively to the assessments of the International Monitoring Commission, and to the ongoing threat from dissident republican paramilitary groups as justifying the continuance of the section in force.[50]

The previous year, the CJ(A)A was enacted on 23 July 2009 with a sunset clause provided within section 8, continued in force for a further year by way of resolution passed by the Oireachtas on 29 June 2010.[51] One year later, for the first time both the 1998 and the 2009 provisions were considered on the same date by the Dáil, albeit by way of separate motions proposed by Minister Alan Shatter; each motion was debated and voted upon separately.[52] The Minister spoke of his 'disappointment' that the 2009 provisions had not proved to be 'of greater benefit in tackling … criminal gangs' and his view that the continued availability of the 1998 provisions was 'essential' as an 'effective response to the threat from terrorist groups', despite the evidence that some of these provisions had not been used on any occasions over the previous year.[53]

Over the years since 2011, successive Ministers for Justice have laid reports before the Oireachtas annually on the operation of the 1998 and 2009 provisions. While opposition to the renewal of the motions has been expressed by some TDs and Senators during the annual debates, each year the motions have been passed; and the relevant provisions have thus continued in force without interruption to date. Indeed, it is argued that during parliamentary debates generally on the motions, greater consideration could have been given to those factors referred to above, as listed by the Hederman Committee as relevant in forming a view as to whether specific provisions should remain in force; such as 'the seriousness of the offence; the inherent complexity of the offence and whether or not extended detention is necessary for the proper investigation of that crime …'.[54]

[49] *Dáil Debates*, 20 June 2000, at www.oireachtas.ie/en/debates/debate/dail/2000-06-20/30/#spk_352.

[50] *Dáil Debates*, 17 June 2010, at www.oireachtas.ie/en/debates/debate/dail/2010-06-17/16/#spk_323.

[51] This renewal was made without any debate or vote in either House: *Dáil Debates*, 29 June 2010, at www.oireachtas.ie/en/debates/debate/dail/2010-06-29/23/; *Seanad Debates*, 29 June 2010, at www.oireachtas.ie/en/debates/debate/seanad/2010-06-29/8/.

[52] *Dáil Debates*, 21 June 2011, at www.oireachtas.ie/en/debates/debate/dail/2011-06-21/27/; www.oireachtas.ie/en/debates/debate/dail/2011-06-21/32/; the same motions were considered over two dates by the Seanad (14 and 15 June 2011).

[53] Namely ss 4, 6, 12 and 17.

[54] Hederman Report (n 6) 7.25–6. See fn 30.

In order to provide more robust parliamentary scrutiny, on each occasion that the motions come before the Oireachtas in future years, it is argued that greater emphasis should be placed in the debates on the content of the reports provided to members by the Minister for Justice under section 18(3) of the OAS(A)A as to the patterns of usage of the relevant provisions. These statutory reports contain instructive information, disclosing the reality that certain provisions are rarely used in particular years. For example, over the 12 month period between 1 June 2018 to 31 May 2019, the report into the operation of the OAS(A)A provisions disclosed that the section 2 provision allowing the drawing of inferences from silence was only used three times; but the section 7 provision making it an offence to possess certain items was used 66 times; sections 3, 4, 6, 8, 9, 12 and 17 were not used at all that year.[55] The report on the 1998 Act for 2020 establishes that section 2 (inferences) was used on 11 occasions over the previous 12 months; the sections 10 and 11 powers were used nine and four times respectively and the section 7 offence 20 times, whereas sections 4, 6, 8, 12 and 17 were not used at all.[56] Similarly, the 2019 report on the CJ(A)A provisions revealed that while 20 arrests were made under the section 72 offence of participating in a criminal organisation and four under the section 73 offence (committing an offence for a criminal organisation), section 71A (directing the activities of a criminal organisation) was not used over that period.[57] The equivalent report for 2020 discloses that 29 arrests were made under section 72, and a greatly increased number of 43 arrests under section 73; but again section 71A was not used over the previous year.[58]

While the reports typically provide information on the number of times each offence has been 'used' and the arrests made under each provision, they do not provide any real detail as to the basis for the annual government assertion that the ordinary courts are inadequate to administer justice. This represents a significant difficulty for legislators – and a notable flaw within the parliamentary scrutiny process, a point strongly asserted during the debates on the 2019 renewal motions, the twentieth occasion on which the Oireachtas considered renewal of the 1998 Act provisions.[59]

VII. OIREACHTAS RENEWAL MOTIONS 2019–2020

Over 12–13 June 2019, resolutions were passed by both Houses of the Oireachtas to continue the relevant provisions in force for another 12 months up to 29 June 2020, with debates focusing on the report furnished by the Minister for Justice and Equality for the year ending 31 May 2018. Speaking in the Dáil on 12 June 2019 to propose the renewal

[55] See the 2019 Report on the operation of the OAS(A)A provisions laid before the Oireachtas on 10 June 2019, accessible at: https://ptfs-oireachtas.s3.amazonaws.com/DriveH/AWData/Library3/JUQdoclaid100619a_170614.pdf.

[56] See the 2020 Report on the operation of the OAS(A)A provisions laid before the Oireachtas on 19 June 2020, accessible at: https://data.oireachtas.ie/ie/oireachtas/libraryResearch/2020/2020-06-24_edocslaid-weekly-listing-15-21-june-2020_en.pdf.

[57] See the 2019 Report on the operation of the CJ(A)A provisions laid before the Oireachtas on 10 June 2019, accessible at https://ptfs-oireachtas.s3.amazonaws.com/DriveH/AWData/Library3/JUQdoclaid100619b_171103.pdf.

[58] See the 2020 Report on the operation of the CJ(A)A provisions laid before the Oireachtas on 19 June 2020, accessible at: https://data.oireachtas.ie/ie/oireachtas/libraryResearch/2020/2020-06-24_edocslaid-weekly-listing-15-21-june-2020_en.pdf.

[59] This also represented the tenth year in which renewal of the 2009 Act provisions had been considered.

motion, Minister for Justice Charlie Flanagan trenchantly expressed his disagreement 'with those who assert that the Special Criminal Court operates contrary to fundamental rights'.[60] He went on to say that:

> Anyone tried in that court has the full range of procedural protections available to him or her, including the Court of Appeal and the Supreme Court. We all look forward to the day when the Special Criminal Court is no longer needed, but regrettably we are not there yet. In the circumstances, I must conclude that these provisions continue to be required and that they should remain in operation for a further 12 months.

Speakers in both Houses over those dates expressed their condemnation of the tragic death of Lyra McKee in Derry.[61] However, several speakers also noted the importance of subjecting the provisions to annual scrutiny, precisely because they represent interference with due process rights of the accused and with the normal standards of criminal justice and referring specifically to the lack of information in the statutory report on why the government still considered the ordinary courts inadequate to administer justice.[62] That point formed the basis for an amendment which Deputy Seán Sherlock of Labour put down in the Dáil, accepting that the relevant sections of the 1998 Act should continue in operation for another year; but seeking to amend the motion as follows:

> for want of any or any adequate information being presented to it, by way of a report under section 18 of that Act or otherwise, in order to enable the Dáil to make an informed finding as to the inadequacy of the ordinary courts to secure the effective administration of justice and the preservation of public peace and order in relation to the offences under sections 6 to 9 and 12 of that Act, declines to resolve that section 14 of that Act should continue in operation from or after 30th June, 2019.

Deputy Sherlock proposed the amendment by reference to the text of Article 38.3.1, which requires that the determination as to inadequacy of the ordinary courts must be made *in accordance with law*; a different standard to that provided elsewhere in the constitutional text, for matters to be determined *by law*.[63] He averred that the scheduling of offences to the OASA was originally carried out by the government on the basis of a volume of information; the existence of this information should be made available to legislators in making their necessary determination under the Constitution. In support of this point, he cited the example of *Kavanagh v Governor of Mountjoy Prison*.[64] He also referred to the Financial Emergency Measures in the Public Interest (FEMPI) Acts, whereby legislators are required to make findings concerning whether 'a serious disturbance in the economy and a decline in the economic circumstances of the State have occurred'. Legislators could make those FEMPI findings by virtue of information provided to them under statute, he

[60] *Dáil Debates*, 12 June 2019, at www.oireachtas.ie/ga/debates/debate/dail/2019-06-12/33/.

[61] This tragic death had occurred on 18 April 2019.

[62] In particular, Deputy Sean Sherlock in the Dáil (12 June 2019), and the author in the Seanad (13 June 2019), at: www.oireachtas.ie/ga/debates/debate/dail/2019-06-12/33/ and www.oireachtas.ie/en/debates/debate/seanad/2019-06-13/13/.

[63] Such as the provisions on the right to vote in local elections under Art 28A.4: 'Every citizen who has the right to vote at an election for members of Dáil Éireann and such other persons as may be determined by law shall have the right to vote at an election for members of such of the local authorities referred to in section 2 of this Article as shall be determined by law.'

[64] [2002] 3 IR 97. In that case the government filed affidavits as to its means of knowledge where its decisions were challenged.

argued, including quarterly Exchequer returns; but no comparable body of information is provided to Oireachtas members on the annual renewal motions as to the adequacy of the criminal courts or the risk of corruption or intimidation of juries. In this context, the statutory report should, he proposed, expressly address the core question of whether jury courts are inadequate to secure the effective administration of justice and the preservation of public peace and order.

Minister Flanagan responded by asserting that:

> It is not the role of the Minister for Justice and Equality to form the minds of Members of the Oireachtas. The reason we are debating here is because I see myself as having a duty to inform the Members of the facts but it is reasonable to assume that Members will engage in their own research, consideration and knowledge, the sum total of which will form the views of Members, including the views of Members as to the operation of normal courts and the capacity to administer justice in circumstances.[65]

A vote on the amendment was lost and the motions themselves passed, so that the relevant provisions were continued in force for another year.[66] When the matter came before the Seanad the following day (13 June 2019), this author repeated the general points raised and argued that legislators should also take cognisance of the patterns of usage and, indeed, non-usage of the different provisions as disclosed in the statutory reports. In respect of the 1998 Act, it was notable that several sections had not been used at all in the past year, and a pattern of non-usage could be discerned over some years.[67] A similar pattern was apparent in respect of the provisions under the 2009 Act where, for example, no arrests had been made under section 71A (directing the activities of a criminal organisation) in the previous year. However, the motions were passed and the provisions continued in force until 29 June 2020.

It could hardly have been foreseen during the June 2019 debates that a bizarre and unprecedented combination of events would transpire over the ensuing year to make the issue of the renewal motions a highly charged one politically. The General Election of 8 February 2020 failed to produce an overall majority for any party, leading to more than four months of negotiations on government formation – a national record – before a programme was finally agreed on 26 June 2020 by three coalition partners.[68] This extraordinary delay in the forming of a new government was exacerbated by the global COVID-19 pandemic which brought about a lockdown of society in Ireland, as elsewhere, between mid-March and June 2020.

Meanwhile, by 3 April 2020, Seanad elections necessitated by the dissolution of the Dáil had taken place, and 49 Senators had been elected by university graduates and through the five vocational panels provided for in Article 18 of the Constitution. However, Article 18.3 requires that the 11 nominated members of the Seanad must be nominated by 'the Taoiseach who is appointed next after the re-assembly of Dáil Eireann following the dissolution thereof'. Because of the lengthy process in negotiating a new government, no Taoiseach was appointed by the incoming Dáil until 27 June 2020. The

[65] www.oireachtas.ie/ga/debates/debate/dail/2019-06-12/33/.
[66] The motion relating to the 1998 Act was voted upon and passed by 63 votes to 21. No vote was called on the motion relating to the 2009 Act. See www.oireachtas.ie/ga/debates/debate/dail/2019-06-12/33/.
[67] Namely those under ss 3, 6, 8, 9, 12 and 17 of the 1998 Act.
[68] Fianna Fáil, Fine Gael and the Green Party.

outgoing Taoiseach, Leo Varadkar, took the view that he was unable to convene a meeting of the Seanad until a new Taoiseach had been appointed and had nominated the 11 additional Senators. This legal interpretation was contested by a group of 10 Senators, who took court action seeking to enable the sitting of the Seanad as constituted by its 49 elected members.[69] The High Court ruled in support of the outgoing Taoiseach's view; but by the date of judgment on 29 June 2020, the new government had been formed, 11 Senators nominated and the Seanad convened to sit for that same date.

While the political uncertainty had continued over the months of May and June 2020, serious concerns had been voiced that it would not be possible for the Seanad to consider and pass the annual renewal motions by the necessary deadline of midnight on 29 June 2020.[70] Meanwhile, the renewal motions were debated by the Dáil before the new government was formed, on 24 June 2020.[71] On that date, the outgoing Minister for Justice committed to conducting a comprehensive review of security legislation, in line with the recommendation of the Commission on the Future of Policing.[72] As a result of this commitment, Sinn Féin did not call a vote on the renewal motions, which passed without opposition. Following the dramatic developments in government formation over the weekend of 27–28 June, the motions were then passed at the first sitting of the incoming Seanad on Monday 29 June, following a short debate.[73] During that debate, this author raised concerns about the lack of substantial information about the basis for renewal and about patterns of non-usage apparent in respect of particular provisions. The incoming Minister for Justice again committed to a comprehensive review of security legislation, and the motions passed without a vote – just a few hours before the midnight deadline.

VIII. CONCLUSION

In anticipation of the promised and very welcome review of security legislation, a brief review of the role of legislators within the OASA statutory framework highlights the need to ensure robust levels of parliamentary scrutiny so that renewal motions are considered in accordance with the Constitution, in particular with Article 38.3.1. It may well be that more enhanced levels of parliamentary scrutiny will be provided for in future, if indeed the OASA framework is to be retained. For example, the continued existence of the SCC could be rendered subject to regular Oireachtas review, as was recommended by the Hederman Committee.[74]

In the meantime, while the current sunset clauses remain in place, legislators should have close regard in the first instance to the report furnished annually by the Justice Minister in order to make a renewal determination 'in accordance with law'. Where the

[69] This author was one of the Plaintiffs; see *Bacik & Ors v An Taoiseach*, High Court, 29 June 2020.

[70] See, eg, M O'Halloran, 'Anti-Terrorist and Criminal Gang Laws may lapse by end of June', *Irish Times*, 19 May 2020 at www.irishtimes.com/news/politics/oireachtas/anti-terrorist-and-criminal-gang-laws-may-lapse-by-end-of-june-1.4256687; see also C Keena, 'Criminal law Acts may lapse if Coalition not formed at month's end', *Irish Times*, 23 June 2020 at www.irishtimes.com/news/crime-and-law/criminal-law-acts-may-lapse-if-coalition-not-formed-by-month-end-1.4285655.

[71] www.oireachtas.ie/en/debates/debate/dail/2020-06-24/3/.

[72] Referred to above: www.policereform.ie/en/POLREF/Pages/PB18000006.

[73] www.oireachtas.ie/en/debates/debate/seanad/2020-06-29/.

[74] Hederman Report (n 6) 9.44.

report discloses a pattern of non-usage in respect of particular provisions, then legislators should inquire as to whether they should simply be repealed. Conversely, if in fact specific provisions are being used extensively and effectively each year by Gardaí, without substantial concerns about encroachment on undue process rights, the Oireachtas should consider taking the step of legislating to repeal the sunset clauses or to continue the relevant provisions in force for a longer period of time, as was done in 2009 in respect of section 11 of the Criminal Justice (Drug Trafficking) Act 1996, referred to above.

When considering the sunset clauses, moreover, the content of the report provided for each annual review should be subject to challenge by legislators, where it fails to identify the basis for the government assertion that the ordinary courts are inadequate 'to secure the effective administration of justice and the preservation of public peace and order'. In response to Minister Flanagan's 2019 comment that Oireachtas members should inform themselves as to this question, it may be countered that much of the information on which the assertion is based will be primarily within the domain of the government. Over 20 years of debates, the general justification of 'security concerns' has typically been presented before the Oireachtas by successive Ministers as the basis for seeking renewal, without any specific reference to particular identified concerns. All too often, Ministers have referred to their own belief that renewal is necessary, in language similar to that used where a Garda Superintendant makes a statutory assertion of belief in membership prosecutions, as discussed above.[75]

The difference, however, is that the Superintendant's assertion of belief is made in accordance with a specific statutory text; and a body of case law has been developed, setting parameters upon the application of the 'belief evidence' provision.[76] No such judicial scrutiny has been addressed to the exercise of decision-making by Oireachtas members on the renewal provisions. Yet, if a renewal decision made by the Oireachtas was grounded on inadequate evidence, or indeed taken without reference to any objective evidence, it might be argued that the renewal has not constituted a determination 'in accordance with law' under Article 38 of the Constitution. Such renewal in force could then be vulnerable to legal challenge by a future defendant before the SCC; albeit that the approach of the courts to the question of whether the SCC should continue in force in cases like *Kavanagh* has tended towards the deferential.[77]

In conclusion, the OASA legislative framework creates an 'extraordinary' criminal justice framework, departing from the fundamental principle of trial by jury for serious criminal offences. Those engaged in carrying out statutory functions within this framework should always be mindful of the need to ensure 'constant insistence upon constitutional due process'. This principle applies to legislators, as much as to judges and practitioners. Oireachtas members must exercise their responsibilities in making annual determinations on the renewal of extraordinary provisions with due regard to the security of the community, and while being mindful of the requirements of constitutional justice. Otherwise there is a risk that the fundamental due process bedrock of our criminal justice system may be undermined, through a process of becoming 'overly habituated to the abnormal'.

[75] The 'belief evidence' provision, in s 3(2) of the Offences Against the State (Amendment) Act 1972.

[76] See L Heffernan and E O'Connor, Chapter 6, this volume.

[77] *Kavanagh v Ireland* [1996] 1 IR 321; *Gilligan v Ireland* [2001] 1 ILRM 473; see also Hederman Report (n 6) 23. See Y Daly, Chapter 11, this volume.

13

A Less Exceptional State of Exception: The Offences Against the State Act as an Emergency Response

ALAN GREENE

I. INTRODUCTION

WHILE THE REST of the world fought the Second World War, Ireland had an emergency. 'Emergency' in the Irish psyche may thus have a whimsical quality to it, evidence of our exceptionalism and tendency to understate the gravity of a situation, in much the same way that the conflict in Northern Ireland that cost over 3,600 lives is known as The Troubles. Yet despite this, the scope of emergency powers available under the Irish Constitution are striking and considerably downplayed by the aforementioned conception of an 'emergency' as a phenomenon of somewhat lesser gravity.

This chapter contends that aspects of the Offences Against the State Act 1939 (OASA) and its subsequent amendments can be conceptualised as an emergency response. However, due to the extremely expansive emergency powers possible under Article 28.3.3 of the Constitution, the establishment of special courts under Article 38.3 and even internment without trial may be conceptualised as 'less exceptional' emergency powers. This status of lesser exceptionality has weakened the 'quarantining effect' of Article 28.3.3, undermining the principle that emergency measures are limited solely to the exceptional situations delineated therein. Even with the constitutional provisions of Article 28.3.3, the OASA demonstrates how normalcy may be calibrated to accommodate what should be conceptualised as exceptional powers, resulting in a de facto permanent state of emergency.

Part II outlines the Irish constitutional approach to emergencies, demonstrating that Article 28.3.3 recognises a classic distinction between normalcy and emergency but also, by separately allowing for the establishment of special courts, the Constitution acknowledges the concept of a 'less exceptional' emergency. Parts III and IV then demonstrates how both the Special Criminal Court (SCC) and the power to intern individuals without trial under the Offences Against the State (Amendment) Act 1940 (OASAA 1940) are manifestations of this less 'exceptional' emergency, facilitated by an overly deferential judicial approach to questions of national security. Part V then argues that the current constitutional model has failed to successfully quarantine exceptional powers to exceptional situations. This chapter concludes by outlining reforms that could ensure sufficient appraisal of emergency powers by constitutional actors other than the executive.

II. THE EMERGENCY PARADIGM AND THE IRISH CONSTITUTION

The fundamental assumption of constitutional emergency powers is that there are exceptional situations that the state must confront; however, the tools necessary to do so should not be permissible under the ordinary provisions of the Constitution. States of emergency take the constitutional shackles off, enabling the introduction of powers that would otherwise be unconstitutional. The ultimate justification of these constitutionally unpalatable measures is that they are necessary – the state has no choice or must choose between the lesser of two evils; however, these powers then negate their own necessity through the elimination of the threat which warranted their introduction in the first place. Emergency threats and the measures needed to defeat them therefore are both conceptualised as temporary aberrations and it is this temporariness that ultimately justifies or excuses emergency powers.[1] By stipulating the conditions that must exist before these powers may be enacted, constitutions attempt to 'quarantine' these exceptional measures, enabling them only when the constitutionally enumerated conditions are deemed to exist. In theory, this avoids these powers being enacted in a period of normalcy, ensuring and preserving a higher degree of rights protection and checks on executive power when an emergency has not been declared.[2]

The Irish Constitution clearly gives effect to this emergency paradigm. Article 28.3.3 provides that:

> Nothing in this constitution other than article 15.5.2° shall be invoked to invalidate any law enacted by the Oireachtas which is expressed to be for the purpose of securing the public safety and the preservation of the state in time of war or armed rebellion, or to nullify any act done or purporting to be done in time of war or armed rebellion in pursuance of any such law …[3]

It continues by elaborating that 'war' includes a conflict in which the state is not a belligerent – a so-called neutrality emergency – and includes the period after the cessation of hostilities until such time that the Oireachtas resolves that the emergency no longer exists.[4] Article 28.3.3 has been amended three times, the first two of which were to expand the definition of 'time of war' to include the aforementioned scenarios. The third amendment prohibited the re-introduction of the death penalty during a state of emergency by inserting into Article 28.3.3 the phrase 'other than Article 15.5.2'.[5] To date, a state of emergency under Article 28.3.3 has been declared twice; first, on 2 September 1939 upon the outbreak of World War II. This was not lifted until September 1976 despite the fact

[1] A Greene, *Permanent States of Emergency and the Rule of Law: Constitutions in an Age of Crisis* (Oxford, Hart Publishing, 2018) 27–30.
[2] See O Gross and F Ní Aoláin, *Law in Times of Crisis: Emergency Powers in Theory and Practice* (Cambridge, Cambridge University Press, 2006) ch 1.
[3] Constitution of Ireland, Art 28.3.3.
[4] Ibid.
[5] Twenty-First Amendment of the Constitution Act 2001.

that all emergency powers enabled by this declaration lapsed in September 1946; instead, the emergency was perpetuated for precautionary reasons, on the basis that the government would be equipped to respond swiftly to some hypothetical threat in the future.[6] The lifting of this emergency in September 1976 was then almost immediately replaced by a new emergency arising from the conflict in Northern Ireland. This was to last until February 1995. Since the enactment of the Constitution in 1937 therefore, Ireland has been in an official state of emergency for almost 56 years; longer than it has been in a state of normalcy.[7]

Article 28.3.3 does not, however, contain the entirety of Ireland's constitutional emergency provisions. Article 28.3.2 allows the government to take 'whatever steps they consider necessary for the protection of the state' in the case of 'actual invasion' and it requires that Dáil Éireann should be summoned at the earliest practicable date if not already sitting. These powers are arguably much wider in scope than the already expansive powers enabled by Article 28.3.3 as they may be introduced by the government without ex ante approval from the Oireachtas. Furthermore, Article 38.3.1 permits the establishment of special courts when 'the ordinary courts are inadequate to secure the effective administration of justice, and the preservation of public peace and order'. The drafting of the Constitution reveals that Articles 38.3.1 and 28.3.3 are closely linked, emerging from the recommendations of the 1934 Constitution Review Committee.[8] There, the 1934 Committee suggested a two-pronged approach to emergency powers: Scheme A which would allow for the enactment of special courts; and Scheme B which would provide for the declaration of a state of emergency for more serious crises.[9] The Irish Constitution therefore does not recognise a wholly clear dichotomy between normalcy and emergency; rather, it recognises different degrees of emergency. There are the most serious emergencies covered by Article 28.3.3 and, indeed Article 28.3.2 in cases of actual invasion; and emergencies of lower intensity which do not amount to 'war or armed rebellion' but nevertheless, render the ordinary courts 'inadequate to secure the effective administration of justice, and the preservation of public peace and order'. This concept of a 'less exceptional' emergency is key to understanding the OASA.

III. THE OASA AND 'LESS EXCEPTIONAL' EMERGENCY POWERS

As a permanent statute, it would be a misnomer to describe the OASA as emergency legislation; nevertheless, the OASA as originally enacted contained six parts, two of which would only come into operation when certain conditions were deemed to exist. These provisions – Part V relating to the establishment of the SCC, and Part VI enabling prolonged detention without trial (internment) – are, ostensibly temporary provisions, designed to respond to an acute crisis and consequently, they may be described as emergency measures. The internment regime under Part VI was itself replaced by Part II of the

[6] A Greene, 'The Historical Evolution of Article 28.3.3 of the Irish Constitution' (2012) 47 *Irish Jurist* 117, 139–140.

[7] Ibid 138–139.

[8] Constitutional Review Committee 1934, NAI/TAOIS s 2979.

[9] Ibid.

OASAA 1940.[10] Despite their exceptional nature, express time-limits on both internment and the SCC are absent and, as we shall see, Part V has been in force for the overwhelming majority of the OASA's existence.

The OASA was the product of a merger of two separate proposed bills – the Special Courts Bill and the Anti-Social Organisations Bill. Davis demonstrates that the OASA has a clear link to the infamous Article 2A of the old Irish Free State Constitution as well as the Public Safety Act 1927 which also had a draconian impact on human rights.[11] Due to this infamous reputation, the government sought to downplay the link as much as possible.[12] Introduced on the same day as what would become the Treason Act 1939, Minister for Justice PJ Ruttledge told the Dáil that the timing of the legislation was a compromise between two views: waiting until an extreme crisis had erupted before introducing the legislation; or introducing the legislation 'when there is absolute calm and quiet in the country. So that it might be discussed in this House calmly'.[13] Ruttledge acknowledged that there was 'comparative quiet in the country over a period' but also pointed to the publication of recent documents attributed to the IRA, challenging the legitimacy of the state and calling on the people of Ireland to complete the revolution started in 1916.[14] Ruttledge further highlighted the deaths of three 'well-known' members of the IRA who died in an explosion in Donegal on 28 November 1938.[15] To justify the timing of the legislation, therefore, the government argued for the necessity of the measures due to a perceived exceptional threat; simultaneously, the perceived calm also alluded to, acted as an attempt to further legitimate the OASA by giving sufficient time for the Oireachtas to debate the legislation. This latter point is particularly important given that the OASA is a piece of permanent legislation. The political conditions of relative calm but also a potential menacing threat on the horizon thus reflect the status of the OASA as incorporating elements of both permanent and emergency measures.

A. The OASA as a 'Less Exceptional' State of Exception

Despite this supposed period of 'relative calm', the OASA was enacted at a time when war was looming in Europe; the government was well aware of this as evidenced by the preparations it had begun to make in early 1939 to amend Article 28.3.3 to cover neutrality emergencies.[16] The OASA was signed into law on 14 June 1939 and it was not long before the 'comparative quiet in the country over a period' was displaced with the first declarations to give effect to Part V and Part VI of the OASA was made in August 1939.[17] This was followed shortly by a declaration of emergency under Article 28.3.3 and the enactment of the Emergency Powers Act 1939 (EPA 1939) on 3 September 1939 upon the

[10] Text to n 57 below.
[11] See T Mohr, Chapter 2, this volume.
[12] F Davis, *The History and Development of the Special Criminal Court 1922–2005* (Dublin, Four Courts Press, 2007) 65–66.
[13] *Dáil Debates* 2 March 1939, vol 74, col 1284.
[14] Ibid.
[15] Ibid.
[16] Greene 'The Historical Evolution' (n 6) 127–130.
[17] SI 249/1939; SI 266/1939.

outbreak of World War II.[18] Prior to the declaration of emergency, the Oireachtas passed the First Amendment of the Constitution Act 1939, amending Article 28.3.3 to allow it to cover so-called neutrality emergencies.[19] In contrast to the timing of the OASA, the First Amendment was specifically delayed to take advantage of a pressing crisis and truncated time period.[20]

The EPA 1939 was a comprehensive piece of emergency legislation conferring on the government vast discretion to enact regulations that did not have to be compatible with the provisions of the Constitution. These regulations included stricter border controls, restrictions on people's movements, requisition of property, new powers of search and detention, and powers to censor the press and postal communications. New offences were also created.[21] While the EPA 1939 was wholly separate to the OASA, evidence from the Department of An Taoiseach files demonstrates that this idea of a less exceptional emergency was key to understanding the relationship between the EPA 1939 and the OASA. As the EPA 1939 did not have to be compatible with the Constitution, this would ostensibly mean that more extreme emergency measures could be enacted under this Act rather than under the OASA which did have to be constitutionally compatible. However, this idea of a 'less exceptional' emergency ultimately damaged the 'quarantining effect' of Article 28.3.3.

This is evident, for instance, from the government's attempts after World War II to end internment for Irish citizens under the Emergency Powers (No 20) Order. A memo dated 7 July 1945 indicated that the Taoiseach wanted to revoke the Emergency Powers (No 20) Order; however, there were still '7 aliens' in detention under this order.[22] It was suggested by Stephen Roche of the Department of Justice that rather than revoking the Order in its entirety, the government should make a new order excluding Irish citizens from the scope of the No 20 Order. A subsequent memo dated 23 July thus confirmed that Order No 20 would be amended so that it would no longer apply to natural born Irish citizens.[23] Here, the government sought to signal a semblance of a return to normalcy. However, the government also feared a heightened threat from the IRA; consequently, a simultaneous proclamation would be introduced bringing into force Part II of the OASAA 1940. There would therefore be two separate internment regimes: one for 'aliens' under the Emergency Powers Act order No 20, and one for Irish citizens under Part II of the OASAA 1940.[24] This second regime under Part II of the OASAA 1940 would remain in force until 1947 and demonstrated that the government considered internment under that Part as somehow less draconian than internment under the EPA 1939.

Even where the 'quarantining effect' of Article 28.3.3 was evident in influencing the shape of the OASA, victories tended to be pyrrhic at best. At their meeting of the 18 March 1947, the government decided that new offences were needed to enforce fuel

[18] Greene 'The Historical Evolution' (n 6) 131.

[19] Under Art 51 of the Constitution, constitutional amendments could be enacted via the ordinary legislative process without the need for a referendum for the first three years after the entry into force of the Constitution.

[20] Ibid, 130–131.

[21] See 'The Emergency Powers Act 1939: Far-Reaching Legislation to Ensure Public Safety' (1939) 5(4) *Irish Jurist* 54.

[22] NAI/TAOIS s 13710A.

[23] Ibid.

[24] Ibid.

rationing and control fuel prices and further, that these new offences should be scheduled offences for the purposes of Part V of the OASA.[25] This would have resulted in individuals accused of offences under the Emergency Powers (Control of Fuel) Order 1941 and the Emergency Powers (Control of Fuel) Order 1942 being tried before the SCC; although the government initially sought to do this without a declaration that the 'ordinary courts were inadequate to secure the effective administration of justice and the preservation of public peace and order'.[26] The Attorney General, Cearbhall Ó Dálaigh, objected however, advising that to schedule offences in the absence of such a declaration would be unconstitutional.[27] For Ó Dálaigh, Part V of the OASA was 'as good a model as could be obtained of the way in which Article 38.3.1 of the Constitution should be applied' and it would be 'undesirable, if not dangerous for dealing with economic offences'.[28] Consequently, he felt that there were some offences that it would be inappropriate for the SCC to try and which were best left to the ordinary courts, albeit deriving their validity from the declaration of emergency under Article 28.3.3. Ó Dálaigh thus considered that the more draconian offences similar to the Emergency Powers (Control of Fuel) Order 1941 and the Emergency Powers (Control of Fuel) Order 1942 were only constitutionally permissible during the more extreme form of emergency envisaged Article 28.3.3. He therefore sought to quarantine these measures to such exceptional situations. He further advised that sentences handed down by ordinary courts were less likely to be interfered with on appeal than convictions and sentences passed by the SCC.

Nevertheless, the government preserved with its chosen course of action and enacted revised scheduled offences under section 6 of the Supplies and Services (Temporary Provisions) Act 1946. The small concession Ó Dálaigh managed to secure was that the Act was accompanied by a declaration that the ordinary courts were inadequate to secure the effective administration of justice and the preservation of public peace and order.[29] Incidentally, Ó Dálaigh would later resign as President of Ireland following ministerial criticism of his referral of the Emergency Powers Bill 1976 to the Supreme Court for a pre-emptive test of its constitutionality, owing to his scepticism over the existence of an emergency as defined by Article 28.3.3.[30]

B. The Special Criminal Court as a Less Exceptional Exception

Part V of the OASA allows for the establishment of the SCC:

> If and whenever and so often as the Government is satisfied that the ordinary courts are inadequate to secure the effective administration of justice and the preservation of public peace and order and that it is therefore necessary that this Part of this Act should come into force, the Government may make and publish a proclamation declaring that the Government is satisfied as aforesaid and ordering that this Part of this Act shall come into force.[31]

[25] Department of Industry and Commerce Memorandum to the Government: Contravention of Control of Fuel Orders and Fuel Prices Orders (18 April 1947) NAI/TAOIS s 14068.
[26] Ibid.
[27] NAI/TAOIS s 14068.
[28] Ibid.
[29] SI 282/1947 – Offences Against the State (Scheduled Offences) (No 6) Order 1947.
[30] DG Morgan, 'The Emergency Powers Bill Reference – I' (1978) 13 *Irish Jurist* 67, 70.
[31] OASA, s 35(2).

These conditions were deemed to exist on three separate occasions: first, during the Second World War from 1939–1946; second, for a brief period between 1961–1962 in response to increased IRA activity; and finally, from 1972 which, again, was originally in response to heightened IRA activity although the SCC continues to be in existence to this day.[32] What was, ostensibly, a temporary court is now a permanent feature of the Irish criminal justice system; indeed, its status has been further entrenched with the expansion of its jurisdiction to now cover certain organised criminal offences.[33]

What makes the SCC distinct from other criminal courts and therefore exceptional is, primarily, the lack of a jury; the court is instead comprised of a bench of three judges. That stated, the qualification requirements for SCC judges is also distinct from that of ordinary courts. Section 39(3) of the OASA allows an officer of the Defence Forces not below the rank of Commandant to be eligible to sit as a judge of the SCC. While the SCC has been effectively demilitarised since 1972, its original formation had an acute degree of military input and control. In *Re MacCurtain*, the applicant argued that his trial by the SCC was unconstitutional as the Court had been comprised entirely of army officers, sat in a military barracks and that he was in military custody.[34] Consequently, the Court was not a special court envisaged by Article 38.3 but a military court as contemplated by Article 38.4.1.[35] The Supreme Court, however, rejected this argument, taking a highly formalistic approach to interpreting Article 38.3.2:

> … Article 38.3.2° empowers the Legislature to prescribe the constitution, powers, jurisdiction and procedure of the Special Courts. The Legislature has prescribed the constitution of Special Courts in s 39 of the Act … it has not been suggested that any member of the Court by which the appellant was tried was not duly qualified under that section.[36]

This formalistic approach means that while the SSC today has been demilitarised, it still remains the case that it is possible under the Constitution to have an SCC comprised entirely of military officials without the need to declare a state of emergency under Article 28.3.3. Section 39(2) of the OASA also gives the power to the government to appoint and remove judges 'at will', demonstrating a high degree of executive control over the composition of the SCC relative to ordinary courts. However, the idea that this gives unfettered power to the government to interfere with or influence the proceedings and decisions of the SCC was rejected by the Supreme Court in *Eccles v Ireland*:

> Whilst, therefore, the Special Criminal Court does not attract the express guarantees of judicial independence contained in Article 35 of the Constitution, it does have, derived from the Constitution, a guarantee of independence in the carrying out of its functions.[37]

[32] SI 142/1972; Davis, *The History and Development* (n 12) ch 7.

[33] Criminal Justice (Amendment) Act 2009, Pt II; See L Campbell, 'The Prosecution of Organised Crime: Removing the Jury' (2014) 18(2) *International Journal of Evidence and Proof* 83; See L Campbell, Chapter 8, this volume.

[34] *Re MacCurtain* [1941] IR 83; G Hogan and G Whyte, *JM Kelly: The Irish Constitution*, 4th edn (London, Lexis Nexis, 2003) 1205.

[35] Ibid. This military tribunal also tried civilians during World War II. See Davis, *The History and Development* (n 12) ch 4.

[36] *Re MacCurtain*, ibid, 90.

[37] [1985] IR 545, 549 (Finlay CJ).

Nevertheless, concerns remain about the scope of this power with Hogan and Walker contending that this provision should be repealed.[38] This recommendation was also made by the Hederman Committee's review of the Offences Against the State Acts 1939–1998.[39]

i. The Threshold for Establishing the Special Criminal Court

The threshold for establishing the SCC under the OASA – when the ordinary courts are inadequate to secure the effective administration of justice and the preservation of peace and public order – mirrors the language of Article 38.3.2. As the drafting papers of the Constitution make clear, Article 38.3.2 was designed to confront crises that do not meet the threshold of an emergency under Article 28.3.3.[40] Despite this lesser exceptionality, the requirement that 'the ordinary courts are inadequate to secure the effective administration of justice and the preservation of peace and public order' would, nevertheless, suggest that a threat must meet a high degree of seriousness before it can justify the introduction of the SCC. In *MacCurtain*, the applicant contended that it was unconstitutional for the Oireachtas to confer on the executive the power to decide when Part V of the OASA should come into force.[41] Duffy J in the High Court, however, rejected this argument on the grounds that:

> The Oireachtas clearly considered the Government to be the authority best situated, from its position and the information at its disposal, to determine whether or not Special Tribunals were necessary in the circumstances set out in the section. In my opinion, the provision that the Government may make such a proclamation when satisfied that the ordinary Courts are inadequate is clearly meant to be an essentially executive decision of the highest executive authority in the State. In my opinion, the Government, in declaring itself satisfied within the section of the inadequacy of the ordinary Courts and of the necessity to set up Special Courts, cannot be said to be acting either in a judicial or in a legislative capacity.[42]

Duffy J, however, went further than simply upholding the constitutionality of the conferral of the power to establish special courts on the executive, finding that there was no need under Part V of the OASA for the executive to provide reasons for its decision that the 'ordinary courts are inadequate to secure the effective administration of justice, and the preservation of peace and order'.[43] This was upheld by the Supreme Court.

In *Kavanagh v Ireland*, this threshold question arose again when the applicant challenged the continued necessity of the SCC in light of the recently declared paramilitary ceasefires in Northern Ireland.[44] The applicant relied upon the pre-1937 case of *R (O'Brien) v Military Gove NDU Internment Camp* where the Irish Court of Appeal

[38] See G Hogan and C Walker, *Political Violence and the Law in Ireland* (Manchester, Manchester University Press, 1989).

[39] 'Report of the Committee to Review the Offences Against the State Acts 1939–1998' *Department of Justice and Equality*, hereinafter Hederman Report.

[40] Constitution Review Committee (n 8).

[41] *Re MacCurtain* (n 34).

[42] Ibid, 86.

[43] Ibid.

[44] [1996] 1 IR 321.

held that civil courts were bound, when their jurisdiction was invoked, to decide whether or not there existed a state of war or armed rebellion.[45] Barrington J, however, dismissed this argument, contending that the issue here was not the existence of a state of war or armed rebellion but a 'specific problem for which the Constitution has made specific provision and the most important thing is to consider that provision and what it means'.[46]

Both *MacCurtain* and *Kavanagh* draw a clear distinction between who has the authority to declare an emergency under Article 28.3.3 and who may decide when special courts are necessary under Article 38.3.1. Article 28.3.3 clearly vests the power to declare an emergency in the Oireachtas, as it renders immune from constitutional challenge 'any law enacted by the Oireachtas expressed to be for the purpose of securing the public safety and the preservation of the State in time of war or armed rebellion …'. Legislation is thus required for a law to come under the protection of Article 28.3.3. In contrast, Article 38.3.1 allows for the establishment of special courts 'by law for the trial of offences in cases where it may be determined in accordance with such law that the ordinary courts are inadequate to secure the effective administration of justice, and the preservation of peace and order'. The words 'in accordance with such law' enables the Oireachtas to confer on the executive or another body the power to declare that the ordinary courts are 'inadequate to secure the effective administration of justice, and the preservation of peace and order'. Barrington J thus concluded that the question of whether special courts should be established is a matter for the legislature and the question of whether Part V of the OASA comes into force is a matter for the government.[47]

Barrington J also upheld Duffy J's finding in *MacCurtain* that the government was under no duty to provide reasons as the ordinary courts have no function to review these reasons provided that these powers have been exercised in a bona fide manner.[48] The difficulty, however, is that without reasons, it becomes impossible to assess whether the decision to establish special courts was bona fide or not. This issue was acknowledged by the UN Human Rights Committee who found that the state had failed to demonstrate that the decision to try Kavanagh before the SCC was based on reasonable and objective grounds.[49] The result is that despite the ostensibly robust wording of Article 38.3.1, the requirement that the ordinary courts are 'inadequate to secure the effective administration of justice, and the preservation of peace and order' has had minimal quarantining effect on the use of the SCC. The SCC is now permanent; part of the architecture of normalcy under the Irish Constitution. Its status has been further entrenched in normalcy following the enactment of the Criminal Justice (Amendment) Act 2009, under which its jurisdiction was extended to cover 'organised crime' or those crimes which do not expressly challenge the political legitimacy of the state.[50]

[45] Ibid, 353; *R (O'Brien) v Military Gove NDU Internment Camp* [1924] IR 32.
[46] *Kavanagh*, ibid. For detailed discussion of the *Kavanagh* litigation see Y Daly, Chapter 11, this volume.
[47] Ibid, 354.
[48] Ibid.
[49] Hogan and Whyte, *JM Kelly* (n 34) 1209.
[50] See A Greene, 'Shielding the State of Emergency: Organised Crime in Ireland and the State's Response' (2011) 62(3) *Northern Ireland Legal Quarterly* 249. See L Campbell, Chapter 8, this volume.

IV. INTERNMENT AND NORMALCY UNDER THE IRISH CONSTITUTION

The provision of special courts was not the only part of the OASA envisaged to be temporary; internment was also provided for by Part VI. Part VI was not permanently in force; rather, it provided that the power to intern individuals to come into effect:

> if and whenever so often as the Government makes and publishes a proclamation declaring that the powers conferred by this Part of this Act are necessary to secure the preservation of public peace and order and that it is expedient that this Part of this Act should come into force immediately.[51]

Part VI mirrored to an extent the language of Article 38.3.2 which allows for the establishment of special courts. Part VI thus allowed for internment when the government considered that the powers were 'necessary to secure the preservation of public peace and order'. Again, we see the idea of a 'less exceptional' emergency arising here, with internment being permissible when it is 'necessary to secure the preservation of public peace and order' but also being permissible without the declaration of a more severe state of emergency under Article 28.3.3 of the Constitution in time of war or armed rebellion. Internment is thus possible in Ireland during a constitutional state of normalcy.

A. The State (Burke) v Lennon

In *The State (Burke) v Lennon*,[52] the applicant challenged by way of habeas corpus his detention at Arbour Hill Military Detention Barracks. In September 1939, the applicant was detained under a warrant issued by Minister of State, Gerald Boland, in accordance with section 55 of the OASA on the grounds that he was satisfied that the applicant was 'engaged in activities calculated to prejudice the preservation of the security of the State'.[53] In the High Court, Gavin Duffy J found Part VI to be unconstitutional, to the surprise of the government. Duffy J found that there was no constitutional provision allowing the Oireachtas to 'disregard the Constitution in any emergency short of war or armed rebellion':

> The Constitution, no doubt, makes exceptions for military law and for special Courts in specified circumstances of danger, but those exceptions do not apply here and I observe that the Constitution does not contemplate internment without trial even by the special Courts set up in time of emergency.[54]

Moreover, the Constitution contained 'no express provision for any law endowing the Executive with powers of internment without trial'.[55] As a result, Part VI had to be tested against the constitutional standards that prevail in normalcy. Duffy J thus found that the Minister making an order under section 55 of the OASA was depriving an individual of their right to liberty and, consequently, was exercising a judicial function, something he

[51] OASA, s 54(2).
[52] [1940] IR 136.
[53] Ibid, 137.
[54] Ibid, 152.
[55] Ibid, 145.

was not constitutionally permitted to do.[56] On this point of the deprivation of liberty, Duffy J expressly asserted that:

> In my opinion, the Constitution intended, while making all proper provisions for times of emergency, did secure his personal freedom to the citizen as truly as did Magna Charta in England.[57]

The Supreme Court upheld Duffy J's decision in *Burke* and a furious government, in response, introduced the Offences Against the State (Amendment) Act 1940 which made what Hogan and Walker describe as 'cosmetic changes' to the internment regime.[58] The main change introduced was that whereas section 55 of the OASA enabled internment 'Whenever a Minister is satisfied', section 4 of the 1940 Act only allowed internment 'Whenever a Minister is of opinion …'. The constitutionality of this change was upheld by the Supreme Court by way of the Article 26 reference procedure. In contrast to Duffy J's repudiation of internment without the declaration of an emergency in *Burke*, the Supreme Court found that while the Constitution did not expressly provide for internment without declaring a state of emergency under Article 28.3.3, the drafters of the Constitution were aware of a number of laws on the statute books that provided for internment. Constitutional silence on the issue of internment, indicated that it was permissible rather than prohibited, notwithstanding the express protection of the right to liberty.[59]

As a result of the Article 26 reference procedure, the internment regime under Part II of the OASAA 1940 is immune from future constitutional challenge.[60] Consequently, the appellant in *Re Ó Laighléis* instead sought to challenge his internment under Part II by way of questioning whether the minister had met the statutorily required threshold of having formed an opinion that he was a particular person engaged in activities which were 'prejudicial to the preservation of public peace and order or to the security of the State'.[61] The Supreme Court rejected his argument, stating that:

> The only essential preliminary to the exercise of the powers contained in section 4 is that he should have formed opinions on the matters specifically mentioned in the section. The validity of such opinions cannot be questioned in any Court.[62]

On this point, the Court in *Ó Laighléis* referred to Lord Atkin's famous dissent in the British case of *Liversidge v Anderson* regarding the internment power in regulation 18B of the Defence (General) Regulations 1939 that allowed the indefinite detention of an individual without trial whenever a minister had 'reasonable cause to believe'.[63] The Court concluded that Lord Atkin regarded reasonable cause for a belief as:

> an objective fact, examinable and triable like any other fact. The contrast he drew was between 'reasonable cause' for a belief and 'mere belief' that a fact exists. His difference with his

[56] Ibid, 148–150.

[57] Ibid, 155.

[58] Hogan and Walker, *Political Violence* (n 38) 217.

[59] Hogan and Whyte, *JM Kelly* (n 34) 1614; Art 40.3.4.

[60] *In the Matter of Article 26 of the Constitution and in the Matter of the Offences Against the State (Amendment) Bill 1940* [1940] IR 470; Constitution of Ireland, Art 34.3.3.

[61] OASAA 1940, s 4(1).

[62] *Re Art 26 and the Offences Against the State (Amendment) Act* (n 60) 479 (per Sullivan CJ).

[63] *Liversidge v Anderson* [1942] AC 206.

> brethren was as to the construction of Regulation 18 B. The Act of 1940 does not require a Minister of State to have 'reasonable cause for his belief; he is authorised to act on his opinion. "Mere belief" is enough. Lord Atkin clearly regarded "mere belief" as a subject state which was not examinable or triable by a court.

This incredibly formalistic reading of Lord Atkin's dissent twists and distorts its true meaning, relying on it to justify rather than condemn indefinite detention at the whim of the executive. Lord Atkin was not simply concerned about the linguistic meaning of 'reasonable cause to believe'; he was not suggesting that had regulation 18B been worded differently, the course of action chosen by the executive would have been tolerable. Indeed, the original wording of regulation 18B allowed for executive detention if the minister was 'satisfied that …' rather than had 'reasonable cause to believe'. Dyzenhaus, however, contends that Lord Atkin's interpretation would still allow review had the original wording been enacted.[64] His argument is based upon the deeper constitutional foundations of the rule of law that underpin Lord Atkin's dissent and his interpretation of regulation 18B. Dyzenhaus builds his argument by engaging with Brian Simpson's critique of Lord Atkin's dissent in *Liversidge*. Simpson describes Lord Atkin's dissent as paying judicial lip-service to the rule of law.[65] Simpson contends that Lord Atkin would have been content with such reasons as the government was willing to supply so long as they were satisfied that the requirement that there was 'reasonable cause to believe' had been met. This was so, notwithstanding the fact that Liversidge's detention was 'at the least, very close to being an example of an order made in bad faith'.[66] Simpson contends that had the government's detention been tested in open court it would have been exposed as bad faith but Lord Atkin was content with such reasons as the government was willing to provide.[67] In this manner, Lord Atkin was willing to cloak the process in a thin veil of legality.[68]

Simpson's interpretation of Lord Atkin's dissent in *Liversidge* would align closely with the Supreme Court's view in *Ó Laighléis*. Both the Supreme Court and Simpson believed Lord Atkin's focus was primarily on the meaning of the phrase 'reasonable cause to believe' and whether the reasons provided by the executive satisfied this requirement. Dyzenhaus, however, disagrees; instead focusing on Lord Atkin's criticism of the majority's rejection of the argument that legislation dealing with the liberty of the subject 'must be construed, if possible, in favour of the subject and against the Crown'.[69] Dyzenhaus thus contends that Lord Atkin's endorsing of this argument shows that Lord Atkin believed that judges should try so far as they can to impose judicial constraints on statutes and regulations in all instances where the liberty of the subject is at stake and not simply in instances of bad faith. In this manner, the judiciary can 'send a message to the legislature (and cabinet) that it is high time for it to put its house in order'.[70] Dyzenhaus

[64] D Dyzenhaus, *The Constitution of Law: Legality in a Time of Emergency* (Cambridge, Cambridge University Press, 2006) 155–156.

[65] Ibid, 149; B Simpson, *In the Highest Degree Odious: Detention without Trial in Wartime Britain* (Oxford, Oxford University Press, 1994) 61.

[66] Ibid.

[67] Ibid, 150.

[68] Ibid.

[69] Ibid, 151; *Liversidge* (n 63) 244.

[70] Ibid, 155.

thus clarifies Lord Atkin's dissent by directing it, not just at the executive who Lord Atkin was primarily concerned with, but at the legislature too. However, it is only the audience that has been altered, not the substance of Lord Atkin's dissent; the principle of interpreting rules in favour of the liberty of the subject remains the same.

In *Ó Laighléis*, the Supreme Court's misuse of Lord Atkin's dissent is even more pronounced, given the express protections afforded to personal rights in the Irish Constitution. While judges in a commonwealth constitutional model such as the UK's, which vindicates the principle of parliamentary sovereignty, are considerably restricted in the degree to which they can construe legislation, the same is not true in Ireland. Legislation must be interpreted compatibly with the Constitution and where this is not possible, it should be declared unconstitutional. Consequently, due to the express protection of personal rights in the Irish Constitution, Lord Atkin's contention that ambiguity in legislation should be resolved in favour of the liberty of the subject is even more compelling. This would entail much more robust obligations on the executive before internment under Part II could be enacted. Unfortunately, the constitutional immunity afforded to Part II of the OASAA 1940 currently restricts the judiciary's capacity to do so. That stated, such immunity does not mean that subsequent judicial engagement with the immune provisions in question must distort novel arguments in such a way as to corroborate the original judgment. While it may be the case that a court has no power to review the constitutionality of the statute in question, in such instances, it may be better, as Dyzenhaus contends, for the courts to admit this and express reservations regarding the immune statute in question and the prior judgment which affirmed its constitutionality; rather than cloaking the law in a thin veil of legality.[71]

B. Lawless v Ireland

On 4 November 1950, Ireland signed the European Convention on Human Rights (ECHR), giving Ireland obligations to protect human rights under international law.[72] In *Ó Laighleis*, the applicant also contended that section 4 of the 1940 Act was incompatible with Article 5 of the ECHR.[73] This challenge failed, however, as the ECHR had not yet been incorporated into domestic law.[74] The failure on this point was, however, inevitable and intentional as the ultimate goal was to reach the European Court of Human Rights (ECtHR). Rebranded as *Lawless v Ireland*, it was the first case to be decided by the ECtHR which may explain the deferential reasoning as the court sought to shore up its legitimacy.[75] In *Lawless*, the ECtHR upheld the declaration of an emergency in

[71] Dyzenhaus, *The Constitution of Law* (n 64) 233.

[72] 'Chart and signatures and ratifications of the Convention for the Protection of Human Rights and Fundamental Freedoms' *Council of Europe* (status as of 16 July 2020) www.coe.int/en/web/conventions/full-list/-/conventions/treaty/005/signatures (accessed 16 July 2020).

[73] *Re Ó Laighléis* [1960] IR 93. See Y Daly, Chapter 11, this volume.

[74] This would not occur until the enactment of the European Convention on Human Rights Act 2003.

[75] BR Dickson, *The European Convention on Human Rights and the Conflict in Northern Ireland* (Oxford, Oxford University Press, 2010) 37. Gross and Ní Aoláin, *Law in Times of Crisis* (n 2) 271.

accordance with the meaning of Article 15, finding that there did exist a public emergency threatening the life of the nation in Ireland for three reasons:

> ... in the first place, the existence in the territory of the Republic of Ireland of a secret army engaged in unconstitutional activities and using violence to attain its purposes; secondly, the fact that this army was also operating outside the territory of the State, thus seriously jeopardising the relations of the Republic of Ireland with its neighbour; thirdly, the steady and alarming increase in terrorist activities from the autumn of 1956 and throughout the first half of 1957 ....[76]

The Court also found that the measures were 'proportionate to the exigencies of the situation' and consequently, Lawless lost. Despite the deferential approach taken by the ECtHR in *Lawless*, the fact that derogation from the Convention was necessary to implement internment suggests that liberty is better protected under Article 5 of the ECHR than it is under the Irish Constitution where no de jure state of emergency was necessary. Part II of the OASAA 1940 thus sends out mixed signals regarding the acceptability of internment under normalcy. Under constitutional normalcy, it is permissible; however, from the perspective of the ECHR, it is not, and a declaration of emergency is necessary. Ireland can therefore, in principle, be under both a state of normalcy from a constitutional perspective and a state of emergency from an international human rights perspective.

V. THE QUARANTINING EFFECT OF IRELAND'S EMERGENCY POWERS

Considering the constitutionality of the SCC and internment in times of official normalcy, Article 28.3.3 has failed to quarantine emergency powers to the exceptional conditions of 'war or armed rebellion'. Of course, in the case of the SCC, this was precisely the point of the two-pronged approach taken to emergency powers by the Constitution. The same, however, cannot be said for internment, the constitutionality of which is the result of an overly formalistic approach to constitutional interpretation. It may be argued that this approach was necessitated as a result of the discrete condition of 'war or armed rebellion' contained in Article 28.3.3. This high threshold may explain why governments have sought to introduce de facto emergency measures without an official constitutional state of emergency, believing that conditions were not severe enough to meet this definition.[77] This argument, however, is based upon the assumption that these discrete conditions actually act as a legal impediment to the declaration of an emergency. To date, the judiciary has been incredibly deferential on the question of the existence of an emergency under Article 28.3.3 to such an extent that the Supreme Court has refused to state whether or not this question is even justiciable.[78]

The result of the jurisprudence on emergency powers, internment, and the SCC is that Irish courts demonstrate an incredibly high degree of deference towards the political

[76] *Lawless v Ireland*, Judgment of 1 July 1961, 3 ECtHR (ser A, 1961) [28].

[77] See text to n 78 below.

[78] *In the Matter of Article 26 of the Constitution and in the matter of the Emergency Powers Bill 1976*' [1977] IR 159, 176; see also A Greene, 'Declaring a State of Emergency under Article 28.3.3 of the Irish Constitution: A Purely Political Question?' in E Carolan (ed), *The Constitution of Ireland: Perspectives and Prospects* (London, Bloomsbury Professional, 2012) 390–91.

branches on questions of national security. There is a clear disjuncture between the restrictive constitutional wording of the respective emergency provisions and the degree to which these provisions have been interpreted and applied by the courts. A narrow definition of emergency therefore does not ensure that emergency powers will be temporary; nor does it mean that a narrow definition of emergency is the cause of the seepage of emergency powers into normalcy in Ireland. Ultimately, the OASA reveals the stark and draconian scope of powers permissible under the Irish Constitution without a declaration of a de jure state of emergency.

There is further evidence that Irish courts are willing to accommodate exceptional emergency powers under normalcy beyond national security crises too. In *Collins v Minister for Finance*,[79] the Supreme Court upheld the constitutionality of the Credit Institutions (Financial Support) Act 2008 and the substantial powers it conferred on the Minister for Finance to commit monies to financial institutions without any financial limit on the extent of the financial support the Minister could advance under section 6 of the 2008 Act. In upholding the constitutionality of the provision, the Supreme Court stressed the exceptionality of the legislation and the 'extraordinary circumstances that constitute the backdrop to and which are reflected in' the legislation. The Court also emphasised that the Act in question could not be 'considered to be a template for broader Ministerial power on other occasions'.[80] In essence, the Supreme Court was attempting to quarantine the precedent of *Collins* to exceptional circumstances. It is essentially an attempt to formulate a constitutional accommodation of emergency powers to deal with financial crises where no such powers are expressly provided for by the Constitution. In turn, *Collins* could potentially be applied in any case law arising from the exceptional powers Ireland enacted to the COVID-19 pandemic in 2020. No emergency could be declared in accordance with Article 28.3.3 as a pandemic does not constitute a 'time of war or armed rebellion'; consequently these exceptional powers had to be compatible with the constitutional parameters of normalcy.[81]

VI. CONCLUSION: SUGGESTIONS FOR REFORM

The wording of Article 28.3.3 is not the primary cause for the seepage of exceptional powers into normalcy; rather, the fact that extensive emergency powers are permitted outside of Article 28.3.3, notably the use of special courts. This is compounded by undue judicial deference and minimal legislative oversight of other forms of exceptional powers such as internment and executive discretion has played a pivotal role in this. Nevertheless, reform of Article 28.3.3 could potentially address this imbalance; in particular, Ireland's constitutional provision of emergency powers could be aligned with Article 15 of the ECHR. Specifically, this would be done in such a way so as to remove the carte blanche powers available under Article 28.3.3; instead, any emergency powers introduced would

[79] [2016] IESC 73.
[80] Ibid, [84].
[81] A Greene, 'Ireland's Response to the COVID-19 Pandemic' *Verfassungsblog* (11 April 2020) https://verfassungsblog.de/irelands-response-to-the-covid-19-pandemic/ (accessed 8 July 2020).

have to be 'proportionate to the exigencies of the situation'.[82] Certain constitutional provisions could also be demarcated as non-derogable; for example, it should be made expressly clear that Article 28.3.3 cannot itself be used to amend the Constitution.[83] The definition of emergency could be used to include phenomena beyond war or armed rebellion; however, were this to be done, it would have to be accompanied by sufficient judicial oversight and express time-limits.

A more synergistic relation between the Irish Constitution and the ECHR on the question of emergency powers would also negate the current paradoxical situation of normalcy under the Constitution but emergency under the ECHR that could arise should the state seek to re-introduce internment under Part II of the OASAA 1940. Despite its constitutional immunity, Part II would most likely be subject to a number of legal challenges. Since the enactment of the European Convention on Human Rights Act 2003, Irish courts are under an obligation to interpret any statutory provision compatibly with the state's obligations under the ECHR, 'so far as is possible'.[84] Where this is not possible, the High Court or the Supreme Court may make a declaration of incompatibility but only 'where no other legal remedy is adequate and available'.[85] On this point, it may be that the courts may not be as deferential towards the executive as they have been on the question of the necessity of the SCC. The distinction between the introduction of internment and the introduction of the SCC depends upon the distinction between 'of opinion' and 'satisfied'. While the constitutionality of Part II cannot be questioned, it still remains the case that the decision of a minister to intern an individual under Part II is still open for review. Here, a future court may wish to consider a more synergistic relation between Irish domestic law and the ECHR, using its interpretive obligation under section 4 of the 2003 Act to ratchet up the degree of rights protection required or, if this is not possible, to declare the provision incompatible with the Convention. On this point, Part II of the OASAA 1940 is clearly incompatible with the right to liberty under Article 5 of the ECHR, as evidenced by the government's decision to derogate from the Convention when internment was introduced in the 1960s.

As noted, we are left with the paradoxical scenario that a state of normalcy exists under the Irish Constitution but a state of emergency exists from the perspective of the ECHR. This sends out the signal that rights are better protected under the ECHR than under the Constitution. Relatedly, while the SCC in its current manifestation does not necessarily raise an issue of compatibility with the ECHR owing to its demilitarised nature, it remains the case that a militarised court of the kind seen in *MacCurtain* is still possible during normalcy under the Irish Constitution. Such a court would, however, raise profound concerns under the ECHR, specifically the right to a fair trial under Article 6. Reform of Article 28.3.3 could also be accompanied by reform of Article 38.3 which would clarify and limit special courts to non-jury courts only but requiring the same personnel and rules of evidence as other courts empowered to try indictable offences. However, this would then raise the question as to whether such a special court was, indeed, exceptional or whether the pretences of temporariness should be dropped and instead this form of special court should be made expressly permanent. At most, what would make this court 'special' would

[82] ECHR, Art 15.
[83] Greene, *Permanent States of Emergency* (n 1) 95–98.
[84] ECHRA 2003, s 2(1).
[85] Ibid, s 5(1).

be the absence of a jury; consequently, this raises the further question of what cases a jury would be unsuitable for, who makes this assessment, and why. At most, removal of the jury should only be done in limited instances of jury intimidation and, as Campbell argues, this possibility is not unique to counter-terrorism cases.[86] There would therefore be no need for such a non-jury court to be 'subsumed within a counter-terrorism paradigm'.[87]

Constitutional reform along the lines suggested above may not cure all ills, however. Like the Irish judiciary, the ECtHR has too often been overly deferential to domestic authorities on the question of the existence of a state of emergency.[88] However, this record does not necessarily mean that all judicial protection must invariably result in such over-deference. De Londras argues that as crises recede, courts tend to 'push back' and become less deferential towards the executive and the political branches.[89] On this point, however, Part II of the OASAA 1940 becomes a particular problem. As it is immune from constitutional challenge, this limits the possibility of the judiciary effecting any push back against internment during normalcy. Ultimately, the possibility of internment under Part II will only end with its repeal by the Oireachtas, something the Hederman Committee was divided over. A minority of the Committee concluded that they could 'conceive of no circumstances in which the use of internment could be justified'.[90] The majority of the Committee did, however, consider internment could constitute a 'legitimate, exceptional response to exceptional circumstances'; however, one member of this majority – Gerard Hogan – argued that internment should only be promulgated pursuant to a declaration of emergency under Article 28.3.3.[91]

The Hederman Committee's disagreement over internment captures the confusion that lies at the heart of Ireland's emergency powers and the concept of less exceptional emergencies. Ireland now has a permanent exceptional court and a permanent legislative regime allowing for the introduction of internment, both of which do not require an express declaration of emergency under Article 28.3.3 of the Constitution. Ireland's constitutional emergency regime has failed to quarantine exceptional powers to exceptional situations and the spread of the SCC to deal with organised crime is a further example of the all too familiar problem of counter-terrorism measures 'creeping' beyond the initial national security threat they were originally invoked to tackle.[92] Emergency powers, even 'less exceptional' emergency powers are designed to be temporary. It is only through negating the necessity of their own existence by defeating the perceived exceptional threat that emergency powers can be legitimated. On this metric, the OASA and the Irish Constitution has failed. Nevertheless, it is unlikely that this failure will result in meaningful reform any time soon.

[86] Campbell, 'The Prosecution of Organised Crime' (n 33) 99.

[87] Ibid.

[88] Dickson, *The European Convention on Human Rights* (n 75); see O Gross and F Ní Aoláin, 'From Discretion to Scrutiny: Revisiting the Application of the Margin of Appreciation in the Context of Article 15 of the European Convention on Human Rights' (2001) 23(3) *Human Rights Quarterly* 625.

[89] F de Londras and F Davis, 'Controlling the Executive in Times of Terrorism: Competing Perspectives on Effective Oversight Mechanisms' (2010) 30(1) *Oxford Journal of Legal* Studies 19, 34 (per de Londras).

[90] Hederman Report (n 39) [5.54].

[91] Ibid, [5.56]–[5.57].

[92] See A Ashworth, 'Crime Community and Creeping Consequentialism' [1996] *Criminal Law Review* 220; O Gross, 'Chaos and Rules: Should Responses to Violent Crises Always Be Constitutional?' (2002–2003) 112 *Yale Law Journal* 1011, 1090–1092; See C Hamilton, Chapter 14, this volume.

14

'Contagion' between the Special and the Normal in Criminal Justice: A Comparative Perspective

CLAIRE HAMILTON

I. INTRODUCTION

'DOING HISTORY', AS Murphy and Whitty[1] argue regarding human rights and criminology, harnesses the ability of historical knowledge to inform current and future criminological choices, better preparing us for the challenges of the present. It is precisely such an attempt at harnessing the lessons of history that forms the subject of this chapter, through an examination of the manner in which the Irish Offences Against the State Act 1939 (as amended) (OASA), as the legislative foundation for most 'special' (emergency) criminal justice measures in the state, fundamentally shaped the development of the 'ordinary' criminal process in Ireland. The specific focus for this discussion will be on 'contagion', defined here as the migration of law and policy from the counter-terrorism to the 'ordinary' criminal justice spheres. Many different labels have been applied to describe the 'contagion' phenomenon, among them normalisation,[2] creep,[3] contamination[4] and transplantation.[5] I have employed the term 'contagion', however, here and elsewhere,[6] given the seriousness with which it conveys the threat to the ordinary criminal justice system. A medical metaphor with its obvious

[1] T Murphy and N Whitty, 'Making History: Academic Criminology and Human Rights' (2013) 53(4) *British Journal of Criminology* 568.

[2] S Kilcommins and B Vaughan, 'A Perpetual State of Emergency: Subverting the Rule of Law in Ireland' (2004) 35 *Cambrian Law Review* 55.

[3] G Appleby and J Williams, 'The Anti-Terror Creep: Law and Order, the States and the High Court in Australia' in N McGarrity and LN Williams (eds), *Counter-Terrorism and Beyond: The Culture of Law and Justice after 9/11* (London, Routledge, 2010).

[4] H Fenwick and G Phillipson, 'Covert Derogations and Judicial Deference: Redefining Liberty and Due Process Rights in Counterterrorism Law and Beyond' (2011) 56(4) *McGill Law Journal* 863.

[5] LK Donohue 'Transplantation' in VV Ramraj, M Hor and K Roach (eds) *Global Anti-Terrorism Law and Policy* (Cambridge, Cambridge University Press, 2012) 67.

[6] C Hamilton, *Contagion, Counter-terrorism and Criminology: Justice in the Shadow of Terror* (London, Palgrave, 2019); C Hamilton and G Berlusconi, 'Counter-terrorism, contagion and Criminology: The Case of France' (2018) 18(5) *Criminology & Criminal Justice* 568.

connotations for public health (and strong contemporary relevance given recent events) also appeared particularly well suited to conveying the risks associated with the spread of policies not only in time (in terms of temporary legislation becoming permanent), but also cross-sectorally. As will become apparent, the Irish case holds important lessons for Western jurisdictions now grappling with counter-terrorism laws in the post 9/11 environment, prime among them the hegemonic power of terrorism and the securitisation agenda more generally.[7] Particularly in the context of a permanent 'war on terror', we may struggle to 'tell the dancer from the dance',[8] and thus the ordinary business of criminal justice from its more politicised cousin. Despite this, the contagion effect is by no means one-way with policies also migrating from the 'ordinary' to the 'special' realm, and thus an increased 'plasticity' of the special and the normal in contemporary times. The role played by human rights in containing 'contagion' is also discussed with a view to reflecting on the challenges faced in addressing similar problems today.

The chapter therefore proceeds as follows. Part II begins analysis of contagion in Ireland from the 'special' to the 'ordinary' criminal justice system through an examination of five key sites. Part III moves the discussion to a contemporary European context through examination of the extent to which post 9/11 counter-terrorism laws have spilled over into the ordinary system, using three case studies of the UK, France and Poland. Part IV highlights the similarities and differences between these case studies and concludes by discussing effective strategies for contesting contagion in the future.

II. THE OASA AND CONTAGION IN IRELAND

Much ink has been spilled on the impact of the security threat in Ireland on the development of ordinary criminal procedure.[9] Daly and Jackson put it very clearly in their recent chapter on the criminal justice process for the Routledge Handbook of Irish Criminology, when they write: 'the OASA 1939 can be viewed as the forebear of a number of measures which illustrate the shift from due process ideals towards a crime control orientation in the Republic'.[10] For those readers unfamiliar, the security threats arose from periodic bouts of paramilitary violence that had blighted occupants of the island since its partition in 1922. The most recent period of political and civil unrest, colloquially known as the 'the Troubles/Conflict', erupted in 1968 and lasted until a 1994 ceasefire paved the way for the signing of the Good Friday Agreement in 1998. The period saw the deaths of over 3,500 people, with many thousands more injured.[11]

[7] Ibid.

[8] Kilcommins and Vaughan, 'A Perpetual State of Emergency' (n 2) 57.

[9] See, eg, D Walsh, 'The Impact of Anti-Subversive Laws on Police Powers and Practice in Ireland: The Silent Erosion of Individual Freedom' (1989) 62 *Temple Law Review* 1099; Kilcommins and Vaughan, 'A Perpetual State of Emergency' (n 2); B Vaughan and S Kilcommins, *Terrorism, Rights and the Rule of Law: Negotiating State Justice in Ireland* (Cullompton, Willan, 2008); and F De Londras and F Davis 'Controlling the Executive in Times of Terrorism: Competing Perspectives on Effective Oversight Mechanisms' (2010) 30(1) *Oxford Journal of Legal Studies* 19.

[10] Y Daly and J Jackson, 'The Criminal Justice Process: From Questioning to Trial' in D Healy, C Hamilton, Y Daly and M Butler (eds) *The Routledge Handbook of Irish Criminology* (London, Routledge, 2016) 287.

[11] For a detailed history, see D Ferriter, *The Transformation of Ireland* (London, Profile Books, 2004).

In Northern Ireland, the authorities responded with emergency legislation authorising controversial measures such as non-jury (Diplock) courts[12] and significantly enhanced police powers. These innovations, among others, gave rise to the argument that the jurisdiction provided a 'testing ground' for the extension of authoritarian powers through the use of repressive technologies and policies soon to be transplanted to mainland Britain.[13] While Hillyard's 'contagion thesis' has been criticised,[14] it appears unarguable that special criminal justice processes pioneered in Northern Ireland have left their mark on British criminal justice. One frequently cited example is the limits on the right to silence for terrorism suspects in respect of interrogation and cross-examination, introduced in Northern Ireland in 1988, and subsequently applied to all criminal suspects under the (UK-wide) Criminal Justice and Public Order Act 1994. Another is the Prevention of Terrorism (Temporary Provisions) Acts, which remained in continuous use from the time of the Birmingham bombing in 1974 to the entry into force of permanent counter-terrorism legislation in 2001.[15] A hindsight view of the evolution of the criminal justice system in the Republic of Ireland also vindicates Hillyard's concerns to quite a significant degree and one does not have to look far for evidence of a process of routinisation of emergency powers. Most striking is the current incarnation of the juryless Special Criminal Court, established in 1972 under section 35 of the OASA to hear cases of a paramilitary nature, and subsequently extended to defendants suspected of involvement in organised criminal activity. As will be discussed further below, other provisions of the OASA relating to, for example, powers of detention have also been replicated in an ordinary criminal justice context, drawing on an important symbolic fusion between subversive crime and 'narco-terrorism'.[16]

One of the closest examinations of this process of 'creep' or 'normalisation' of counter-terrorist legislation has been conducted by two Irish criminologists, Kilcommins and Vaughan, as part of a wider examination of law 'in the shadow of the gunman' as they term it.[17] For them, rather than a single Schmittian moment of exception,[18] the normalisation of the exception in Ireland has been achieved through a series of small steps, or 'a steady accretion of views which go largely unchallenged'.[19] They identify five areas where this process of normalisation has occurred, which, given their relevance to the instant discussion, merit some elaboration here.

[12] See further J Jackson and S Doran, *Judge Without Jury* (Oxford, Oxford University Press, 1995).

[13] P Hillyard, *Suspect Community: People's Experiences of the Prevention of Terrorism Act in Britain* (London, Pluto Press, 1994).

[14] A Mulcahy, 'The "Other" Lessons from Ireland? Policing, Political Violence and Policy Transfer' (2005) 2(2) *European Journal of Criminology* 185.

[15] For commentary see L Zedner, 'Security and Counter-terrorism' in L Zedner, *Security* (London, Routledge, 2009). See also C Pantazis and S Pemberton, 'From the Old to the New "Suspect Community": Examining the impact of recent UK counter terrorism legislation' (2009) 49(5) *British Journal of Criminology* 464 for a discussion of the Muslim 'suspect community' in Britain.

[16] See C Hamilton, 'Organised Criminals as "Agents of Obligation": The Case of Ireland' (2011) 17(4) *European Journal on Criminal Policy and Research* 253.

[17] Vaughan and Kilcommins, *Terrorism* (n 9).

[18] C Schmitt, *Political Theology: Four Chapters on the Concept of Sovereignty* (Cambridge, Massachussets, MIT Press, 1988).

[19] Kilcommins and Vaughan, 'A Perpetual State of Emergency' (n 2) 73.

A. Garda Holding and Information Gathering Tactics

The OASA, uniquely in the Irish criminal justice landscape at the time, made provision for detention for the purposes of interrogation. In the absence of any general power of detention for serious criminal offences, Gardaí began from the late 1970s onwards to use section 30 of the OASA, to arrest and detain suspects for offences covered by the Act (known as 'scheduled' offences) when their real interest related to an 'ordinary' offence. Indeed, Hogan and Walker note that *most* persons wanted for serious crime were arrested and detained in this manner up until the commencement of the general detention provisions under the Criminal Justice Act 1984 in 1986.[20] Many of these individuals were not ultimately charged with an offence, fuelling concerns about abusive practices under the legislation.

B. Extra-ordinary Measures and Non-paramilitary Activity

When the use of such 'holding charges' under the OASA came to be challenged before the courts the Supreme Court upheld this practice provided there was a link between the two charges and the Gardaí, in good faith, suspected the accused of the scheduled offence.[21] This requirement was further watered down in *People (DPP) v Howley*,[22] where it was held that a link between the scheduled and non-scheduled offence was not necessary and the primary motive for the arrest did not need to be for the subversive offence. These decisions can be seen as particularly serious in terms of their implications for contagion given that the list of offences 'scheduled' under section 30 is not confined to paramilitary style offences (such as membership of an unlawful organisation) but includes generic offences such as possession of a firearm.

C. The Retention of the Non-jury Special Criminal Court for Non-paramilitary Activities

As noted above, the non-jury Special Criminal Court remains in operation today, despite its initial justification on grounds of jury intimidation from paramilitaries, and the greatly improved political situation in Northern Ireland. Its use for organised crime offences was justified by the Offences Against the State Review Committee in 2002[23] on the rather 'whimsical'[24] basis that 'attempts have been made to tamper with juries in high-profile criminal trials in the ordinary courts',[25] and has been formalised through the introduction in 2009 of a provision that certain serious organised crime offences should be presumptively tried in the Court.[26] While, to the tremendous credit of the DPP, very

[20] G Hogan and C Walker, *Political Violence and the Law in Ireland* (Manchester, Manchester University Press, 1989).

[21] *DPP v Quilligan* [1986] IR 495.

[22] [1989] ILRM 629.

[23] By a majority of the Committee. Three members, including the chair, dissented.

[24] Kilcommins and Vaughan, 'A Perpetual State of Emergency' (n 2) 64.

[25] *Report of the Committee to Review the Offences Against the State Acts, 1939–1998* (Dublin, Stationery Office, 2001), hereinafter, Hederman Report, 9.36.

[26] Criminal Justice (Amendment) Act 2009, s 8.

few offences are tried under this section, the Special Criminal Court remains a 'stain on the legitimacy of the Irish criminal process'[27] and has attracted criticism from international human rights bodies such as the UN Human Rights Committee.[28]

D. Seizing Criminal Assets without Requiring a Criminal Conviction

Another clear example of emergency procedures transcending the exceptional realm can be located in legal mechanisms providing for forfeiture of assets without a criminal conviction. Legislation enabling this was passed in record speed following the murder of journalist Veronica Guerin in June 1996, and permits the Criminal Assets Bureau (CAB) to confiscate assets worth more than €13,000 on the civil standard a proof without the safeguards normally attending criminal proceedings.[29] According to Kilcommins and Vaughan, the 'primary impetus' for this model derived from the Offences Against the State (Amendment) Act 1985 which allows for forfeiture of property of unlawful organisations and its vesting in the Minister. In introducing the 1996 legislation, the then Minister for Justice, John O'Donoghue, referred back to the 1985 Act and the decision in *Clancy v Ireland*, upholding its constitutionality, as providing a 'clear and direct precedent for legislation of this type'.[30] Apropos Kilcommins and Vaughan's argument, and particularly their suggestion that a 'special zone … in which normal laws do not apply … [will] expand to incorporate more and more normal crime'[31] it is instructive to note that the threshold value of property that can be seized by CAB has recently been lowered from €13,000 to €5,000 by the Proceeds of Crime (Amendment) Act 2016.[32]

E. The Acceptance of Supergrass Testimony in the Ordinary Criminal Justice System

Another development strongly associated with the period following Veronica Guerin's murder is the establishment of a Witness Protection Programme to facilitate the prosecution of a number of high profile individuals operating in the world of organised crime, the first such programme in the history of the state. Among the many worrying features of the programme as it was applied in Ireland was the potential for fabrication and exaggeration, the lack of a requirement for corroboration, the lack of a legislative framework or guidelines and the fact that most of these cases were heard in the non-jury SCC. The members of the so-called 'Gilligan gang' who participated in the

[27] Daly and Jackson, 'The Criminal Justice Process' (n 10) 293.

[28] See, eg, UNHRC Concluding Observations on the Fourth Periodic Report of Ireland (2014). Available at: http://daccess-dds-ny.un.org/doc/UNDOC/GEN/G14/141/79/PDF/G1414179.pdf?OpenElement (accessed 17 April 2020). See Y Daly, Chapter 11, this volume; M Coen, 'International Human Rights Law: A Flavour of its Impact on the Irish Criminal Justice System' in S Egan, (ed) *International Human Rights: Perspectives from Ireland* (Dublin, Bloomsbury Professional, 2015) 333.

[29] Proceeds of Crime and Criminal Assets Bureau ('CAB') Acts 1996.

[30] *Dail Eireann*, 2 July 1996, vol 467, col 2409.

[31] Kilcommins and Vaughan, 'A Perpetual State of Emergency' (n 2) 73.

[32] See further: L Campbell, Chapter 8, this volume; L Campbell, *Organised Crime and the Law: A Comparative Analysis* (Dublin, Bloomsbury Professional, 2013).

programme were described as 'supergrass'[33] witnesses, in a manner akin to the arrested paramilitaries in Northern Ireland who gave evidence against their compatriots, often in exchange for immunity from prosecution. The somewhat hypocritical attitude taken by Irish politicians to the use of such witnesses given the strong condemnation of such practices in Northern Ireland in the 1980s is noted by Vaughan and Kilcommins as further evidence of a process of normalisation from the extraordinary to the ordinary sphere.[34]

While the above five sites capture much of the contagion effect in the Republic of Ireland, there remain other provisions of the OASA which, in times of penal crisis, have been reached for by the authorities as solutions to serious (primarily 'gangland') criminal activity. To the five areas discussed above, for example, we can add several other sites where the exceptional provisions pioneered in the OASA gradually became the norm. In the period following the murder of journalist Veronica Guerin in 1996, for example, *detention and investigatory powers* under sections 30 and 52 of the OASA were replicated in sections 2 and 7 of the Criminal Justice (Drug Trafficking) Act providing for a seven-day detention and incursions on the right to silence respectively. Likewise in 2007, following the murder of two individuals at the hands of organised crime gangs in Dublin, a new Criminal Justice Act extended a seven-day detention to firearms and other serious offences, and provided for wide-ranging incursions on the right to silence. We see a similar pattern following the murders of Shane Geoghegan and Roy Collins in Limerick in 2008–09, with the introduction of a provision allowing Gardaí to give *opinion evidence* on the existence of a criminal organisation in organised crime cases, again mirroring provisions under section3(2) of the OASA (Amendment) Act 1972 allowing Gardaí to give evidence of an accused's membership of an unlawful organisation.

More generally, it is interesting to contemplate the extent to which the public, and criminal justice agencies in Ireland, have become inured to the existence of emergency measures and habituated to their use. Such a 'criminology of the extraordinary' as Kilcommins and Vaughan describe it, may go some way to explaining the somewhat indifferent approach taken to liberty safeguards[35] and the continued tendency in Ireland to apply provisions aimed at serious crime far beyond the initial justificatory context. An example given by Daly and Jackson is section 16 of the Criminal Justice Act 2006 providing for the introduction into evidence (in breach of the hearsay rule) of prior hearsay evidence at trial in a situation where the witness refuses to give evidence. This provision was introduced in the wake of the high-profile collapse of the Liam Keane murder trial in Limerick following the apparent intimidation of witnesses but has been applied far beyond it.[36]

[33] See S Greer, 'Supergrasses in the Legal System in Britain and Northern Ireland' (1986) 102 *Law Quarterly Review* 198; S Greer, *Supergrasses: A Study in Anti-Terrorist Law Enforcement in Northern Ireland* (Oxford, Clarendon Press, 1995).

[34] Kilcommins and Vaughan, 'A Perpetual State of Emergency' (n 2) 70, 71.

[35] Paul O'Mahony describes this as 'the general atmosphere of neglect and indifference towards issues of personal freedom'. See P O'Mahony, *Criminal Chaos: Seven Crises in Irish Criminal Justice* (Dublin, Round Hall, 1996) 34.

[36] See *DPP v O'Brien* [2011] 1 IR 273.

III. CONTAGION IN EUROPE AFTER 9/11

Turning now to contagion in a contemporary European context, this section presents the results of an Irish Research Council funded research project examining the impact of counter-terrorism measures on the criminal justice systems of the UK, France and Poland.[37] As above, the aim was to explore a seepage or 'trickle down' effect between counter-terrorism measures and control measures aimed at 'ordinary' crimes as well as to examine the hegemonic power of terrorism and the securitisation agenda more generally. To this end, the 'contagion' concept was broken down into three categories, drawing on, inter alia, Donohue's[38] typology of 'transplantation'. The first category, 'the use of terrorism as a picklock', can be described as the potential of terrorism to leverage broader, usually controversial, reforms. Thus, the period following the commission of a terrorist attack may present something of a 'window of opportunity' for governments with the heat of the emergency providing political cover for previously controversial legislative measures. The second category may overlap with the first but, rather than seeking to apply exceptional security provisions to areas *unrelated to terrorism*, it targets *terrorism* and terrorist-related behaviour through broadly drawn ('blank cheque') legislation.[39] The contagion effect to other areas of the criminal justice system therefore occurs in the implementation stage although it is a direct consequence of the drafting process. The final category concerns the role of counter-terrorism legislation, through the creation of a new constitutional or legislative template, in diluting core procedural safeguards, thereby becoming 'the new normalcy'.[40] What follows below is a summary of the main findings of the research project in all of the case study jurisdictions under these three headings.

A. Use of Terrorism as a 'Picklock'

As discussed above, the need to combat terrorism very often serves to smooth the path of contentious legislation with a much wider reach. For example, the UK Government's response to 9/11, the mammoth, 14-part Anti-Terrorism, Crime and Security Act 2001, contains provisions smuggled into the Act with an apparent lack of connection to terrorism, such as a requirement on public authorities to disclose information to each other for the purposes of *any* criminal investigation. These provisions were first proposed by the government in its Criminal Justice and Police Bill earlier in 2001 but had to be dropped

[37] See Hamilton, *Contagion* (n 6). The countries were selected based on a 'most-different' design in order to test the validity of the 'contagion' thesis across a range of different settings. The most important differentiating factors in this regard were experience of terrorism and membership of the European Union so that the comparator countries include both older democracies/established Member States of the European Union with long histories of responding to terrorism (England and France) and newer democracies/members with little exposure to the phenomenon (Poland). The author would like to acknowledge the generous support of the IRC New Horizons scheme.

[38] Donohue, 'Transplantation' (n 5).

[39] Ibid, 71.

[40] LK Donohue, *The Perilous Dialogue* Georgetown Public Law and Legal Theory Research Paper No 12–028, (Georgetown University, 2009); Kilcommins and Vaughan, 'A Perpetual State of Emergency' (n 2).

in the face of stringent criticism in the House of Lords.[41] While the French response to 9/11 was more muted, probably on account of their already robust counter-terrorism apparatus, the amendments to the French law on daily security nevertheless contained provisions of more general application modifying sensitive provisions of the Code of Criminal Procedure.[42] More recently, evidence of this type of contagion can be seen in the contentious area of surveillance and media freedom. Against the background of the recent terrorist attacks in Europe, for example, the Investigatory Powers Act 2016, a controversial act known as the 'Snooper's Charter', was justified by the UK Government as essential to keep the UK 'safe from terrorists'.[43] The Act's provisions essentially replicated measures contained in the ill-fated 2012 Communications Data Bill, which was ultimately blocked by the Liberal Democrats and has since been found incompatible with EU law.[44] Similar tactics can be observed in France where the Charlie Hebdo attacks of January 2015 provided political cover for the introduction of legislation that served to authorise highly intrusive surveillance on a variety of grounds among them the protection of economic interests, the maintenance of public order and prevention of 'organised criminality'. The Fédération Internationale des Ligues des Droits de l'Homme (FIDH)[45] has argued that the expansion of the grounds for authorising intelligence collection 'amounts to the generalisation of an exceptional – and highly objectionable – system of derogations that legalise large-scale surveillance'. In Poland a series of reforms to police powers, the laws on illegally obtained evidence and surveillance have been justified by reference to the Paris and Brussels attacks in November 2015 and March 2016 respectively.[46] Despite these official pronouncements, the attempt to invoke the jihadi terrorist threat as a justification for the legislation was overwhelmingly dismissed by interviewees we spoke to as a pretext or 'Trojan Horse'.[47] As regards surveillance, the threat has been used to consolidate sweeping powers far beyond the terrorism context in the hands of the Internal Security Agency (ABW), with no independent oversight mechanism. The June 2016 Counter-terrorism Act, described by Amnesty International as containing 'some of the most draconian surveillance powers in the EU',[48] allows the ABW, inter alia, to maintain

[41] A Tomkins, 'Legislating against Terror: The Anti-Terrorism, Crime and Security Act 2001' (2002) Summer *Public Law* 205.

[42] Loi no 2001-1062 du 15 novembre 2001 relative à la sécurité quotidienne, Art 23. For criticism, see *Commission Nationale Consultative des Droits de l'Homme* (CNCDH), *Avis sur les dispositions législatives proposées par le Gouvernement en vue de renforcer la lutte contre le terrorisme.* (Paris, Commission Nationale Consultative des Droits de l'Homme, 2001).

[43] Home Office, 'Investigatory Powers Bill receives Royal Assent' 29 November 2016 [press release]. Available at: www.gov.uk/government/news/investigatory-powers-bill-receives-royal-assent (accessed 17 April 2020).

[44] M Spurrier, 'The People vs. The Snoopers' Charter' [press release] 10 January 2017. Available at: www.libertyhumanrights.org.uk/news/press-releases-and-statements/people-vs-snoopers%E2%80%99-charter-liberty-launches-crowdfunded-legal (accessed 17 April 2020).

[45] Fédération Internationale des Ligues des Droits de l'Homme (FIDH) *Counter-terrorism measures and human rights: When the exception becomes the norm.* (Paris, FIDH, 2016) 28.

[46] Deutsche Welle, 'Poland joins Hungary in planning stringent anti-terrorism laws in wake of Brussels attacks' 24 March 2015. Available at: www.dw.com/en/poland-joins-hungary-in-planning-stringent-anti-terrorism-laws-in-wake-of-brussels-attacks/a-19141781. See also justification of the provisions of the Counter-terrorism Act at: www.rpo.gov.pl/sites/default/files/Projekt%20ustawy%20antyterrorystycznej%20-%20wersja%20z%205%20maja%202016_0.pdf.

[47] Interviews with human rights activists, academics and senior persons in the Polish human rights commission were held on 16, 17, 18 and 19 January 2017.

[48] Amnesty International, *Dangerously Disproportionate: The ever-expanding national security state in Europe.* (London, Amnesty International, 2017) 34.

a list of persons suspected of being involved in terrorism-*related* activities (see below) for the purposes of accessing data held by government agencies. There was a striking level of consensus amongst the experts we spoke to in Poland that these provisions would likely be used for political purposes.[49]

B. 'Blank Cheque' Legislation

One of the best illustrations of this second category of contagion is probably the use of section 44 of the UK Terrorism Act 2000, which introduced powers of stop and search without the need for any prior suspicion in areas where it was considered 'expedient' for the prevention of acts of terrorism. In practice, it was applied primarily in London where a continuous rolling authorisation under section 44 remained in place from 2001 to 2010. While this power was ultimately found to be unlawful by the European Court of Human Rights in 2010,[50] at its height section 44 was used more than 250,000 times in a single year, including against journalists and peaceful protestors, with *no* resulting prosecutions for terrorism offences.[51] Similarly, in France, while the broad drafting of terrorism and terrorism-related offences has a long history,[52] the emergency laws enacted following the November 2015 attacks have led to numerous reports of abusive applications against environmental activities, labour protestors and also in the ordinary criminal sphere.[53] In relation to the latter, FIDH[54] reports that most of the searches authorised by the Prefecture (local authority) under the state of emergency were carried out by members of the drugs squad, in an effort to 'boost the number of searches conducted and opportunistically issue search orders for persons linked to ordinary crimes by claiming the existence of a direct link between drug trafficking and terrorism'. These claims, by members of the *Union Syndicale des Magistrats* are supported by the statistics from the Ministry of the Interior which reveal that out of the 576 legal proceedings opened on foot of the over 4,000 searches carried out under the state of emergency only six have been initiated by the specialist national anti-terrorist unit.[55] Looking to Poland, the Counter-terrorism Act of June 2016 cited above is a paradigmatic example of what may be termed 'blank cheque' legislation. The Act extends the definition of terrorism to include 'terrorist incidents', described by the government as including occasions in which: a Polish citizen 'comes into contact' with a person 'feared' to be involved in terrorism-related activities; travels to or from regions where an armed conflict involving organisations deemed to be

[49] See above n 47 for interview details.

[50] *Gillan v UK*, (Application no 4158/05), European Court of Human Rights.

[51] J Hodgson, *Legitimacy and State Responses to Terrorism: The UK and France* (Legal Studies Research Paper No 2013–30, Warwick School of Law, 2013).

[52] See further Hamilton and Berlusconi, 'Counter-terrorism' (n 6).

[53] Amnesty International, 'France: Unchecked clampdown on protests under guise of fighting terrorism', [press release] 31 May 2017 available at: www.amnesty.org/en/latest/news/2017/05/france-unchecked-clampdown-on-protests-under-guise-of-fighting-terrorism/; Amnesty International France, 'COP21: Les Militants Écologistes Pris Pour Cible', 16 December 2015, available at: www.amnesty.fr/liberte-d-expression/actualites/cop21-les-militants-ecologistes-pris-pour-cible; Amnesty International, *Dangerously Disproportionate* (n 48) 16.

[54] FIDH (n 45) 19.

[55] CNCDH, *Statement of Opinion on the State of Emergency*. (Paris, Commission Nationale Consultative des Droits de l'Homme, 2016).

engaged in terrorism-related activities is ongoing; or simply loses his or her ID documents while abroad.[56] Amnesty International[57] has argued that these activities, 'taken alone, could hardly be considered credible and sufficient evidence that a person was involved in terrorist activities'. Indeed, given that these very loose definitions underpin the exercise of surveillance powers and powers of pre-trial detention under the Act, it is arguable that the provisions do not comply with the principle of legality.[58]

C. The 'New Normal'

Much could be written under this heading concerning what Zedner[59] terms the 'terrorisation' of the criminal law, ranging from the development of new coercive measures outside of the criminal process, to challenges to the principle of open justice, to moves towards a system of *a posteriori* rather than *a priori* review. In the UK, one of the main legislative innovations was the introduction in 2005 of 'control orders', that is, civil orders imposing severe restrictions on liberty short of house arrest, but with the threat of criminal sanctions for breach.[60] While these orders have since evolved into somewhat less restrictive orders termed 'Terrorism Prevention and Investigation Measures' (TPIMs),[61] we may note the introduction in 2007 of the Serious Crime Prevention Order (SCPO), another civil preventative measure closely modelling the control order, applying to crimes as wide-ranging as drugs trafficking, fraud, tax offences or simply participating in activities of a (vaguely defined) 'organised crime' group.[62] A related issue is the 'special advocate' procedure used in control order/TPIM hearings where, due to the sensitive nature of the evidence adduced in court, counsel are unable to take instructions after they have seen the evidence.[63] This practice has spread very quickly to a large number of other areas such as asset-freezing cases and parole hearings so that 'there are no fewer than 22 different types of court hearing in which special advocates can be used'.[64]

Similarly, in France the 'hegemonic tendency' of counter-terrorist legislation is much in evidence, particularly in relation to organised crime, with an almost

[56] Rozporządzenie Ministra Spraw Wewnętrznych i Administracji w sprawie katalogu incydentów o charakterze terrorystycznym. Dziennik Ustaw, No 0, Location 1092, 2016.

[57] Amnesty International, *Dangerously Disproportionate* (n 48) 25.

[58] See Martin Scheinin, (former) UN Special Rapporteur on the promotion and protection of human rights and fundamental freedoms while countering terrorism, Report to the Commission on Human Rights, E/CN.4/2006/98, para 46: 'The first requirement of article 15, paragraph 1, [ICCPR] is that the prohibition of terrorist conduct must be undertaken by national or international prescriptions of law. To be 'prescribed by law' the prohibition must be framed in such a way that: the law is adequately accessible so that the individual has a proper indication of how the law limits his or her conduct; and the law is formulated with sufficient precision so that the individual can regulate his or her conduct.'

[59] L Zedner, 'Terrorizing Criminal Law' (2014) 8(1) *Criminal Law and Philosophy* 99.

[60] Prevention of Terrorism Act 2005.

[61] Terrorist Prevention and Investigation Measures Act 2011.

[62] Serious Crime Act 2007.

[63] See further J Jackson, '*The Use of Special Advocates in Countering Terrorism: Human Rights, Best Practice and Procedural Tradition*' in G Lennon, C King, and C McCarthy (eds) *Counter-Terrorism, Constitutionalism and Miscarriages of Justice* (Oxford, Hart Publishing, 2018) 99.

[64] *Hansard* (1 March 2010), above n 42, col 739 (Andrew Dismore) cited in Fenwick and Phillipson, 'Covert Derogations' (n 4).

'reciprocal'[65] relation between the two areas. A 2004 Act, aiming to adapt the justice system to new forms of crime, applied the procedural tools that were originally confined to terrorist offences to this wider range of crimes, among them an array of covert surveillance measures (eg secret observation, interception of communications); powers to conduct night searches in places of residence; an extended period of detention (96 hours); and delayed access to a lawyer.[66] This is particularly problematic when the highly fluid nature of the definition of organised crime in France is considered. As Hodgson notes, '[a] group of boys who come together in order to steal another boy's bus pass would fall within [it]'.[67] Perhaps the ultimate blurring of the exceptional and the ordinary in France occurred with the recent counter-terrorism law of 30 October 2017 (SILT) that permanently transposes into French law powers exercised by the authorities during the two year state of emergency, such as the imposition of house arrest and surveillance measures.[68] Referring to these measures recently, the UN Special Rapporteur on the promotion and protection of human rights and fundamental freedoms while countering terrorism described them as constituting 'a de facto state of qualified emergency in ordinary French law'[69] and also expressed concern that they will be applied in other contexts, such as public demonstrations and environmental protests. In Poland, on the other hand, this type of contagion appears to have less relevance owing to the recent origins of much of their counter-terrorism law. Moreover, recent crises in the administration of justice in that jurisdiction make challenge through the courts difficult, and therefore the creation of constitutional templates increasingly unlikely.[70]

While space does not permit a full exploration of the extent of the implementation of the laws discussed above, it is worth noting that there have also been marked differences in the application of these laws, emphasising the need for comparative research to examine the law in practice as well as the law in the books. Contagion has thus occurred in all three jurisdictions but to varying degrees and according to pre-established legislative patterns, practices and political cultures.[71] For example, France has been much more draconian than the UK in the application of its counter-terrorism measures, both in terms of the prosecution of terrorism-related offences and in relation to the use of administrative measures.[72]

[65] Hodgson, *Legitimacy and state responses* (n 51).

[66] Loi no 2004-204 du 9 mars 2004 portant adaptation de la justice aux évolutions de la criminalité (Loi Perben II).

[67] Hodgson, *Legitimacy and State Responses* (n 51) 18.

[68] Loi no 2017-1510 du 30 octobre 2017 renforçant la sécurité intérieure et la lutte contre le terrorisme (SILT).

[69] United Nations Special Rapporteur on the promotion and protection of human rights and fundamental freedoms while countering terrorism, *Preliminary findings of the visit: UN Special Rapporteur on the promotion and protection of human rights and fundamental freedoms while countering terrorism concludes visit to France*. (Geneva, 2018).

[70] As result of recent reforms of the administration of justice and the following Constitutional Tribunal crisis, the Commissioner for Human Rights has withdrawn challenges to the Counter-terrorist Act of June 2016.

[71] See further on this F Foley, *Countering Terrorism in Britain and France* (Cambridge, Cambridge University Press).

[72] See further Hamilton, *Contagion* (n 6).

IV. CONCLUSION

A. Contemporary Contagion: 'Old Wine in New Bottles?'

Discussing the process of normalisation in Ireland some years ago Kilcommins and Vaughan argue that, while much of this has taken place 'against a backdrop of Ireland's particular history in the twentieth century, there are lessons for many western countries now attempting to grapple with anti-terrorist laws in a post 9/11 milieu'.[73] In drawing out these lessons, and concluding this chapter, we may make a number of observations.

The first, deceptively simple but important, point is the continued relevance of the concept of contagion in contemporary Europe. As discussed in the sections above, the Irish experience of abusive application of broadly drafted provisions such as section 30 of the OASA continues to find a resonance in the very wide use of suspicionless stop and search powers in the UK and the opportunistic application of French emergency laws to drugs offenders. Similarly, the bureaucratic tendency to return to tried and tested solutions in the exceptional realm in responding to serious crime (as evidenced by the extension of non-jury trial, forfeiture of assets and exceptional criminal procedures to organised crime in Ireland) finds a contemporary application in the rapid spread of the UK special advocate procedure and the 'reciprocal' relationship between organised crime and terrorism in France. The tendency of emergency laws to remain longer on the statute book than the demands of the situation require is also neatly exemplified by the recent state of emergency measures now permanently embedded in ordinary French law. Even beyond the instant study, comparative accounts from countries such as Norway[74] and Australia[75] are quickly accumulating and detailing the substantial impact of counter-terrorist legislation on the criminal justice system more broadly. Speaking at a recent event in the Royal Irish Academy in Dublin, Fionnuala Ní Aoláin,[76] UN Special Rapporteur on Counter-Terrorism and Human Rights, was forthright in her view that counter-terrorism law emanating from the UN Security Council was 'increasing and encroaching' in ways that are largely invisible to citizens. Such work prompts further legal and criminological reflection on the connections, both normative and practical, being forged between 'exceptional' and 'ordinary' legal regimes in a seemingly permanent 'war on terror'.

The second point is to acknowledge that while clear parallels exist between past and present, Ireland and Europe, important differences are also at play in the contemporary outworkings of the contagion process. The first of these is the increasingly synergistic relationship between the special and normal in recent times, owing perhaps to a more general deprioritisation of due process values in recent decades.[77] In this more inhospitable environment, ordinary serious crimes may *already* be subject to harsh measures, and

[73] Kilcommins and Vaughan, 'A Perpetual State of Emergency' (n 2) 56–57.

[74] EJ Husabø 'Counterterrorism and the Expansion of Proactive Police Powers in the Nordic States' (2013) 14(1) *Journal of Scandinavian Studies in Criminology and Crime Prevention* 3.

[75] R Ananian-Welsh and G Williams, 'The New Terrorists: The Normalisation and Spread of Anti-Terror Laws in Australia' (2015) 38(2) *Melbourne University Law Review* 362.

[76] F Ní Aoláin, 'Emergency Laws, Counter-terrorism and Human Rights', 21 November, Royal Irish Academy.

[77] C Hamilton, *The Presumption of Innocence in Irish Criminal Law: Whittling the Golden Thread* (Dublin, IPA, 2007); M Tonry, 'Symbol, Substance and Severity in Western Penal Policies' (2001) 3(4) *Punishment & Society*, 517; D Garland, *The Culture of Control* (Oxford, Oxford University Press, 2002).

thus contagion may occur in both directions, 'trickle up' as well as 'trickle down'. Witness, for example, the extension of powers to compel evidence and produce documents from the field of serious organised crime to terrorism in the UK Terrorism Act 2006 and the application to terrorist suspects in the Counter-Terrorism Act 2008 of notification requirements previously imposed on sex offenders.[78] Even the hybrid civil/criminal model upon which the control order was based was forged not in the hot crucible of national security politics but in the rather more anodyne context of anti-social behaviour.[79] Highlighting such borrowings from the 'ordinary' to the 'special' realm, Walker[80] makes a case for the 'plasticity' of what is both 'special' and 'normal' in criminal justice. Similarly, in France, Lazerges and Henrion-Stoffel[81] trace the trend towards pre-emption in contemporary counter-terrorism law to the inclusion as far back as 1994 in the ordinary criminal code of a range of offences criminalising risky behaviour. A second difference perhaps concerns the more fluid political context in which counter-terrorism measures are now invoked, in particular the rise of right-wing populism and the revival of nationalistic rhetoric in democratic countries. While governments will play the politics of security, just as they have always done, this type of 'security populism',[82] which 'is premised on the vilification of outsider groups' and has increasingly relied on 'systemic Islamophobia'[83] merits particular scrutiny in terms of its implications for contagion. As discussed above, despite very low prevalence rates, 'terrorism' seems to have played a crucial role in the series of dramatic law reforms pursued by the populist Law and Justice Party in Poland since 2015, highlighting the need for careful attention to vague counter-terrorism laws as 'picklocks' or gateways to abuse.

The third, critical issue concerns the social contestation of contagion and how we may seek to contain further 'creep and contamination'[84] going forward. The Irish case presents as particularly instructive in this regard as, while challenges to the status and mandate of the SCC itself have largely been unsuccessful,[85] the courts have in other ways sought to push back against excessive securitisation. In this regard Kilcommins and Vaughan[86] identify several decisions of the Irish superior courts as evidence of what they describe as the 'counterweight of law', and the potential of the judiciary to resist the steady drift towards 'a penal dystopia in which the exception becomes the norm'.[87] Prime among these is the decision in *People (DPP) v Ward*[88] where a man convicted of the

[78] K Roach, 'The United Kingdom Responds A Legislative War on Terrorism' in K Roach (ed), *The 9/11 Effect: Comparative Counter-Terrorism* (Cambridge, Cambridge University Press, 2011).

[79] As Shami Chakabarti, then director of Liberty, commented at the time, 'It seems to me that we would not be living with the chilling spectre of the anti-terror 'control order' (indefinite punishment based on secret intelligence) if we had been more critical of his older cousin, the Asbo' See L Casey and S Shakrabarti 'Mob justice or yob control?' *The Guardian*, 19 March 2005.

[80] C Walker, 'Terrorism Prosecution in the United Kingdom' in F Ni Aolain and O Gross (eds), *Guantanamo and Beyond* (Cambridge, Cambridge University Press, 2013) 265.

[81] C Lazerges and H Henrion-Stoffel, 'Chronique de politique criminelle: Le déclin du droit pénal: l'emergence d'une politique criminelle de l'ennemi' (2016) 3 *Revue de science criminelle et de droit pénal comparé* 649.

[82] L Laarus and B Goold 'Security and Human Rights: Finding a Language of Resilience and Inclusion' in B Goold and L Lazarus (eds) *Security and Human Rights* (Oxford, Hart Publishing, 2019).

[83] Ibid, 8.

[84] Fenwick and Phillipson, 'Covert Derogations' (n 4).

[85] For a detailed discussion of these challenges, see Y Daly, Chapter 11, this volume.

[86] Vaughan and Kilcommins, *Terrorism* (n 9).

[87] Kilcommins and Vaughan, 'A Perpetual State of Emergency' (n 2) 78.

[88] Court of Criminal Appeal, Unreported, 22 March 2002.

high profile murder of journalist Veronica Guerin in 1996 had his conviction set aside on the grounds of concerns over the integrity of protected witness ('supergrass') testimony. Another example can be found in the quashing of the conviction of Colm Murphy for conspiracy (on grounds of suspected interference with interview notes and the introduction of inadmissible evidence of previous convictions), despite him being the only person ever to be tried for the Omagh Bombing.[89] In their later work, Vaughan and Kilcommins argue that it is the judicial 'habitus' in Ireland that remains 'attuned to the primacy of rights',[90] suggesting it is rather the articulation of rights within a due process orientated legal *culture* (what Loader[91] has described as the 'cultural lives of rights') that hold the key to resistance.

In a post 9/11 milieu, it may be argued that in many contexts human rights have shown themselves both adaptable and vulnerable to the pressures associated with the pursuit of security. Writing about the UK, leading human rights scholar, Conor Gearty[92] admits, with admirable candour, that 'human rights law in the United Kingdom has largely accommodated these security-oriented changes and the effect of this has been to render them seemingly compliant with rather than inherently hostile to human rights principles'. The same may be said at an international level, where it may be argued that human rights have broadly failed in their task of containing the 'increasing and encroaching' approach to terrorism risk propagated by bodies such as the UN Security Council.[93] The case of Ireland, accepting that some resistance to contagion has been successfully mounted as discussed above, therefore raises important questions for comparative lawyers, criminologists and social scientists more generally, regarding the conditions in which *successful* appeals to rights may be made. Writing in relation to another Enlightenment concept, that of 'proportionality', Nicola Lacey, argues:

> where it 'works' to limit punishment, this is because of its articulation of, and resonance with, deeper conventions, normative systems, political institutions, and social structures. The challenge, accordingly, is to try to understand the conditions under which proportionality both gains its appeal and has some potential to limit power: whether through consensus within a powerful epistemic community such as a judiciary, and/or through its being situated within detailed rules, doctrines and institutional arrangements.[94]

Applying the same reasoning to rights and their ability to act as effective counters to security in the Irish case and beyond, it is perhaps only when these complexities are more fully understood that the 'lessons of history' discussed at the beginning of this chapter will truly be learned.

[89] For discussion of further examples outside the terrorist context, see S Kilcommins, 'Crime Control, the Security State and Constitutional Justice in Ireland: Discounting Liberal Legalism and Deontological Principles' (2016) 20(4) *International Journal of Evidence and Proof* 326.

[90] Vaughan and Kilcommins, *Terrorism* (n 9) 163.

[91] I Loader, 'The Cultural Lives of Security and Rights' in BJ Goold and L Lazarus (eds), *Security and Human Rights* (Oxford, Hart Publishing, 2007).

[92] C Gearty, *Can Human Rights Survive?* (Cambridge, Cambridge University Press, 2006) 125.

[93] See further C Hamilton and R Lippert, 'Governing Through Human Rights in Counter-terrorism: Proofing, Problematization and Securitization' (2020) 28(1) *Critical Criminology* 127–145. See also C Hamilton 'Sword or shield? The Influence of International Organisations in Criminal Law Policymaking' (2018) 142 *Revista Brasileira de Ciências Criminais* (*Brazilian Journal of the Criminal Sciences*) 67.

[94] N Lacey, 'The Metaphor of Proportionality' (2016) 43(1) *Journal of Law and Society* 27.

Index

www.ingramcontent.com/pod-product-compliance
Ingram Content Group UK Ltd.
Pitfield, Milton Keynes, MK11 3LW, UK
UKHW050944290926
15470UKWH00005B/1623

9 781509 931996